M000311357

DESIGNING ONE NATION

Designing One Nation

The Politics of Economic Culture and Trade in Divided Germany

Katrin Schreiter

OXFORD UNIVERSITY PRESS

Oxford University Press

Oxford University Press is a department of the University of Oxford.
It furthers the University's objective of excellence in research, scholarship,
and education by publishing worldwide. Oxford is a registered trade mark
of Oxford University Press in the UK and certain other countries.
Published in the United States of America by Oxford University Press
198 Madison Avenue, New York, NY 10016, United States of America.

© Oxford University Press 2020

All rights reserved. No part of this publication may be reproduced, stored
in a retrieval system, or transmitted, in any form or by any means, without the prior
permission in writing of Oxford University Press, or as expressly permitted by law, by
license, or under terms agreed with the appropriate reproduction rights organization.
Inquiries concerning reproduction outside the scope of the above should be sent to
the Rights Department, Oxford University Press, at the address above.

You must not circulate this work in any other form and you must impose
this same condition on any acquirer.

Library of Congress Cataloging-in-Publication Data
Names: Schreiter, Katrin, author.
Title: Designing one nation: the politics of economic culture and
trade in divided Germany / Katrin Schreiter.
Description: New York: Oxford University Press, 2020. |
Includes bibliographical references and index. |
Identifiers: LCCN 2019056854 (print) | LCCN 2019056855 (ebook) |
ISBN 9780190877279 (HARDCOVER) | ISBN 9780190877286 (PDF)
Subjects: LCSH: Germany (West)—Relations—Germany (East) | Germany (East)--
Relations--Germany (West) | Germany--History--1945-1990. |
German reunification question (1949-1990) | Germany--Economic conditions--1990-|
Industrial design--Social aspects--Germany. | Functionalism in art--History.
Classification: LCC DD258.85.G3 S37 2020 (print) | LCC DD258.85.G3 (ebook) |
DDC 943.087--dc23
LC record available at https://lccn.loc.gov/2019056854
LC ebook record available at https://lccn.loc.gov/2019056855

1 3 5 7 9 8 6 4 2

Printed by Integrated Books International, United States of America

S|H
M|P

The Sustainable History Monograph Pilot

Opening up the Past, Publishing for the Future

This book is published as part of the Sustainable History
Monograph Pilot. With the generous support of the
Andrew W. Mellon Foundation, the Pilot uses cutting-edge
publishing technology to produce open access digital editions
of high-quality, peer-reviewed monographs from leading
university presses. Free digital editions can be download-
ed from: Books at JSTOR, EBSCO, Hathi Trust, Internet
Archive, OAPEN, Project MUSE, and many other open
repositories.

While the digital edition is free to download, read, and share,
the book is under copyright and covered by the following
Creative Commons License: CC BY-NC-ND 4.0. Please
consult www.creativecommons.org if you have questions
about your rights to reuse the material in this book.

When you cite the book, please include the following
URL for its Digital Object Identifier (DOI):
https://doi.org/10.1093/oso/9780190877279.001.0001

We are eager to learn more about how you discovered this
title and how you are using it. We hope you will spend a
few minutes answering a couple of questions at this url:
https://www.longleafservices.org/shmp-survey/

More information about the Sustainable History Monograph
Pilot can be found at https://www.longleafservices.org.

To Paolo,

everything is better together.

CONTENTS

CONTENTS

ACKNOWLEDGMENTS

It is a great pleasure to express my appreciation to the individuals and institutions who helped me in the process of writing this book. First and foremost, I would like to thank Oxford University Press and the terrific Susan Ferber and Alexandra Dauler for believing in this project when it first landed on their desks. I am especially indebted to the two anonymous reviewers who gave crucial suggestions and encouraging comments that have contributed tremendously in transforming an interdisciplinary, multi-archival project into a proper book manuscript.

The majority of the research was funded by grants from the University of Pennsylvania and its School of Arts and Sciences. The Penn Program on Democracy, Citizenship, and Constitutionalism Graduate Fellowship allowed me a carefree year of writing and welcomed me into an inspiring interdisciplinary setting. I owe much as well to the support of Thomas Childers, Kathy Peiss, Paul Betts, and Catriona MacLeod whose comments and encouragement were particularly valuable in developing this book manuscript. At King's College London, I not only found a new intellectual home at the departments of German and of European and International Studies but also a thriving interdisciplinary environment that supported my continued research on this book by funding frequent visits to archives in Germany.

As the saying goes, it takes a village to raise children, and it takes equally as many people to finish a book project of transnational scope. During my research in Germany, a number of people provided me with invaluable support. First, I would like to thank the friendly staff of the Bundesarchiv in Koblenz and Berlin for their help in locating rare materials. Kerstin Schenke and Gisela Haker have greatly assisted my research and filed extensive requests on my behalf for early document access. Special thanks go to Helge Aszmoneit at the Rat für Formgebung in Frankfurt who provided me with personal contacts and expert knowledge about all things design in Germany. The staff of the Politische Archiv at the Foreign Office of the Federal Republic helped tirelessly with tracing early postwar-era files, while staff at the Werkbund Archiv der Dinge in Berlin, the Staatsarchiv Dresden, and the Stadtarchiv Stuttgart offered their expertise in filling in gaps in the national record. Similarly, I am grateful to the foundation Haus der Geschichte der Bundesrepublik Deutschland Berlin for the opportunity to peruse their Sammlung industrielle Gestaltung, a treasure trove documenting GDR industrial design initiatives. Special thanks go to Thorsten Krause and Anja Schubert, who helped with locating visual materials under complicated circumstances. Helen Streilein offered support at the archive of the Association for Consumption, Market and Sales Research in Nuremberg. I am indebted to Uta Brandes, Michael Blank, Axel Bruchhäuser, Michael Erlhoff, Peter Frank, Rolf Heide, Karin Hirdina, Günther Höhne, Rudolf Horn, Bernd Göbel, Martin Kelm, Karin Kirsch, Lore Kramer, Peter Maly, Detlef Mika, Herbert and Rotraud Pohl, and Renate Sigwart who generously invited me into their homes and workplaces. Their indispensable personal accounts offered valuable insights into the practice of design in Cold War Germany. The generous support of the furniture production and retail companies Deutsche Werkstätten Hellerau, Interlübke, Möbel Wallach, Hülsta, Tecta, and Walter Knoll provided the opportunity to see firsthand what I was writing about. In England, I was assisted by the knowledgeable staff of the University of Brighton Design Archives in researching the institutional nature of German Cold War design globally. Without the selfless and enthusiastic support from these institutions and individuals, this book would have never come into being.

Early drafts of book chapters have received feedback from colleagues on numerous occasions, among them panels at annual conferences of the German Studies Association and the American Historical Association, colloquia and research seminars at Freie Universität Berlin, King's College London, and the Institute for Historical Research at the University of London, and the GHI Transatlantic Doctoral Seminar at the Friedrich-Schiller Universität Jena. Probing questions, excellent suggestions, new leads, and thoughtful comments from attendants contributed greatly to how what started out as doctoral research has been reconceptualized and has grown over the years into the book that is in front of you. Here I would like to thank especially Jeremy Aynsley, Erica Carter, William Glenn Gray, Christina von Hodenberg, Konrad Jarausch, Eveline Kilian, Jan Palmowski, Eli Rubin, Benedict Schofield, Catherine Smale, Elizabeth Stewart, Richard Wetzell, and Michael Wildt, who kindly offered their expertise and critical advice.

Over the years, many friends have accompanied me on this journey, and their support, friendship, and sound advice over countless dinners and coffee breaks sustained this project. Special thanks goes to Julie Davidow, Jacob Eder, Julia Gunn, Chelsea Johnson, Reena Vaidya Krishna, Chase Richards, and Kerry

Wallach, who also read and commented on early drafts. Several family members in Hamburg, Wiesbaden, and Stuttgart hosted me during my research abroad. Thanks to Monika and Thomas Busch; Michael, Andrea, Daniel, and Dennis Busch; Christine and Horst Otto; and Vincent Hochreiter for their hospitality.

I am particularly grateful to my parents, Susanne and Manfred Schreiter, and my sister, Sabine Schreiter, for their unfailing support and encouragement. Their constructive outlook on life puts the trials and tribulations of academia into perspective. My late grandmother Ilsemarie Busch, born in 1920, lived through ninety-nine years of German history. Her quiet optimism and ability to find joy in the simple things have informed much of my curiosity about Germany's 20th century. Most of all, I owe thanks and love to Paolo Aversa, without whom this project would have never come to completion. Its failings, of course, are entirely my own.

ABBREVIATIONS

AA	Federal Ministry for Foreign Affairs, West Germany
AiF	Office of Industrial Design 1972–1990, East Germany (ZfF/ZfG)
BDI	Federation of German Industries, West Germany
BMB	Federal Ministry for Intra-German Relations 1969–1991, West Germany (BMG)
BK	Office of the Federal Chancellor, West Germany
BMG	Federal Ministry for Pan-German Affairs 1949–1969, West Germany (BMB)
BMWi	Federal Ministry for Economic Affairs, West Germany
CDU	Christian Democratic Union
CoID	Council of Industrial Design, Britain
COMECON	Council for Mutual Economic Assistance
CSCE	Conference for Security and Cooperation in Europe
ČSSR	Čzechoslovak Socialist Republic
DAMW	German Office for Standardization and Product Testing, East Germany
DIHT	German Industry and Commerce Board, West Germany
DM	West German Mark
DWH	Deutsche Werkstätten Hellerau
EEC	European Economic Community
ESS	Economic System of Socialism
FDJ	Free German Youth, East Germany
FRG	Federal Republic of Germany
GDP	Gross Domestic Product
GDR	German Democratic Republic
GfK	Society for Consumption Research, West Germany
HfG Ulm	Ulm School of Design
HO	National retail organization, East Germany
ICSID	International Council of Societies of Industrial Designers
IDZ	International Design Center

IM	Unofficial Informant (Stasi)
IMM	International Furniture Fair, Cologne
MDW	Modular furniture system produced by DWH
MfAA	Ministry for Foreign Affairs, East Germany
MfS	Ministry for State Security, East Germany (Stasi)
MIA	Ministry for Domestic and Foreign Trade, East Germany
MoMA	Museum of Modern Art, New York
NES	New Economic System of Planning and Management
NSDAP	National Socialist German Workers' Party
R&D	Research & Development
RfF	Design Council, West Germany
SED	Socialist Unity Party
SMAD	Soviet Military Administration in Germany
SPD	Social Democratic Party
Stasi	State Security Service, East Germany (MfS)
StäV	Permanent Representative Mission, West Germany
TSI	Trust for Intra-Zonal Trade, West Germany
UN	United Nations
UNESCO	United Nations Educational, Scientific, and Cultural Organization
VBK	Association of Artists in the Applied Arts
VEB	Nationalized/socialized companies, East Germany
VEH-DIA Möbel	Nationalized Organization for German Domestic and Foreign Furniture Trade
VNIITE	All-Union Scientific Research Institute of Industrial Design, Soviet Union
VVB	Association of Nationalized Companies, East Germany
ZfF/ZfG	Central Institute for Design 1963–1972, East Germany (AiF)
ZK	Central Committee of the SED

Introduction

Designing One Nation

E X ORIENTE LUX, EX OCCIDENTE LUXUS." Light from the East, luxury from the West. Polish writer Stanislaw Jerzy Lec has been credited with coining this laconic aphorism to capture the magnetism of the two dominant Cold War ideologies. After the collapse of the German Democratic Republic (GDR), West German design critics reappropriated the phrase in discussions about East Germany's material legacy.[1] They used it triumphantly, because from their point of view luxury had eclipsed the light. Western economic liberalism, so it seemed, had won the war of ideologies.[2] They used the phrase cautiously, because the lost socialist utopia, the extinguished light, carried the potential to ignite nostalgia among East Germans, a longing for a past civilization that, by 1992, had been taken over by the West. They used the phrase because the aphorism so fittingly encapsulated the Cold War struggle in divided Germany, the confrontation of two diametrically opposed socioeconomic systems: the principled, moralizing socialist economy in the East and the lavish, affluent capitalist economy in the West. Entrenched as these cultural critics and their contemporaries were in the political mindset of the Cold War, emphasizing difference had always been a way to ensure the international recognition of separate German identities. In fact, it is impossible to understand the Federal Republic of Germany (FRG) during the decades of division without the GDR, and vice-versa. Their domestic and international politics, economic policy, social progress, and cultural development substantially derived from the tension created by the sheer presence of the other. Ironically, their attempts at expressing difference unintentionally created a shared code of ideological inscription in everyday German life.[3]

After the Third Reich delegitimized nationalism as a valid form of identification, both German states faced a search for acceptable political values. Nationalist approaches that stressed German exceptionality had become unacceptable. The West German decision to remove the first stanza from the German national

1

anthem is just one example; Germany could no longer aspire to stand "above everything in the world."[4] Moreover, heavy Allied involvement in state-building and policy development left the population with a sense of insecurity about the origins of their state(s), further hindering their identification with postwar Germany. In an effort to create a valid political culture, governments followed the people literally into their homes with highly politicized debates about German living standards. In election campaigns, the first chancellor, Konrad Adenauer, capitalized on the general social uplift created by the "economic miracle" of swift West German industrial recovery, while East German leaders Walter Ulbricht and later Erich Honecker promised similar material everyday comforts with the New Economic Policy (1963) and Unity of Economic and Social Policy (1971) programs. In cooperation with cultural and economic elites, they relied on everyday aesthetics to create distinct national domestic cultures and emphasize ideological demarcation as integrative concepts. Economic progress would promote the new political order in both national and international contexts. It would also substitute for traditional nationalism by providing the population with values that yielded a sense of belonging. This importance of economic success for political legitimacy of the two Germanys in the East-West competition has long been acknowledged.[5] On closer examination, however, this period of delineation should be understood as a prelude to the détente of the 1970s. Seeing that the signing of the German Basic Treaty in 1972 "normalized" the antagonistic relationship between the two German states, a long-term analysis that extends to 1989 can provide insights into a more diverse political utilization of German material culture—and thus into the internal German relationship—than has been recognized so far.

One of the ways the FRG and the GDR developed and maintained the new national identity was by instilling material culture, specifically interior design and furniture production, with strong political messages. However, the emerging aesthetic did more than just modernize the respective parts of Germany. What started as a Cold War competition for ideological superiority in the field of economics quickly turned into a shared, politically legitimizing quest for an untainted postfascist modernity. In the process, they resurrected the "Made in Germany" brand to mark a rehabilitated, divided-yet-peaceful Germany that yearned for membership among modern industrial nations. Following furniture products from the drafting table into the homes of ordinary Germans offers insight into how converging visions of German industrial modernity created shared expectations about economic progress and living standards. These shared expectations shaped a system of values at the juncture of economic and sociocultural politics, an economic culture that bound the two Germanys together. Implemented as policy, it projected internationally a pan-German interest.

That the striving for difference created similarity in how East and West Germans negotiated their country's division is a paradox that warrants explanation. Examining this phenomenon highlights historical interconnections between the two Germanys in product design, economic structure, corporate ethos, trade, and consumer society. All of these are part of economic culture, which political scientist Paul Egon Rohrlich explained as the need to understand "the perceptual predisposition of national populations, based on cultural value systems" as the motivation behind policymaking.[6] From this perspective, the legitimating norms for policymaking spring from contexts other than politics in society, yet they become visible through analysis of issue interpretation, policy formation, and implementation. It puts the focus on the people as historical actors, rather than on the state structure, to explain policymaking. In the case of postwar Germany, this concept offers an approach that transcends the starkly contrasting systems of state socialism and market capitalism. In doing so, it underscores similarities in the activities of a network of politicians, entrepreneurs, and cultural brokers, and how they envisioned and realized economic policy in the two German states in their efforts to regain economic stability and political influence in Cold War Europe's order.

Like other capitalist and socialist societies throughout Europe, both the Federal Republic and the GDR embarked on finding solutions to postwar reconstruction problems, most notably scarce housing and furnishing, and shared their findings in the myriad European design exhibitions, among them the Milan Triennal and the Jablonec International. Many of those solutions involved the mechanization of craft industries and ensuing standardization, which were economically efficient but were criticized by contemporaries for their monotony, thus hindering cultural diversity as well as societal refinement. Both German states created institutions that not only defined the new industrial design profession but also invested in consumer taste education that promoted certain national aesthetics. Meanwhile, in the later postwar decades, growing notions of individualism and social distinction across all social strata pushed designers, industrialists, and politicians to find more bespoke solutions. Especially in state socialism, the apparent contradiction between collectivist maxims and individualistic desires preoccupied high-ranking politicians of the power-monopolizing Socialist Unity Party (Sozialistische Einheitspartei Deutschlands, SED). Efforts at creating ideologically conforming consumer habits reveal personal responses and show how the ideas that consumer education initiatives promoted became pervasive among the population. Naturally, the availability and affordability of desired products were key to the success of these ideas.

Despite the centrality of trade in shaping the German-German relationship, especially after the 1972 Basic Treaty, it has received relatively little scholarly attention. Economic treatments of GDR history have focused on the shortcomings of the command economy in order to explain the country's comparatively sudden collapse in 1989.[7] Over the past three decades, the question of its forty years of relative political stability, peaking in the 1970s, has remained a scholarly focus. Controversies emerged over the stabilizing factors of communist rule.[8] Yet the extent to which the GDR leadership secured this "golden decade" through its special relationship with the Federal Republic goes unnoticed or, when looking at trade credits, is oversimplified to portray the GDR as a passive receiver, instead of as an active agent in the marketplace. Alternatively, the Federal Republic's economic success has diverted attention to Western integration and the development of the European common market.[9] The FRG's economic relationship to the GDR has been deemed insignificant, which is true in terms of its trade balance but not in terms of pan-German cultural influence and national politics. The following pages describe an asymmetric relationship in which economic and political priorities developed at times into conflicting and contradictory dynamics. For the West, the political aspect of intra-German trade outweighed its economic benefits, and for the East, economic necessity trumped the official policy of ideological differentiation.

Details are sparse about East Germany's efforts to deepen trade with the West. Indeed, the GDR capitalized on the territorial incertitude and the lack of a postwar peace settlement that would have defined borders. With the help of the Federal Republic, it gained special status for trade with the European Economic Community (EEC). Through the Protocol on Intra-German Trade, East German goods and services were exempt from tariffs that other non-EEC countries had to pay. Western customers bought, often unknowingly, East German products in department stores and through mail order catalogs, enjoying low prices courtesy of an eastern economic infrastructure that focused on mass production. By the 1970s, the Federal Republic had become an indispensable trade partner for the GDR, second only to the Soviet Union. From the West German perspective, the structurally lagging GDR economy offered opportunities for a gradual normalization of German-German relations. Hence these links ran deeper than simple economic transactions; they were inherently political, illustrating not only the place of East-West trade in the permeability of the Iron Curtain but also pointing to its significance in stabilizing the GDR. Moreover, in catering to foreign markets, GDR industries and their designers eventually aligned themselves with western tastes and aesthetics, which risked undermining cultural distinction efforts on the national level.

Beyond uncovering hitherto understudied dimensions of German-German relations, the economic culture perspective contributes to the literature of postwar German history in a number of methodological and thematic ways. First, many cultural studies of Cold War Germany evaluate economic performance exclusively based on consumer satisfaction.[10] It is, however, crucial to consider the aspirations for and perceptions of cultural modernization alongside its actual materiality. Including specific values in the discussion of economic performance reveals the significance of a shared history, cultural norms, and economic practices in the German postwar context. Hence this work is not just about competition for preeminence between East and West Germany, but it is also about the rediscovery of forgotten similarities. Vying for economic and ideological superiority and earnest efforts for a German-German cultural rapprochement were not mutually exclusive.

Second, the economic culture approach, based as it is on cultural value systems, illuminates the complex interaction of German state and nonstate actors across and beyond national borders in international organizations. Numerous avenues of communication made the inner-German border permeable and allowed for the transfer or exchange of ideas, goods, people, and, of course, interpretations of material culture. This book thus brings together scholarship on East German and West German design and consumption, which, like most of the historiography on postwar Germany, have heretofore developed largely separately.[11] West Germany's apparent untainted economic success has not only served as a benchmark against which to measure the East German past but has also allowed Germany's eventual integration into the Western system of capitalism and liberal values to take on the semblance of a predetermined outcome.[12] Moreover, scholars' tendency to focus on just one part of Germany has led to the assumption that the two countries developed in very different, indeed contrasting, ways, with a particular interpretation of industrial modernity in the East being labeled "socialist modern."[13] Yet studying the two Germanys alongside each other underscores how much—and at what points—they influenced each other. Against the backdrop of state policy, the dynamics among designers, entrepreneurs, retailers, and ordinary Germans can show when and why these actors competed or cooperated over the question of what modernization meant for the GDR, the Federal Republic, and the relationship between the two countries.

Designing One Nation thus seeks to offer a narrative that, as historian Konrad Jarausch describes, "break[s] out of the strait-jacket of parallel stories" and instead looks at mutual influence and internal relationships without losing sight of ideological differences.[14] Addressing the Cold War from the German perspective, a focus on trade and design offers a detailed look at instances of exchange and even cooperation in Europe across the Cold War divide.[15] Such moments of German-German agreement came to the fore especially during the so-called Second Cold War in the early 1980s, when the Soviet-American relationship deteriorated and set the stage for Germany's gradual diplomatic emancipation. The two German states employed the constructive message of product design to communicate alternatives to nuclear deterrence for European security and peace. These initiatives show that German elites consciously used economic and intellectual resources to normalize East-West relations, which eventually undermined the Cold War status quo and helped to pave the way for unification. The tentative endpoint, the unification of 1990, meanwhile, must be examined without the teleological assumption that East and West Germany are easily identified as one nation. After all, almost nobody in Germany, East or West, believed that reunification would be possible up until the point when it actually happened.[16]

And yet, in examining a process of rapprochement there are always the pitfalls of teleology that undermine the exploration of patterns of past developments. Convergence theory of the 1960s predicted the inevitable harmonization of capitalist and socialist countries.[17] Facing the same challenges of the industrial age, the theory assumed, both systems would solve their respective problems with similar technological means that eventually would create the same social and political modernity. East and West Germany might seem like ideal candidates for testing this theory. Yet, convergence implies a kind of linear development that glosses over the complex internal relationship that bound the two German states together. In fact, East German social scientists rejected the theory, as it hollowed out the raison d'être of the socialist project. It was seen as a Western, anticommunist plot, and in particular during the years of détente the GDR felt as a result that it needed to double down the demarcation effort in the ideological struggle with the West.[18] In going beyond parallel histories of convergence, changing and constantly renegotiated values and norms become visible in economic and foreign policy, in processes of production and consumption, in applied aesthetic concepts as well as in institutional and individual agency in the economic culture of partition. Approaching the German-German past through episodes of mutual provocation and cooperation in the field of economic policy therefore allows for a clearer picture of the tensions that fueled their trajectories.

At the center stands the question of how the two Germanys turned a competitive situation, the implementation of legitimizing socioeconomic orders, into a diplomatic tool for reconciliation.

The sources that shed light on this question come from diverse political, economic, and cultural institutional archives, published sources, oral histories, and visits to factories and retailers. Among other official sources, the book incorporates previously inaccessible documents on the activities of the West German Ministry for Economic Affairs (Bundesministerium für Wirtschaft, BMWi) and the Permanent Mission (Ständige Vertretung) in East Berlin that detail the mechanisms and behind-the-scenes bartering of the intra-German trade. Design archives in combination with the papers of the FRG and GDR foreign offices helped to establish how the two German states operationalized trade and material culture in international organizations for diplomatic goals. Meanwhile, design magazines, interior design advice literature, and exhibition catalogs offer insights into the changing meanings of material aesthetics. Interviews with former East and West German designers and politicians were instrumental in closing gaps in the archival documentation of technological and aesthetic development in product design, which the GDR referred to as industrial design much earlier than the West.[19] Visual sources from a number of sociological studies and design journals provide a rare glimpse into the homes of East and West Germans, exposing their levels of taste appropriation and expressions of individuality. In addition, visits to furniture manufacturers and retailers helped to establish their technological, material, and infrastructural challenges. These wide-ranging sources connect the sphere of policymaking to policy implementation in the everyday lives of East and West Germans. The fact that the furniture industry developed similarly in terms of mechanization and labor intensity in the two Germanys, save for the difference in resource availability and investment stagnation in later decades, allows for a close examination of comparative developments in production and consumption. It is, for instance, unlike the automotive industry, which had disabling structural and competitive inequalities that would render any comparison futile from the outset.

The analysis of postwar Germany's economic culture unfolds in five thematic chapters. Wartime destruction offered an empty canvas for material reinvention in Germany after the end of the Second World War. Chapter 1 follows the rise and fall of disciples from the famous Bauhaus school and members of the architecture and design association Werkbund in the institutionalization of national product aesthetics in the late 1940s and early 1950s. Their goal to create a forward-looking cultural and economic vision for Germany, which would distance it from the politicized aesthetics of the Third Reich, relied initially on the modernist mantra "form follows function." The GDR soon abandoned simplistic design in favor of highly ornamented styles to ideologically demarcate itself from the West. In the late 1960s, this GDR cultural policy was reversed, though not for purely economic reasons during a period of industrial standard-ization as previous scholarship has proposed. Instead western debates about functionalism's dogmatism enabled the GDR intelligentsia to reclaim modern aesthetics for the socialist planned economy.

Turning discourse on official aesthetics into practice set both German states on a track toward "nation branding." The term describes the efforts of a network of designers and producers to create a narrative of political significance around their products. Chapter 2 offers a behind-the-scenes look at this translation pro-cess in the furniture industry. In particular, it underscores the business ethos of small- and medium-sized enterprises, the backbone of Germany's industry, in both economic systems. Ultimately, this demonstrates that durable designs and quality materials were favored in both economic systems, although execution varied according to resources.

Domestic economic structures were not the only way in which national brand similarities were discovered and maintained. By the mid-1960s, the two German production cultures started to converge in a rationalized, streamlined aesthetic. It was not the case that, when faced with the same economic problems, capitalist and communist systems inevitably arrived at similar solutions. Rather, while the FRG successfully regained a reputation for excellence in interior design, the need for foreign currency in the GDR eventually led to a search for customers in the global market. This economic reorientation gave incentives to East German designers and producers to cater to western trends and tastes. Chapter 3 reveals how intra-German trade, strategically financed by the Federal Republic, played a significant role in undermining the Cold War division in Europe and paved the way for East-West cultural rapprochement.

With a focus on material culture as a means of diplomacy, chapter 4 demon-strates how industrial design became an important part of trade as a lingua franca in the German Question and offered space for exploration of alternatives to eastern and western alignment. The analysis builds on a growing literature on German cultural diplomacy and expands design histories by exploring industrial design's—and related questions of export trade's—operationalization for diplo-matic purposes in the context of German division.[20] It examines cultural activ-ities in the International Council of Societies of Industrial Designers (ICSID) and the friendly competition that emerged from it in the context of talks about cultural cooperation following the German-German Basic Treaty in 1972. Despite attempts by the Federal Republic to isolate East Germany, the GDR succeeded in using membership in international organizations as stepping-stones toward international recognition. It is here that the potential for a "third way" between eastern and western integration emerged in German foreign policy.

Beyond the spheres of production and trade, consumers constituted an important factor in economic culture. Contemporary politicians and industrial designers were concerned about the taste levels among the population and implemented a multitude of strategies, such as publications and design exhibitions, to educate consumers from the 1950s onward. Not only were consumers the target of prescriptive elite taste education, but I argue in chapter 5 that they also presented a benchmark for success in establishing particular domestic cultures that expressed respective political and economic goals. Interestingly, despite the apparent differences between what economist János Kornai has named the socialist "economics of shortage" and the western market economy of abundance, similar narratives about functionalist aesthetics emerged in East and West German homes. They reveal a conservative modernism shaped by traditional elements in social and housing policy that translated into moderated production designs and consumer tastes.

The Cold War determined the context for the difficult relationship between the Federal Republic and the GDR, and the partition left Europe with the question of whether or not Germany should be able to unite and what role it should play in the region. While this "German Question" lost its political urgency after the peaceful unification of 1990, it is still part and parcel of its Cold War history.[1] The lens of economic culture and related questions of design, trade, and consumption in combination with the political dimensions of the German Question offer an intriguing alternative to traditional Cold War histories of Germany that emphasize rivalry. In revealing similarities and instances of collaboration, it refocuses Germany's Cold War history on the special relationship between the two German states. The findings help to explain the relative stability of the division over four decades and illuminate the comparatively smooth transition to unification in 1990. Moreover, they show how, in particular, West Germany—underneath thick layers of Western integration and international politics that strived to isolate the GDR—invested in sustainable economic and cultural policies that kept alive ties across the Iron Curtain, in the end designing one nation.

CHAPTER I

Form Follows Function

Industrial Design and the Emergence of Postwar Economic Culture

I N 1967, WALTER GROPIUS, founder of the Bauhaus School and then émigré to the United States, wrote a letter to the Federal Ministry for Economic
Affairs (Bundesministerium für Wirtschaft, BMWi) to intervene in the
debate about state funding for design institutions. Expressing his astonishment
about West Germany's limited use of design resources to enhance the national
prestige of its production, Gropius warned that the federal government was
making an enormous mistake: "More than ever, I am convinced that the solution to cultural-political questions touched upon by design belong at the center
of public interest, not the periphery." After all, design institutions such as the
Deutscher Werkbund and the Bauhaus had once asserted Germany's international leadership in modernist aesthetics, the architect maintained. Convinced
that the Bauhaus tradition had been appraised "inaccurately" by the political
and cultural elites in Germany, he identified "a lack of connections to powerful
figures in government and economy after the war" as the real reason for this
negligence.[1]

Gropius's intervention came at a moment of cultural crisis in West Germany
that placed the rational-modern aesthetics of functionalism at the center of public political debate. Material culture was one of many battlefields on which the
1968 generation challenged the conservative reconstruction values of Adenauer's
Germany. Disappointed by how little two decades of efforts at cultural reinvention had achieved in terms of creating a truly democratic West German society,
social movements demanded a more honest examination of Germany's national
culture, not least in regard to the Nazi past. Their requests led to the realization
that, because Adenauer had prioritized Western integration and Cold War competition with the GDR over dealing honestly with the legacy of the Third Reich,
postwar aesthetics had lost their impetus for true democratic reform. This in

turn enabled the GDR eventually to reclaim modern, functional aesthetics and production ethics for the socialist project in the East. Curiously, the cultural crisis in the West put the two German national aesthetics on a path of convergence.

While the late 1960s were thus a watershed moment in pan-German aesthetic development, the expatriate Gropius could not have been further from the truth in his evaluation of industrial design's significance in postwar Germany. An analysis of institutionalization processes in cultural and economic politics of the immediate postwar years on either side of the Iron Curtain reveals how deeply interlinked and invested the interwar design elites were in the construction of postfascist societies. In fact, interior design and questions pertaining to the creation of new ways of living in East and West Germany received much attention as well as resources from the governments due to pressing demands for housing and, consequently, furniture.

Meanwhile, the war-scarred economy required efficient use of limited resources. Officials looked for structural solutions that could cultivate an economic culture built on greater coherence among the different participants in the production and consumption processes. Both Bonn and East Berlin supported proposals to develop institutions that would professionalize designers, acquaint producers with the merits of quality, or "good," design, and educate consumers in questions of style and taste to create the "right" demand within the scope of available resources. Contrary to Gropius's assertion that interwar design and its proponents had been forgotten, the members of the Werkbund and Bauhaus in particular pioneered this material cultural reinvention in both Germanys. Moreover, the rational aesthetic philosophy of interwar modernism served as a common point of reference in East and West Germany, alternating between an ideal to aspire to and a foil to reject, but in either case shaping German postwar culture. While the discourse first focused on aesthetics as the visual communicator of societal change and progress, this was not an entirely cultural undertaking. Despite vast changes in levels of prosperity and general public well-being on either side of the border over the first two postwar decades, the discursive concepts that tied the idea of "good design" to sensible economics remained stable.[2]

What happened during this period of design institutionalization in the years from 1945 to 1967 that led Gropius to assume that postwar West Germany had neglected the legacy of Bauhaus modernism? To answer this question this chapter follows debates surrounding the politicization of aesthetics as well as their institutionalization in East and West Germany from a comparative perspective. It does so to illuminate the cultural and economic reconfiguration of two divergent German political systems, marred by their National Socialist past, whose attempts at rehabilitation extended from the public sphere all the way into the homes of the population. As a unified future moved out of reach with the introduction of the West German Mark (Deutsche Mark, DM) or D-Mark in 1948, the two German states explored diverging aesthetic options to develop identities for their part of the country. Cultural concerns about reconstruction design and living standards, often fought out in the field of economics, increasingly mirrored domestic and international tensions over the question of Germany's division. It is thus important to consider how developments in both German states influenced each other.

At the same time, the reconstruction challenge connected the two Germanys to debates that were happening in other societies, illuminating the European dimension of postwar cultural and economic reform. For instance, Swedish and British design institutions inspired the German institutionalization process and served as a point of reference for both the West German Design Council (Rat für Formgebung, RfF) and the East German Central Institute for Design (Zentralinstitut für Formgestaltung, ZfF; renamed Amt für industrielle Formgestaltung, AiF, in 1972). Britain established its Council of Industrial Design "to promote by all practicable means the improvement of design in the products of British industry" in 1944.[3] Dedicated to quality control, consumer education, and national trademark promotion, this institution would be decisive in shaping a cohesive aesthetic for British national design and projecting a modern image abroad.[4] Turning a war economy to peacetime production presented a parallel challenge, and thus the Germans were eager to learn. But the fact that in Germany this process began under Allied occupation added another layer to the debate. Both American and Soviet occupiers attempted to envelop their part of Germany culturally into their sphere of influence, which remained a contentious issue domestically and internationally throughout the reconstruction period.

Looking at political action and reactions on both sides of the Iron Curtain highlights exchanges across the increasingly fortified inner-German border and tenable analysis of how these exchanges shaped structural and cultural developments in East and West Germany. It also furthers understanding of how political and structural differences influenced the ability of modernism's disciples to realize their vision of postfascist modernity in democratic and socialist societies. Cultural exchange across the Wall has been documented before, often as influenced by Americanization or Westernization.[5] While Western influence certainly figured largely as a backdrop to Germany's postwar consumerist turn, Americanization is a less helpful concept when looking at industrial design as a professional field, as it threatens to overemphasize Allied influence in this area of

German cultural development and to underplay the legacy of interwar aesthetics in the German-German relationship. East German designers in particular have been portrayed as uninspired copyists, who followed Western trends to answer public demand and were thus complicit in the regime's strategy to bribe the GDR population via consumer goods in return for political support.[6] Such a view eclipses GDR design's creative potential while focusing on the East's consumer good production output, which admittedly remained inferior throughout the Cold War due to the lack of appropriate machinery and quality materials, and mismanagement. In fact, a rich and visionary discourse took place in the GDR that far exceeded West German thinking about the material environment and its place in postwar society. Tracing the politics of German postwar design in both national cultures underscores mutual fertilization, while revisiting assumptions about East German achievements, or the purported lack thereof, that have developed in public memory.

The Long Shadow of National Socialism: Reinterpreting German Modernism

Historical scholarship on German industrial design has established that aesthetics did not change very much from 1925 to 1965: "What did change . . . was the cultural meaning and representation of design, as the very same objects were embraced by dramatically incongruous political regimes as visual markers of their specific political projects," historian Paul Betts explains.[7] This time frame brackets the heyday of modernism referenced in Gropius's comments, a time of great influence for the German architecture and design reformers of the Deutscher Werkbund and the Bauhaus. The Werkbund, an association of architects, artists, and aesthete industrialists founded in 1907, had a long tradition of involvement in German cultural politics. It adopted "social aesthetics" as its cause, which the association promoted via exhibitions, competitions, and publications until the National Socialist regime absorbed it into its cultural organizations in 1933.[8] Founded by Walter Gropius in 1919, the avant-gardist Bauhaus school has become synonymous with German modernism in architecture, photography, painting, and product design.[9] Germany's politically tumultuous first half of the twentieth century continuously affected how the Werkbund and the Bauhaus operated in changing political environments.

Since the Wilhelmine period, Werkbund activities had focused on forging ties to political circles to fund their vision of modernity based on the moral and educational value of everyday objects.[10] They reacted against the mechanizing elements of industrialization, which had been perceived as a threat to traditional craftsmanship and the cultural value of goods since the second half of the nineteenth century. Werkbund members, theorists and practitioners alike, looked to reconcile industrial production (standardization) and design (spiritualization) in aesthetic, social, and economic regards. They strove to achieve a quality of objectivity "through adopting a rational approach to form-giving, guided by the requirements of engineering and technology, which were deeply respected."[11] Emphasizing the use of quality materials and simple, functional shapes, the association promoted the concept of "good design" as a middle ground between alienating mechanical asceticism and abundant decoration to introduce a material culture of modern everyday objects.[12] In later years, the credo "form follows function" united the Bauhaus with these Werkbund ideas.

The post–World War I era saw an expansion and radicalization of such design conceptions, which developed traction particularly in urban planning and public housing.[13] The Great Depression abruptly ended a period of state-supported architectural experimentation in 1929, leaving many ideas for the industrial age unexplored, and the Werkbund henceforth struggled with its association with this vision of failed industrialism.[14] The movement thus came under attack both from the political left and right. Werkbund ideals for industrial modernism presented a provocation to cultural conservatives who feared that industrialization would do away with distinctly German culture. On the left, radical Marxists condemned Werkbund elites for being detached from the masses and wasting their talents on designing luxuries.[15] With the Nazi seizure of power, the Werkbund ceased to exist as a private association and was brought first under the jurisdiction of Joseph Goebbels's Reich Chamber of the Visual Arts (Reichskammer der bildenden Künste) and later under that of the Reich Chamber of Culture (Reichskulturkammer).[16] Despite their different political perspectives, Werkbund industrial modernism and Nazi culture, with its agricultural "blood and soil" ideology, proved to be compatible at least in the realm of industry, rationalization, and propaganda.[17]

It was this aesthetic and political legacy against which the Werkbund had to reconstitute after World War II. Indeed, its problematic involvement with the Nazi regime was something that the Werkbund desired to leave in the past. In contrast, the 1933 closure of the Bauhaus and the resulting emigration of most of its teachers freed the Bauhaus legacy from any allegations of complicity with the Nazi regime. In postwar West Germany, the term "Bauhaus modernism" carried an antifascist connotation, rendering it initially a safer aesthetic reference than

"Werkbund functionalism" in the public sphere. Bauhaus modernism served as shorthand for everything that National Socialism opposed.[18] As a result, this term distinguished the Federal Republic culturally from the Third Reich, but it also released both theoreticians and practitioners of industrial design from any inherent necessity to seriously consider design's sociopolitical function. Moreover, modernism's association with an untainted past made it difficult for the intellectual elite to critique the aesthetics and their political instrumentalization in postwar Germany. Associated with Western democratic values, art historian Frederic J. Schwartz concludes, Bauhaus aesthetics left the Federal Republic without the necessary reference points, concepts, or terminology to move beyond its past.[19]

Nevertheless, the devastated and bombed-out cities offered the Werkbund a new beginning and manifold opportunities for imprinting its principles on postwar material culture. In a turn away from the visual politics of fascism that emphasized the aestheticization of the relationship between people in the public arena, such as Albert Speer's grandiose productions for the National Socialist German Workers' Party (Nationalsozialistische Deutsche Arbeiterpartei, NSDAP) mass rallies, the postfascist campaign focused on the private sphere.[20] In an effort to overcome the administrative and economic divisions imposed by Allied occupation, the Werkbund joined forces with former Bauhaus students in both the eastern and western zones of Germany to encourage the institutionalization of industrial design with the deliberate goal of maintaining a unified cultural identity.[21] Yet the aesthetic continuity with Weimar functionalism in spite of political change posed challenges for the successive regimes on German territory: how to instill new meaning into the relationship between politics and design, between people and things, when the material culture, for all intents and purposes, looked the same?

Immediately after the war, the Werkbund re-established regional groups in the eastern and western occupation zones in cities like Dresden, East and West Berlin, Düsseldorf, and Stuttgart. The association quickly gained official recognition with the western authorities. By the summer of 1948, regional governments subsidized the Werkbund group *West-Nord* with DM 10,000 annually and the Bavarian cultural ministry generously gave its regional group DM 60,000 per year.[22] Public financial support signified an acknowledgment of design as a constitutive part of the reconstruction effort and an early flirtation with modernist aesthetics in the West. Such official cooperation considerably facilitated the Werkbund's later involvement in the foundation of a West German design council that would continue the association's mission to prevent the production of kitsch and educate the consumer about the "right" consumption.

The Werkbund bid for aesthetic leadership in the Federal Republic with two domestic culture exhibitions mounted in Cologne and Stuttgart in 1949. *New Dwelling* and *How to Dwell?* showed modernist solutions for small families in the bombed-out cities in Germany's west. Northern European, Swiss, and American influences were immediately visible. Any confidence in once-powerful Werkbund ideals existed only in the exhibitions' reliance on abstraction for the product placement in the displays.[23] Promoting pure minimalism in furnishings, *New Dwelling* prescribed Germans modesty in their consumer behavior. The exhibition encouraged moral choices based on a collective commitment to counter the corrupting influence of materialism, false abundance, or pretentious ornamentation.[24] The Werkbund tied its tradition of taste education (*Geschmacksbildung*) to its struggle against kitsch, which had long been associated with social decay.[25] Photographs from this exhibition show multifunctional room settings that are best described as empty. This decorating style stemmed from the poor state of the German economy, underscored by an outdated prewar product range peppered with barely finished prototypes. But it also expressed the Werkbund's renewed search for socially responsible aesthetics. A poster proclaiming "Werkbund is no Luxury" (*Werkbund ist kein Luxus*) advertised a reincarnation of the failed interwar mission: to make affordable and well-designed products for the masses.[26] The Economic Administration for the Tri-Zone publicly embraced the Werkbund effort, which heralded the dawn of national solutions to problems of Germany's postwar housing crisis.[27] Earlier that year, the Economic Administration had entered negotiations with the Werkbund about a "committee for design," but this had not come to fruition because of unsettled finances and an alleged lack of dedication on the part of the Werkbund. Nevertheless, Werkbund members publicly announced the idea for a national "council for industrial design" at their annual congress in June 1949 in Cologne, underlining again their claim to cultural leadership in the everyday.[28] With West Germany still under Allied occupation, the realization of such a council, however, hinged on the restoration of a German-led government to power and the right motivation for investment in cultural politics at the national level. Such motivation eventually materialized with the growing reappearance of German products on the global market.

Meanwhile, the Werkbund groups in the Soviet zone of occupation increasingly lost their political influence. The Soviet Military Administration in Germany (SMAD) cemented political leadership with the SED in 1946, a first step

FIGURE 1.1. Graphic designer Hanns Lohrer designed this poster
advertising one of the first postwar Werkbund exhibitions,
the *How to Dwell?* show in Stuttgart, 1949. Photograph courtesy
of Werkbundarchiv—Museum der Dinge Berlin 020627.
© Hanns Lohrer succession.

toward the party dictatorship that would emerge in 1949.[29] Irritated by the coercive centralization of most cultural fields, prominent Werkbund members, such as industrial designer Wilhelm Wagenfeld in East Berlin and architect Egon Eiermann in Dresden, emigrated to the West. Others committed to the Werkbund and Bauhaus principles holding stronger socialist ideals, such as industrial designers Mart Stam and Horst Michel and architect Selman Selmanagic, remained in the eastern zone.[30] The SMAD opened schools for the education of designers, beginning with the Weimar University for Architecture and the Arts in 1946. Weimar, significant as the location of the first Bauhaus school, thus remained a postwar center for artists, architects, and designers. Horst Michel, an experienced member of famed architect and interior designer Bruno Paul's studio, started an industrial design program there.[31] Provincial Weimar turned out to be the perfect setting to reconstitute East Germany's material culture, offering Michel and the university the opportunity for diverse partnerships with local industries.[32]

In contrast to his West German counterparts who had practically unlimited possibilities in their approach to industrial design, Michel found his work increasingly circumscribed by socialist ideology and constraints of nascent political centralization. The challenge lay in materially expressing the immaterial virtues of socialism, which, Michel recognized, entailed not only the aesthetic education of designers but also the education of consumers to create the right demand for a socialist domestic environment. In Michel's eyes, durability, honesty, effective use of materials, reduced storage and transportation costs, and the avoidance of moral decay and pretension of value appreciation via "unauthentic" materials or embellished surfaces marked good socialist design.[33] These qualities fit perfectly with the eastern occupation zone's plans for industrialization of crafts in large-scale production. At the same time, they closely aligned with the Werkbund vision in the West, equally concerned with the moral perils of kitsch. To Michel, kitsch embodied the reverse of socialist ideals, a complex concept of profit-induced diversity that differs from today's definition of kitsch as cheap trumpery. Like other twentieth-century cultural critics, Michel blamed kitsch on capitalist industrialization and mass production:

It seems to be necessary to fight increasingly rampant kitsch and its inherent waste of resources at the level of the state and to influence the quality of products from crafts and industry. The multiplicity of shapes, more or less resulting from financial greed, the amassing of dishonest pomp on appliances of the everyday and basic commodities, as well as the wasting of resources mean an exploitation of the people and dissipation of the people's wealth.[34]

Anticipating the later GDR economic motto "if only good is produced, nothing bad can be sold," Michel drafted a "Law Against the Exploitation of the People by Kitsch" and introduced it into the Thuringia regional parliament in 1947.[35] While the Kitsch bill did not pass, he successfully introduced a quality seal for crafts and applied arts in Thuringia: a white lily and hammer in a blue circle. Retailers recognized the merits of the seal and priced these products higher, which in turn incentivized industry and crafts to produce better products. With the cooperation of local companies, Michel also assembled household wares and ceramics in large juried shows that created criteria for socialist good design. This practice continued in later years during standardization and *Sortimentsbereinigung*, an effort to reduce the number of models for a given product to increase Plan efficiency and industrial output.[36] These episodes illustrate Michel's involvement in ideological debates about production and kitsch even before the official founding of the German Democratic Republic. While his principled take on socialist good design aligned with economic policy, his aesthetic sensitivities would soon clash with official stylistic development under Soviet influence.

Between 1946 and 1948, the SMAD worked toward the centralization of cultural politics in cooperation with its German partners.[37] Here the SED hoped to ensure uniformity in the political reorganization process that accompanied the growing German division. By May 1948 the SED announced an all-encompassing claim to cultural leadership at the party's Culture Conference (*Kulturtag*): "[The Culture Conference] has illustrated the character of the Party as a party of culture in the broadest sense of the word as well as the leading intellectual force in Germany's democratic reconstruction."[38] Henceforth, principles of party control, rather than artistic and aesthetic concerns, guided East German cultural and educational policies. Consequently, the *Kulturtag* marked the end of any assumed or aspired cultural unity between East and West. The decision to pursue a "socialist" culture in the eastern zone of occupation allowed the SED to model its part of Germany on the Soviet example, in contrast to the liberal cultural fabric of the Federal Republic. These contrasting approaches to cultural policy set the stage for similarly divergent national aesthetics in East and West Germany during the reconstruction period.

Separate Economies, Separate Design

The nascent cultural division between East and West deepened as the Western Allies took measures to solidify the war-damaged German economy. The Marshall Plan and the currency reform of 1948 cemented the separation, creating two German economies. Acting against the Allied agreement on Germany's economic unity at the 1945 Potsdam conference, Britain, France, and the United States merged their occupation zones and treated this territory of the so-called Trizone as a single economic unit while de facto excluding the Soviet zone of occupation.[39] Eventually, the subsequent Soviet blockade of Berlin between June 1948 and May 1949, challenging joint control over Berlin, effectively foreclosed Allied cooperation in Germany and complicated the status of Berlin. These events dashed hopes for a unified future and left Germany to emerge as the ideological battleground of the Cold War.

When East Germany achieved statehood as the German Democratic Republic in the fall of 1949, cultural delineation from the West became a pressing ideological concern. The construction of a national identity by the GDR included the socialist remaking of society and all its underlying structures. Toward these ends, early state socialism and its artistic proponents took a comprehensive approach to the human environment, discussing new ways of feeling, thinking, and living specific to the working class.[40] Such efforts followed the example of the constructivists in the Soviet Union of the 1920s, an avant-garde movement that had shifted the focus from art for art's sake to an active engagement in processes of sociopolitical restructuring inspired by the goals of the Bolshevik Revolution. The constructivist understanding of artistic production rendered every aesthetic decision a political one.[41] Aesthetic expressions were meant to impact the population in its evolution toward revolutionary consciousness.[42] Art and the material environment therefore played an important role in the education of the socialist individual and the creation of collective socialist identity.

While the constructivist bond between politics and culture had remained strong under Stalin, the carefully crafted relationship between art and the everyday was replaced by material culture that favored form and emotionality over function, a style commonly known as socialist realism.[43] Socialist realist architecture, for instance, explored extremes, achieving monumental, heavily ornamented, and pompous aesthetics.[44] Instead of integrating art into the everyday, under Stalin art came to dominate the design of everyday objects, betraying the ideas of the Bolshevik avant-garde. The GDR arrived at similar juncture in its

socialist aesthetic development about twenty-five years later, an outcome predetermined by the Soviet example.

During the years of occupation, the SMAD demanded German recognition
of Soviet cultural superiority.[45] While Soviet influence remained considerable
after 1949, East Germans increasingly commanded their own state apparatus
and decision-making, at least in regard to domestic policies. Consequently, the
SED faced the task of creating the parameters of a German socialist culture,
which not only encompassed high culture forms of the arts in literature, painting, and music but also the culture of everyday life. Industrial design, the material manifestation of socialist thought and its realization at the crossroads of
applied arts and economic planning, became part of this aesthetic reinvention.

East Germany's socially conscious approach to cultural rebuilding did not go
unnoticed in the West.[46] After Werkbund member Wilhelm Wagenfeld, one
of Germany's most influential Bauhaus-trained designers, had left the East, he
warned Hermann Veit, the minister of Economic Affairs of Baden-Württemberg, in 1949: "I am from Berlin and, therefore, from the Germany beyond the
zone border. I have seen that we can counter the East only with a new intellectual world and, thus, with new social empathy and thinking."[47] Wagenfeld
understood the intellectual appeal of socialism as he himself held leftist political
views and had remained loyal to the Werkbund mission that promoted designers' social responsibility. Most important though, by suggesting that western
material culture was to be inscribed with moral meaning, Wagenfeld pointed to
the need for a deeper rethinking of social and cultural structures to counter the
lure of socialist material collectivism. At the same time, his remarks show that
industrial design became a competitive field in the German Cold War, which
began to shape the West German discourse in contrast to the quickly developing
socialist alternative in the East.

Wagenfeld's warning to the Baden-Württemberg administration echoed
West German intellectuals' earlier antifascist campaigns for a complete break
with the German past. Their vision included an alternative material and social philosophy that stood in opposition to the so-called war-mongering forces
of nationalism and capitalism. They envisioned a social revolution that would
give birth to a humanized, non-Marxist Germany in the middle of a united
Europe led by the young generation with "its perceived condition of alienation
from the German past."[48] Yet this radical new beginning did not occur. Instead,
supported by the Western Allies, the older Weimar generation took control in
Bonn and quickly marginalized the leftists in the newly established capitalist
economic system.

This power shift emerged most clearly in West Germany's foreign trade ambitions. As the country gradually reintegrated into international economic circles as a contributor to the reconstruction of Europe, West Germans longed to rekindle export relations and publicized their adherence to Western capitalist principles and peaceful economic competition.[49] To test the waters, the Trizone participated in the Decorate Your House exhibition in New York in early 1949. It was the first time since World War II that the occupiers granted German industrialists permission to take part in an international trade event. In his opening remarks to the German industry show catalog, Ludwig Erhard, the director of the tri-zone economic administration, expressed his hope that the West German display would prove to the world that "the German people's only desire today is to strive diligently for the improvement of human and social welfare and to show that they have kept their strength and ability for the accomplishment of this desire despite all the mistakes and the terror of the previous decade."[50] Yet Erhard downplayed the materialistic and commercial components of Germany's participation in the fair, thereby missing an opportunity to establish a cultural bond based on shared attitudes toward trade and consumption with the West, particularly the United States. Instead, he placed German economic recovery in a moral and social context, thus emphasizing the ethical importance of aesthetic reinvention. New German aesthetics, he pronounced, should display industriousness and efficiency in the service of the common good, which implied a rejection of the pompous aesthetics connected to the public displays of National Socialism. Moreover, Erhard's statement expressed the perhaps naïve sentiment among the West German political and economic elites that economic prosperity could replace, if not redeem, the vices of the Third Reich in public memory. In this way, politicians began to instill German products with symbolic meaning that went beyond economic values, but fell short of a progressive social vision.

Erhard embraced these material promises for a better future and promoted them abroad as new West German virtues. He described the New York exhibition displays as conveying the "honest work of German hands and minds."[51] The German trade show participation in New York thus marked a watershed moment in cultural diplomacy, which was henceforth wrapped in a rhetoric that equated aesthetic quality and material reliability with moral deliverance from the Nazi past, which, it was hoped, would improve West Germany's international standing.[52] These initial years of western economic activity coupled with a new morality laid the foundation for a West German democratic identity based on economic success that came to fruition during the "economic miracle" of the late 1950s and 1960s.

While the catalog clearly presented the message of a recivilized Germany, the material content of the New York displays failed to convince its intended audience.[53] Showcasing curved, heavy recliners and an embellished display cabinet made of mahogany, the German exhibition received reviews that ranged from ridicule to outrage at what was regarded as impractical, pompous kitsch.[54] Insecure about what kind of aesthetic could best demonstrate Germans' reformed postwar attitudes, exhibitioners relied on best-selling Bavarian arts and crafts and Louis XV–style furniture. Such bold designs with extravagant use of materials, though, felt inappropriate amid the postwar scarcity of resources and living space. Critiques centered on the impression created of a culturally backward and arrogant Germany, the failure to break culturally with the Nazi past, and Germany's abandonment of its heritage of international modernism.[55] It gave cause for concern that products "made in Germany" could again gain a negative reputation on the global market.[56] After this opprobrium in New York, West Germany's political and industrial elites finally realized that aesthetic reinvention warranted more organized approaches.

The Struggle to Institutionalize Modern German Aesthetics

The following period from 1950 through 1953 proved critical in German state-directed industrial design as intensifying cultural debates led to the creation of design councils in East and West. After decades of lobbying, the Werkbund goals finally intersected with government interests in the early 1950s to create a modern German identity. Notably, the acknowledgment of the economic dimension of design in both Germanys resulted in the same conceptual shift: Both the East and West German governments created central institutions dedicated to the development of national aesthetics.

In stark contrast to the centralized state administration in the East, the federal organization of West Germany assigned the individual states authority for culture, education, and regional economic development. Within this pluralistic and decentralized state-building process, lobbying became a strong feature of West German political culture. The Werkbund aimed its lobbying activities at making the institutionalization of industrial design a governmental priority. The creation of a national Werkbund umbrella organization in 1950 under architect Hans Schwippert's leadership decisively shaped the course of events.[57] This united Werkbund successfully impressed upon the Adenauer administration the notion that a centralized governmental institution should oversee West Germany's commodity aesthetic. With its close ties to Bonn's political elite—Theodor

Heuss, the first president of the FRG, was a member—the Werkbund members were able to discuss the idea with representatives of the Federal Ministry of Economics and to win the support of parliamentarian Arno Hennig (Social Democratic Party, SPD) for the design council plans in the Bundestag.[58] In October 1950, Werkbund member Heinrich König was invited to bring the plans for a national design council before the Bundestag Committee on Cultural Policy. Reminding the parliamentarians of the embarrassment at the New York exhibition, König connected Germany's international reputation to domestic reconstruction needs: "Instead of handy, functional, and comfortable things to furnish the small apartments of public housing, producers offer heavy, pompous show-pieces of impractical arrangement." König concluded that it created a situation in which "production continued with no regard to the real needs of the masses."[59] While economic connections between design and export rates dominated the ensuing discussion, the limited mentions of aesthetic considerations emphasized shaping a national style. Referencing national brands of world renown, such as Murano glass, Brussels lace, and French luxury commodities, expert witness Max Wiederanders reminded the committee to demand quality production that German consumers could trust. Although assimilation to foreign tastes was thought to increase exports, he regarded this to be of secondary importance as German workmanship in quality products would speak for itself.[60] What was needed, according to the Werkbund and its supporters, was a national institution capable of executing a prescriptive and holistic aesthetic reform program. Yet, gaining unlimited support for a national design council proved difficult in the early years of the FRG, because it countered the trend of cultural decentralization.

At the same time, the heightened anticommunism of the early Cold War as well as the existence of the East German socialist alternative made the parliament suspicious about leftist influences on national aesthetics. Given this parliamentary apprehension and its historic connections to leftist reform movements, the Werkbund changed its strategy to complement the government's two main interests in industrial design: export increase and the diplomatic value of material culture. At subsequent parliamentary hearings in 1950 and 1951, Werkbund representatives again invoked the embarrassment of the New York fair to stress the economic gains that the Federal Republic could acquire through the national organization of design activities. Eventually, the evident economic opportunity trumped concerns about undermining cultural federalism as the Bundestag voted in favor of the initiative with only one opposing vote in 1951.[61] This vote swiftly formalized the Federal Republic's claim to Weimar modernism, ensured

Werkbund control over design politics, and set the country on the path to finding a West German aesthetic that could withstand Americanization.

Indeed, the Western Allies, particularly the American military administration, intensified efforts to integrate West Germany culturally into the ranks of Western democratic nations. Financed by the Marshall Plan for Western Europe, the traveling exhibition *We Build a Better Life* introduced modern home design to the West German population in 1952. During its three-week run, it drew half a million visitors in Berlin (40 percent of them from the East), Hanover, and Stuttgart. The exhibition catalog announced that "the same taste, same needs, and same interests bond the Atlantic community tightly together."[62] This "same taste" was a commitment to a modernist aesthetic reminiscent of the Bauhaus, with clear lines, sparsely furnished rooms, and the limited use of patterned fabrics and ornamented household wares. Many of the objects had been recycled from the annual "good design" exhibitions at New York's Museum of Modern Art (MoMA), as Edgar Kaufmann Jr., curator of its industrial design department, had been hired for this Marshall Plan initiative by the US State Department.[63] Much effort went into subduing the impression of cultural Americanization. US information officers stressed the inclusiveness of the aesthetic in press releases, and West German media conveyed the message: "There are different versions of one style and one way of life typical for a 'western bourgeois' household. Nothing is foreign to us, whether it comes from Berlin or Los Angeles, from Stockholm, Sicily or New York."[64] Nevertheless, many of the modern kitchen appliances had been imported from the United States and were unattainable by the average West German at the time.

In general, West German attitudes toward American patronage in industrial design were conflicted. US influence could not be completely avoided in the early years of the Federal Republic as American funding cofinanced a number of public institutions. For example, industrial designer Walter Kersting, an outspoken US critic, registered his concerns that American funding for the Ulm School of Design (Hochschule für Gestaltung Ulm, HfG Ulm) in Baden-Württemberg would give Americans control over German design. In a 1951 letter to Ludwig Erhard he wrote, "Above all, the idea that the United States will guide us to a new culture of design is no gain for the German reputation in the world."[65] Instead, Kersting pleaded for the founding of an exclusively German industrial design school, but to no avail. Eventually, Inge Scholl joined with Swiss designer Max Bill, a Bauhaus student and head of the Swiss Werkbund, in 1953 to found the school with American support that would provide a model for responsible political education. Its curriculum was to address the materialization of politics

FIGURE I.2. Interior of the Marshall Plan exhibition *We Build a Better Life* that traveled to Germany in 1952. It combined an Eames chair in the middle flanked by two Danish ones, and a table lamp designed by Isamu Noguchi for Knoll International. Photograph courtesy of Werkbundarchiv—Museum der Dinge Berlin D7020-7039. Photographer unknown.

through design, giving design a moral authority in defining the character of postwar life.[66] The goal was to "educate a democratic elite as a counterforce against the tides of intolerance."[67] The HfG Ulm labeled itself the "New Bauhaus" in 1955, thus signaling to the world that antifascist resistance and international modernism were alive and well in the Federal Republic.[68] It moreover reinforced West Germany's claim to Bauhaus modernism as its cultural heritage. Financed mainly by the Scholl Foundation, the project was also funded by the regional government of Baden-Württemberg and the American high commissioner, John J. McCloy. Despite taking American money, HfG Ulm quickly developed a design vision with an anti-American stance that objected to Western mass consumerism. Bill, Scholl, and Scholl's graphic designer husband Otl Aicher strove to develop designs that were driven by rational and systematic thinking, rather than style and fashion. "Within this," art historian Jeremy Aynsley has observed about Ulm design, "the notion of timelessness was invoked as an important criterion, defined against the phenomenon of conspicuous consumption and in-built obsolescence of the American system of industrial styling."[69] The HfG's story illuminates how the FRG, caught between the Western Allies' vision for a new Germany and the ever-present communist alternative of East Germany in the early reconstruction years, needed its own strong institutions to shape its postfascist identity.

Encountering similar reconstruction challenges, the GDR fought its battles over the cultural policy of aesthetics that had the potential to turn East Germans into socialist citizens. In the early 1950s, the so-called Formalism Debate, an ideological-artistic dispute involving SED politicians and artists, discussed a more holistic approach to the aesthetics of the socialist material environment. Deeming socialist realism the official aesthetic, the party announced a radical reorientation of all areas of cultural activity at the Third Party Congress in July 1950.[70] By displaying cultural coherence with the Soviet Union, the GDR government strove to present a contrast to West Germany. Yet, from the beginning, socialist realism also connected artistic expression to the task of enlightening and ideologically reeducating the working population in the spirit of socialism. Stressing modes of socialist production and class struggle, socialist realism focused on everyday work heroes, who built the socialist utopia, to inspire popular ideological identification. Folk culture, materially articulated in artisanal traditions, provided German national substance to the style.[71] At the same time, East German politicians, led by State Council chair and general secretary of the SED Walter Ulbricht, a cabinetmaker by trade, denounced modern functionalism as artless, international, and cosmopolitan. Its lack of ornamentation, according to the SED, signified the missing element of national culture, and the reduction of its design to simple shapes made this aesthetic formulaic. The fact that West Germany embraced functionalism as its official aesthetic only reinforced the GDR's political and ideological resolve to reject interwar modernism.

For a centrally organized state, East Germany's cultural reorientation had far-reaching consequences for the freedom of artistic expression. To protest what was effectively censorship, the artistic community publicly challenged the party's sweeping decision, but with minimal success. Over the course of three years, the government repeatedly defended its stance in newspapers and at public events. In this way, the Formalism Debate became less cultural and increasingly political in content. Alignment with the Soviet bloc outpaced the search for a homegrown modern socialist aesthetic that Horst Michel and others had begun and, eventually, the nationalistic values embedded in the realist aesthetics of

FIGURE I.3. Apartment with sample furniture in the first completed building at
Weberwiese in Stalinallee, 1952. Bundesarchiv 183-14563-0005.
Photograph: Heinz Funk.

cultural Stalinism held sway. In January 1954, the GDR Council of Ministers
commanded the furniture industry to develop aesthetically pleasing furnishings "based on the national cultural heritage."[72] Reminiscent of the style and
ornamentation of the so-called founders' period (*Gründerzeit*, c. 1870–1890),
German cultural heritage in the GDR was thereafter to be expressed in artful
decorations, curved lines, and expensive handicraft techniques. For instance,
East Germany's first major public housing project in East Berlin, the Stalinallee, showcased wedding cake–style facades, heavily adorned with sculptures and
mosaics depicting workers and farmers. A coherent vision for the apartments'
interiors followed in a 1952 exhibition held in the first finished high-rise. The
furnishings were bulky with patterned upholstery fabric. Pleated lampshades,
lace curtains, and squat-shaped porcelain added a curious petit-bourgeois atmosphere.[73] This emphasis on ornamentation came to represent simultaneously a
search for a politically untainted past, a demonstration of integration into the
Eastern Bloc, and cultural delineation from West Germany.

    While some historical analysis has cast doubt on the political significance of
the Formalism Debate—for instance pointing to the possibility that the SED
used it to create the illusion of a participatory pluralistic public sphere—there is
evidence of ideologues and functionalist designers, architects, and artists being

publicly embattled.[74] First, a number of applied art schools founded on Bauhaus teaching principles already existed in East Germany by 1950 led by steadfast socialists like Michel. The country depended on these schools to create consumer goods for reconstruction and thus wielded considerable influence. Second, the fact that the debate lasted approximately three years and was conducted in public speaks volumes about the earnestness with which politicians and cultural elites immersed themselves in the making of East German official culture.[75] Interpretations of the Formalism Debate as a predetermined affair risk to miss the initial stage in negotiations between designers and the state over the place of interwar modernism in GDR design and the struggle against an unfamiliar culture of Soviet provenance.[76]

Although praised in the initial reconstruction phase, Bauhaus modernism and its students comprised the main target of the political campaign against "formalism." Despite the risk of losing their livelihood, the GDR Bauhaus disciples resisted state intervention in artistic expression. Mart Stam, a Dutch architect appointed as the first director of the new School for Applied Arts (Hochschule für angewandte Kunst) in Berlin Weissensee in 1950, became the most prominent casualty of the conflict. Stam had introduced the Bauhaus curriculum and methods in Weissensee. A socialist idealist, he had worked with architect and urban planner Ernst May on the New Building (*Neues Bauen*) public housing projects in Frankfurt on Main in the 1920s and helped build the industrial cities of Magnitogorsk, Makeyevka, and Orsk in the Soviet Union between 1930 and 1933.[77] Stam additionally founded and headed the Weissensee Institute for Applied Arts (Institut für angewandte Kunst), the first inception of the East German design council.[78] When cultural Stalinism gained the upper hand in the Formalism Debate, Stam and his wife left the GDR in 1953, disenchanted with the country where he had hoped to contribute his vision for a socialist way of life to a true Marxist state.

Stam's departure simultaneously marked the end of the Formalism Debate and the beginning of the institutionalization of cultural Stalinism in East Germany. The remaining Bauhaus community viewed this development critically. In a surprisingly candid 1985 interview, Bauhaus-educated Selman Selmanagic, a highly regarded urban planner, interior designer, and architect, who had worked with Stam at both the Weissensee Institute and the School, lambasted the transformation of the institute into a government agency after Stam's emigration.[79] He saw Walter Heisig, Stam's successor at the Weissensee Institute, as a person "without comprehension," who "designed florets on ceramics and such kitsch."[80] Labeled as "German cultural heritage," this naïve representation of reality was henceforth the official aesthetic of the GDR. However, the practical influence of the institute on broader culture remained limited under Heisig's leadership and he does not appear to have been a strong force in the search for an East German national aesthetic.[81] The remaining Bauhaus disciples in East Germany left Berlin and went into artistic exile in the provincial centers of the GDR.[82] For example, Stam's student Martin Kelm started the independent Halle Institute for Design and Development with fellow Stam student Günter Reissmann in 1958. Many years would pass before East German disciples of modernism and their vision for the "workers and peasants' state" regained political influence.

As it faded in the East, functional modernism was gaining political and cultural influence in the West after the Bundestag resolved to create the design council on 4 April 1951, to enhance the Federal Republic's image abroad and promote the country's exports.[83] The council's tasks, such as advising industry, helping to re-establish Germany's competitiveness at international exhibitions and trade fairs, supporting design education in applied arts schools and professional training, and instructing traders and consumers about quality and design, imbued it with extensive influence over industry and consumers.[84] The Werkbund seemed to have finally reached its goals of being the arbiter of West German good taste and reviving the prewar reform project.

Centralization of cultural power in the hands of the Werkbund, though, was counteracted by two factors: funding and personnel decisions. Industrial design, emerging as a new profession in postwar Germany, competed for state funding with the fine arts. While the Federal Ministry of the Interior supported the arts financially, industrial design did not fall under their jurisdiction.[85] The connections politicians drew between industrial interests and design considerations resulted in the subordination of this new council for design (Rat für Formgebung) to the Ministry for Economic Affairs (BMWi). This decision, primarily based on budget considerations, inherently linked design to the promotion of products for export. In June 1953, the RfF was established in Darmstadt, Hesse, as a non-profit organization. West German economic interests, rather than the Werkbund's cultural hegemony, subsequently played a key role in determining the state's plan for the design council. The Werkbund could only effectively influence the planning of international exhibitions. This initial and fundamental conflict continued to generate strong infighting among different factions in the design council until the Werkbund officially withdrew from it in 1968.

The second factor undermining Werkbund influence from the start pertained to the selection criteria for RfF board membership. The original goal had been to create an advisory body of distinct personalities that took on cultural leadership in the young republic. Yet the BMWi quickly abandoned this plan and, instead, pushed for including representatives from all economic fields. Minister of Economics Ludwig Erhard (1949–1963, Christian Democratic Union, CDU) initially appointed to the council sixteen designers and industrialists, almost all of whom were Werkbund members and aesthete industrialists. But Erhard then appointed twenty more unsalaried consultants—representatives of varying concerns such as crafts, labor unions, consumer organizations, and public administration—which caused discord between the government and the initial council members.[86] The Werkbund especially objected to the appointment of Eduard Schlafejew as council director. Schlafejew had been a competent economic administrator in Erhard's BMWi, which, in their eyes, made him a "puppet of industry" who lacked design expertise.[87] Instead of an innovative and modern aesthetic mission, the Werkbund lamented, the council would become a pawn for economic interests, a "second Federal Trade Office."[88] This, the Werkbund feared, would strip the design council of cultural assertiveness and diminish its leadership in material culture.[89] Lobbyist König, worried about a loss of control and influence, likened the situation to the Werkbund's first experience with failing state-cooperation in the Weimar Republic under the Reich art supervisor (*Reichskunstwart*).[90] After more than a year of negotiations with the ministry and threats of withdrawal from the project altogether, the Werkbund eventually chose to compromise. Leading members decided to work within the ministerial framework, which they believed to be a watered-down version of *their* design institution.[91] They accepted Schlafejew's appointment on the condition that longtime Werkbund member Mia Seeger be named general secretary.

With Seeger's appointment, the Werkbund gained lasting artistic influence over the RfF. Seeger was an experienced "cultural broker of German modernism" whose organizational work included important Werkbund exhibitions, most notably the 1927 architectural exhibition Weissenhof Settlement (*Weissenhofsiedlung*) in Stuttgart.[92] The legal status and the funding of the design council, however, remained contested between the Werkbund and government. In a pamphlet introducing the council and its agenda, the presidium labeled it a government-initiated "self-administrated organization" instead of a state institution. Both the federal government and the Bundestag had operated "from the assumption that broad segments of the German economy will recognize the importance of industrial design and support it."[93] In the end, it became clear that Bonn supported the council only due to Werkbund connections to the economic elites represented in the Federation of German Industries (Bundesverband der Deutschen Industrie, BDI). After initial hesitation, West Germany's business community strongly supported the RfF. Large companies, such as Siemens and AEG, set up a foundation for industrial design, from which the design council drew some funds.[94] Through overlapping membership the BDI was well represented in the Werkbund and vice versa.[95] This overlap in membership further demonstrates that only a small group of designers and entrepreneurs shaped the inception of West Germany's central design institution. Bonn's increasing involvement in setting up the council, however, disabused industry of the notion that it could control the council, and therefore limited industry commitment in the long run.

Without wholehearted industry support the design council had major financial problems throughout its first two decades of existence. In its first five years from 1953 to 1957, the RfF received a moderate DM 70,000 annually.[96] By comparison, the GDR later financed its design institution with state subsidies of 796,000 East German marks (*Ostmark*, M[97]) in 1963, its first fiscal year.[98] The British Council of Industrial Design had an annual budget of over DM 6 million, of which the state provided 3.5 million by 1967.[99] At that point the RfF budget had grown to DM 220,000—still only a fraction of the funds available to the British Council of Design that year and less than a third of what the East German industrial designers had had in its first year of operation. In part this stemmed from West German industry bodies reneging in later years on their formal promise to support the RfF financially.

In the GDR, the creation of a central design institution comparable to the RfF began with the Weissensee Institute for Applied Art in 1952. In contrast to the West, the East initially thought design to be purely a part of the cultural development of a socialist society. The initial positioning of the institute under the Ministry for Culture indicates that the East German government still categorized industrial design as applied arts and not as an asset to economic development in the early 1950s. This notion possibly stemmed from the country's focus on heavy industry in the early years of reconstruction, because of its importance for fulfilling the reparations that the Soviet Union demanded. And yet, by allocating most of its resources to coal mining and steel production, the GDR also emulated the economic principles that had catapulted the Soviet Union from the agricultural to the industrial age. However, this policy neglected consumer industries at the expense of living standards within the GDR.[100] This meant an unfortunate delay in gratification for the hard-working population that suffered under consumer product shortages, while work norms simultaneously increased in 1952 and 1953 through these measures of economic Sovietization.[101]

In the wake of Stalin's death in the spring of 1953, this economic policy underwent a partial shift. The post-Stalinist New Course announced on June 9 reversed some of the measures, yet the work quotas remained in place and fueled the pent-up frustration among the population.[102] Construction workers began a protest against the work norms on 16 June, and the demonstration spread from Berlin throughout the country the following day. The spontaneous uprising of some five hundred thousand people was put down with the help of Soviet tanks.[103] In the aftermath of the bloody protests, the SED became even more aware of the political dimension of living standards. Public support, the regime learned, could be gained by improving the population's material situation. This led to an emphasis on consumer products, exemplified by the shop window competition in divided Berlin in the 1950s.[104]

The sealing of the German-German border on 13 August 1961 further heightened the political significance of consumer products. The Wall not only stemmed the tide of westward mass migration, but also temporarily cut off the flow of western goods into the GDR. This blockage aggravated the GDR's supply problem, and it underscored the line between prosperity in the West and scarcity in the East. Investment in consumer product development became a new priority. The hope was that an official industrial design institution would create a distinct aesthetic in commodities that would represent an East German national identity and at the same time stave off popular desires for western goods. This endeavor was helped by international developments. In the wake of the Cuban Missile Crisis in 1962 the United States and Soviet Union implemented a policy of peaceful coexistence between the Cold War blocs. The military de-escalation reinvigorated the ideological competition in other fields, among them consumer products and their design. GDR officials noted: "Peaceful coexistence has at its root the decisive, forceful battle against all manifestations of bourgeois ideology. Specific artistic problems are also to be classified in this broader political context."[105] That year, the newly founded Council for Industrial Design (Rat für Industrieform), a link to industry, joined the Weissensee Institute at the Ministry of Culture to implement state initiatives in the field of industrial design and to "supervise their realization through economic institutions, trade organizations and specialized institutes."[106]

At this critical point, Mart Stam's student Martin Kelm utilized the centralized industrial design effort to increase the political responsibilities of the Weissensee Institut für angewandte Kunst under the new name of Central Institute for Design (ZfF) in 1963.[107] Shortly thereafter, the ZfF under Kelm's leadership began its ascent to prominence within the East German planned economy, foreshadowing the eventual success of functionalist design within East Germany's production industries. The ZfF was the first East German government body committed to forging a cohesive aesthetic that also exercised increasing influence in the economic planning process. Thereupon, throughout the 1960s, industrial design became more deeply anchored in the economic structures of the GDR.[108] In 1965, the ZfF moved to an institution dedicated to standardization and product testing, the German Office for Standardization and Product Testing (Deutsches Amt für Messwesen and Warenprüfung, DAMW), a transfer that significantly changed the perception of industrial design's role in the East German economy. The SED leadership began to see industrial design as part of a scientifically measurable process that enhanced products and optimized their competitiveness on the international market, rather than simply as a superficial beautification process.

The leadership change deposing Walter Ulbricht from power in 1971 facilitated Kelm's rise on the career ladder. The new First Party Secretary General Erich Honecker, for whom Kelm's wife worked as personal secretary, turned the ZfF into a government institution in its own right in 1972 and renamed it the Office for Industrial Design (Amt für industrielle Formgestaltung, AiF). Kelm had already been a member of the Council of Ministers, but as the director of the Office, he officially joined the economic planning apparatus. This gave him far-reaching authority in design decisions with power over other ministers.[109] Two laws ensured that the central design institution remained the main arbiter of taste in the GDR and became crucial stepping stones for Kelm's lasting influence over East German industrial design and the prevalence of the functionalists. First, the 1965 law required all nationalized companies (Volkseigene Betriebe, VEB) in the production industries to employ designers and, second, the 1973 law obliged all factories to "outsource" their industrial design work exclusively to the AiF.[110] Whereas few people in the GDR design scene had praised Kelm's artistic vision—in fact, some even criticized him as "uninspired"—he definitely was known to the political elite as a superb bureaucrat with excellent connections.[111] Günther Mittag, a member of the Politbüro since 1958 and secretary of economics in the Central Committee since 1962, took Kelm under his wing.[112] Mittag oversaw Kelm's dissertation about the role of industrial design in socialism and vouched for his party credentials as well as his aesthetic vision for a socialist way of living.[113]

The ascent to power of a functionalist like Kelm was noteworthy for completely contradicting GDR cultural policy. The 1965 transfer of the ZfF from the Ministry of Culture to the DAMW had seemed logical in the contemporary economic climate of standardization and production streamlining. Yet an interpretation of this event as the natural outcome of the East's progress toward economical production aesthetics would undervalue the ideological determination with which the political elite had shaped the discourse on socialist realist aesthetics. In fact, the SED apparatus was painfully aware of the ideological inconsistencies among industrial designers and their lack of loyalty to the official party line. In 1964, the Culture Department at the Central Committee of the SED (Zentralkommittee, ZK) reported, "Revisionist attacks from the applied arts against the cultural policies of the Party [that] are supported by some members of staff of the ZfF" to the secretariat. The industrial designers argued "against a connection between applied arts and our socialist ideology as well as against the designer's task being to work according to the newly developing aesthetic necessities of socialist men."[114] Fearing that these challenges from within would break applied arts away from the "edifice of socialist aesthetics" and could even result in attacks on the principles of socialist realism in the fine arts, the Central Committee demanded a strict response to bring the ZfF back in line. Instead, the problem was avoided by relocating the institute from the realm of culture to the DAMW. Kelm and his unruly institute were essentially "kicked upstairs" to avoid further meddling in cultural politics, though Central Committee members knew that "the supporters of this wrong opinion [that applied arts and ideology should be separated] will interpret the Central Institute breaking away from the Ministry of Culture as a confirmation of their opinion."[115]

The conflict between the Central Committee and industrial designers over the implementation of socialist cultural principles points to a lively ideological debate around socialist realism in the 1960s. Indeed, the SED never achieved full aesthetic control in the field of industrial design. The ideological deviance of the ZfF indicates that there was space for practical arguments that favored functionalism on the basis of its more economical use of resources, which stood in contrast to the expensive embellishments of Stalinist aesthetics. Rather than this constituting a break away from Soviet socialist realism in official policy, as others have proposed, the late 1950s and early 1960s in fact saw a softening of aesthetic guidelines only in practice, albeit not in discourse.[116] Nevertheless, it was evident to the SED government that representative wedding cake buildings, such as the houses on Stalinallee, were costly, work-intensive, and required scarce resources, such as marble and hard wood, that the GDR could not afford for public housing. The turn to prefab housing blocks in the late 1950s, starting with Neu-Hoyerswerda in 1959, was only later followed by a rethinking of the interior, including a general shift toward functionalist furniture design in the mid-1960s.[117] Thus, the practical dilution of cultural Stalinism in the GDR occurred only some years after Nikita Khrushchev's de-Stalinization in the Soviet

Union, as Ulbricht's personal taste for power delayed the Thaw in East Germany.[118] Modernist design would not be officially rehabilitated until later in the decade, and it took until the 1970s for Kelm to be able to furnish the interiors of Honecker's state guesthouses using Bauhaus designs.[119]

Politics of Design: The Rise and Fall of Functionalism

Whereas the GDR experimented with dramatically different German styles during the first two postwar decades, the Federal Republic developed its national aesthetic incrementally, continuously testing international reaction. International representation was at the core of the RfF's mission and it took most of the 1950s for it to create a clear vision for the postwar reinscription of everyday material culture. The design council dismissed the international style of *Nierentisch* organicism, which was popular among West German consumers at the time, and established a design style based on functionalist principles. The development of the council's aesthetic was apparent in the contrast between the 1954 Milan Triennial, the 1957 Milan Triennial, and the 1958 World Exposition in Brussels. An increasing emphasis on humility and transparency distinguished the postwar state from the monumental architecture and folk home design that had characterized the Third Reich aesthetic.[120]

In these exhibitions, the RfF decreased the number of arts and crafts objects and increased the industrial design goods on display. By 1958, the materials featured in the German pavilion at Brussels were clean and modern, such as glass, tubular steel, concrete, and wood.[121] While viewed with suspicion by West Germany's own national media, this new, subdued aesthetic won acclaim from the foreign press and international audiences for its openness and simplicity. Captivated by its "spiritual functionalism," the *London Times* hailed the West German pavilion as elegant, transparent, and radiant.[122] Paranoia about international perception had led to a West German cultural policy that embraced dependable and high quality products for the improvement of daily life as ambassadors of the Federal Republic's emerging economic culture and national identity. In Brussels, the German emphasis on everydayness decidedly contrasted with the attention-seeking displays of other nations.[123] The groundbreaking exhibition successfully linked West German industrial design with postfascism and set new standards for how the Federal Republic used interior design and architecture to communicate its postwar identity abroad in the Adenauer era.[124]

Despite this international acclaim, the work of the RfF came to a complete standstill between 1964 and 1965. The Federal Republic's government remained

FIGURE 1.4. Transparency and leveled perspectives in the West German pavilion at the 1958 Expo in Brussels. Photograph courtesy of Werkbundarchiv—Museum der Dinge Berlin. Photographer unknown.

reluctant to turn the design council into a proper public agency, and the council was dependent on business involvement and private sponsorship.[125] In 1965, RfF president Ernst Schneider, at the time also president of an industry-led industrial design interest group called BDI Committee for Industrial Design (Arbeitskreis für Industrielle Formgebung), wrote to the Minister of Economics Kurt Schmücker to convince him that the council would be able to tackle its growing challenges if given new organizational and financial footing. To this end, Schneider set the council's national significance in global perspective: "The idea that the Rat für Formgebung fulfills a socio-political function has been recognized as a state task and honored as such in the Federal Republic as well as in many other industrial countries."[126] But the government refused to take on what it perceived as the responsibility of the specific industries that would financially benefit from the council's work. After almost two years of unproductive negotiations and mutual accusations, the BDI Arbeitskreis attained administrative control over the RfF in early 1967. Schneider served as president, porcelain manufacturer Philip Rosenthal as his deputy, and architect Fritz Gotthelf as managing director of both institutions, decisively diminishing Werkbund influence. With this step, the RfF lost its independence and freedom from private interest.[127]

Following this crisis, funding for the council resumed and the extension of the council's official responsibilities was reassessed. The ministry, though, saw little promise in the proposed changes based on the work of the last three years, which had been limited by the ongoing power struggles. Only two-thirds of the budget had been spent in 1966 and 1967. Schmücker's successor Minister of Economics Karl Schiller and his advisors at the BMWi criticized the council's personnel structures as a continuing impediment to greater efficiency and success and supported only a few practical proposals, such as the creation of a national industrial design prize (eventually endowed as Bundespreis "Gute Form" in 1969), an industry-initiated International Design Center (Internationales Design Zentrum, IDZ) in West Berlin, and triennial global exhibition tours of excellent German design.[128]

Werkbund members began to fear that their cultural ideals would be sidelined or undermined by industry interests, which led to a public falling-out between the Werkbund and the BDI Arbeitskreis in 1968–69. The Werkbund maintained that the public design council had been swallowed up by private interests and demanded a "complete institutional and personnel separation" from the BDI Arbeitskreis and reassertion of the RfF's democratic legitimacy.[129] However, the organizational structures, including Schneider's joint presidency of both institutions, remained unchanged.[130] In the end, the Werkbund representatives resigned from the RfF in the summer of 1969. Its board of directors published a statement lamenting that "the Werkbund cannot identify with the Rat für Formgebung as it had once been able to" under the circumstances.[131] The feeling was mutual. A promotional pamphlet that the RfF produced in 1989 about its history and purpose completely omitted the Werkbund's integral role in the inception of the design council.[132]

Alongside these battles over design council leadership, functionalism as a sociopolitical and moral agenda underwent a crisis in the Federal Republic. Prominent participants in the 1950s discourse on architecture and design, who had enthusiastically embraced the credo "form follows function" as the spirit for West German reconstruction, became uneasy about neofunctionalism as a revisionist official aesthetic in the 1960s. The debate revolved around the shift in functionalism from a social program—aimed at reforming societal stratification through material uplift—into an iconic style that papered over persisting social relationships.

The origins of the philosophical void can be traced back to the previous decade, when even Werkbund members, once firmly committed to the language of social uplift, struggled to find any underlying welfare concepts in West Germany's striving domestic culture. For instance, in anticipation of the 1957 Interbau architecture exhibition in Berlin, a key event in international modern public housing construction, the RfF previewed the furnishings for one of its projected apartments at H55, an interior design summit in Hälsingborg, Sweden. Instead of explaining how the design would improve living conditions for the population, however, in the catalog Mia Seeger attributed the interior design solutions to the fact that both the exhibition space and the H55 concept had restricted the German committee to space-saving furniture.[133] There was no mention of a vision for a reformed postwar German domestic culture, a democratization of design, or material redistribution.

Given her professional background working with progressive architects and designers, Seeger should have been able to articulate a new West German social outlook on design, that is, if there had been one. Her expertise in the field of reform aesthetics only underscored the de-emphasis on the social question in West German domestic culture. Other European countries, particularly Scandinavian ones, were better able to communicate the postwar challenges in public housing and general welfare. In comparison, West German postwar functionalism looked insubstantial and had lost its reform vision.

Even earlier in the 1950s, the new ideological threat from the GDR, the socialist alternative across the border, had exposed leftist ideals to criticism in the Federal Republic. Attacks on reform design as a guiding principle had come from within the Werkbund, among others, in the so-called Bauhaus Debate of 1953. Cologne church architect and Werkbund member Rudolf Schwarz published an essay in which he rejected Bauhaus rationalism for the rebuilding of Germany.[134] He targeted the Bauhaus and Gropius's avant-garde projects as un-German and communist. Instead, he promoted a conservative "modernism of the middle."[135] His contemporaries rushed to the defense of Gropius and the Bauhaus, though none of them were Werkbund members.[136] Schwarz's attacks contributed to the successive diminishing of leftist reform ideas in the Federal Republic's postwar design and architecture, and his populist comments exemplify a pervasive anti-communism in Adenauer's Germany.

The prevalence of this sentiment is indirectly confirmed by the absence of social reform ideas in West German design institutions and their teachings, which created generations of "socially unconscious" designers. Rolf Heide, one of Germany's most influential neofunctionalist designers to date, began his career in 1950 as a cabinet-maker and went on to study architecture at the Muthesiusschule in Kiel, an institution of higher education named after Werkbund founder Hermann Muthesius.[137] His colleague Peter Maly followed a similar path, beginning a cabinet-maker apprenticeship in 1955 and later studying at the technical college for interior design in Detmold.[138] When asked about the social vision behind their designs, both responded that they made things to be beautiful, not socially responsible.[139] Admired and critically acclaimed designers, Maly and Heide also embody the absence of a social philosophy in the West German discourse on material culture.

The HfG Ulm, Germany's only educational institution founded on the assumption that material culture necessarily represented political consciousness, is a prime example of the institutional repercussions of this change in intellectual climate. Ulm had developed a philosophy of aesthetic and material austerity that became its trademark in the years of want. However, the sudden and strong public criticism of design without a social message in the 1960s led to the school's eventual downfall at the height of the economic miracle.[140] Situated on a hill overseeing the city, the school was not only physically but also conceptually removed from the life of the people "below." The HfG Ulm was an institutional stronghold of die-hard functionalism that correlated with the RfF's aesthetic postwar vision for a culturally and economically liberal Federal Republic. Rejecting popular taste and consumer demands as guiding principles in the design process, Ulm found itself increasingly criticized in the press.[141] In particular, a damaging article about the institute in the West German political magazine *Der Spiegel* caused the Baden-Württemberg government to review its financial commitment to the school.[142] Tensions in the relationship between Ulm's design principles and wider societal trends led to it losing funding from the regional government in 1968, and the HfG Ulm closed its doors that November. The criticism of Ulm was not the only one leveled against elite institutions or functionalism.[143] 1967–68 witnessed worldwide social change and rejection of a democratic consensus, which the HfG Ulm and the RfF claimed to materially express in their aesthetics of good design. The closure of the Ulm institute marked disillusion with the moral power of functionalism as a distinct West German aesthetic. Ulm's modern aesthetic rigidity, nonetheless, had a tremendous influence on German material culture through, for example, the school's collaboration with the electric appliance producer Braun, its corporate design for the German national airline Lufthansa, and its design for the elevated trains of the city of Hamburg. The school's closing showed, however, that functionalism had run its course by the end of the decade.

German intellectuals from the political left, motivated by the general population's rising concerns about capitalism's shortcomings, contributed to the critique of neofunctionalism. The escalating Cold War arms race and the politics of nuclear deterrence had shown that trade and collective prosperity had failed to fulfill the promise of world peace.[144] Modernist design, which from its inception had attempted to temper industrial production with human artistic sensitivity, began to represent the failure of a humanistic capitalist order. This was especially catastrophic in West Germany, where democratization had become closely intertwined with the concept of Western economic integration and social advancement. In his 1965 critique of "Functionalism Today" at the annual Werkbund conference, leftist philosopher and Frankfurt School member Theodor Adorno chastised the inhumane postwar application of modernism.[145] A renowned critic of mass culture, he historicized the functionalist rejection of ornamentation, emphasizing that one era's indispensable design feature could easily be seen as obsolete ornamentation by the next generation. Yet this did not mean that functionalism as a stylistic concept had any claim to an aesthetic truth.[146] To Adorno, the functionalist demonization of historical styles uncovered it as a political dogma. The prescriptive idea inherent in functionalism, the defined relationship between form and utility, Adorno argued, rendered the functionalist object "unfree." The remedy, he suggested, would be for society to create more humane objects by opening up materiality to unknown functions.

As the debate continued in subsequent years, the West German design periodical *Form* published a series of articles that grew increasingly critical of functionalism. The articles highlighted some of its shortcomings as a design style. One fundamental problem was that the designers considered to have fathered functionalism, Henri Labrouste and Louis Sullivan, who had coined the phrase "form follows function," had never actually defined what function meant: the practicable, the useful, or the technically optimized?[147] On closer examination, functionalism started to look more like an ideology than an aesthetic truth. Contributors to this discussion demanded the sacrifice of the "sacred cows" that had been labeled "good design" in divided Germany since the 1950s. By 1969, *Form* pronounced "grandpa's functionalism" dead.[148] Thus, functionalism, with its fetishization of geometric forms, durability, utility, and (in theory) need-based consumption, was revealed to be inherently production-oriented, while ignoring the consumer.

At this very point Bonn withdrew its commitment to the RfF, marking the end of West Germany's crisis of functionalism. In an effort to salvage the national functional aesthetic, the debate moved on to consider Adorno's proposed extended functionalism, one that designs objects to serve humanity rather than maltreat it with sharp edges.[149] Already in 1950, designer Wilhelm Wagenfeld had worried that the Federal Republic would lose sight of the social significance of materiality on its path toward capitalism. Wagenfeld's concern could not only be seen in the language of functionality but also in the teachings of his contemporaries. To theoreticians and practitioners of design, this demonstrated that, for two decades, West German material culture had failed to pursue an agenda that stood for human improvement.

Interestingly, functionalism's western crisis enabled the East to finally reconcile its economic and cultural policies and claim the once opposed aesthetic for the socialist project. In general, any motivation to think about the human aspect of design at this point, it seemed, originated from the socialist Germany. Within socialism, designers intrinsically considered how their designs improved the human condition, while limited resources forced them to find economical solutions.

Yet also in the East the philosophical and aesthetic elements of postwar design remained subject to criticism, and they underwent constant change from the reconstruction years onward. Ulbricht had purged Weimar modernism and its disciples from GDR institutions by 1954, but it proved difficult to enforce a cultural consensus around socialist realism in the applied arts. Kitschy products, combining styles such as rococo, classicism, and *Biedermeier*, were produced for the cultural rebirth of the East German state. This style also favored ornamentation over functionality and hygiene, an especially important consideration for household wares. Kitsch and petty-bourgeois coziness (*Gemütlichkeit*) were privileged over economic considerations and production ethics.[150] Some cultural critics remained at odds with the new cultural doctrine, such as Horst Michel, who proclaimed that "the person who buys Rococo china in 1950 shows bad taste."[151] He reiterated this position in 1952 at the first conference for interior design at the Deutsche Bauakademie: "This [cultural policy] cannot end in providing 'princely' furniture to the working people. We shouldn't talk them into things that look like bourgeois riches, instead we need to give them real riches that serve humanity."[152]

Given his opposition to the aesthetics of socialist material culture, it is somewhat surprising that Michel remained an influential figure in the GDR. His work gained recognition abroad in 1957 when the West German Institute for New Technological Form (Institut für neue technische Form) in Darmstadt organized an exhibition featuring the designs of Michel and his Weimar colleagues. West German designers perceived these Weimar designs as the East's return to functional shapes, celebrating the emergence of a "functionalist German style" on both sides of the German-German border.[153] However, this was a premature celebration of shared aesthetics. At the Culture Conference of 1957, the SED renewed the claim for a socialist-realist culture, declaring cultural work a political issue that concerned the very fabric of the working class. The following year the political leadership connected cultural reform with its economic goals at the Fifth SED Party Congress in East Berlin.

In the spring of 1959, the Bitterfeld Conference, a writers' conference that included representatives of the government, the SED, workers, and the intelligentsia, discussed the prospects of assimilating workers and farmers into socialist realism. A resulting program that aimed at overcoming the previous separation of the arts and workers became known as the Bitterfeld Path (Bitterfelder Weg). The Bitterfeld Path included industrial design as a field of applied arts and suffused all areas of the economy to avoid the pitfalls of profit-oriented mass production that, according to the SED leadership, ignored social responsibility.[154] The Bitterfeld critique of capitalism played an important role in the regime's strategy to counteract suspicions of socialist mass production and promote the possibility of responsible socialist serial manufacturing. In the same vein, Michel wrote the pamphlet "The Industrial Designer on the Bitterfeld Path," in which he criticized the lack of cooperation between designers and workers in socialist production, but used this reasoning to target socialist-realist kitsch. Arguing that only the laborers knew their own needs, Michel maintained that the state should rely on them to eliminate the production of "commodities that do not comply with our *Zeitgeist*. Bourgeois kitsch, modernist Formalism, decadence and snobbism are not befitting for us."[155]

Meanwhile, economic planners struggled with the implications of economic socialism for the population's consumption habits. This discourse paralleled the cultural debates at the Bitterfeld Conference and aligned centralization, rationalization, and standardization with Ulbricht's cultural vision. Fears that a rigid restructuring of production would flatten the cultural value in socialist materiality led to the question of how to retain a "domestic culture despite standardization."[156] At the first standardization show in Leipzig in 1959–60, the GDR interior design journal *Kultur im Heim* (*Culture at Home*) discussed how to combat the impression that standardization would necessarily lead to uniform apartment furnishings.[157] Alongside pictures of the first standardized living room furniture sets, the journal asked its readers, "Would you have guessed that these are standardized pieces?" However, no matter how tasteful the execution, standardization and streamlining of the product range logically resulted in limited choices for consumers.

To quell consumer discontent, the ZfF needed to justify the monotony of standardization. By introducing the ideas of leftist cultural intellectual Giulio Carlo Argan into the debate, designers and policymakers tried to reconcile uniformity with individuality. Designer and ZfF employee Ekkehard Bartsch quoted Argan's formalistic critique of Weimar modernity, stating, "When industry exclusively reproduced shapes that were meant for crafts, that is as singular pieces, monotony resulted from the repetition of these formal specialties." On the contrary, he argued, standardization celebrated the generalized shape because "the machine has no other job than to make a thousand pieces of it" and thus "identity and not uniformity results, because every object will keep the character of an original."[158] According to this interpretation, uniformity was only present in form because of its assigned function. Identity, on the other hand, was inherent in standardization, because it was left to the owner to ascribe a product's specific function, thus leaving the object to fulfill individual expectations:

> The individual can develop freely and creatively only on the basis of standardized production. Only when humans stop seeing the fruits of their material ambitions as a marker of their social status and attitude will they finally be able to benefit from technological innovation. Products become real servants of his [*sic*] existence, he himself stands in the center, not his supporting equipment.[159]

This position had much in common with Adorno's suggestion for an extended functionalism that made the human being the central category for evaluating the functionality of an object. Argan is thus an essential stepping stone in the discursive realignment of eastern and western aesthetics. Although the FRG and the GDR faced very different challenges in changing social relations through material culture, by the mid-1960s they had arrived at similar ways of thinking about the place of objects in industrial society.

In practice, however, GDR planners and designers soon realized that efficiency-oriented organization of mass serial production rendered a small number of furniture models ubiquitous. This, in turn, led to the feared "moral deterioration" of the individual designs and thus a loss of their cultural identity.[160] The challenge was to find a compromise between industrial productivity and sociocultural demands. It was neither in the interest of the GDR leadership nor its goal to make public and private life entirely uniform; it always wanted to keep up the appearance of a dictatorship with a human face.

What all of these contradictions between design dogmata and production practice brought about was an increasing insecurity about what GDR design actually embodied ideologically and, in turn, how this ideology could be expressed materially. It is thus no surprise that even with the benefit of hindsight seasoned East German designers failed to make sense of 1960s GDR design. This is visible in a concept for a 1990 AiF design retrospective entitled *From Bauhaus to Bitterfeld*. While the curators concluded that the diversity of permissible forms increased in the early 1960s, they had difficulties explaining the formal, if arbitrary, limits to artistic expression that continued to exist. For instance, they were unable to satisfactorily explain official disdain for designer Hubert Petras's cylindrical, plain white vases, which had been exhibited at the fifth Dresden Art Exhibition in 1962. In the end, the curators pinned the critique on the design's lack of joie de vivre: "The strict, compromise-less cylinder shapes delineated themselves from shallow industrial mass production. Yet officials agreed that they ran counter to the optimistic attitude towards life of a civilized people with a happy future."[161] While the vases fulfilled antikitsch requirements, they apparently failed to show the right uplifting spirit that the leadership demanded for GDR material culture. Each object, it seems, was judged on its own merit and sometimes arbitrarily censored without considering what socialist material culture tried to achieve, namely a contribution to the cultural-ideological education of the New (Wo)Man. A response to needs, the avoidance of kitsch, and timeless designs immune to moral decay—these were the maxims of the time. In fact, Petras's designs fit that bill.

Cultural policy in the 1960s slowly but steadily moved away from socialist realism and toward modern idioms, which confronted arbiters of taste such as Michel with the opposite extreme—fashionable and modish designs with an aesthetic life span of only a few years.[162] In response, Michel shifted from

FIGURE 1.5. After the Fifth German Art Exhibition in Dresden,
Karl-Heinz Hagen wrote a propaganda article for Neues Deutschland,
criticizing Hubert Petras's cylindrical vases as "artless" in 1962.
Petras Roehren-03, Günter Höhne, 2008.

criticizing backward-looking stylistic historicism to warning against exaggerated originality and avant-gardism. Michel reiterated his concerns in 1964 on
the occasion of the ZfF's reorganization under the DAMW, which included the
implementation of standardized design criteria for technological product evaluation. Pointing out that quality in mass production was difficult to maintain,
he rejected the argument advanced by producers and retail that "products are
designed badly because of popular taste and demand."[163] The guest books from
a 1965 interior design exhibition attest to the fact that at least parts of the population appreciated moderately modernist-inspired designs. Fifteen thousand

visitors saw *Modern Dwelling* in Hoyerswerda, and for the first time in a decade, their opinions were not only recorded but also were used to evaluate the success of a new, holistic exhibition concept that offered the atmospheric effect of a decorated room.[164] Not so surprisingly, the modern way of living found broad acceptance.[165] Michel suggested that the efforts previously undertaken to achieve better designs had been insufficient. After all, "in every type of taste, in every style, tasteless products exist. It is the task of the designer to create something decent in every individual or seasonally conditioned taste," he maintained.[166] Rejecting doctrinaire one-sidedness that favored a specific style or slavishly followed official cultural policies, Michel saw material socialism play out in the relationship between the product and its user. With the standardization of product ranges, he hoped to have more control over what was produced as well as distributed to the East German home.[167] This did not foreclose diverse styles, as long as they moderately interpreted a taste or fashion. Michel did not believe in coercion and taste dictation. Rather he strove to enlighten retail buyers and consumers to positively influence production through the right demand. Michel thus helped establish a modern vision during the reconstruction years and the Bitterfeld Path in the late 1950s and early 1960s, but he was unable to leave a mark on the Formalism Debate between 1951 and 1953 and the later years of modish production. In these phases, which overlapped with heightened Cold War tensions and deteriorating German-German relations, moderation contradicted the ambitions of the GDR, a country that tried to propel its economy forward with centralization and Five-Year Plans. A distinct national culture and socialist mass production presented two ways in which East Germany aimed to gain a higher profile in the postwar world and to compete with the Federal Republic.

Toward the end of the 1960s, amid the crisis of functionalism in the Federal Republic, the GDR finally gained greater clarity about how to align its cultural and economic outlook. Here again East German industrial design elites took the lead, suddenly and publicly embracing the leftist politics of interwar modernism. On the occasion of the GDR's twentieth anniversary in 1968, the ZfF organized an exhibition that positioned GDR design at the intersection of the Bauhaus/Werkbund tradition and Soviet constructivism. The exhibition's historical section addressed a range of artistic expressions that the GDR designers saw themselves indebted to: 1840–95 historicism and eclecticism, 1895–1915 arts and crafts reform movements and stylistic art such as art nouveau and neoclassicism, and 1918–33 new objectivity, expressionism, and functionalism.[168] This exhibition concept was the first to include the latter two among the roots of socialist design in East Germany. In a break with previous cultural policy, the exhibition text also paid special attention to the leftist politics of some of the Bauhaus's protagonists.

In the 1970s, after functionalism's gradual rehabilitation in the previous decade, the East German design magazine *Form und Zweck* (*Form and Function*) became the forum for a discussion about the merits and the pitfalls of functionalist design. This critical debate was not dissimilar to the 1960s exchanges in the West German design periodical *Form*.[169] The term "good design" now found usage on this side of the Iron Curtain as well, but it gained a different meaning.[170] GDR good design embodied two sides of the same coin: It used resources and labor efficiently, while at the same time it was dedicated to fulfilling the needs of the population without providing dispensable luxury. With economic considerations shaping the conversation, the East German functionalism debate was less politically loaded and instead presented a historic perspective on German modernism's original intentions. Cultural critic Karin Hirdina intervened in this debate, reclaiming the legacy of western functionalist dogmatism for socialism in 1975: "In fact, defined as a program and a method, not as a style, functionalism represents a Utopian vision of a non-capitalist order of relationships between Man and his environment. Strictly speaking, functionalism does not work in the capitalist system. It does not affirm capitalism, it transcends it."[171]

East German designers and politicians thus slowly regained confidence in their modernist heritage, a development epitomized by the reopening of the Bauhaus Dessau in 1976.[172] What seems like a long overdue realization to the outside observer took the GDR leadership two decades to understand: The good design principles of utility, resourcefulness, and timelessness were perfectly matched to the GDR discourse on a socialist domestic culture. In contrast to West Germany, the social program of interwar modernism fit neatly into the state ideology.[173] In the GDR, design debates had always involved morality, because everyday culture was understood as a central part of a holistic approach to creating a socialist society. Hirdina's practical, or in Adorno's words "extended," understanding of functionalism refrains from creating stylistic maxims and taste regimes.

A decade and a half after Michel's Darmstadt exhibition had triggered premature declarations of German-German aesthetic rapprochement, GDR state approval and the eventual alignment of cultural goals and economic planning resulted in East German interior and furniture design free from earlier contradictions and ambiguities. This revitalization of interwar design principles also marked the first steps toward an all-German economic culture.

CHAPTER 2

Producing Modern German Homes

The Economy of Nation Branding

IN TURNING THE DISCOURSE on official aesthetics into economic success both German states engaged in practices of "nation branding."[1] The term describes a branding effort at the national level that substantially follows similar logics as those that develop the specific properties of a product brand. Such branding evolved in the postwar period from simply harnessing firm reputation to employing symbolic values, such as cultural or historical factors.[2] Coherent communication was crucial for the success of branding. To reinvigorate the "Made in Germany" brand, a network of designers and producers created a narrative of political significance around their products. In the furniture industry, their narrative moved meaning from "the culturally constituted world to the consumer good," associating established cultural categories and principles with home furnishings.[3] Nation branding is thus part of collective sense-making in economic culture, by which economic actors invoke a "structure of values that reacts to economic indicators and constructs domestic economic mechanisms."[4] It is a cognitive process that narratively manifests national policy-legitimizing norms and values in consumer products based on cultural perception.

Politicians adopted the practice of assigning greater meaning to everyday objects, because it fit the political climate of the Cold War period, when an important component of German-German relations emphasized competing ways of living. This German Cold War over living standards constituted part of the 1950s East-West confrontation in Europe, as threat of mutual destruction in the ongoing superpower arms race increasingly yielded to a competition for popular support tied to economic prosperity. Both sides had an interest in keeping the Cold War "cold" in Europe and thus sustained a minimal level of communication and exchange. But even here, provocations remained the rule rather than the exception, as Richard Nixon and Nikita Khrushchev showed during the famous Kitchen Debate at the American National Exhibition in Moscow in July 1959.[5] In short, material well-being became a proxy for political prowess in the East-West conflict.

Similar to a product brand, the products of national domestic culture were intended to offer both German populations a sense of identity as well as promote their cultural achievements abroad.[6] A coherent aesthetic that bolstered that narrative, however, hinged upon strategic cooperation and communication among the political leadership, designers, industrialists, and consumers in East and West Germany respectively—which proved quite difficult to accomplish. Rival ideas about German modern domestic culture undermined the necessary narrative coherence for the promotion of East or West German "corporate identity" at home and abroad, which left the two German states vulnerable to external influences and set the stage in the late 1960s for their unintended aesthetic convergence.[7]

A focus on industry reveals the breakdown of the national aesthetic narrative in practice. The practical dilution of the initial postwar cultural Stalinism in East Germany and rigid functionalism in West Germany in production industries in fact ran in parallel by the 1970s. The problem was one of political rhetoric versus economic reality: Why, after decades of invoking German-German cultural delineation, did both states fail to assert an official style, a particular East or West German "national aesthetic" in workshops and homes? Taking into account the fundamental structural differences between the economic and political systems of the FRG and GDR, this chapter traces how policymakers interacted with the industrial sector to link ideologically conforming ways of living to economic reconstruction and prosperity. Norms and values behind economic and political mechanisms in East and West Germany explain what impaired the consistent implementation of official aesthetics in furniture production. In the process, both Germanys moved toward a shared idea of economical production and comfortable living.

The Role of Economic Success and Political Legitimacy in the West German Struggle for Aesthetic Coherence

It might be expected that the German-German competition for superiority in industrial design and production would have first and foremost a unifying effect on either economy. The East and West German design councils certainly aimed each to define and defend one coherent national aesthetic to strengthen the economic reputation of the FRG and GDR respectively at home and abroad. Yet, at times, domestic actors—the government, regional administration, and industries—followed differing or even opposing agendas in the national economy. These diverging forces undermined the creation of a cohesive national brand.

Of course, the fact that Germany has always had a regionally diverse culture partially explains the context in which the struggle for national product aesthetics developed.[8] As the tradition of tensions between region and center predated the German partition of 1945, a strong culture of regionalism already existed in both Germanys when they reached statehood. In the years after the war, the cultural element of regionalism was reinforced by the new economies. In contrast to the centralized war economy of the Third Reich, new economic planning organizations were anchored at the regional and municipal level.[9] The significance of regional administrative thinking in the economy also had implications for the implementation of cultural policy in the postwar period, particularly in West Germany. Without local institutional cooperation, the realization of a unified product aesthetic was highly unlikely. Centralized approaches, namely the institutionalization through a design council that defines and executes cultural and economic policies for the entire nation, strove to disable regionalism and activities which economically assisted one region or favored a regional aesthetic identity over a coherent national style in the long run.

From its inception in 1951, the West German design council RfF, as a national institution, stood in direct conflict with the regional reorganization of the economy. The contradictory notion of cultural and economic centralism in a federalist political system was contested by politicians and apparent to contemporaries. "It may seem surprising that government-controlled agencies should act as arbiters of taste in industrial design and assume a frankly partisan or even doctrinaire attitude in promoting modern design," observed art historian Lorenz Eitner in 1957. "This is possible in Germany (where the State has often played an active role in such matters) because since 1945 the weight of official approval has come to rest on the side of modern art, modern architecture, and modern design."[10] Indeed, the permissiveness vis-à-vis the RfF based on a social and political consensus on modern design that the council claimed to represent in the 1950s. Initially, it was successful in projecting this image at home and abroad. However, because of the decentralized organization of West Germany's economy and the fact that much of the council's funding came from the private sector, informal agreement with industry about which aesthetics could best encapsulate the spirit of a postwar Germany was crucial to the RfF's success.

To a large extent, the design council's bid for leadership in the Federal Republic's material culture was critically linked to the success of the social market economy. Economic prosperity contributed greatly to public support for the young democracy and thus to West Germany's internal and external political legitimacy.[11] Since many Germans had experienced the stock market crash of 1929 and the resulting depression, which made them suspicious about democratic rule in the postwar period, economic progress and the acceptance of a new democratic state went hand in hand.[12] Therefore, the unprecedented social improvement that resulted from the economic growth of the 1950s encouraged the population to identify with the FRG.[13] The work of the RfF was part of this project, yet it would have remained inconsequential without the cooperation of industry.

Fortunately for the design council, organized industrial interests, represented by the Federation of German Industries (Bundesverband der Deutschen Industrie, BDI), shared the belief that the state and private interest needed to collaborate to achieve economic recovery. In fact, the BDI became a trusted ally in the conservative Adenauer government's economic policies early on.[14] In 1950, a lack of capital, multiple allied production restrictions, and decreased domestic demand caused the unemployment of more than two million workers. As the social market economy experiment threatened to fail, American pressure to institute some degree of state regulation of the economy grew as well. In a step to avoid reversing the liberal elements of the postwar economy, Adenauer turned to industrial associations for help. Consequently, the BDI took on the task of distributing scarce resources and organizing exports.[15] Corporate traditions thus found their way back into the market economy of the Federal Republic, which raised the question of whether the republic would be able to withstand strong economic corporatism in the long run.[16] With regard to industrial design, the answer to this question was clearly no.

The role that industry played in West Germany's cultural revival cannot be overemphasized. The philanthropic committee of the BDI, the Culture Committee (Kulturkreis), awarded fellowships and organized art shows to support the arts in Germany from 1951 onward.[17] BDI lawyer, art enthusiast, and CDU member Gustav Stein largely initiated this cultural engagement and invoked the historical responsibility of entrepreneurs as patrons of the arts. Convinced that art could function as a social force to connect people, he strived to prevent the negative experience of the Weimar Republic from repeating itself. He strongly believed that infusing everyday life with cultural objects could prevent the disintegration of society.[18] While the Kulturkreis members' taste in art was as diverse as its membership, the BDI followed official aesthetics in its award practices and thereby became Germany's biggest patron of abstract modern art and, later, industrial design.[19] Big businesses such as Thyssen, Krupp, and Reemtsma reinvigorated the concept of the collector-benefactor in the new republic.[20] Yet the motivation behind this kind of cultural philanthropy was not entirely altruistic. Patronage helped the industry enhance its image, which had been badly damaged during years of collaboration with the Nazi regime.[21]

Evidently, the modernist consensus that the RfF encouraged found approval and support from the business elites, and the relationship became mutually beneficial when the design council connected business and large-scale customers. Holding a gatekeeper role, the RfF served as a source of information in particular for government institutions, which were in dire need of office furniture, mess kits and flatware for cafeterias, and art to decorate the administrative buildings in West Germany's new capital.[22] By advising to prestigious construction projects in Bonn and numerous international exhibitions, the design council possessed considerable influence between 1952 and 1965. With the BDI and the RfF promoting the same modernist aesthetic, this more or less voluntary cooperation under the leadership of Economic Minister Erhard strengthened the national brand.

Yet early on, the BDI sowed the seeds for an eventual divergence. In 1952, it established an independent project similar to the design council, the Committee for Industrial Design (Arbeitskreis für Industrielle Formgebung). Fourteen of the thirty-six associations represented by the BDI were present at the constituting assembly of the Arbeitskreis, demonstrating industrialists' considerable interest and work on issues of form and design. This initial success quickly led to the BDI becoming involved in a second, more pragmatic area of design activism.[23] It organized special shows of selected, well-designed products at the annual industrial fairs in Hanover, Frankfurt, and Cologne.[24] And in order to publicize its work more prominently, the BDI Arbeitskreis started the non-profit organization Industrial Design (Industrieform) in the city of Essen, which focused on displaying well-designed products.[25] Gustav Stein became a prominent figure in this process, working behind the scenes to give willing industrialists the opportunity to advertise their wares in these two different venues. In particular Industrieform's permanent exhibition with industry-sponsored displays aimed at improving sales by educating the public about good design. Within three years of its opening in November 1955, more than 492,000 visitors had viewed the exhibition.[26] This popular demand to learn about the features of modern furnishings and appliances encouraged the industry to maintain its own efforts, in parallel to its cooperation with the RfF, well into the 1960s.

Nevertheless, the increasingly aggressive role of industry in questions of design eventually disrupted the peaceful cooperation between cultural politics and enterprise. Rivaling the mission of the RfF, the BDI Arbeitskreis attempted to take the lead in the education of designers and the promotion of rational and socially responsible industrial design.[27] The furniture industry branch of the BDI, for instance, hosted a press reception in 1960 at which presenters elaborated on topics such as "On good and bad taste," "Serial furniture and its significance for today's apartment," "Thoughts on the issue of 'modern,'" and "On the meaning of furnishing."[28] Such issues were at the core of contemporary debates in the applied arts, a domain that the Werkbund traditionally considered to be their expertise. The industry-controlled initiatives eventually led to diminished commitment to the RfF. Industry's willingness to cooperate with the Werkbund members in the design council seems to have decreased proportionally as independent BDI projects grew in significance.

By the mid-1960s, the activities of the BDI Arbeitskreis, reconstituted as the BDI Design Committee (*Gestaltkreis*) in 1965, signaled an eventual divergence between state and business interests.[29] Entrepreneurs pinned this on a difference of opinion over the purpose and direction of German industrial design. The secretary general of the Study Group of Industry for Product Design and Product Planning in Stuttgart implicitly criticized Bonn's lack of practical thinking: "Our study group came together to help members replace abstract intentions with methodological thinking. The group members no longer want to talk about the cultural-political goals of the design concept, but want instead to search for practical ways to realize these."[30] While in earlier years the visions of the RfF and the BDI had overlapped when industry supported the idea of moral recovery via aesthetics, they came apart once repairing the country's international image was deemed unnecessary and West German products had regained their good reputation in the global market. At this point, the business community returned to a profit-oriented interpretation of design.[31] Consequently, West German industry moved away from the dogmatic rigidity of postwar functionalism and toward catering to consumer tastes.

This shift coincided with strife between the Werkbund and BDI factions on the board of the RfF, which came to a head between 1967 and 1969. The design council's formal restructuring of 1967–68 that brought the RfF under BDI control played out as a hostile takeover. It seems as though the BMWi was largely responsible for the breakdown of the relationship between the Werkbund members and the BDI representatives in the RfF, as the minister's rejection of earlier requests for more financial state support left the public design council little choice but to seek money elsewhere and under new terms in order to continue its work. As a result, the mission of the design council became increasingly industry-oriented at the expense of its cultural foundations.[32] Coupled with a weak management since Mia Seeger left as RfF general secretary in 1967, the design council lost its independence. Strictly speaking, the official aesthetic promoted by the RfF henceforth only existed in government-sponsored foreign trade industrial shows or other international exhibitions as part of West German cultural diplomacy.

Regional actors took advantage of the state of distraction that the RfF's infighting caused. A growing number added their own voices to the debate about good design in the 1960s. Munich's *Neue Sammlung*, a tax-supported gallery of modern design, and regional chambers of commerce, especially that in Stuttgart, not only maintained permanent collections of well-designed products but also assembled traveling exhibitions. In addition, West German cities founded a network of *Wohnberatungen*, information centers equipped with pattern books where interior designers counseled West Germans on how to furnish their apartments. By 1961 *Wohnberatungen* could be found throughout the Federal Republic, many of them funded by public housing agencies or local chambers of commerce, though the *Wohnberatungen* in West Berlin, Mannheim, and Munich also received Werkbund money.[33] Most of the initiatives for a modern "German" taste correlated with the furnishing boom of the 1960s, when 40 percent of all households were buying furniture.[34] Fueled by such demand, the 1960s and 1970s became the most exciting decades in West German furniture development. For the RfF, however, this meant ample competition for aesthetic leadership in interior design.

Aside from maintaining their own collections of "good design," the *Länder* chambers of commerce created regional design centers that served local industry and rivaled the RfF in influence. Two among them, the design centers in Stuttgart (Baden–Württemberg) and in Essen (North Rhine–Westphalia), developed powerful ideas for industrial development in regions that were already more economically successful than the rest of West Germany. In the 1970s, Stuttgart's design center even applied repeatedly for independent membership in an international design organization, the International Council of Societies of Industrial Design (ICSID), where the RfF was a founding member and representative of German interests. Relations between the Stuttgart Design Center and the RfF hit a new low when the latter became involved in Stuttgart's ICSID candidacy process. Throughout the Cold War, most countries appointed only one design society to this international organization in order to project a cohesive nation brand in the realm of industrial design. Stuttgart's application triggered an exchange between the ICSID board and the RfF in which information about the relationship between the design council and the Stuttgart Design Center was solicited in an effort to determine membership fees. If the council vouched for a close relationship, the Stuttgart Design Center would pay reduced fees. But Herbert Ohl, RfF's technical director and ICSID board member, was unwilling to do so. "I should think also," Ohl sarcastically added, "that they would themselves not like to be regarded as part of the Rat für Formgebung, since we are a national institution."[35] Ohl's reaction was indicative of irreconcilable differences between the two institutions on the matters of regional and national industrial design policy. The higher membership fees, as Ohl well knew, had not been budgeted for by Stuttgart's center, and he knowingly jeopardized a stronger West German presence in this international body for the sake of national brand cohesion. Nonetheless, the Stuttgart Design Center reached an agreement with the ICSID and became a member in 1979 without Ohl's support.

These episodes make it abundantly clear that the West German design council failed to maintain its leadership of the nation brand as time went on. The growing number of participants in the industrial design discourse, the diverging objectives between industry and state interests, and the lack of sustained support from the government undercut RfF activities and curtailed the council's ability to exert influence over production aesthetics and the West German brand.

Modernizing the GDR Brand: Streamlining, Mechanization, and Standardization

In contrast to the Federal Republic, central planning, nationalization of industry, and collectivization of craft businesses in the GDR should have facilitated the creation and maintenance of a coherent nation brand based on socialist realist aesthetics.[36] But this process remained incomplete until the very last days of the GDR.[37] Moreover, the GDR only belatedly moved industrial design matters from the Ministry of Culture to the German Office for Standardization and Product Testing (DAMW) in 1965, finally anchoring it in the centralized planning structures.[38] The fact that this institutional restructuring was done in order to keep industrial designers from further interfering in SED cultural policy, rather than to acknowledge that designers could contribute to savvy economic policy, says much about the limitations that the design council ZfF faced. In fact, the development of economic policy from the 1953 New Course to

Ulbricht's New Economic System of Planning and Management (Neues Ökonomisches System der Planung und Leitung, NES) rather tells a story of struggle
in the creation of a coherent aesthetic in GDR production culture, in which the
ZfF only occasionally appears.

While the partition of Germany created favorable conditions for the West
German economic miracle, the eastern side was left wanting. Traditional agricultural areas in the east were cut off from industry in the west, especially the
Ruhr region, southern parts of Lower Saxony, the Rhine-Main region to the
Rhine-Neckar region and the region surrounding Stuttgart in the south. The
GDR held industrial centers in Thuringia and Saxony, but northern East Germany had close to none. It also lacked a waterway like the Rhine river system,
which easily transported consumer and bulk goods to the northern European
ports, thus facilitating West German overseas trade. The shipping industry on
the Elbe River, for instance, was disrupted by the inner-German border and predominately served to supply West Berlin.[39] Meanwhile, because of its location at
the edge of the Eastern Bloc, the GDR lost its importance in the east-west trade
once the Iron Curtain came down. Moreover, the Federal Republic possessed
most of the coal and ore reserves, while the resource-rich areas in the east had
been surrendered to Poland after 1945. West Germany also had a larger percentage of climatically favored and consumer-oriented agricultural areas, as well as
ice-free ports.[40] Finally, the partition spared the west from having to support the
agrarian east. These factors, coupled with a modified free-market economy, left
West Germany well positioned to quickly increase production, satisfy consumer
demand, and regain foreign markets, which triggered an industrial boom that
lasted well into the 1960s.[41] The Federal Republic's success posed a great challenge to the economically weaker GDR, even though it was the most successful
Eastern Bloc economy.

The GDR also suffered disadvantages as it shouldered the lion's share of
Soviet war reparation claims.[42] After postwar negotiations between the Allies
failed, the Soviet Union extracted a minimum of 10 billion dollars' worth of
machinery and products from the eastern zone of occupation. Until 1949, entire factories were relocated to Soviet territory.[43] The Saxon furniture company
Deutsche Werkstätten Hellerau (DWH) was completely dismantled down to its
workshop lamps and light bulbs, which were transported eastward along with
expensive machinery.[44] The need to pay reparations also led to the restructuring
of large-and medium-sized industry, which, together with large land holdings,
had been largely nationalized during occupation. As the Soviet Union asked in
particular for goods from the automotive and heavy engineering sectors, these

industries expanded with the Plans of 1949–50, 1951–55, and 1956–60, while investments in light industry and food production slowed.[45] Furniture production therefore had to re-establish itself largely without large-scale investment plans in the 1950s. Yet as this industry was central to housing reconstruction, living standards, and consumer satisfaction—topics closely linked to East Germany's political legitimacy—it offers great insights into how the GDR leadership became increasingly influenced by the West German "other." Despite SED promises of economic improvement, West German prosperity set an unattainably high benchmark for the GDR. Explanations for the failure of the centralized GDR economy commonly center on often contradictory Five-Year Plans.[46] Politics trumped economics in the planning process, and recent scholarship points to efficiency—or rather the lack of it—as an important analytical category for understanding the role of political leadership in the socialist planned economy.[47] Companies learned to navigate East Germany's centralized economy by hiding their real capacities with the goal of being assigned the lowest possible production quota with the largest possible resource allocations.[48] The entire system further diminished productivity and encouraged wastefulness by disabling principles of market competition both domestically and internationally, where the state's monopoly on foreign trade stifled innovation from the outset.[49]

One central problem in enforcing a national brand in the GDR industrial production continued to be individualistic firms and regional identity. While opportunistic behavior of companies and local operatives undermined quantitative goals and labor efficiency, there was opposition to cultural policy in the light industries as well. For instance, one of the country's largest furniture collectives, the Saxon furniture complex Dresden-Hellerau that had been built around the core company DWH, opposed the SED's socialist realist diktat and continued to design furniture with its signature simple, modernist aesthetic as long as it could.[50] DWH's founder, Karl Schmidt, had been an influential leader in the turn-of-the-century workshop movement (*Werkstättenbewegung*) and a founding member of the Werkbund.[51] Bruno Paul, a famous art nouveau interior designer and architect, had conceived DWH's first serial furniture program, the "Growing Apartment" (*Wachsende Wohnung*). It offered different furniture pieces that could be assembled as a living or dining room set according to the customers' individual needs and brought modern design to the middle classes.[52] Although DWH became nationalized in 1951, Schmidt's aesthetic philosophy and production ethics remained in force. DWH continued to produce the *Wachsende Wohnung* as Model 558, until it was discontinued because of mounting political pressure in 1958.

To curtail Hellerau's popular modernist influence, Ulbricht himself became involved early on. In 1953, he personally stopped the publication of a booklet about DWH on the grounds that the furniture photographs in the book contradicted the SED's official aesthetic guidelines.[53] The market, however, liked the practical furniture that Hellerau produced. For example, when a home furnishing exhibition in East Berlin's Alexanderplatz in 1953 showed models that tended to bulky proportions and lacked stylistic cohesiveness, visitors asked instead for Paul's *Wachsende Wohnung* and demanded furniture that they considered to be well-proportioned and affordable.[54] Increasingly, however, producers found their design options limited by the Construction Academy of the GDR (Bauakademie der DDR), a scientific institution in charge of construction and architecture. The Bauakademie took control of furniture design development as well, reviewed product catalogs, and, if deemed necessary, dictated specific models in line with socialist realist style. Following the Minister Council's order to the furniture industry on 21 January 1954, which required that furniture aesthetics invoke the German cultural heritage, it created development departments, so-called *E-Stellen*, that reported to the Bauakademie with the directive to execute aesthetic guidelines.[55] In order to avoid economic and political marginalization or even closure, DWH started to integrate style elements in line with official cultural doctrine into new designs, a change in strategy to appease the SED. Most of Hellerau's workers, it seems, disliked the change, as they indicated their preference for modern aesthetics during a viewing of these new furniture designs.[56] That October, the DWH head of development emphasized that, while his department endeavored to follow official guidelines in developing a socialist domestic culture, "it ought to be our goal to maintain Deutsche Werkstätten [Hellerau]'s noted good style or, rather, to win it back."[57] Surely, DWH was only one site of resistance the SED encountered in the production sector.[58] Yet it offers important insight into the mechanisms that were put in place to control the creative process in the furniture industry and ensure aesthetic cohesion in the national brand. Ulbricht's censorship of the company and the increasing controls on production aesthetics meant to stifle the individual character of businesses such as DWH were followed by further collectivization of industry in 1958–59.[59]

At the Fifth Party Congress in 1958, Ulbricht declared the new goal for the East German economy: to surpass West Germany in per capita consumption.[60] Workforce mobilization was a crucial part of this plan. Letters to the workers called on them to join the effort to eradicate overlapping production and waste of resources. At the height of the Berlin Crisis in 1959, one of these open letters was addressed to "Furniture Workmen in the German Democratic Republic": "In this situation, West Germans look to us. They observe how we live. Our successes in the social and cultural arena are great and lack an equivalent in the Bonn Republic. We have made progress in the field of material consumption as well. And it is in material consumption where we must advance faster to overtake West Germany."[61] For workers in the furniture industry, the connection between the socialist way of life, expressed in *Wohnkultur*, and the fruits of their labor was especially evident.

The idea behind accelerating the development and production of a distinctly socialist furniture culture, forward-looking and comfortable, aimed at counteracting images of abundance coming from West Germany.[62] To this end, Ulbricht announced further integration and concentration of nationalized small and medium industry within their district through the Association of Nationalized Companies (Vereinigung Volkseigener Betriebe, VVB). Since earlier collectivization processes had created even more regional activity, the new association was intended to effectively control regional industry, steer production aesthetics, and maximize efficiency by creating intermediate-level institutions located between the Planning Commission and enterprise that could organize industry transregionally.[63] The new administrative units coordinated production by redistributing "tasks to allow greater specialization, standardization and the use of spare capacity," and by taking greater control over research and development, which was previously located at the individual company level or, in the case of collectivized state-owned industry, at the core company.[64] However, the introduction of the VVBs ended up creating rivals to the central planning institutions. Focused on their own industry, the VVBs did not uphold a cohesive narrative of nation branding. Furthermore, the VVBs of the same industry remained subdivided in districts across the GDR, a fragmentation that would become increasingly difficult to overcome with growing specialization and compartmentalization between and within districts.

The Thuringian furniture industry was the first to unite private and state-owned furniture companies in the Gera and Jena area under the name VVB Möbel Zeulenroda/Thüringen in 1959.[65] It combined sixteen VEBs and six semi-state owned companies, and twenty-two private enterprises among others in Eisenberg, Gera, Greiz, Jena, Lobenstein, Pößneck, Rudolstadt, Saalfeld, and Zeulenroda.[66] Cooperative relations between enterprises of all ownership forms, the underlying theory suggested, would yield increased resource efficiency and organize entire industries horizontally. The 1959 open letter to the furniture industry workers had already announced Zeulenroda's future as a *Musterbeispiel*, a model for specialization and cooperation among firms of different ownership forms.[67] Zeulenroda had been chosen because its core company specialized in stylistically overwrought furniture (*Stilmöbel*), a natural fit with the official East German socialist realist production aesthetic of the 1950s. It offered a promising case study for the streamlining of the furniture industry alongside the successful implementation of cultural centralization in the GDR.

Yet by 1962 the myriad of ownership forms in the GDR economy continued to complicate concentration efforts (see table 2.1). Of 14,520 furniture-producing companies, 13,698 were in private hands, of which 13,542 were small crafts and trade. The fragmentation caused labor inefficiency: about 96 percent of smaller furniture companies, employing 48 percent of the manpower, produced only 34 percent of the national production volume. In addition to the apparent untapped labor potential, the fragmentation also caused a technological challenge. As a big portion of companies were artisan businesses, they could rarely be transformed into large-series producers (*Großserienproduzenten*). However, from the 1950s onward, the ultimate goal of any restructuring of the furniture industry had been mass production to fulfill growing consumer demands.

In 1964, the VVB Möbel began yet another attempt at restructuring furniture production, based on a report which found that, until 1963, furnishings constituted only about 2 percent of the GDR's total industrial production but showed great promise as an export industry—15 percent of all export consumer products came from the furniture industry.[68] The report pointed out that East Germany's outdated technological standards and lack of investment had lowered the country's international competitiveness. Furthermore, it noted, a large variety of styles and models inhibited economies of scale. For example, there were between 1,200 and 1,400 different furniture models in the upholstery sector. Every time a company switched to a new model, processes, machines, and tools needed to be recalibrated, which meant an interruption in production.

The 1964 structural reform aimed at addressing these shortcomings, shifted investment strategies to mechanization and modernization of furniture manufacturing, and opened a new chapter in supplying national retail and foreign trade. It eliminated the fragmentation of production through company mergers, cut down on specialized production by increasing mechanization, incorporated modern processing and manufacturing technologies, used materials that corresponded to international quality standards, and implemented serial mass production.[69] The Planning Committee increased annual investments to the furniture industry from 30 million Ostmark in 1964 to 50 million Ostmark from 1966 onward.[70] The funds were exclusively allocated for machines fit for

TABLE 2.1. Ownership forms in the East German furniture industry, status 31 December 1962

Form of ownership	Production volume in million MDN	Share (%)	Number of companies	Share (%)	Number of employees; excl. apprentices	Annual average (%)
GDR total	1,730	100.0	14,520	100.0	92,250	100.0
Industry total	1,143	66.0	563	4.0	48,015	52.0
State-owned (VEB)	866	50.0	178	1.3	32,705	35.5
Partially state-owned (HSB)	218	12.6	228	1.6	11,670	12.5
Privately owned	58	3.3	156	1.1	3,590	3.9
Industrial co-operative	1	0.1	1	0	50	0.1
Crafts total	587	34.0	13,957	96.0	44,235	48.0
Crafts co-operative	225	13.0	415	3.0	14,325	15.5
Private small trade/crafts and small industry	362	21.0	13,542	93.0	29,910	32.5

SOURCE: BArch, DE 1/ VS II 12173, concept, "Zur Entwicklung der Möbelindustrie der Deutschen Demokratischen Republik Berlin," September 1964, p. 1. NOTE: MDN (*Mark der Deutschen Notenbank*) is an abbreviation for the East German currency, or *Ostmark*, in the 1960s.

serial production; existing factory buildings had to suffice, as the investment plan was aimed solely at raising standards of technology.[71]

The 1964 reform also deepened the restructuring of regional clusters of industry. It created combines (*Kombinate*) throughout the 1960s, which basically replaced the VVBs as mid-level control bodies. However, clustering and coordination were only successful in traditionally dense industrial areas. Big companies focused on the mass production of serial furniture, while small crafts businesses were to respond to short-term changes in demand and fill gaps in the product range.[72] Consequently, companies specialized either in a particular model or furniture ensemble, in certain technological processes or steps in the production process, or in assembling certain parts.[73] Where industry was thinly spread out, these attempts at concentration, cooperation, and specialization did not take hold. Nevertheless, the modernization and rationalization measures shifted the emphasis in nation branding activities: Instead of the backward-looking "keeper of German heritage" narrative, the modernization effort reconnected East Germany's cultural vision to that of other industrialized countries in a forward-looking way.

The 1964 furniture industry reforms were an integral part of the NES (1963–68), which continued in modified form under the name Economic System of Socialism (Ökonomisches System des Sozialismus, ESS) until 1971, when the Politburo aborted this economic program and returned to the authoritative Plan. Ulbricht's NES program aimed at allowing more flexibility for all levels of planning—most notably by giving individual companies greater discretion—and at working toward greater efficiency and growth. It recognized the limits of socialist economic thinking as the GDR strove to re-enter international markets after a period of extreme isolation following the erection of the Berlin Wall.[74] Economic levers played an important role in NES, which attempted to combine central planning with indirect steering of enterprise via mostly monetary incentives. These economic levers, including net profit deductions, taxes, prices, and the cost and availability of credit and fund formation, became methods for indirectly aligning enterprise with the Plan.[75] Bonuses and other financial incentives were aimed directly at motivating the workforce. Nevertheless, the introduction of market elements stressed quantitative as well as qualitative performance.

The Planning Commission expected the furniture industry to produce a complete and continuous range of functional and modern furnishings to meet domestic demand and export commitments. During the 1964 reforms, it demanded "superb quality, technologically state-of-the-art" furniture that should contain a higher "moral" value, meaning that it should be more durable, have greater functionality, and be simpler and lighter in construction.[76] These new guidelines revised the previous emphasis on ornamentation and arts and crafts techniques in furniture production. GDR furniture industry was thus encouraged to implement simpler aesthetics, which taste reformer Horst Michel and other former Werkbund members and Bauhaus disciples had envisioned back in the late 1940s. Part of the plan was to compensate for a scarcity of natural resources and quality materials by modernizing furniture design. Chipboard and fiberboard, new surface materials, and chemical manufactures were used to reach these new standards. Rather than traditional materials like wood, the planners favored man-made materials, such as plastic and synthetics for drawers, doors, frames, and entire chairs.[77] But more than just an economic program, this new focus on chemistry had cultural aims as well. Horst Redeker's 1960 pamphlet "Chemistry adds Beauty" (*Chemie gibt Schönheit*) set the tone for this period.[78] In the furniture industry, synthetic materials were mainly used in finishing treatments and cushion foams. While the ultimate goal was, literally and figuratively, to enhance the socialist surface, this mostly resulted in a glossing over of the lack of quality materials underneath. In this way, the leadership changed the GDR national brand to one of forward-looking synthetic modernity in the mid-1960s.

Eventually, the scientific ideas that accompanied the centralization measures of the 1964 reform impacted industrial design rhetoric. Internal ZfF communication shifted emphasis from cultural directives to questions of socialist scientific progress.[79] The main prerequisite for the institute's work remained the improvement and design of the "socialist way of life," but urgent technological and economic considerations surpassed purely cultural concerns. One challenge that remained was how to define the everyday needs of this "socialist way of life." Ulbricht vaguely described the function of domestic culture in his presentation on "Basic Tasks for the Year 1970" in connection with the ongoing GDR housing crisis: "The quality of housing influences work productivity and development of the socialist identity. People reproduce their labor mainly in housing areas. With the evolution of a socialist mode of life, though, qualitatively new demands on housing develop."[80] The design of the home and of kitchen furniture was to be purposeful and pragmatic in order to free up time to do "more pleasant and useful things, such as cultural activities or educating ourselves."[81] Aesthetic considerations too impacted this practical approach: "Bad shape and color effects in tools, home textiles or furniture limit our joy of habitation."[82] The government thus understood the home to be an important part of the workers' state, a place of recuperation and recovery from and for work as well as a space for self-improvement. Aesthetic concepts continued to play a great ideological role in shaping Germans into good socialists. However, determining these visual markers of a socialist way of life more concretely was left to the ZfF. By turning the aesthetic reconstitution of East German material culture into a scientific experiment, the GDR aligned its conception of the human environment with the scientific-economic interpretation of socialism that prevailed in the Eastern Bloc in the 1960s. This was an effort to catch up with Khrushchev's rationalization of the Soviet everyday, which proclaimed technology as the locus of communist modernization.[83]

Alongside the structural reorganization and scientification of the East German furniture industry, more efforts were made to standardize production. Those measures included the standardization of furniture measurements in cooperation with the construction industry, the nationwide streamlining of assortments (*Sortimentsbereinigung*)—a specific type of product range rationalization based on cultural and political motivations—and tight quality control.[84] *Sortimentsbereinigung* dramatically reduced the numbers of models in the market and was a crucial prerequisite for the furniture industry to venture into mass production. In this way, the ZfF hoped to simultaneously achieve greater productivity and conserve raw materials.

This rethinking of furniture included machine-produced boards and self-mounted furniture series. Economic planners found the answer to their problems in modular storage furniture (*Schrankwand*). Ironically, at this point the leading furniture combine Zeulenroda with its stylistically fraught furniture fell out of favor with the political leadership, and the SED reconciled with DWH, which it had previously viewed with suspicion. The furniture "modularization" program that Rudolf Horn designed for the Dresden-Hellerau combine in 1966, called Model German Workshops (Modell Deutsche Werkstätten, MDW), perhaps best embodies this new strategy. Instead of creating one variant of a hundred types, Horn changed the underlying concept to producing a hundred variants of one furniture type, substituting one distinct function with multiple functions for a piece or part of furniture. Wooden boards and panels constituted the basis of the construction concept, which relocated production from the work-and resource-intensive furniture industry to the wood prefabrication industry that simply provided the panels.[85]

The program was based on a vertical modular grid that optimized storage functionality and warehouse turnover. The pieces measured 96 mm vertically and 600 or 800 mm horizontally and included shelves, doors, tabletops, desktops, and drawers. Its aesthetic appeal lay in the combination of matte-finished surfaces on the basic structure and shiny veneers with real-wood visual appearance on the front. MDW became a best-selling item because of its modularization, availability, flexibility, and the degree of customization it allowed the final user. Consumers could assemble the pieces at home themselves. The system's simple modular assembly and disassembly made it easy to move the furniture to a new location or to add supplementary parts as needed. MDW basically grew, or shrunk, over the course of the consumer's life. Horn redesigned it twice in

FIGURE 2.1. A studio photograph of East German system furniture
Modell Deutsche Werkstätten (MDW) with larch veneer. Designed by Rudolf Horn
for VEB Möbelkombinat Hellerau in 1967/1972. SLUB/Deutsche Fotothek,
Friedrich Weimer, 1976.

FIGURE 2.2. The *Schrankwand* became a popular solution for bed and living room
storage in both German states. Hülsta modular furniture series Universa in mahogany
and white wood, catalog no. 5002. © Hülsta-werke Hüls GmbH & Co. KG, 1978.

the 1970s and 1980s, ensuring its production until the collapse of the GDR.[86] It eventually incorporated upholstery modules from neighboring companies and combines. MDW and its supplier network thus perfectly embodied the division of labor that rationalization had brought to the modernization of the East German furniture industry. MDW was one of the longest-selling and most successful furniture lines before Ikea products became a global phenomenon.[87]

MDW also entailed a complete rethinking of relations between production, retail, and fitting. Retail had to be reorganized to provide first-time buyers with *Wohnberatung*, interior design counseling that would create the best solution for any given house, apartment, or room. Stores had to offer assembly in a timely manner, though consumers could choose to assemble the pieces themselves without professional help. However, Horn envisioned close cooperation between furniture stores and industry. He quoted Ulbricht's guidelines from the Seventh Party Congress in 1967: "It is here that retail fills out its role as contributor to the People's economy—for the good of the economic efficiency."[88] *Wohnberatungen* had existed in the GDR before, but the projected MDW counseling exceeded prior institutions in scale and ambition, revealing a systematic attempt to promote both an aesthetic and a utilitarian vision to the broader public.[89]

Although NES and the Chemical Program incentivized a host of reforms in the furniture industry, enabled investments, and facilitated greater coordination—for which MDW was an exceptionally successful example—not everything went according to plan. In hopes of increasing the potential for innovation, NES gave combines and VEBs more freedom with regard to product development and planning. This leeway, however, made quality control more difficult, and thus necessitated extra incentives for industry to produce goods consistent with the official aesthetic. It is here that the ZfF used its industrial design expertise to participate in the economic planning process. As a unit of the DAMW, it issued a new quality seal for "Good Design" and awarded medals at the semi-annual Leipzig trade fair from 1964 onward. Winning companies could increase prices for their domestic retail and export products and thus reach their annual production quota faster. However, the measure did not achieve the desired effect, because the economic levers introduced by the NES did not eradicate self-interested company behavior. By 1970, the SED party organizations in the furniture industry blamed poor quality of products and lack of innovation on the VEB and combine directors. They requested an end to the "ideology of omission," the tendency to mass produce only those furniture designs that required the least material and labor resources.[90]

Family Businesses and Aesthete Entrepreneurs

The 1964 restructuring of the GDR furniture industry was closely related to the state of West Germany's furniture production. Investments in mechanization technology had propelled the Federal Republic to the top of storage furniture-producing nations, while education and professional training had given West German products a reputation for quality workmanship and innovation.[91] West Germany's successes became the implied benchmark for the GDR furniture industry in the 1960s. To complete the modern brand narrative, however, the GDR planners, despite concentration measures that theoretically increased control over the design process, still depended on the cooperation of the industrial sector, just as western design councils needed to work hand in hand with entrepreneurial elites. The results of these efforts were mixed, and both risked losing a key actor in their brand narrative endeavor: the entrepreneur.

In the postwar era, a number of German family businesses that produced furniture grew from small firms that competed in niche markets into international companies. Nonetheless, the families maintained their ownership as well as their influence on business culture and leadership. Alongside big industry, the family business has been identified as one of the two routes to Germany's industrial modernity.[92] The economic strength of small-and medium-sized businesses, the so-called *Mittelstand*, shaped West German capitalism, while they played a less important role in the GDR.[93] There the social capital and economic prowess of entrepreneurial families were frequently overlooked because of the policy focus on state-owned companies and large production clusters.

Owners' financial and personal involvement in family and *Mittelstand* businesses often created specific organizational structures.[94] Specialized regional networks of artisanal work emerged through associational cooperation, a "decentralized industrial order," before and alongside big business, strengthened by the distinctive social ethos of the *Mittelstand* entrepreneurs.[95] In West Germany, most of the furniture industry was clustered in Baden-Württemberg, Bavaria, and North Rhine–Westphalia.[96] Through mechanization and mutual support in regional networks, the industry found creative ways to sustain itself even during economic downturns, such as the oil crises of the 1970s, and the onset of market saturation. Whereas 40 percent of the population in the Federal Republic bought furniture during the furnishing boom of the 1960s, just 20 percent did at the beginning of the 1980s. Yet the expenditures doubled from DM 318 to DM 646 per purchase.[97] This was partially due to collaborations between different branches of the industry. For example, upholstery and storage furniture manufacturers together created attractive modular programs that offered solutions for the entire house and enticed consumers to spend more money in a single purchase. Technological progress contributed to the sustainability of medium-sized furniture production as well. By the 1980s, the industry mechanized with remarkable speed, resulting in greater output using less manpower.[98] Most of these firms were still medium-sized companies with workforces of less than one hundred.

In the realm of design, the personal involvement of family members and the ability to draw on regional artisanal skills often made family businesses drivers of innovation. The North Rhine–Westphalian furniture company Interlübke exemplifies how timeless designs, quality production, and long product life span became the cornerstone of family business success. Founded by brothers Hans and Leo Lübke in 1937, the company became a household name by the 1960s. Based on the ideas of Swiss interior designer Walter Müller, the Lübke brothers developed an "endless" closet and shelving system in 1963 that revolutionized the West German living room. The *Schrankwand*, a modular furniture system, could be rearranged or added to as needed, just like the MDW storage solution in the GDR a few years later. While there were other people working on similar solutions to provide flexible storage in the living room, the Lübke closet system, called Interlübke 63, won over consumers with its durability and simple elegance. Interlübke did not follow trends or listen to consumer surveys but rather relied on its own taste to create progressive and modern high-end furniture.[99] As trendsetters, the Lübke family represented the ideal type of aesthete industrialists in the Federal Republic: a family business that excelled in quality design and whose interests eventually aligned with the aesthetic mission of the RfF. However, companies that could afford to cater only to a selective and exclusive clientele with expensive, modern taste were the exception also in the Federal Republic.

Even during periods of enormous growth, the *Mittelstand* ethos remained visible in the firms' political activism. Members involved in the BDI Arbeitskreis often came from small-and medium-sized enterprises and family companies.[100] The smaller scale of their businesses allowed *Mittelstand* entrepreneurs to combine traditional craftsmanship with serial production. They were in general more likely to consider questions of design alongside production ethics that valued premium materials and durability, and less prone to Americanize their business methods than their big business counterparts.[101] In the postwar decades, American production and management methods, such as rationalized mass production to increase profit margins, systematic data collection to maximize productivity, and mass distribution, including marketing techniques, to create demand, had become influential in German big business.[102] While German industrialists were fascinated by the productivity and prosperity of US industries, they rejected American production practices that consciously cut short product life span with superficial styling and mediocre materials and construction.[103] Instead, German *Mittelstand* entrepreneurs shared a belief in quality materials and timeless shapes with other European countries that had adopted reform ideas from social design movements, such as the Swiss Werkbund (1913) and the Dutch De Stijl (1917), into their national value system in the first decades of the twentieth century. The furniture industry particularly upheld these standards because technologies of wood processing had not advanced enough to mechanize production entirely, and for the most part small series production prevailed. West German furniture production thus combined aesthetic characteristics with social responsibility by necessity as well as by intention. This value system persisted until well after reconstruction and was reaffirmed in 1965 by the BDI. Gustav Stein summarized the position as follows: "If everybody took part in the conscious quality reduction coming out of America, then there is only one recipe for success for us: technological quality with its 'Made-in-Germany' seal shaped by 'good design as a quality factor.'"[104] Business elites thus saw their products as part of a national brand that stood for high standards with a commitment to affordable value. From their point of view, German aesthetics and production ethics stood in opposition to those associated with American methods.

Like industrialists in the Federal Republic, the economic planners of the GDR idealized quality design and quality products. East Germans upheld durability and social responsibility as the underlying principles of production. This is supported by the fact that the DAMW established quality control benchmarks and mechanisms with the goal of prolonging product life span.[105] This policy was partially motivated by the scarcity of consumer goods. Increasing demand, so the idea went, could be stemmed if the available goods remained in households long enough. For instance, economic planners expected living room and bedroom furniture to last fifty years, a view they shared with a sizable part of the wider population. As late as 1984, almost a third of East Germans maintained that furniture should be bought only once in a lifetime.[106] The fact that Germans in East and West opposed the American "throwaway society" thus suggests that Americanization cannot explain all facets of Germany's postwar cultural and economic development.

In East German socialism, the space for entrepreneurial activity shrunk during waves of intensified collectivization and expropriation in the 1950s,

1960s, and 1970s, in spite of the fact that private ownership persisted in segments of the arts and crafts. In response, East German companies steadily migrated westward in search of better economic and more liberal political conditions. As early as 1953, about one in seven East German industrial firms, more than four thousand in total, had moved to the Federal Republic, taking their skilled workers and managers with them.[107] This exodus marked an enormous brain drain, as the average GDR refugee was young, educated, and highly adaptable.[108] Loss of talent hampered the country's technological-scientific development and damaged its industrial progress. This migration flow was only halted by the construction of the Berlin Wall in August 1961.

Innovation, while desired among East German entrepreneurs and family business owners, found little space in the socialist economy as NES and ESS drew to a close in 1970. The new national brand narrative of synthetic modernity that was deeply anchored in industrial research and development (R&D) put even more pressure on the Planning Commission to keep up with the international industrial competition. With a mix of paranoia and hunger for success, the GDR increasingly fostered its technological development through industrial espionage.[109] However, the practice risked turning away potential allies in the national brand narrative and increasingly undermined the entrepreneurial spirit of *Mittelstand* business owners.

Such spy activity intersected with entrepreneurial expertise in the family business Bruchhäuser in Güstrow, Brandenburg. The firm was founded by Werner Bruchhäuser and his son Axel joined, after earning an engineering degree, to manage technical development and marketing. During the standardization efforts of the early 1960s, the DAMW took note of the high quality standards and continued improvement of production technology in the Bruchhäuser company.[110] By the late 1960s, this enterprise, a private company with majority state shareholding, produced couches, chairs, and other seating that were successful on the western export market.[111] The case of Axel Bruchhäuser offers an illustration of how a financially well-situated middle-class family that seemed to have come to an understanding with local and national party operatives could feel stifled by the state's one-size-fits-all policy solutions to advance East German technical production.

In 1969, Axel Bruchhäuser requested assignment as *Reisekader*, a person who was granted official permission to travel outside of the GDR for business or political purposes without undergoing the long visa process.[112] This would allow him to visit the Federal Republic to meet with his business contacts in the western furniture industry. His father, Werner, had been a *Reisekader* ever since the company started exporting furniture to West Germany in 1966, and it may have been either the request for the second travel permit for one firm or the fact that the father had not proven to be a good and reliable Stasi (Ministry for State Security) informant that put the Bruchhäuser family on the radar of the GDR intelligence service.[113]

After long deliberations, followed by an extensive background check, the Stasi decided not only to grant Axel the travel permission but also to hire him as an unofficial informant (*Inoffizieller Mitarbeiter*, IM), a collaborator of the intelligence service.[114] His research in synthetic fillers for upholstery cushions coupled with his engineering knowledge made him an ideal candidate for industrial espionage. Moreover, Axel had never openly criticized the regime, had a clean record in the required socialist youth mass organizations, and had become an expert in chemical technology. Even the fact that he had not been politically active and came from a middle-class family helped his case. The Stasi concluded that this "bourgeois" profile would make western business partners more likely to trust and speak openly with him.[115] Once his IM training was complete, the Stasi showered Bruchhäuser with financial incentives to work for them.[116]

For two years everything went smoothly. Bruchhäuser and his father both went on trips to Western Europe and reported back to the Stasi on the political, economic, and social situations of their host countries. Specifically, Bruchhäuser's mission consisted of collecting

> operational intelligence regarding offensive economic activities in the economic realm, the infiltration of the adversary structure, intelligence of adversary companies and their centers of interference, accumulation of scientific-technological information and documents from non-socialist countries, recruitment of western economic cadres, and intelligence on operationally interesting persons from non-socialist countries.[117]

The list reveals that investigating external "interference" in the GDR economy seems to have taken precedence over uncovering foreign industry secrets. But informant Bruchhäuser provided the Stasi mostly with technological information about West German businesses that worked in the field of polyurethane chemistry and not with intelligence about suspected western economic warfare. He also went to the IMM Cologne Furniture Fair in 1970 and 1972 to evaluate and report back on the international standards of technological development in furniture production.

In 1972, after Erich Honecker had succeeded Ulbricht as general secretary of the SED, the entrepreneurial situation in the GDR took a turn for the worse.

Already majority-owned by the state, the Bruchhäuser family business became expropriated under the auspices of a new nationalization policy. Having endured partial expropriation in 1960, this was more than the Bruchhäuser family was willing to accept.[118] A few weeks after the announcement of the nationalization policy, the Stasi inadvertently sent father and son simultaneously on trips to western countries, giving them an opportunity to flee the GDR. Reuniting in West Germany, they joined forces with an old business contact in Lauenförde, Lower Saxony, and proceeded to take over a furniture company called Tecta, which they converted to specialize in Bauhaus designs and other high-end furniture.[119] Taken by surprise, the Stasi tried to force the Bruchhäusers to return to the GDR by holding Axel's mother and his three sisters hostage. For two years, the Stasi followed their every step but eventually gave up in 1974.

This episode shows to what lengths the GDR went to catch up technologically with the West, especially the Federal Republic. The Stasi risked involving father and son in their IM program and provided transportation as well as funds to enable them to deepen their business contacts in the West. Moreover, Bruchhäuser's mission also illuminates the suspicion and paranoia with which the GDR leadership viewed the FRG. Nevertheless, the investment in Bruchhäuser could have paid off. Axel did report back on new ideas about how to combine chemical components that could substitute for scarce natural resources such as wood or fillers in cushions.[120] Among the East German projects that his expertise and industrial espionage facilitated were the new synthetics works in Schwedt. In a letter he sent to a friend in Güstrow after he had fled the GDR, Bruchhäuser pointed out that the technological standard in Schwedt was tremendous and that people in the West were "tearing their hair out seeing how little such technological expertise was put to use" in the GDR.[121] This inability to fully benefit from captured industrial secrets may be traced back to shifting power relations in industrial development since the late 1960s. To be in full control of the R&D process and to monopolize information, the Stasi cut official lines of international, and at times even internal, communication and substituted technological and scientific exchange with industrial espionage. Instead of incremental change through experimentation, R&D departments were ordered to copy illegally procured western products. This meant that industrial espionage became the sole source of progress in key industries for the GDR's modernization, such as microelectronics, and that these industries were always a step behind the international competition.[122] As Bruchhäuser's story illustrates, this was also true for the chemical industry, an increasingly important contributor to furniture production.

The way in which the SED handled industrial research thus suppressed both home-grown innovation and the entrepreneurial spirit.[123] Espionage surely informed technological development in the GDR furniture industry, though fully taking advantage of these advances depended on visionary entrepreneurs. However, such figures had been lost to the other side due to the expropriation and surveillance policies of the state. Whether *Mittelstand* industrialists physically emigrated to the West like Bruchhäuser or refused to cooperate, the government lost a crucial building block in the nation branding process.

Consumer Reception and Market Research

Postwar nation branding and the narratives it created around products established a direct link between correct production and the "right" consumption. In the case of West Germany, over the course of the 1950s the brand had become national by design, but shared its modern edge with design work done in other European countries. In the East German case, the branding message changed from presenting the GDR as the keeper of traditional German aesthetics in the 1950s to articulating a socialist synthetic modernity more international in character in the 1960s.[124] Successful implementation of these narratives in everyday life via consumption necessitated the inclusion of the population in the brand. Here we see the efforts of industry and state-supported design institutions diverge again. Increasingly, industry's vision for design as part of the national brand had a pragmatic and hence a more inclusive emphasis than that of state institutions when it came to listening to consumer opinion. Meanwhile, the RfF design council in the West and the ZfF, the DAMW, or the Bauakademie in the East attempted to streamline or even control specific interior design aesthetics. The difference in approach was guided by customers' buying power alongside market research that facilitated producers' acceptance of different tastes and purchasing decisions.

From the early days of the GDR, design educators made a great effort to include the population in the branding of postwar East Germany. Interior design shows offered an opportunity for design visionaries to directly interact with the general public. In 1952, the Institut für angewandte Kunst (the later ZfF) organized an exhibition of modern household goods that presented the official vision of the SED leadership. At its *Industrial Products of Today* show the institute asked the population to assess the displayed products, considering it an "important democratic cultural task" to judge the current industrial production "with the goal of influencing their further development and of scrutinizing those distributers and buyers who brought the mediocre and the bad instead of the best into retail."[125] The GDR thus strengthened the link between production and consumption by actively involving consumers in writing a national narrative, at least until the Formalism Debate and its aesthetic diktat curtailed the conversation.

Shortly after the Formalism Debate, the GDR design council's exhibitions often stood in stark contrast to the official style guidelines. Customers left angry comments in response to the displays in the guestbook of the 1956 show *Industrial Products—Functional and Beautiful* at East Berlin's Alexanderplatz. They felt misled by the modern sample furniture in the exhibit that were not being mass-produced at that time. It further highlighted the drab offerings in stores and uncovered the shortcomings of East German consumer goods production. One visitor even called the exhibition a "smoke screen" hiding the bleak state of the socialist interior design industry.[126]

This guestbook offers testimony to popular discontent by the second half of the 1950s, once it became clear to the population that the GDR leadership would be unable to deliver on reconstruction-period promises.[127] Visitors' frustration with the apparent inability to put modern products in East German stores resulted in pilgrimages to West Berlin. "It's always the same. Retail, that is the government, has only to blame itself if we go to the West to see or even buy well-designed products!" one visitor remarked, deeply disappointed after having seen such unattainable furniture displayed in the exhibition. "This [exhibition] is proof that we also have such things. Where can I buy the nice little upholstered lounge chairs from Hellerau?"[128] Consumer comments cleverly employed ideological rhetoric to engage and challenge economic planners: "Fulfilling personal needs is the best cultural education (*Kultur-Erziehung*). How can we benefit from the most beautiful exhibition if everything is destined for export?"[129] Most of the commentators signed their critique with their full names and addresses, which indicates that they neither feared repression nor punishment for their candor. "This book with its contents can be described as an 'arraignment'; an arraignment because it uncovers openly and consistently the idleness of retail and partially even that of the industry," reads one of the last comments, summarizing the general tone of responses in the guestbook.[130]

Ten years later, in 1965, at the furnishings show *Modern Dwelling* in Hoyerswerda, similar comments about retail's failure to embrace modern furniture again appeared in the guestbook. The show's visitors especially blamed retail buyers and proposed that "the HO and Konsum buyers of Hoyerswerda should acquire good taste by seeing the original [in this exhibition]. Hopefully then there will be good products available in our stores."[131] Assuming buyers had been whiplashed by the Formalism Debate and the oft-changing SED style directives, the public urged them "to buy and act bravely!"[132] Ample evidence exists that many GDR citizens preferred modern idioms to the opulent kitsch of socialist historicism. It is safe to say that the leadership and the populace did not agree on a single style for German socialism in the 1950s and the first half of the 1960s. Representing large state-owned retail organizations, HO and Konsum buyers grew insecure; they either safely complied with the SED guidelines on socialist realism or simply followed their often uneducated personal taste. By the mid-1960s, when the national brand narrative changed to a synthetic modernity that included simpler, functional designs, production and retail had to undergo a complete restructuring in order to fulfill this new vision.

In the long run, economic organization by districts seems to have caused consumption disruption and inhibited modernization. The industry in each district was supposed to cover the consumption needs of the entire region, which posed fewer problems in regard to foodstuffs or articles of personal hygiene and clothes than with furniture. Despite efforts to align the furniture aesthetic across the GDR via cultural policy, each of the furniture combines maintained its own specific style. The inflexible organization by district severely limited interdistrict exchange of goods, which negatively affected the availability of specific furniture sets and add-on systems across the country at the close of the 1950s.[133] For somebody who had decorated a home in the district of Dresden with ready access to the very particular furniture of Hellerau, moving to, for instance, Schwerin at the Baltic Sea coast meant either starting over, going to the expense of furnishing the home with new furniture, or adding pieces of furniture produced in the new home district, potentially compromising the previous aesthetic vision. While these problems might seem trivial, they negatively affected the quality of life in the GDR and the popular support for the national brand.

In an effort to improve domestic economic planning, the GDR established a market research institute in 1962 to coordinate supply and demand.[134] The increasing interest in consumer demand had originated with the New Course and was reaffirmed by the 1958 Fifth Party Congress, which heralded gradual shifts away from an economy exclusively based on heavy industry.[135] As early as 1953 GDR retail sales personnel were already writing down daily comments and criticisms of customers and sending the feedback up the levels of the economic planning apparatus, which were then summarized for the Planning Commission. As paradoxical as conducting market research in a centrally planned economy might sound, the Institute for Consumption Research (Institut für Bedarfsforschung), renamed Institute for Market Research (Institut für Marktforschung) after 1967, contributed tremendously to the configuration of Five-Year Plans. It conducted polls among consumers, compared past production rates with actual demand, and calculated and analyzed the predicted consumption of goods to perfect the Plan. The institute saw its mission as one of "understanding and explaining the antagonism between production and consumption, supply and demand, communal and individual interests, communal and individual consciousness" via consumer motivation research.[136] In this way, market researchers searched for ways to address discrepancies in the socialist "planning of the market." Foreseeing business landscapes in five-year increments based on this data presented an insurmountable task, yet the planning apparatus continued to attempt to reach budget conclusions and anticipate demand despite recurring proof that both the consumer and the producer estimates were off.[137] Nonetheless, the presence of a market research institute in a planned economy speaks to the GDR's attempt to balance ideological boundaries and the uniformity of standardized materiality with consumer behaviors.[138]

By 1971, a period when prefabricated housing blocks had become the preferred building form in the GDR, consumers continued to prefer functionality over pomp and ornament.[139] According to a market survey, half of the population liked the new add-on furniture systems, such as MDW. More than 40 percent of the population liked the idea of extra storage for clothes in the living room. Among consumers who had a one-bedroom apartment, where the parents used the living room as their bedroom, this number almost doubled. With regard to interior design taste, the population was split down the middle. While 49 percent favored a cohesive style for their living room furniture, 44 percent preferred to have different styles or shapes in supplemental small furniture, such as side tables or flowerpot stands. Regarding dining tables and chairs, the percentage of consumers preferring aesthetic cohesion with their storage furniture (*Behältnismöbel*) was even higher at 53 percent. Eighty-two percent indicated a preference for natural materials in their furniture, especially real wood.[140] The findings of the study indicated to the economic planners that the population had specific ideas about their living environments, with a preference for modern design idioms made of natural materials that enabled maximum flexibility and practicality.

Synthetic materials, increasingly applied in accordance with the Chemical Program and modernization concepts of the mid-sixties, did not make the list of preferences, indicating that the narrative of synthetic modernity failed to find full support among the GDR population. Antiques and inherited wooden furniture also continued to be a substantial part of GDR interiors. When the Council of Ministers later encouraged this trend to combat a shortage in raw materials and consumer products in the 1980s, these makeshift solutions were absorbed into the brand narrative.[141] For instance, the interior design magazine *Kultur im Heim* and such articles as *"Biedermeier* in the Modern Building?" (*Biedermeier im Neubau?*) and "Second-hand Furniture" (*Möbel aus zweiter Hand*) promoted the appropriate incorporation of old furniture into socialist living environments.[142] The key to keeping the home "socialist," they suggested, was to avoid treating the piece as ornamentation, no matter how historic or precious, and instead to assign it a specific function.

GDR consumer research also illustrates how popular attitudes toward home furnishings changed over time. The number of households that wanted to replace their furniture more than doubled from 21 percent in 1971 to 43 percent in 1984.[143] While this figure is still comparatively low, it indicates the growing expectations of material well-being among the East German population in the later years of the GDR. Honecker's consumption-oriented promises of the Unity of Economic and Social Policy program at the Eighth Party Congress in 1971 had likely spurred expectations. Nevertheless, the planned economy failed to fulfill these hopes for improved furniture availability. While the nonfulfillment of production quotas was one factor here, this was significantly compounded by the fast progress in prefabricated housing that led to increased demand.[144] The public housing programs of the 1960s through 1980s started a large migration from decaying inner-city housing to these new high-rise apartments on the outskirts of cities, which often necessitated the purchase of additional furniture.[145] Although the production capacity was great enough to cover the unexpected demand even when unfulfilled production quotas are taken into account, East Germany's increasing dependence on export revenues meant that a large percentage of the national production was instead sent abroad. The furniture industry eventually failed to keep up with both domestic and export demand.

As the supply gaps widened, the population grew increasingly disgruntled. In *Eingaben*, complaint letters to the communal, regional, or national leadership, consumers decried their plights with the retail sector.[146] *Eingaben* were not consistently retained, but from a number of preserved letters it appears that the population mainly used them to criticize and not to compliment the goods supply. They offer insight into how GDR consumers negotiated with the political leadership over its failure to provide adequate material comfort. *Eingaben* performed a particular rhetorical function, with highly stylized content. It followed a general pattern where GDR citizens first presented themselves as righteous socialist citizens and then threatened to appeal to higher levels of the administration, quoting political leaders to legitimize their appeals.[147] These letters were part of a carefully crafted illusion that suggested to consumers that they could bring their concerns directly to the people in power, an emulation of direct participatory democracy and another "smoke screen" employed by the government to maintain domestic stability. Just like the guestbooks at design exhibitions, *Eingaben* functioned as pressure valves where consumers could release their frustrations, without the SED having to actually make changes in the slow-moving economic system.[148] They seem to have gained traction only in *Prisma*, a popular GDR television program that featured complaints and forwarded *Eingaben* to the responsible people, which annoyed economic planners and policymakers.[149] Ironically, *Prisma* did more of a disservice to consumers, because it took the focus away from the wrongs in the system and directed it instead toward individual cases that, after some moralizing on national TV, industry and retail were able to fix. For quite a long time, the leadership succeeded in creating the impression that the socialist economy was able to fulfill demands, but the cracks in the facade were exposed in the late 1980s. The Ministry for District and Food Industries, which was responsible for the furniture industry, reported for the first six months of 1987 that the tone of the *Eingaben* became more acrimonious.[150] Rather than the complaints being framed by the acceptable limits of ideological discourse, some *Eingaben* openly challenged the purported advances of socialism. In a letter to the furniture collective Dresden-Hellerau, the Licht family from Dresden complained that 15 percent of the delivered parts for a self-assembled children furniture set were faulty and concluded that "we cannot imagine that customers in the non-socialist West would be content with this. Yet we deem the damage that is done to the population's trust in the products of our socialist industry more severe."[151] This and other *Eingaben* show the extent of pent-up frustration among the public and that the SED's mechanisms of population control began to fail by the late 1980s.

In the market economy of the Federal Republic, consumer demands necessarily shaped attempts to forge a cohesive aesthetic. In 1954, the Institute for Opinion Polling Allensbach conducted a survey about consumer tastes in furniture among females over eighteen years of age.[152] The results revealed the challenge that West German industrialists and official arbiters of taste faced as they dealt with diverse tastes in their quest for aesthetic revival. The overwhelming majority, 60 percent of the women interviewed, preferred flowered kitsch, dark woods, and curved lines on living room buffets and recliners. Thirty percent liked what could be described as subdued modern or Swedish style with clear lines, blonde woods, and unadorned surfaces, the style closest to the functionalist aesthetic of the national brand. Only 7 percent of the respondents, mostly younger women between the ages of eighteen and twenty-nine, showed interest in the organic shapes of 1950s American-influenced, "international" design. A further breakdown of this group reveals that better educated female wage earners and entrepreneurs from mid-sized towns favored the modern idioms (Swedish and International styles). These numbers revealed a slowly growing trend toward modern, simple aesthetics among wealthier consumer brackets. Industry intended to accelerate this trend through taste education initiatives, such as the *Wohnberatungen* and industry-sponsored permanent exhibitions of well-designed objects.

Yet attempts to streamline West German taste in interior design met with little success. In 1963, sociologist Alphons Silberman conducted a similar study in the city of Cologne and the small town of Bergneustadt. Respondents again preferred an aesthetic that was bulky and ornamented, especially those in the higher income brackets.[153] A few years later in 1969, the by then industry-led RfF started a quality initiative similar to the economic levers employed by economic planners in the GDR, awarding outstanding designs from industry and design students that reflected official aesthetics with a government-endowed prize, also named "Good Design" (*Gute Form*) like that of the GDR.[154] The idea was not bad, as West Germans regarded good quality to be the most important factor in their furniture purchasing decision.[155] However, the prize failed to get noticed by West German audiences and was often confused with the much older Good Industrial Design (*Gute Industrieform*) quality seal awarded annually at the Hanover Fair.[156] Subsequently, the winning designs were showcased in a traveling exhibition sent around Western and Eastern Europe to highlight West German ingenuity, unfolding more impact abroad than at home.

Aside from policies, design, and production, retail played an important role in supporting or undermining nation branding efforts. As in the GDR, the availability of modern designs depended largely on their distribution through buyers and retail organizations, which became the object of inquiry for the Nuremberg Society for Consumption Research (Gesellschaft für Konsumforschung, GfK).[157] In the spring of 1972 the GfK conducted the first research on furniture retail and distribution with a view to offering the industry better data on the challenges ahead. It found that due to increasing production capacities and a growing number of competitors (close to 10,000 retail businesses were counted) the struggle for customers already intensified.[158] Over a period of six years, the market further expanded from over DM 9 billion in sales in 1972 to over DM 15 billion in 1978. The furniture industry grew steadily in the *Länder* of Bavaria, Baden-Württemberg, and North Rhine–Westphalia; the latter expanded from 2,532 retail businesses in 1972 to 2,990 in 1978. Despite the economic downturn after the 1973 oil crisis, the furniture sector remained highly competitive, which meant that industry and retail increasingly followed consumer tastes, instead of implementing the national brand narrative.[159]

One of the largest German retailers was the Neckermann mail order business, which sent out catalogs to ten million West German homes in the early 1970s. Asked how Neckermann conceptualized its product line, Eckart Rittmeyer, its head buyer, responded that the company did not perceive itself as educating consumers but rather that it allowed demand to dictate the choices in the catalog. Unfortunately, he continued, designer furniture and low prices seldom matched up, but even if they did, he thought that the RfF jury for the Good Design prize was too avant-garde in its tastes and missed the mark with respect to both the needs and demands of the population.[160] Gerhard Krahn, the general manager and partial owner of the small furniture store Gessmann and the larger furniture center Europa-Möbel in Frankfurt, shared Rittmeyer's view. Whereas the typical Gessmann customer was usually well-to-do, Europa-Möbel catered to the lower-income strata. Asked to speculate about the promises of functional furniture at affordable prices, Krahn said that it would not change lower-income consumer behavior, "because this furniture with clear lines doesn't offer enough on an emotional level."[161] He also pointed out that even the affluent often preferred stylized furniture over functional furniture. However, Krahn observed that the functional avant-garde designs eventually began to sell at the Gessmann store and, increasingly, at the Europa-Möbel center.[162]

In the end, despite all the effort devoted to educating consumers about good design, West German policymakers never succeeded in completely eradicating the bulky-style furniture commonly known as *Gelsenkirchner Barock*, a kind of opulent Biedermeier that came to embody German popular taste during the economic miracle.[163] Middle-income groups especially liked to demonstrate their affluence with heavy, wooden furniture, elaborate patterned fabrics, and numerous knick-knacks. To this social group, functionalism and good design represented the scarcity and shame of the postwar years that most Germans wanted to leave behind. While the Federal Republic understood the centrality of prosperity in its postwar narrative of nation branding, the selected aesthetic style did not fit the self-image of a large segment of the population. By the early 1970s, though, a noticeable change in taste took place, as demand for and affordability of modern furniture increased, evidenced by the international success of Ikea.

In both Germanys, then, similar struggles over centralized cultural policy, regional economic organization, and popular reception shaped and necessarily altered the nation branding narrative over the course of forty years. Policymakers, designers, industry, retail, and consumers came to the market with different expectations. Paradoxically, the efforts to create national brands by infusing German homes, East and West, with styles that conformed to their respective narrative continued to bring the two aesthetics closer together, particularly because the underlying norms and values regarding product quality remained similar. The emphases on durability over modishness and technological precision over superficial styling are features with which German product design and engineering have become synonymous. Even if GDR production failed to uphold these principles in practice because of shortcomings in the socialist economic system, officials continued to demand world standard quality. It is, in fact, this proud "Made in Germany" brand that exemplified the aspired economic culture in both Germanys.

CHAPTER 3

Intra-German Trade and the Aesthetic Dialectic
of European Integration

AT THE 1963 LEIPZIG TRADE FAIR, West German industrial designer Friedrich Koslowsky approached leading East German politicians and economic planners with his idea for a "House of Life" in East Berlin. His proposed furniture store project would offer East German producers the possibility of presenting their products to West German buyers. Based on the hope that trade across the border, and thus a shared material culture, would overcome Germany's physical partition, he sought to build bridges between the GDR and the Federal Republic that went beyond mere economic contacts.[1] Koslowsky's plan never came to fruition, but his concept of cultural rapprochement through trade was one of many contemporary efforts to combine progress and German politics to preserve the notion of a common economic culture.

Moreover, intra-German economic contacts proved to be equally important for the efforts by the two German states to rebuild themselves as internationally significant export nations. With the immediate postwar needs for housing and furnishings fulfilled, both German states shifted their attention to export industries, which included the intra-German trade. Exploring how this trade "preserved rudimentary structures of all-German economic unity" and how the two Germanys instrumentalized it for strategic and tactical goals in the German-German relationship can offer insight into their respective stance on national unity.[2]

The change of economic policy from reconstruction to trade pitted the two economic systems directly against each other in a competition for economic superiority, while at the same time the interconnected economic infrastructure glossed over the Cold War division. The latter was aided by the pan-German principles firmly anchored in West Germany's Basic Law and Germany Policy (*Deutschlandpolitik*) that claimed the territory of the GDR as part of the postwar German state. Bonn's position in the German Question relied on two principles:

the Federal Republic's policy of nonrecognition (*Nichtanerkennungspolitik*) and its claim to sole representation (*Alleinvertretungsanspruch*) vis-à-vis the GDR, which the Hallstein Doctrine implemented globally.[3] The Federal Republic welcomed economic interactions with East Germany precisely because they offered an opportunity for East-West dialogue that did not necessitate official political recognition of the GDR. Like Koslowsky, Bonn regarded trade not only as a way to maintain ties but also as a way to transfer cultural ideas. In terms of trade and economic development, East Germany often looked toward the West in later decades, playing into West German policies when it served their own economic interest. In spite of very different motivations, intra-German trade emerged as a lifeline for a shared German economic culture and shaped broader European economic foreign policy.

Limiting the analysis of cultural-economic transfer to the two German states, however, would not account for the increasing complexity of economic policy after the Federal Republic entered the European Economic Community (EEC) in 1957. Commitment to a future of Western European unity held the potential for conflict with German attempts to uphold connections between its two parts. The contested territorial situation and the special nature of intra-German trade made the GDR practically an unofficial member of the Common Market, which caused tensions between the Federal Republic and the other EEC member states. The fact that intra-German trade permeated the Iron Curtain places any discussion of it squarely in the context of economic exchange between the Cold War blocs in Europe, rendering exports a fundamental element of economic foreign relations.[4] Therefore, this chapter examines how export trade shaped East and West Germany's national brands as they used it to project their reformed postwar image abroad. At the same time, European economic integration brought with it cultural change that culminated in a convergence of German aesthetics in the 1980s. This process ultimately led both to adapt their aesthetics to changing economic and political climates on the international markets and connected them to broader European ideas of modern culture.

An examination of West German attempts at balancing European integration with the German Question brings into focus aesthetic convergence of East and West German design in the *Mittelstand* furniture industry. Friedrich Koslowsky never built his House of Life, but his vision to erect cultural bridges via product exchange was realized through the intra-German trade and the European Common Market. The Federal Republic's economic foreign policy with pan-German interests at its core not only created economic dependencies in the East but also facilitated German-German economic cooperation that undermined the Cold

War division of Europe. It presents the GDR as an early example of Europeanization that reached beyond the Iron Curtain, and thus beyond the borders of the Common Market.[5]

Traditionally, historians have discussed Europeanization as the colonial impact of European values and technology on other regions of the globe.[6] But with the increasing interest in the structural and political growth of the European Union, debates about supranational policymaking and its effects on member states relocated the concept within the borders of the European Union with a focus on institutionalization and policy implementation.[7] Although the following analysis explores identity formation through industrial design from a standpoint closely tied to European economic integration, it looks beyond the borders of the EEC. It extends the analysis of processes of Europeanization to consider the mutual transfer of cultural values in economic interactions with the GDR by understanding Europe as a social and cultural community in constant flux that is constructed through discourse and social practice.[8] In the realm of industrial design, this approach examines how European economic integration affected material culture as an expression of national identity.[9] While the two German states maintained their special relationship in intra-German trade and used it to influence the population on the other side of the border, they also changed their cultural outlook through interactions with Western Europe. At the end of this process, both Germanys contributed to a modern European aesthetic that did not follow one dogmatic style but rather produced stylistic diversity.

When East Meets West: Encounters at the Leipzig and Cologne Fairs

It was no coincidence that Koslowsky proposed his plan for the House of Life at the Leipzig fair. Ever since the German partition, trade fairs had functioned as sites of East-West encounters. In the competitive Cold War climate, the fairs also gained political significance as places for comparison between the two Germanys' alternative visions of modern material identity and technological advancement. At the same time, the countries used the fair to keep the transfer of ideas open. For the furniture industry, the Leipzig Fall Fair and the International Furniture Fair in Cologne evolved into important arenas for the promotion of East and West German *Wohnkultur*, on which both countries based claims to political legitimacy and economic preeminence. The interplay between aesthetics and ideology instills material markers of economic culture, in this case interior design products, with the ability to communicate cultural values and social relations that go beyond the mere exchange value of the objects in question.[10] In this way, purely economic transactions gain cultural and political significance.

As a locus of concentrated encounters between consumer products and the general public, fair displays could thus achieve a visual effect that combined economic and representative interests. In the early twentieth century, fairs had transitioned from sale fairs (*Warenmesse*) to sample fairs (*Mustermesse*). Whereas trade remained the main incentive for holding a fair, producers increasingly limited themselves to exhibiting samples instead of selling on site.[11] As a result, exhibitioners paid more attention to the composition of their product displays, which showcased advances in design and technology. Appealing displays certainly advertised the exhibited goods, but they also represented the political order that had produced them. Accordingly, producers became ambassadors of either East or West German cultural identity and values, which placed their products and the messages they conveyed to the public at large under scrutiny. Both German states were fully aware of the larger issues at stake. For example, while attending the 1960 Cologne Furniture Fair, West German intra-zonal trade representatives noticed displays of GDR system furniture, which were priced well below West German furniture of similar quality and aesthetics.[12] This caused surprise and unease among Bonn's trade specialists. Without the pressure for high profit margins, the GDR pricing policy made commodities affordable to the low-income strata of the population, thus threatening to convince West German consumers of the GDR's socialist-egalitarian promises.[13]

Hosting a commercial event that advanced market principles became an ideological challenge for the Soviet zone of occupation early on. To circumvent this problem, the Leipzig Fair reinvented itself as a political event.[14] The administration claimed that the fair was of paramount importance in bringing about German economic unity (*deutsche Wirtschaftseinheit*) and presenting German goods to the world. In a pamphlet published in 1947, the fair administration spoke of a "compulsion for export" should reconstruction efforts and the revival of economic life in Germany become a success. To reach this goal, the two German states needed to work together. Preproduction for export products on the other side of the zone border tied the two economies together. If fair activities and economic promotion continued to be hindered by occupation zone borders, the pamphlet argued, it would inadvertently hurt "the German product" and contradict pan-German interests.[15]

The 1947 Leipzig Fair pamphlet offers early evidence of eastern pragmatism in navigating the different economic orders emerging in occupied Germany. It should be seen against the backdrop of the American reconstruction aid plan for Europe that resulted in the Marshall Plan in 1948. The eastern zone held the position that only a unified economic policy could secure Germany's survival and reemergence as a global brand. To drive the point home, the brochure related anecdotes about the Soviet occupation zone's true efforts for German economic unity from the prior fair: "Passengers on special trains from all parts of Germany understood their unhindered passing at the zone borders as a symbolic act: a dividing line was crossed and, finally, there was space for dealings and action once again."[16] Similar spatial analogies connecting East and West Germany appeared throughout the pamphlet, culminating in the exclamation "Contemplation of the whole!" (*"Besinnung auf's Ganze!"*) that paid lip-service to the East's purported commitment to German unity.[17] Likewise, economic representatives of the western zones welcomed Leipzig's all-German activity as a way to improve intra-zonal trade. Leipzig complemented similar efforts to preserve economic ties at western trade fairs, such as Hanover or Cologne.[18] Nevertheless, both German economic systems mutually depended on each other for the rebuilding of viable economies during the reconstruction. Relatively poor in natural resources, they developed strong export industries whose success was based on finishing processes that added product value. With the focus on the fairs as places for encounter, both sides acknowledged the initial interdependence of the occupation zones for economic recovery.

While the Leipzig fair was immediately invested with political significance during the occupation years, the fair in Cologne seemed to emerge in a less contentious context. When Cologne reopened its doors to visitors for the first postwar fair in the fall of 1947, it not only competed with the Leipzig fair but also with other fairs in the western zones of occupation, such as Frankfurt or Hanover.[19] In contrast to the Soviet funding for the Leipzig fair, Cologne received no financial support from the occupation authorities. The necessity to be self-sustaining and profitable eventually led to the discovery that specialized fairs brought in more revenue for Cologne. Therefore, cities in the West German zones of occupation divided up these special-interest fair events among them in order to ensure sufficient attendance by the general public as well as industry and retail experts.[20] One such event was the International Furniture Fair (Internationale Möbelmesse, IMM), introduced in the spring of 1949.[21] The early years of German division thus saw activities on both sides of the border that intended to maintain economic ties and to create spaces for East-West encounters.

Glossing over the emerging division ended with the institution of the *Deutsche Mark*. The West German currency reform in 1948 de facto foreclosed economic unity and further politicized German-German trade. The Soviet Union reacted to what they understood as a separatist policy by American and British occupation authorities with a blockade of western access to the eastern zone including West Berlin, which brought intra-zonal trade to a complete halt in June 1948.[22] In response, the economic administration of the western occupation zones decided to withdraw its representatives from the Leipzig fair, although they feared that this might cause the fair to lose the status of an all-German trade institution.[23] This was exactly what happened. By the time the Berlin blockade ended in 1949, eastern efforts at an all-German economic recovery had ceased. In successive years, the fair implemented barriers that limited participation of western companies. Subsequently, Leipzig developed an exposition-like character, providing the Eastern Bloc with a platform for self-representation. Contemporaries described Leipzig as a "GDR performance show."

Once hopes for German unity were dashed by separate state foundations in 1949, the GDR joined the Council for Mutual Economic Assistance (COMECON, sometimes referred to as CMEA) in 1950 and built its own national economy independent of West Germany.[24] East Germany financed industrial development mostly through trade in the Eastern Bloc, a political process that often denied economic rationality.[25] The government held a monopoly over foreign trade, which meant that the VEBs, VVBs, and combines had little or no control over import and export decisions.[26] Trade became closely connected to the GDR's quest for international political recognition.[27] Accordingly, fair organizers aggressively internationalized the event again in the mid-1950s.[28] In the late 1950s and early 1960s, the GDR increasingly used it to display the reputed superiority of the socialist order, not least in contrast to the commodities of the West German economic miracle. This deliberate politicization of Leipzig raised questions about the political symbolism of West German fair participation in the context of its nonrecognition policy vis-à-vis the GDR. Trading with the GDR could be interpreted as West Germany's unofficial recognition of the other German state. Furthermore, trade relations could potentially stabilize the weaker East German economy. On the contrary, the Federal Republic supported these economic interactions precisely because they offered an opportunity for East-West dialogue that did not necessitate official political recognition. Throughout the Cold War the Federal Republic considered intra-German trade relations as a political rather than an economic interest. In the early years of this trade, its volume and revenue remained relatively low. Yet intra-German trade grew over the course of the 1960s and 1970s as it became an increasingly important tool in the German Question.

The Federal Republic's refusal to acknowledge the GDR remained the guiding principle in its dealings with the eastern part of Germany. To reinforce its position, the Ministry of Economic Affairs (BMWi) handled intra-German trade through an extra body, the Trust for Intra-Zonal Trade (Treuhandstelle für Interzonenhandel, TSI), rather than the foreign trade administration.[29] Meanwhile, the GDR, denying the FRG's claim to sole representation and asserting its own nationhood, handled intra-German trade through the Ministry for Domestic and Foreign Trade (Ministerium für Innen-und Außenhandel, MIA). These structural demonstrations of diametrically opposed politics in regard to German economic and political unity proved an ongoing bone of contention but did not prevent the two German states from trading with each other. In the West German case, the disagreement even spurred Bonn's commitment to this economic cooperation as Bonn hoped to use it to undermine East Germany's demarcation policy. In fact, the negotiations between the TSI and the MIA were the only nearly consistently intact channel for communication between the two German governments across forty years of division.[30]

The Berlin Agreement of 1951 established the basis for intra-German trade. The United States at first rejected the idea, requesting guarantees for the free movement of goods between the Federal Republic and West Berlin and the end of Soviet interference with West Berlin traffic. Ludwig Erhard, however, insisted that the negotiations should be conducted by German authorities and aimed for a quick resolution to reestablish economic ties that the Berlin blockade had severed.[31] The 1951 agreement fixed the exchange rate between the *Ostmark* and the D-Mark at equivalency, and so-called Swing credits served as a financial instrument to overcome the economic oddities of German division.[32] These credits were interest-free, short-term intergovernmental loans intended to stabilize trade between the two German states that remained relatively insignificant until the 1970s. The *Ostmark* was only a domestic currency, purposely restricted by geography and backed by the Wall, and the GDR had a fictional currency for international trade, the *Valutamark*.[33] Every year or two, the TSI and the MIA negotiated stock lists of goods and services that were traded according to their exchange value under three different accounts. To facilitate East German requests for goods and services not listed on the stock lists, the additional account "Sonderkonto S" arranged cash payment in D-Mark.[34] In theory, the principle of reciprocity regulated German-German economic affairs, such as fair-based trade. American concerns about East Germany and the Soviet Union taking advantage of West German desires to rekindle East-West trade were not unfounded, however. Whenever possible, the GDR did not uphold reciprocity and used the economic agreement as a lever in negotiations with the West. In addition, the Soviet Union only acknowledged the status of Berlin in the quad-ripartite agreement of 3 September 1971.

In practice, East German protectionist behavior limited the stock lists and shaped strategic decisions about which West German industries received permission to participate in the Leipzig fair throughout the 1950s. The trade fairs served as the stage for a constant behind-the-scenes wrangling between the states over economic relations, and West German industry entered into an uneven relationship. To protect the domestic furniture industry, at the time a vibrant crafts industry on the verge of mechanization, from the dominant western competition, the SED denied western furniture producers access to the Leipzig fair. By 1960, only one West German furniture company had gained permission to exhibit its products in Leipzig, allegedly thanks to its low price range.[35] Meanwhile, West German officials did not take similar actions to protect domestic industrial interest against GDR competition at the Cologne fair. Constituents of the National Lumber Industry Association (Hauptverband der Deutschen Holzindustrie und verwandter Industriezweige e.V.) complained about the large presence of East German furniture businesses at the 1960 IMM. In a letter posted to the BMWi after the event, the association pointed out a lack of state-implemented regulations for East German exhibitors in Cologne, while the GDR government systematically excluded virtually all West German producers from the Leipzig fair.[36] They urged the BMWi to intervene on their behalf by similarly restricting East German fair participation in Cologne. The ministry responded that the state chose to refrain from regulating the private enterprise that organized the fair, invoking the liberal principles of the social market economy. Up to that point, the ministry explained, it had only advised the organizers to admit exhibitioners from the "Soviet zone" in the interest of expanding inter-zonal trade, provided that eastern traders did not abuse the event with provocative political demonstrations.[37] It quickly became evident that these imbalances in trade and fair representation signaled as much Bonn's economic decision-making as its political strategy in the context of the German Question. It also revealed a fundamental problem for West German companies: in trading with the East, they subjected themselves to dealing more or less directly with the middle and upper echelons of the GDR economic planning apparatus, not their firm counterparts, without having matching support from their own government.

Indeed, corporative attempts to balance out intra-German trade on a macroeconomic level had failed before. In February 1960, representatives of the furniture industry and the BMWi had met at the Cologne furniture fair to discuss

intra-German trade. The furniture industry delegates blamed the mismatch
between East and West German furniture exports on the fact that the ministry did not press the case of furniture in trade agreements with the GDR. The
BMWi offered to solve the problem by listing furniture separately in the next
trade agreement and by insisting on the principle of reciprocity at upcoming
intra-German trade negotiations.[38] This was a well-meaning attempt to appease
national industry, but separate negotiations between the West German furniture industry and the GDR foreign trade representatives revealed that solving
the matter to the satisfaction of all parties involved would be difficult.[39]

In a meeting with the industry-specific Nationalized Organization for German Domestic and Foreign Furniture Trade (Volkseigene Handelsunterneh-
men Deutscher Innen- und Außenhandel Möbel, VEH-DIA Möbel) the following day, West German furniture industry representatives learned that the
GDR furniture industry was incapable of covering its own domestic demand.
Theoretically, the VEH-DIA Möbel claimed, imports from the West should
close the gap. Unfortunately for industry in the Federal Republic, the GDR
chose to prioritize heavy industry. In fact, until 1971, the GDR avoided imports
of finished and consumer products, such as furniture that could be produced by
East German companies, to save scarce foreign currency for much-needed raw
materials.[40] Instead, the GDR pushed exports to the West to earn foreign currency. By 1958, East German furniture exports totaled 835,000 accounting units,
which increased steadily over the 1960s.[41] Such fast growth of GDR furniture export can be traced back to the industrial concentration and collectivization that
started in 1958, which created enormous production capacities.[42] Hiding behind
the mechanisms of the planned economy and putting their national interest first,
the East German delegates exploited the differences between the two economic
systems to complicate the principle of reciprocity in intra-German trade. The
VEH-DIA Möbel delegation ironically advised the West German furniture industry to participate more frequently at the Leipzig fair to resolve the imbalance.
A collective display with West German products "of average pricing and average taste" would surely help create demand, and only such demand might make
possible a budget allocation for furniture in the next economic plan. However,
the VEH-DIA Möbel qualified, it would take at least a year of negotiations and
planning to win this privilege at the Leipzig fair for the West German furniture
industry.[43] As puzzling as this contradictory behavior of fair officials and the
VEH-DIA Möbel may seem, the West German furniture industry eventually
did gain greater access to the Leipzig fair via these intra-German trade negotiations. Whereas the need to protect domestic industry remained a priority, the

GDR could not risk losing the economic exchange with the West and thereby access to western currency.

While East German companies were able to promote their products at the IMM in Cologne without limitation, they focused their promotional efforts domestically on the semiannual Leipzig fairs, which slowly grew in importance for East-West trade. In 1964, the GDR Council of Ministers decided to award gold medals to further "heighten the political prestige of the Leipzig Fair and to underpin its significance as an international trading node."[44] The national industry could set higher prices for winning products for domestic retail as well as for exports.[45] Nonetheless, the award system benefitted most directly the state, by furthering its international reputation as a leading industrial nation. In fact, the SED instituted a ratio for medals awarded, distributing awards between the GDR, other socialist countries, and the nonsocialist countries, with the goal of presenting East German industry in a favorable light.[46] At the 1970 Leipzig Fall Fair, the GDR awarded its own industry thirty-five gold medals for outstanding and technologically progressive products. The Soviet Union received the second highest number with twelve gold medals.[47] That year's official (and hence confidential) fair report on the state of research and innovation in East German domestic industries, however, contradicted outright this show of socialist economic superiority: "The number of new and enhanced designs is completely insufficient, and their quality is at best equivalent to world standard."[48] By overemphasizing its achievements, the GDR attempted to convince the international community that the East German planned economy could keep up with the innovations in design and technology displayed by Western competitors. To that extent, the Leipzig fair fulfilled its diplomatic function.[49]

Dealing with the Devil: German-German Trade

BMWi hesitance to become involved in enforcing the principle of reciprocity attests to the political nature of West Germany's trade with the East. Western strategy for maintaining relations with the GDR was based on three official aims: helping the population in the East, maintaining a degree of German economic unity, and safeguarding the uninterrupted traffic between West Berlin and the Federal Republic.[50] In reality, Bonn also used this strategy to regulate East German contacts to other Western nations and leveraged it when the GDR leadership behaved uncooperatively. At the height of the Berlin Crisis in 1960, for instance, the Federal Republic unilaterally terminated the Berlin Agreement after the GDR restricted West Germans' passage into East Berlin. However, the dispute was resolved and the agreement reinstated subject to renegotiation before the new trade year began by 1 January 1961.[51]

The GDR meanwhile perceived West German economic policy as "economic warfare," pointing to early trade embargos on raw materials for the military in-dustrial sector in the 1950s and the discouragement of West German firms from fair participation in Leipzig during the Berlin Crisis in 1960 and after the build-ing of the Berlin Wall in 1961. In general, the East German Ministry for Foreign Affairs (Ministerium für Auswärtige Angelegenheiten, MfAA) complained, the West continued to dictate the terms of economic engagement and interfered in GDR trade relations with third states.[52] These trends were only exacerbated with the renegotiation of the Berlin Agreement later in 1961, which abolished the limits on stock lists, simplified the accounts structure, and increased the flexibility of Swing credits.[53] In the process, the GDR economy grew dependent on West German trade in order to support struggling consumption-oriented industries. Because it was the GDR's second-largest trade partner after the Soviet Union, goods and loans from the FRG became a crutch to a planned economy that failed to fulfill the consumer promises of the Fifth Party Congress and Ul-bricht's NES on its own. While the Federal Republic perhaps had not counted on this particular dependency of the GDR as the outcome, it was surely not an unwelcome one.

Intra-German trade then became an increasingly important tool in the Ger-man Question over the course of the 1960s. Nonetheless, the way in which it helped stabilize the East German regime contradicted the CDU-led "policy of strength" position vis-à-vis the GDR throughout the conservatives' rule in the Federal Republic. Foreign observers, such as US senator Hubert Humphrey, speculated about how Bonn reconciled eastern trade relations with its critique of the Limited Test Ban Treaty in 1963, a Soviet-American agreement that limited nuclear tests to relax tensions caused by the arms race.[54] To him the subsidized West German trade with East Germany showed similar political motivations for relaxation in the German Cold War, which rendered the critique of Ameri-can global détente efforts hypocritical. The handling and implementation of the intra-German trade on either side of the border thus tells a story of a paradoxical western *Deutschlandpolitik* in the early 1960s and steady political antagonism that occurred alongside growing economic interdependence.[55] Once the social democrats entered the government in 1966, some of these contradictions were resolved. Foreign minister Willy Brandt's New Eastern Policy (*Neue Ostpolitik*) of the late 1960s eventually ushered in a period of détente and aligned economic exchanges across the inner-German border with national politics. Based on a new foundational premise of "two states in one German nation," it ended the isolationist policy of the Hallstein Doctrine. Thus changing course from the conservative Adenauer government's isolation of the GDR to cooperation and accord, the Federal Republic instrumentalized German-German exchange in the realm of culture, economy, and humanitarian aid for rapprochement in the German Cold War.[56]

The Swing credits went from being almost insignificant to being an instrument of political bartering once Honecker introduced his Unity of Economic and Social Policy at the Eighth Party Congress in 1971. The program attempted to increase the East German living standard by ameliorating decades of underdevelopment in consumer goods production through investments financed with foreign credit. A couple of years into this new policy, economic planners realized that the early emphasis on heavy industry had compromised the light industry structures beyond recovery. Western goods and money started to seep into the East German economy to fill the gaps.[57] West German furniture became a staple at the Leipzig Fall Fair, thanks to three specialized product shows—the Interscola for school furniture, the Intacta for interior home design, and the Expovita for sports and leisure-time activities (*Freizeitgestaltung*)—that served as venues for western products.[58] Already in the fall of 1971 the combined display area of all represented industries from the Federal Republic and West Berlin made the FRG the second-largest participating nation, second only to the GDR.[59] Overall, the atmosphere at the fair that year was described as "thoroughly friendly."[60] For the first time since 1946, politicians refrained from the traditional polemics against the Federal Republic in official speeches, and GDR minister of foreign trade Horst Sölle invited for the first time the West German state secretary to his reception at the Leipzig city hall.[61] This change in tone developed against the background of German-German talks over a new footing for their relationship, which culminated in a "treaty concerning the basis of relations between the Federal Republic of Germany and the German Democratic Republic" (Basic Treaty) in 1972.

In preparation for the Basic Treaty negotiations, the Federal Republic reviewed the effectiveness of its trade policy toward the GDR. Trade by credit had become the law of the land, which created mostly one-sided dependencies: The GDR depended on West German money to finance its imports, and the Federal Republic required the GDR to use the credits to procure exclusively West German products. Accounting units usually documented the exchange, which eliminated most of the actual money flow. In this way, the GDR received DM 2.5 billion worth of raw materials, preproduction and subassembly parts, and services from the FRG in 1970 alone.[62] However, to maintain this level of trade the following year, the TSI estimated that the GDR had to raise its debts by another 500 million accounting units, because it had received 418 million units more than it delivered to the FRG in the previous year.[63] East German short stockage, the incapability to deliver certain in-demand products due to ill-guided Five-Year Plans, partially caused the trade imbalance.

Moreover, the GDR followed a calculated import-export strategy. The GDR exported finished products to profit from high added value, while it mostly imported semifinished products and raw materials such as steel (32.4 percent of the annual imports) and subassemblies (34.6 percent of the annual imports) from the FRG that contained less or no added value.[64] Finished products only constituted 6.3 percent of the GDR's annual imports in 1971.[65] Had the West German business community at large known this statistic, the BMWi would likely have faced complaints from domestic industrial associations again. Bonn instead masked the imbalance by utilizing separate statistical methods for German-German trade and foreign trade. Trade statistics on the GDR offered information about the industrial origins of products, yet they did not specify the degree of finishing. Although the ministry claimed that this method was to politically contrast the two kinds of export on paper, the practice obscured the fact that the West German side delivered goods of lesser value, and thus more of them, to East Germany, while the GDR delivered mostly finished products of higher worth and fewer of them.[66]

Despite all of these favorable conditions for the East, by 1971 the GDR had accumulated a debt of 1565.9 million accounting units, or DM 1565.9 million. West German officials privately welcomed these debts as a political guarantee for the persistence of German-German relations.[67] This dire picture already existed before the industrial investment strategy of the Unity of Economic and Social Policy program faltered. Bonn knew that the GDR would not have the funds to buy the machines necessary to continue building up its capital equipment industry to further develop the consumer goods program. A FRG economist analyzing the situation looked skeptically at alternative solutions to East Berlin's dilemma, pointing to the traditional interconnectedness of the two German economies and the GDR's dependency on West German spare parts and fittings. Consumer goods production relied heavily on machinery originally built in the Federal Republic.[68] Without natural resources to sell for foreign currency, the GDR faced the dilemma of financing increased consumer goods production with the export of finished products, thus sending abroad the very items that its own population needed.[69]

Yet in the end, the funds from consumer goods exports were needed to finance imports of steel and other construction materials for Honecker's second
ambitious project: the housing program.[70] These simultaneous and contradictory investment projects for 1972 precluded the option of a significant reduction
of iron and steel purchases in order to avoid further debts. From a West German perspective this would have been prudent policy if GDR economic planners
wanted to have the means to import western consumer products in quantities
that would even come close to covering the demand for commodities among the
East German population.[71] And above all, buying on credit changed the focus of
the GDR economic policy from long-term growth through investments to the
short-term policy of borrowing and, subsequently, to the "immediate exigency
of debt reduction" by the 1980s.[72] As a consequence, the Federal Republic in
fact partially financed Honecker's economic reform program.[73] Western trading
partners, first and foremost West Germany, continued to grant the GDR loans
and credits until the entire system came close to collapse under enormous debts
in 1988–89.[74]

In reaction to the Basic Treaty signed in 1972, the GDR fell back into a pattern of deep distrust and paranoia in its relationship to the Federal Republic
and Western influence at large. Representations of Western culture and affluence were again perceived as threatening by the mid-1970s, when it became clear
that Honecker's economic policy failed to produce the desired results. Fearing
that displays of the West German lifestyle would threaten the GDR's precarious economic and political stability, the East German government explicitly
prohibited fairgoers from exploring western stands in Leipzig in 1974.[75] Only
industry specialists, with the express permission of their companies or combine
director, and accompanied by their colleagues, could visit exhibitions of western
companies. In confidential talks with the West German GDR Trade Board, the
SED admitted to taking such measures, explaining that East Germany's general
foreign currency shortage warranted tight control over consumer demand.[76] Evidently, complex relationships between political aesthetics, economic policy, and
everyday consumption had developed within the realm of intra-German trade.

The latter point was especially evident to the GDR's industrial designers.
Maintaining business on the export market required a certain degree of adaptation to Western tastes. Coinciding with both Honecker's plans to increase consumer goods production and relaxed German-German relations in the context
of Basic Treaty negotiations, the Federal Republic experienced a "furnishing
wave," caused by a general rise in wages during full employment in the 1960s
and early 1970s.[77] Large buyers, such as the Kaufhof department stores and

the Neckermann mail order business, increasingly relied on large production capacities in East German industries to meet the demand. Although the mail order businesses had direct connections to East German furniture combines, the BMWi oversaw these trade relations and monitored their progress closely.[78] Noting that in the past the GDR had seldom fulfilled special orders, Kaufhof representatives remarked in a meeting with the ministry that this attitude was changing in the early 1970s, when the GDR became more receptive to western taste. East German bedroom furniture of the lower-to-middle price range that met the necessary quality standards especially attracted West German consumers. Kaufhof would also have ordered sofas, armchairs, and desks, but the Plan proved inflexible in responding to specific requests. In addition to East German industrial inflexibility, the GDR transportation system proved unreliable. For example, Deutrans, the GDR's state-owned cargo company, delayed deliveries to the FRG in 1971 because, allegedly, their trucks were needed during the fall harvest to transport potatoes from the fields to the towns.[79] Under such unreliable circumstances, standardized, easily transportable storage furniture turned out to be the most consistent export product.

Notwithstanding logistic challenges, furniture exports to the West continued to increase, with the Federal Republic as the main receiving market. In the first quarter of 1972 alone, trade with West Germany grew by 18 percent over the same time period in the previous year. But the domestic shortage of consumer products was not the only unwarranted effect of Honecker's ambitions. The export-oriented nature of East Germany's furniture production eventually came at the expense of national aesthetics. Increasingly, western preferences seeped into the guidelines for industrial designers as the GDR economy opened up to export markets in the West. As a result of the interplay between demand and subsequent reorientation of production design, what I call the dialectic aesthetic of intra-German trade, East German industrial designers found their vision of socialist product culture jeopardized by the aesthetic requirements of export. In a 1975 interview, designer Horst Michel pinned what he perceived as the demise of German socialist materiality on West Germany's mail order giants, such as Neckermann or Quelle.[80] Their buyers, he was convinced, undermined his and his disciples' efforts to create a morally responsible product culture in the GDR. With this observation, he indirectly criticized the cultural and economic leadership for turning the GDR production system into a magnet for western bulk buyers. Collectivization and regional concentration of industry had created large industrial clusters and combines whose raison d'être was large series mass production. This production order, ironically, matched ideally the supply needs of western retail chains. Michel complained that large businesses like Neckermann pushed prices down and thus forced East German industry to use low-quality materials, which also compromised the functionality of the products. Michel seems to have forgotten, however, that it was first the lack of capital investments and subsequent backward production standards in the East German furniture industry that resulted in attracting these West German large retailers serving the low-income population. High-end furniture producers and retailers usually refrained from cooperation with East German combines because their customers demanded expensive woods and state-of-the-art production methods, neither of which the GDR economy could offer. Even Deutsche Werkstätten Hellerau (DWH) could not keep up with western standards. In the 1980s, it mass-produced wooden chair designs for the West German luxury brand Interlübke, but it could only produce one design, because it did not own the machinery necessary for details on bent parts that the other designs required.[81] While Michel astutely spoke to the creative potential of industrial designers and the skills of the furniture workers, the interplay between East German technological backwardness, scarce materials, and the resulting focus on low-end furniture ended in the mass production of low-quality goods.

The global economic downturn of 1973 further complicated German-German trade. The crisis hit the West German economy hard, particularly industries that relied on oil and the chemicals derived from it, such as cushion foam for upholstery furniture. In the autumn of 1974 the Bavarian Upholstery Association complained to West German minister of economic affairs Hans Friderichs about a new set of imbalances in intra-German furniture trade.[82] Specifically, the association demanded to be granted the same 6 percent tax reduction that the federal government gave to East German companies. In its response, the BMWi attributed this competitive advantage for East German products to the "special quality of the intra-German trade."[83] The turnover tax reduction served as a means to create incentives for western buyers to order eastern products and was intended by the ministry as a measure to level the playing field for GDR export industries.[84] Because of "budget concerns, the tax system, and European Community agreements," Friderichs explained, such a turnover tax reduction could not be applied to domestic industries, even if they were in financial distress.[85] He furthermore pointed out that the East German exports of upholstery products corresponded to only 1.8 percent of domestic production, which, he assumed, would not affect the market noticeably.

Nevertheless, West German industry, especially in federal states neighboring the GDR, such as Bavaria, did have cause for concern. The erratic nature of

FIGURE 3.1. By the 1960s large furniture industry clusters developed in the GDR and the FRG. The competition from Thuringian and Saxon furniture clusters close to the inner-German border with Bavaria caused particular concern for the local furniture industry.

TABLE 3.1. West German imports of East German furniture, 1980–1981

January–June	1980 in m AU	1981 in m AU	Real increase in m AU	In percent
Sofas and divan beds	14.7	29.0	+14.3	97.3
Wardrobes	0.3	4.4	+4.1	–
Chests of drawers	1.9	4.6	+2.7	142.1
Living room furni-ture systems	5.3	6.4	+1.1	20.8
Kitchen chairs	5.4	6.0	+0.6	11.1
Armchairs	20.8	12.4	-8.4	40.0

SOURCE: Schaefer, *Ergebnisse des IdH im 1. Halbjahr 1981,* 24 August 1981.
NOTE: m=millions; AU=accounting units.

trade between the GDR and the FRG by the early 1980s shows how Friderichs's generalizations about upholstery import amounted to misinformation or only momentary truths. In any case, the furniture sector was in the fastest-growing position in the lumber product trade between East and West Germany.[86]

Tables 3.1 and 3.2 offer a glimpse into the flexibility required on the part of West German buyers in dealing with the fluctuating GDR planned economy. Bulk production and differing Plan priorities could result in the overproduction of certain furniture in any given year. In 1981, this happened to be sofas, which resulted in a 97.3 percent growth of sofa exports to the Federal Republic. The following year the pattern changed to armchairs, with an increase of 154 percent, while sofa export returned to the 1980 level. Giant furniture retailers such as Ikea and RKL Möbel found themselves confronted with these wild fluctuations in their East German product supply.[87] The West German competition, small-and medium-sized furniture producers such as the members of the Bavarian Upholstery Association, suffered when GDR furniture erratically flooded the West German market. The fact that Bonn did not take action on behalf of this industry and tolerated the GDR inconsistencies further confirmed West Germany's political interest in the intra-German trade.

To justify its actions, the GDR turned the western trade partners' concern about eastern reliability on its head. At a conference on the "situation of the global economy" in the fall of 1981 in Hamburg, Jürgen Nitz, a representative of

TABLE 3.2. West German imports of East German furniture, 1981–1982

January–June	1981 in m AU	1982 in m AU	Real increase in m AU	In percent
Armchairs	12.4	31.5	+19.1	+154
Add-on furniture	–	23.8	+23.8	–
Kitchen tables	–	11.9	+11.9	–
Wooden bed rests	8.1	11.5	+3.4	+42
Sofas and divan beds	29.0	14.9	-14.1	-49

SOURCE: Schaefer, Ergebnisse des IdH im 1. Halbjahr 1982, 23 August 1982.
NOTE: m=millions; AU=accounting units.

the East Berlin Research Institute for Politics and Economy (Institut für Politik und Wirtschaft), explained to a bemused western audience how the capitalist path in the global economy continued to disappoint the socialist nations.[88] The disconcerting results, he explained, threatened GDR trading interests: the slowing-down of industrial growth; the relatively slow accumulation of capital after the oil crises; chronic inflation in capitalist countries that was detrimental to socialist economies; stagnant wages that throttled demand for import products from socialist countries; and the increasing instability of capitalist currency, which made credit negotiations difficult for the GDR.[89] These crises, Nitz contended, negatively affected global trade between East and West; and East Germany, as well as other socialist countries, would not accept the blame for the consequences. While pointing to the shortcomings of capitalism, the GDR displayed little concern about the structural quirks in the planned economy and its focus on political goals, rather than mutually beneficial trade, that negatively affected the Western European countries.

Moreover, to gain political advantage in trade negotiations, the GDR did not shy away from manipulating Plan statistics to conceal the real state of its economy from Western countries. The BMWi and the Federal Ministry for Intra-German Relations (Bundesministerium für Innerdeutsche Beziehungen, BMB) usually looked to the Plan, in combination with GDR foreign and intra-German trade statistics, to leverage West German trade policy diplomatically. However, the Plan often reflected political aims rather than economic probabilities, leaving the ministries to rely on GDR trade policy patterns to estimate real outcomes. For example, in the 1981 Plan directive, the Planning Commission estimated impossible growth in the production sector, which, western economists realized, was a statistical trick on paper to balance and conceal the import purchases necessary to uphold the current standard of living in the GDR.[90]

By the 1970s, West German money and consumer products increasingly seeped into a socialist Germany that desperately tried to gain popular support by raising the standard of living. While this created deepening dependencies, the GDR won a reliable source of credit, which funded the economic policies of the SED leadership and created the illusion of a flourishing socialist consumer society. In addition to the political significance of the financial and economic cooperation between the two German states, their collaboration clearly undermined the division of Europe between the Eastern Bloc and the partners of the transatlantic alliance.

Creating the Common Market

The specific characteristics of intra-German trade, such as the high degree of interdependence in production industries and special tax cuts, differed greatly from international norms of foreign trade. When the Federal Republic joined the EEC, intra-German trade carried high potential for problems in the Common Market. A triangular relationship joining East and West Germany and the EEC member states spun a complex web of economic and political interests dominated by the German Question. The 1957 Protocol on Intra-German Trade formed the basis on which the two German states engaged in the most profit-oriented manner with other European nations and shaped a Europe that from the very beginning accommodated German special interests. Therefore, examining political goals in conjunction with the economic interests that were carried out over the German division also helps in understanding the economic culture of this export-import triangle and the aesthetic market incentives which resulted from it.

The European market has been critical to West Germany's economic foreign relations. France, Italy, Belgium, the Netherlands, and Luxembourg took about 35 percent of Germany's exports in the 1950s, but the vibrant economies of these nations also presented competition.[91] In 1955, the Federal Republic identified Italy, Belgium, Norway, and Sweden as its main competitors in the furniture export market. A BMWi market analysis found that the rate of export orders for furniture slowly accelerated, mainly from Western Europe, but from overseas as well, where the demand for seating furniture was particularly high. Rising packaging and shipping costs made trading goods overseas less lucrative, which kept the number of successful competitive contracts low. In Western Europe, however, the postwar demand for all kinds of furniture was high.[92] Nevertheless, economic analysts worried about the German furniture industry's inability to "jump over the tariff wall" within Europe.[93] The fact that the German industry had cut itself off from the international market from 1933 to 1945 had encouraged other nations to build their own industries. As a byproduct of this process, the report stated, these countries had developed strong national tastes that rendered any mention of "a global furniture market situation" that corresponded to distinctive aesthetics pointless. Italy and Belgium emerged as the main competitors; while their technical production costs were not lower, they had lower labor costs. Analysts saw the only chance to overcome these hurdles in "exporting especially high-quality products that neither the national industry of the target markets could produce nor Italy, Belgium, Norway or Sweden could export there at the same qualitative level and with the same design aesthetic."[94] This export strategy developed alongside the FRG's early attempts to create a national aesthetic in industrial design.

The early 1950s also offered an opportunity to employ economic relations in the service of reconciliation in Western Europe. France's fear of West Germany's reemergence as a dominant power was replaced by trust in the stabilizing effects of cooperation and multilateralism. Paris hoped to steer West German foreign policy away from national interest toward European integration.[95] The Franco-German rapprochement implemented in the realm of coal and steel eventually included Italy and the Benelux.[96] These first steps toward a shared European economic sphere enabled West Germany's success as an export nation that excelled with the establishment of the EEC on 1 January 1958. The integration into the Common Market solved most of West Germany's furniture export problems by abolishing tariffs between EEC members, leveling the playing field among German, Italian, and Belgian furniture producers in the European market, and rendering the Scandinavian countries less competitive. The open Common Market accelerated industrial modernization with the support of American investments and technology, which was one reason for the Federal Republic's later superiority in the EEC. Social stability under the conservative, welfare-oriented Adenauer governments promised foreign investors safe profits and offered them a gateway into the Common Market.[97] The West German infrastructure offered a dense network of railways and highways, an outstanding communication system, and the most efficient inland waterway in Europe.[98] These favorable conditions turned the Federal Republic into a true competitor in the EEC, compelling German industry to acquire more capital and to accelerate its peaceful expansion.

From the very inception of the EEC, the German Question stood at the center of Bonn's relations to other member states. The FRG demanded special stipulations for intra-German trade, which other members feared could adversely affect the community. Accordingly, the 1957 Treaty of Rome contained a "Protocol on intra-German trade and related issues" stipulating that German-German trade remained unaltered by the EEC agreements.[99] However, paragraph 2 of the protocol required all EEC states to relate any trade with "German territories outside of the territory of the Basic Law," that is to say the GDR, to the other members, and to take precautions that any agreements with the GDR would not contradict the principles of the Common Market.[100] Furthermore, paragraph 3 of the agreement stated that each member state was allowed to take action against injurious interaction between another member state and East Berlin.[101]

While trade with the GDR theoretically counted as foreign trade, the country could not be treated like any other third party. Its special status due to the open German Question and West German nonrecognition required bilateral agreements signed at the level of nonstate actors, such as foreign trade associations. Its special status foreclosed a common EEC trade policy toward East Germany by definition. In theory, the principles of protocol paragraphs 2 and 3 applied to the Federal Republic as well, but Bonn exempted itself, claiming as its guiding foreign policy the notion that "in all of its actions, the government of the Federal Republic assumes the *political and economic unity of Germany*, whose realization is only obstructed by factual, but not legal reasons."[102] For the Federal Republic, the protocol regulated all trade between East Germany and the European partners, interpreting it to mean equal treatment for all German territories.[103] From this point of view, trade between the GDR and any of the EEC members did not constitute foreign trade. When in 1961 the European Council of Ministers attempted to include EEC-GDR trade relations under Article 111 of the Rome Treaty, which regulated foreign trade, Bonn demanded a clause exempting the Federal Republic from all of the council's decisions vis-à-vis the GDR.[104]

Not surprisingly then, one of the first foreign trade disagreements in the EEC came about in relation to the Eastern Bloc and European trade credits. The Berne Union had implemented the limit of state-backed credit to five years with a gentleman's agreement between Western countries to create fair trading conditions across the Iron Curtain.[105] In accordance with Western containment policy, this agreement strove to prevent the Soviet-led bloc from playing Western trade partners against each other for political or financial gain. Together with the United States, the Federal Republic had been timid about overstepping the Berne Union rules. Admittedly because of its geographic situation, among Western countries West Germany already consistently ranked first in trade statistics with the Eastern Bloc generally and the GDR specifically as table 3.3 shows.[106] Bonn looked confidently toward the future, reassuring itself that the kinds of goods the GDR required and the kinds of goods it produced made West Germany a unique and essential trading partner for years to come.[107] By 1964, however, a number of Western countries, among them Japan, the UK, Italy, and France, broke the Berne agreement and granted the East European socialist countries credits ranging from seven to fifteen years. Worried about keeping its prominent status in trade with the East and its leverage over East Berlin, the Federal Republic started an initiative to streamline EEC foreign trade policy toward the Eastern Bloc. At the same time, the BMWi defended its own generous credits for the GDR, stating explicitly that "intra-zonal trade is an instrument of reunification policy," reemphasizing the political nature of German-German trade.[108] While Bonn felt no need to further justify its special interest in these trade relations, the government feared that the GDR could find financial support elsewhere, thus jeopardizing the carefully crafted interconnections between the two German economies. At a conference with other EEC members, West Germany proposed two options that would apply to all members: extending the limit to state-backed credits by two years or upholding the original Berne Union agreement. Bonn's attempts to shape Europe's global trade policies to protect its own special relationship to East Berlin were stopped by Italy, which preferred to debate these matters at the Berne Union or the OECD in order to come to a binding agreement for all Western nations.[109]

While Bonn protected its political goals regarding intra-German trade against rival European interests, the East German economy greatly benefited from its de facto integration into the European market. By trading with Western Europe through West German middlemen, the GDR benefitted, like EEC members, from the removal of internal tariffs on certain products in 1968. A German-German exchange of blows in 1970 brought to light how much the GDR profited from West Germany's EEC membership. The minister for intra-German relations Egon Franke estimated publicly that the GDR earned DM 400 to 500 million per year because of its economic relationship to West Germany.[110] With Franke's statement, the Federal Republic reminded the GDR of its economic dependence on West Germany. Moreover, his remarks implied

TABLE 3.3. Trade results between NATO states and the GDR (in million US $)

Country	Exports/Deliveries to the GDR					Imports/Deliveries from the GDR				
	1961	1962	1963	1964	1965	1961	1962	1963	1964	1965
Belgium/Luxemburg	11.52	13.68	14.28	8.76	11.88	14.16	16.92	19.68	22.92	26.36
Denmark	12.36	21.84	14.40	18.36	24.60	15.84	16.32	17.04	20.76	23.88
France	21.48	15.96	18.12	26.28	69.00	8.4	8.52	12.60	14.28	15.96
Greece	6.48	4.56	4.92	6.57	9.50	2.64	3.96	4.80	6.11	8.42
Iceland	0.96	0.72	0.96	0.36	1.68	1.92	1.68	1.20	2.40	2.88
Italy	10.80	7.92	12.96	13.32	16.08	14.28	11.52	12.36	14.88	14.16
Netherlands	16.08	9.24	12.12	15.60	19.92	17.2	17.64	23.28	30.24	32.76
Norway	6.0	6.12	7.32	15.96	10.08	8.40	7.68	6.00	9.84	11.88
Portugal	0.36	0.36	0.48	0.48	0.60	0.24	0.24	0.24	1.56	0.36
Turkey	4.68	1.32	5.64	4.92	9.24	6.12	4.32	5.76	8.16	9.36
Great Britain	27.48	27.00	22.44	17.04	23.16	18.72	18.48	21.12	29.04	33.60
NATO Europe (w/o FRG)	118.20	108.72	113.64	127.65	195.74	108.24	107.34	124.08	160.19	179.62
Canada	1.56	0.12	1.20	10.92	14.04	0.96	0.84	1.08	1.37	1.44
USA	2.76	1.68	6.36	19.92	12.60	2.52	3.00	3.24	6.72	6.48
FRG (intra-zonal)	216.75	213.53	214.89	287.13	297.78	235.62	228.62	255.58	257.11	315.69
NATO total	339.27	324.05	336.09	445.62	520.16	347.34	339.80	383.98	425.39	503.23

SOURCE: BArch, B102/245208, Results of Trade between NATO States and the GDR (in Mio US $).

that it would be prudent for East Germany to stop pushing for recognition as a separate state under international law, a goal that the GDR fervidly pursued in the 1960s and early 1970s.

Not surprisingly, the depiction of East German economic growth as an outcome of West German European integration politics offended the GDR government. In a public message, the Council of Ministers defended the socialist economy against the "capitalist imperialism" of the Federal Republic by pointing to its trade relations with the Soviet Union and other socialist countries.[111] Indeed, the Soviet Union was East Germany's biggest trade partner. Member countries of the Eastern Bloc's COMECON usually traded roughly three-fourths of their exports within the COMECON area.[112] In 1962, for instance, only 11 percent of GDR exports went to the Federal Republic, and 14 percent to other Western nations.[113] The lagging domestic potential of smaller members such as the GDR or the Čzechoslovak Socialist Republic (ČSSR) made them heavily dependent on Eastern Bloc trade. Yet the principle of sovereign planning meant that national Five-Year Plans remained uncoordinated among member states, which often caused supply shortages. This in turn necessitated short-term covering of purchases from the more flexible nonsocialist economies. Furthermore, commodities within the COMECON were exchanged for kind, not money.[114] Accordingly, no hard currency found its way into the GDR via this trade. For foreign currency, East Germany depended on credits and trade with the West.

The GDR was not the only Eastern Bloc country that had realized this. In the early 1970s, the Soviet satellites pressured the Soviet Union into establishing official contacts between the COMECON and the EEC. The Soviet Union gave in to these demands spearheaded by Hungary and Poland in 1973 to maintain cohesion and "reduc[e] some centrifugal tendencies" in the COMECON.[115] Just like the GDR, these countries already entertained trade relations with the EEC and had a vested interest in deepening these contacts. This policy change aligned with contemporary Soviet détente efforts and ensured a level of coordination that left the Soviet Union in control of Eastern Bloc trade with the West. On the other hand, EEC-COMECON contacts played also into Western détente efforts, showing that European integration was compatible with other institutional solutions in the 1970s, such as the Conference for Security and Cooperation in Europe (CSCE), for overcoming the Cold War divide in Europe.[116]

Just as Minister for Intra-German Relations Franke had foreseen, the Eastern Treaties (*Ostverträge*) the Federal Republic signed with the Soviet Union, Poland, and later the ČSSR, and the Basic Treaty with the GDR threatened East Germany's special status in the European statutes. The question of a unified

EEC eastern trade policy resurfaced immediately in 1970 with the signing of the Moscow and Warsaw treaties. The EEC thought that if the Soviet bloc recognized European cooperation not only de facto but also de jure, a more cohesive and effective European economic policy would be viable, which could possibly contribute to the extension of the EEC to other Western European countries. With East-West détente and the GDR's international recognition on the horizon, West Germany's European partners wanted to renegotiate the status of intra-German trade. Once the Basic Treaty was signed in 1972, the other member states grew increasingly impatient with the Federal Republic.[117] Pushing for the complete abolition of the 1957 Protocol on Intra-German Trade, the European Commission acknowledged the new political reality of two German states and insisted that the GDR was a third country.[118] West Germany meanwhile maintained that the Basic Treaty had not further deepened the German-German division. The question of German unification remained open, Bonn argued, because the two German states still did not consider each other foreign territory and thus intra-German trade would remain an important bond between them.[119] In order to ease European concerns, however, Bonn pointed to trade statistics. The percentage of intra-German trade in contrast to West German EEC trade was small, while the trade between the EEC partners and the GDR had decisively increased in recent years. Intra-German trade, as it had developed over the 1960s, was unlikely to grow given the GDR's difficulties in reciprocating, and the danger of GDR price-dumping practices was negligible for the Common Market, since East Berlin at this point kept prices high to reap larger profits.[120] Accordingly, from the West German point of view, there was no reason to nullify the protocol.

The situation changed considerably, however, after Honecker's consumer turn of 1971 gained momentum, normalizing the use of Swing credits in intra-German trade, which radically transformed the size of German-German trade.[121] At the same time, EEC skepticism about West Germany's claim to a special relationship between Bonn and East Berlin grew. In 1974, Belgium demanded that the community should implement measures to monitor intra-German trade.[122] The same year, the Netherlands complained that the Federal Republic interrupted the free-trade zone, stopping imports of GDR products sent through other EEC countries into West Germany.[123] Bonn reacted strongly, insisting on upholding the regulations of paragraph 1 of the protocol on intra-German trade. The federal government justified this stance with the continued political interest in keeping German-German economic exchanges as direct and as frequent as possible in order to thicken contacts between East and West Germany.[124] When bilateral negotiations failed to produce agreement, the Benelux countries began a grievance procedure.

While the Benelux countries rightfully questioned Bonn's loyalties, the real bone of contention was the tariff exemption for East German products. The European Court of Justice had declared these to be products "not of German origin" for the purpose of EEC trade policies after the GDR's formal recognition by EEC members had made it a third country in 1974.[125] Yet, due to the special nature of intra-German trade, the GDR paid no tariffs for products crossing the border into the Federal Republic.[126] Once inside the EEC zone, East German goods could continue to move around the EEC without further taxation, skewing the principles of the Common Market and hurting national industries as well as wholesale networks. Consequently, the West German position that connected the German Question to intra-German trade came under close scrutiny by the EEC. The Benelux countries furthermore hinted at West German economic profiteering from intra-German trade as a transit hub for distribution of eastern products. Because of the customs and other tax exemptions as well as established dealership networks, West Germany could sell East German goods to other member states with higher margins. Moreover, the system of intra-German trade through product bartering tied to exclusive credit agreements necessarily conflicted with the free trade principles of the Common Market.[127] Had the products entered under the usual tariff laws through other EEC member states, they would not have enjoyed this competitive advantage. In order to avoid legal action while guaranteeing the uninterrupted political priority of intra-German trade, the Federal Republic proposed a compromise: a license agreement that allowed for DM 10 million worth of GDR products to be brought into West Germany through other EEC countries. This proposal represented a maximum amount that, so Bonn hoped, would neither enable East Berlin to supply West German demand exclusively through third countries nor possibly create a political lever for the GDR.[128] In the end, the 1951 Berlin Agreement principles of intra-German trade, revised for greater flexibility in 1961, remained in place until German-German economic and monetary unity on 1 July 1990.

Despite the risk of disagreement in the EEC, time and again Bonn prioritized the well-being of German-German relations over European agreements. Yet this rapprochement policy triggered widespread domestic critique from liberals and conservatives. In a public hearing before the parliament in 1977, sociologist Ralf Dahrendorf described the lack of clarity in Bonn's *Deutschlandpolitik* in combination with European integration as "explosive."[129] Active pursuit of European political unity would necessarily preclude German unification, Dahrendorf maintained, because none of West Germany's neighbors had a strong political or economic interest in seeing Germany reunite. Similarly, political scientist Hans-Peter Schwarz criticized the policy of rapprochement, noting that the Basic Treaty had taken the German Question out of the East-West conflict and German policies had fallen by the wayside.[130] On the contrary, this analysis of intra-German trade in relation to the EEC integration explicitly reveals the political power and economic significance of the unresolved German Question for West Germany's European politics, and how it reinvigorated German-German economic and cultural ties well beyond 1972.

Aesthetic Convergence in the Common Market

The integration of the EEC increased the interaction of East and West German import and export economies through the loophole of intra-German trade, permeating the Iron Curtain with capitalist market principles and Western aesthetic styles. West German stubbornness thus not only worked to uphold bonds between Germans, but also contributed to a convergence of aesthetics between East Germany, the Federal Republic, and EEC countries. Although both German states had striven for their own national identity in design aesthetics during the reconstruction years, other countries' styles and tastes affected German material culture alongside growing trade.

German furniture, with its legacy grounded in interwar modernism, remained a contender on the global market and, after initial struggles, continued to be an important export good for both the GDR and the FRG after the Second World War. It is thus not surprising that the annual IMM fair in Cologne became the most important furniture marketplace in the world. Within intra-German trade, the furniture traveled mostly from East to West, but on the global market, both countries gained important positions as furniture export nations. Already in the early 1960s, the GDR proclaimed itself the world's largest furniture export nation, if only in percentage of total annual production rather than real profits. It exported 40 percent of its furniture production to twenty countries, at a time when the standardization and mechanization of the GDR furniture industry had only begun to gain momentum.[131] If nothing else, this high percentage of export furniture underscores East Germany's chronic domestic underprovisioning in the realm of household goods and domestic culture. In comparison, West Germany reached the status of the world's largest furniture exporter in absolute numbers alongside Italy by the early 1980s, with DM 3 billion in sales, which was about 17 percent of its annual furniture production.[132]

As the Federal Republic imported the same amount of furniture from other countries, its market was saturated.

In the GDR, the aesthetic incentives of the Common Market worked mostly through export goods production, slowly undermining socialist material ideals. To the East German office for quality control, the DAMW, the fact that exports to the West increasingly determined the appearance of commodities in East Germany was even more disturbing than the obvious gap between the claims and the realities of its production. East Germany's inflexible planning mechanisms made the production of export furniture and domestic design inseparable. Once set on a furniture model, the regional industry structured the distribution of raw materials and ordered the machines needed to realize only these designs. Changing the design meant a halt in production until necessary material and technological changes were made. These impediments crippled innovation to the degree that industry reports after 1970 regularly included remarks on the old-fashioned look of GDR furniture.[133] While these products should not have been awarded the official seal of quality "Good Design," exceptions were made for poorly designed furniture in the export business. The DAMW's realistic assessment that earning foreign currency was more important "because we cannot force our design principles on the foreign buyer" exemplifies how economic necessities suppressed socialist fervor, designers' creativity, and innovation.[134]

The furniture at the 1970 Leipzig Fall Fair, in particular, failed to live up to the DAMW's expectations. "The requirements of a socialist living culture cannot be met with these [export] models," the fair's report declared.[135] While the East German upholstery section at the fair did display "joy of experimentation," it was often a result of West European customers' requests.[136] Indeed, archival evidence suggests that the GDR actively pursued West European customers. For example, by the 1960s the ZfF had sent its staff to trade fairs in the West to report on the technological quality and design of the capitalist competition.[137] The new travel agreements of the Basic Treaty facilitated this. Short trips to West Berlin to visit exhibitions at the newly opened International Design Center (IDZ) or to view the range of products at West German furniture stores increased exponentially after 1972. Most of the documented visits to the IMM in Cologne fall into this time period as well and include representatives from the furniture industry. Such observational activity entailed a certain degree of adaptation to Western aesthetics. Indeed, West German producers feared the eastern economic competition on the European market. In 1974, the Bavarian Upholstery Association accused East German combines of "slavishly" imitating West German designs and selling their furniture on Western markets at cut-rate prices.[138] The federal government, however, saw this transfer of cultural ideas as a way to impress western aesthetics upon the East German population and to increase the GDR's western economic dependency, thereby taking another step toward a shared economic culture.

The ZfF's successor institution, the Amt für industrielle Formgestaltung (AiF), institutionalized the practice with a product card index in 1974. The index cataloged furniture systems predominately from Scandinavia, the Federal Republic, Switzerland, and Italy, with an occasional Russian model thrown in to inspire the export models that headed east.[139] The firms in the card index were producers of extreme examples of classy, high-priced designer furniture like Interlübke, nothing one would expect in a "workers' and peasants' state." In the process of cataloging the Western furniture, GDR industrial designers compared their products with those of the West, which, ultimately, hindered the development of a distinct East German aesthetic. The tendency toward comparison sharply contrasted with the GDR's goal of convincing the West of the East's superior quality and comfort of life. The GDR intelligentsia incorporated this Westernization of style into the socialist framework of the state without hesitation. Cultural critic Karin Hirdina hurried to make the form fit the ideology, claiming in 1975 that "functionalism represents a Utopian vision of a non-capitalist order of relationships between Man and his environment."[140] Results remained substandard nonetheless. All too often GDR production mashed together the natural look of Sweden, the functionalist purism of West Germany and Switzerland, and the playful avant-gardism of Italy in the cheap export furniture offered in West German mail order catalogs like Neckermann.

The most important lesson learned from trips to the West pertained to materials rather than design. Upon his return from the 1979 IMM in Cologne, Gert Großpietzsch, the head of the Dresden-Hellerau combine's product development department, recommended that the combine should refocus on producing expensive furniture to maximize its revenues and to target these unexplored parts of the western market.[141] In terms of materials, he reported, the trend was toward natural looks with a high demand for solid woods and wooden veneers, which were the exact materials that the Chemical Program had abolished in the GDR. Instead, the synthetic alternative to veneers, so-called decorative foil, which went through multiple varnishing and polishing processes after its application on chipboard, compromised the overall aesthetic of the East German furniture production.[142] With the shortfall of Honecker's Unity of Economic and Social Policy, the material dreams of Großpietzsch and his designer colleagues remained out of reach, leaving East Germany to continue its low-end quality

production strategy. By 1985, only about 8 percent of the Federal Republic's furniture imports came from the GDR.[143]

In the case of the Federal Republic, trade and a nascent collective vision of
Europe as a cultural space brought European trends into West German designs.
The Federal Republic's accession to the status of the world's largest furniture
exporter, grossing DM 3 billion in 1981, developed in parallel to its place as an
equally high importer of foreign-made furniture.[144] Consequently, domestic
producers followed the lead of the European market demand in order to maximize sales. Foreign influences thus found their way into the department stores
and homes of the FRG, slowly affecting the overall national aesthetic. While
consumption shaped and reproduced dominant ideas about the appearance of
material culture, artistic influences brought new ideas into the Common Market. West German domination of the international furniture market coincided
with the "designer decade" of the 1980s, which brought the aesthetic qualities
of material culture, alongside a renewed appreciation for ornamentation, back
to the forefront.[145] Cultural events, such as the Venice Biennale of 1980, greatly
impacted industrial furniture design once more to a degree that had last been
seen in 1958 at the Brussels world exposition. The Venice Biennale marked the
arrival of postmodernism in Europe. Although postmodernism mostly developed in architecture, many of its participants were engaged in interior design as
well. As lifestyle design stores mushroomed, design reentered public discourse
on consumption. Moreover, design infiltrated all areas of public and private life
via collaborations between traditional brands, such as Alessi or WMF, and the
most creative minds in the applied arts, turning everyday utility objects into
design objects.

A radical design movement from Italy illustrates the playfulness of this postmodern decade and its implications for West German furniture design.[146] Inspired by art deco and pop art, the virtuoso movement Memphis (1981) entered
the design scene under the leadership of Ettore Sottsass. While the extreme
shapes were not enthusiastically received by the population due to their limited functionality, their influence can be seen in German museums. Wolfgang
Flatz' lightning chair and table (1982), displayed at Hamburg's Arts and Crafts
Museum, drew inspiration from the movement. Furniture mass production
referenced these exaggerated shapes, for example emulating urban skylines in
top pieces of wardrobes and shelves. Especially in West Germany, this playful
movement broke down into geometric forms exemplified by Peter Maly's Zyklus
furniture (1984), pieces that have become German classics. In the GDR, similar shapes emerged with Herbert Pohl's Metropol furniture for the East Berlin

FIGURE 3.2. West German interpretation of postmodern:
"Zyklus" furniture designs by Peter Maly, 1984.
Photograph: Foto COR.

furniture combine, which the AiF approved and recognized with the "Good Design" prize at the Leipzig fair in 1988. The Metropol program never entered mass production, because the GDR collapsed before the model could be integrated into the next Plan.[147] Nevertheless, opening up to European influences further increased aesthetic similarities between the two German states as well as between them and the rest of Western Europe.

Germany's own original take on postmodernism drew markedly on historical elements.[148] In contrast to the architectural deconstruction movements elsewhere in Europe, East and West Germans rehabilitated urban apartment buildings dating back to the nineteenth century. The rediscovery of the classic architecture of an aesthetically untainted German past came alongside a postmodernist critique that aimed at the core of postwar German national design. In this rejection of modern aesthetics, which encompassed the Werkbund, the Bauhaus, the HfG Ulm, and the late functionalism of large-scale housing programs

FIGURE 3.3. East German interpretation of postmodern with Asian influences. "Metropol" furniture designs by Herbert Pohl for VEB Möbelkombinat Berlin, 1986. Photograph: Bernd Neumeier.

and city transportation systems, the strong sense of aesthetic continuity since the 1920s that they represented came under attack again.[149] Such critique of functionalist modernism affected German furniture designers as well. In 1982, an East German report from the Cologne fair explained that the Spartan aesthetics and rigid lines of West German functionalism had gone out of fashion in the West. Instead, "lines of emphasized elegance with a tendency to individualism" attracted the consumer.[150] Successful West German furniture producers such as Interlübke and Hülsta recovered elements that evoked the mass appeal of art nouveau. Within Europe, this furniture style was historically one of the most successful aesthetic concepts that straddled the divide between crafts and mass production. Its many international names alone indicate the vibrancy of style in the fields of architecture, art, and decorative arts as well as the scope of its circulation: *Jugendstil, Stile Liberty, le style moderne, arte nova, arte joven*, and

FIGURE 3.4. Hülsta furniture with art nouveau influences at the IMM in Cologne, 1982. Bundesarchiv DF7/1072. Photograph: Gerhard Wetzig.

Nieuwe Kunst, to name but a few. The return to historical styles did not constitute a novelty but rather brought the postmodernist and the style enthusiast in Germany closer together, while simultaneously creating bridges to more opulent French and Italian styles. In the process of European economic integration, then, awareness of a European culture and identity began to emerge.

It is important to note that design as an economic factor also received attention at the European level. For the first time in its comparatively short history, the EEC awarded an industrial design prize in 1988. The award recognized small-and medium-sized companies that excelled in the categories of quality design and corporate identity. This prize illustrated, first, that design had become by the late 1980s a critical factor in the success of European products of *Mittelstand* businesses that still constitute the backbone of European national economies. The design prize marked, second, the culmination of cultural-economic competition for markets within the European Community that encouraged the acceptance of other national aesthetic concepts. In the call for submissions to the 1988 EEC design prize, organizers underscored the pan-European nature of this event. In particular, the competition's three objectives emphasized the concept of a shared European design culture: (1) to stimulate interest in design in European/EEC industries; (2) to illustrate the nature of the design process and how it can be used as a tool for industrial innovation; and (3) to promote European/EEC design outside of Europe.[151]

The 1980s thus were a turning point in the effort to forge a European cultural space. As plans for a cultural television event demonstrate, industrial design served as a building block for European identity. The pan-European project *La Casa Europea—European Design Day on European TV* aired on the same day in all EC member countries. It consisted of discussions, lectures about objects, interviews, and design presentations. Organizers pushed for a cohesive European aesthetic that communicated the "growing together" of the Western European countries. Among other things, they used the event "to offer design as a European identity."[152] Aiming to prove to a European audience that Europe had grown into a tight-knit network of different locations and activities, the television program proposed Europe as an open space. Industrial design helped to create this European public sphere, serving as a framework for European innovation to explain "Europe as a real and artificial world."[153] This conception of Europe as a cultural space and its integrative force even brought about deliberations for a communal EC cultural policy vis-à-vis the GDR.[154]

Not everybody shared in the excitement about the concept of a European design. In 1989, the West German design council RfF restructured itself under new leadership. Dieter Rams, known as the mind behind the rebranding of Braun and its evolution into one of the leading technological design companies worldwide, volunteered to serve as president of the disorganized design council. In an effort to bring the RfF back to its rightful place at the core of West German industrial design policy, he started a fundraising campaign among industrialists and entrepreneurs. In a letter asking for financial support, Rams pointed to other countries' design activities and the integration of the European market as motivation for rejuvenating the West German brand. The goal was to heighten awareness of German design by expanding its presence abroad, thus giving German design its rightful recognition as an important export.[155] Rams intended to continue the RfF's quest for a national identity predicated on its industrial design.

The preoccupation with a national brand, informed by the tense German-German relationship even in the context of European economic integration, suggests that the Federal Republic could only commit fully to Europe after the resolution of the German Question in 1989. This point is further supported by the sequence of subsequent events leading up to reunification and the manner in which this process was negotiated with Germany's European neighbors in 1990.[156] Yet this is not to say that the EEC was of no significance to the German-German rapprochement process. To the contrary, European economic integration and European cultural trends paved the way for convergence between East and West Germany. Dahrendorf's description of Bonn's pursuit of European integration as "explosive" for its *Deutschlandpolitik* reverberates in historical accounts that present Adenauer's policy decisions about German unity and Western integration in the 1950s and 1960s as highly contradictory, if not mutually exclusive. However, with the long-term perspective of the economic culture approach it seems that EEC trade agreements reinforced the special nature of intra-German trade, and in a roundabout way helped to deepen German-German economic interaction and interdependencies. The initial moments of German aesthetic development toward a shared design aesthetic can similarly be found in the integration of the Common Market and the incentives it gave to pursue "modern" tastes and styles, no matter how diverse.

CHAPTER 4

From Competition to Cooperation

Cold War Diplomacy of German Design

W HEN THE WEST GERMAN embassies reopened in the early 1950s,
countless perplexed letters from around the world arrived in Bonn.
Staff requested guidance about what to do with emblems of the
Third Reich. The embassy in Rio de Janeiro faced a peculiar conundrum in
1952, as it inherited a set of eagle-and-swastika-adorned silverware. Estimated at
a value of DM 115,000, a lively letter exchange between the Rio embassy and the
Federal Ministry for Foreign Affairs (Auswärtiges Amt, AA) developed about
the NSDAP party symbol.[1] Eventually it was decided that a local Brazilian jew-
eler should remove both eagle and swastika.

In varying geographical and geostrategic contexts, West German ambassadors
learned quickly how central material representation of the new postfascist narrative of transparency and simplicity was to the country's success abroad. This
was particularly true when it came to the task of opening up export markets for
engineering and consumer products with high added value, the core of the West
German export industries. In countries where the Federal Republic's trade consisted of mostly cheap products, tremendous efforts were made to improve the
reputation of the German national brand. Ambassador Dr. von Hentig reported
from Djakarta in 1953 that the embassy's Mercedes 300 had been the single best
investment for economic promotion activities, together with a modern sterling
cutlery set made by the company C. Hugo Pott: "The cutlery has found highest
admiration and acknowledgement among international and Indonesian-Dutch
circles. It may be described without hesitation as the most beautiful, even far
superior to President Sukarno's state silver. . . . In this artistic accomplishment
lies proof that we are not only technologically but also artistically superior."[2]
His exchanges with the AA illustrate a high awareness of industrial design's
importance for economic relations among the diplomatic corps in the early years

of the Federal Republic. For instance, von Hentig politely declined German textiles offered to him through AA contractors, as these could "not even compete with the quality of the most affordable of mass-produced hand-knotted Indian carpets and fabrics."[3] Instead, he preferred to furnish the representational spaces in the embassy with interior design solutions from the Vereinigte Werkstätten in Munich, the pre-1945 sister company of the Deutsche Werkstätten Hellerau (DWH) in Dresden, known for its modern and functional aesthetic. The embassy in Paris chose furniture designs from the Werkstätten as well, as they expressed a "dignified modesty."[4] The potentially positive effect of displayed humility and artistic excellence underpinned the diplomatic work that the AA began in an effort to reintegrate the Federal Republic into the world economy and, eventually, re-establish the country's importance in international politics.

From the early days of the Federal Republic the symbolic significance of German materiality for foreign relations and trade was thus well understood. What is more, it became a medium through which diplomats communicated their anxieties about Germany's past and their hopes for a better future based on mutually beneficial interests, such as trade and cultural exchange. Material cultural foreign policy became intrinsically linked to the economic culture of the home country, the structures, values, customs, skills, technologies, and materials visible in the products of German industry. In fact, the BDI and the German Industry and Commerce Board (Deutscher Industrie und Handelstag, DIHT) spearheaded West German foreign trade policy. In some cases they even preempted the reopening of official diplomatic relations with other countries to recommence foreign trade speedily. The two economic organizations coordinated their efforts to show a united front and aligned their ambitions with Adenauer's foreign policy. They supported western integration and a confrontational *Ost-* and *Deutschlandpolitik* even if trade with the Eastern Bloc would have been lucrative.[5]

These fundamentals complicated German-German relations during the Cold War, a piecemeal effort to "coexist" in a geopolitical situation marked by rising superpower tensions. Faced with deadlocked ideological positions, Germans eventually realized that they needed new ways to interact in order to salvage what was left of the cultural and economic bonds between them. Like economic reconstruction and intra-German trade, alternatives to eastern and western alignment were also explored in diplomatic usages of German material culture as both Germanys fiercely competed for legitimacy and recognition in the international arena.[6] In the beginning, the Federal Republic shared its modern style in interior design with other members of the Atlantic community. Its fresh and functional aesthetics placed West Germany among the advanced and progressive nations in the innovative fields of engineering, technology, and design. Meanwhile, cultural Stalinism of the 1940s and early 1950s, economic planning, and the politicization of product development delayed East Germany's cultural aspirations until the mid-1960s. Impelled by the economic logic of export markets, the GDR eventually made progress in the production of modern furniture that was able to find customers in East and West. Thus, the research suggests that East and West German attempts at expressing ideological and systemic difference ironically created a shared code inscribed in material culture that would eventually further German-German rapprochement.

Within the bipolarity of the Cold War, the political significance of aesthetics in everyday objects has been well established.[7] Taking the focus off the superpowers to interrogate the specifically German cultural politics behind the aestheticization of separate identities—proletarian in the East and cosmopolitan in the West—highlights German interests in the global Cold War. It is in the operationalization of industrial design for diplomatic purposes, in which economic culture and foreign policy directly connect. In order to show how material culture emerged as a recognizable language in the intra-German relationship and what functions it served, this chapter integrates the material with the diplomatic ambitions of the two German states. In this way, East and West German cultural-political strategies that sought to negotiate a German-German modus vivendi through the medium of domestic culture can be connected to the complex history of Cold War German diplomacy within the framework of international industrial design exhibitions, international design organizations, and direct German-German cultural exchanges. At the center stands the question of how both Germanys turned a competitive situation, the aestheticization of their respective political orders, into a diplomatic tool for rapprochement.

Part of what allowed material culture to mediate German-German relations was the deeply ingrained self-understanding of Germany as a "nation of culture" (*Kulturnation*) that survived the 1949 division. The term originated with early German conservatives who substituted the lack of a nation-state in the nineteenth century with the term *Kulturnation* to describe "one people united by custom, language, poetry and music, and a common tradition in which all these factors defined a unique German history."[8] Both sides utilized German aesthetic traditions to overcome or suppress the horrors of the Third Reich and employed them to display moral improvement. This operational understanding of aesthetics was the lowest common denominator upon which communication between the FRG and the GDR functioned. While both Germanys shared one cultural heritage of Goethe, Beethoven, and Dürer, the ideological Cold War shifted focus from high culture to lifestyle and *Wohnkultur*. Industrial and product design, a material expression of progress and membership among modern nations, thus became an integral part of their competitive foreign relations efforts.

International Exhibitions and the Diplomatic Significance of Material Culture

Early in the 1950s, both Germanys established a tradition of competitive international industrial exhibitions.[9] The aesthetic and artistic elements were underpinned by economic strategies and the search for international partners. In the 1960s, East and West German design councils began working toward establishing more formal relations with European nations on the other side of the Iron Curtain. Both German states aimed to demonstrate material progressivism and economic prowess to the opposing bloc. The lingering German Question and East Berlin's legitimization efforts pitted East and West German material culture against each other.

Prior personal and professional friendships facilitated the Federal Republic's entry into this new stage of Cold War design diplomacy. The general secretary of the RfF, Mia Seeger, together with her Polish counterpart, Zophia Szydlowska, the head of the design council Instytut Wzornictwa Przemyslowego, proposed the first exclusively West German industrial design exhibition in the Eastern Bloc.[10] The two women had met at the 1960 Milan Triennial, where the German and Polish displays were adjacent. When Seeger saw the final blueprints for the exhibition space, she noticed a wall that separated the Polish exhibition from the German one. She immediately wrote to Szydlowska and put her disappointment about the Polish demarcation in the most diplomatic terms: "If I read your layout correctly, then you have erected a wall against the German section, your section against ours. This would greatly hinder the flow of visitors. In no way do we need a wall."[11] The wall was never again mentioned and a lifelong friendship between the two women ensued. In the following years, they made an invaluable contribution toward constructive East-West exchanges in industrial design. For instance, in 1965 Szydlowska informed Martin Kelm, the head of the East German ZfF, about the industrial design work done in West Germany.[12] The friendship of Seeger and Szydlowska demonstrates how interpersonal relations effected links across the Iron Curtain many years before Chancellor Willy Brandt's New Eastern Policy initiated official reconciliation with Poland.[13]

In 1967, the RfF organised "Industrial Design from the FRG," the first West German industrial exhibition to travel the Eastern Bloc since 1949. It stopped in the Polish cities of Warsaw and Krakow first, and then moved on to Sofia in Bulgaria, and Zagreb in Yugoslavia. The RfF promoted this event as part of a series of Western European and Scandinavian exhibitions that visited the Eastern Bloc. Yet considering Germany's special position in Cold War Europe, it took particular "cautious and balanced good will" on all sides to make this project happen.[14] Once the exhibition opened its doors to Polish visitors, aspects specific to the Federal Republic's relations with the East surfaced. The underlying message of the show was that of Western abundance and technical superiority, consistent with western Cold War cultural diplomacy. In a design journal review, Peter Frank, an exhibition supervisor and staff member close to Mia Seeger, reported his uneasiness regarding the excitement that Polish visitors expressed when seeing the exhibition objects: "As exhibition custodian, I receive the admiration of visitors with somewhat ambivalent feelings. The exhibition is more than simply a specific design show." And he elaborated: "It is, like every other documentation of a country's national design standards, understood as a representation in its broadest sense. Perhaps design exhibitions are especially fitting for this purpose, particularly if they make evident that industrial design expresses more than just the immediate technological and economic level."[15] Frank only realized the show's combined effect of abundance and technological advancement once it was on display.[16] He also noted that the West German products either were complete novelties in Poland or representative of a different economic and social context. For example, a bachelor kitchenette embodied a particular Western lifestyle, whereas from a communist viewpoint, it must have seemed like a waste of resources for a social oddity.[17]

Two incidents heightened the diplomatic payoff West Germany derived from this event. First, GDR industrial designers scheduled a visit to Poland for one of their regular bilateral exchanges during the two-week period of the FRG exhibition in Warsaw. This afforded East German designers the opportunity to acquaint themselves with West German products that they had before only seen in print.[18] West Germany, meanwhile, could once again show off its superiority in product design. While the unexpected visit from the GDR delegation surely gave great satisfaction to the RfF, the friendship between Seeger and Szydlowska yielded an even bigger success for West German diplomacy. After the show's opening in 1967, Szydlowska organized a dinner party to honor her dear German friend, to which the Federal Republic's chargé d'affaires in Poland was invited— his first official invitation to a Polish event.[19] With this exhibition the Federal

Republic not only showcased its material culture but also made an important step toward rebuilding diplomatic relations in the Eastern Bloc.[20]

West Germany's activities in the Eastern Bloc triggered East German anxieties about its own reputation as the most technologically advanced industrial country in the Soviet sphere of influence. To be trumped by Bonn in the realm of product design and consumer culture in front of its socialist friends, as East German politicians feared, could potentially lead to a loss of prestige in the COMECON. Within months of the West German traveling exhibition, the ZfF hastily put together its own exhibition to feature GDR state-of-the-art interior design. The show *Function—Shape—Quality* traveled through the Eastern Bloc for two years, imitating the route of the West German exhibition by starting in Warsaw and then progressing to Krakow. The ZfF modeled the size and concept of the exhibition after what the Federal Republic had presented just months earlier.[21] Instead of stressing difference and superiority, as the Federal Republic's exhibition had done, the GDR attempted to win over their Polish audiences with a message of solidarity.[22] Positioning industrial design as a common challenge for all socialist nations, the GDR sought to appeal to mutual interests in the ideological and practical problem-solving process within the COMECON. The exhibition's intended audience, however, included professionals beyond the Eastern Bloc, as invitations were sent to numerous Western design councils and design schools.[23] Consequently, this exhibition aimed to declare the state of industrial design in the GDR—in practice and theory—to both friend and foe, as well as signal the GDR's commonalities with other socialist nations, where it subsequently toured.

As the title *Function—Shape—Quality* suggests, the show's focus linked aesthetics to functionality. It was the first GDR display to feature design as an important quality of industrial production. It thus expressed the consumer turn in East German economic policy, which led planners and designers to pay more attention to the relationship between humans and their material environment. More than 150 objects and group exhibits, thirty photographic displays, and eight models provided a comprehensive overview of contemporary East German industrial design.[24] Visitors were greeted by an introductory display that covered German design history between 1900 and 1933. The timeline omitted the Nazi period in accordance with the foundational myth of the GDR, which emphasized a clear break with the Third Reich.[25] The next part of the exhibition introduced the German arts and crafts tradition and provided an overview of current design education in the GDR. The rest of the exhibition addressed significant aesthetic challenges in socialist societies: design solutions that "integrated the cultural and the utility value of the product" for work environments, domestic spaces, and leisure, reflecting the state-dominated life of the socialist citizen.[26]

The show's ideological component was especially apparent in the accompanying catalog. It explained the role design ought to play in socialist societies: "The world that humans shape has a shaping influence on them in return. The properties, benefits, and shapes of man-made objects stimulate people's behavior and relationship to the world." This stimulation would result from "usage, that is the experience of the objects' material, construction, and function, which come together in the design, leads in the end to the unlocking [of] new human senses and to the activation of satisfaction, pleasure, and joy of living."[27] Although the explanation may sound like a definition of hedonistic consumption, the relationship between humans and their material environment was central to the mid-1960s understanding of production and consumption in the GDR. The idea of "humanistic socialism" put humans at the center of design, with the goal of creating an environment that served the needs of the population. The degree to which a product fulfilled these needs determined its ideological value.

Generally speaking, the catalog revised many of the more extreme ideological stances that the GDR had taken in the 1950s and early 1960s. The historical section even exonerated the Bauhaus, which had been erased from East Germany cultural memory during the Formalism Debate between 1950 and 1953. Instead of the previous official critique labeling Weimar modernism as cosmopolitan and formalist, by 1967 the ZfF had crowned the Bauhaus the highest developmental stage among a series of design initiatives coming from the East German territory. The catalog text for the *Function—Shape—Quality* exhibition in Moscow two years later even integrated the Bauhaus into leftist, that is, socialist, opposition to the Hitler regime, pointing out that the Nazis closed down the design school as a "hotbed of cultural Bolshevism."[28] One of the pieces displayed, Horn's modular furniture program MDW, epitomized the newfound sense of modernist tradition and a humanistic outlook on production, as it allowed consumers to accommodate individual needs of their changing personal as well as spatial living situations by adding on.

Polish media extensively advertised the show during its run from 11 December 1967 until 20 January 1968, and numerous Polish politicians and designers visited the displays. Newspaper reviews reveal that the exhibition's novelty, unlike its West German counterpart, was not the display of unfamiliar products, since East German products were mostly available on the Polish market. Rather, the fascination lay with the display's explanation of the development of a design culture and its subsequent appropriation by industry.[29] The integration of design into the economic planning process, epitomized by the ZfF's 1965 relocation from the Ministry of Culture to the DAMW, was especially admired by the Polish press. At the specialist symposia framing the exhibition, GDR representatives emphasized the economic benefits of functionalist industrial design, while the catalogs stressed its cultural value. The crucial takeaway from the industrial exhibition was the GDR's move toward resolving the evident contradiction between the ideological superstructure and its practical application inherent in the economic culture of the 1950s and early 1960s.

The mid-1960s then were a moment in which the GDR revised its ideological position vis-à-vis functionalism in its cultural diplomacy. After a decade of aesthetic divergence from the West and internal political contradiction, ideology and social considerations surrounding industrial design merged in humanistic socialism. The new interest in individual needs increasingly paved the way for consumer-oriented design and the rediscovery of Weimar modernism as a leftist aesthetic. This rehabilitation of the Bauhaus tradition in East Germany signaled once more the GDR's commitment to artistic and economic competition with the Federal Republic. The demise of socialist realism in the East occurred alongside the crisis of functionalism in the West. At the same time, individual solutions, such as the MDW furniture program, enabled increasing standardization of production, which in turn helped preserve resources. Yet, the mismanagement of the planned economy would eventually ruin this moment of convergence. As a result, the GDR remained an "economy of scarcity," in which consumers waited for years to attain coveted furniture, cars, and other technical equipment.[30]

To claim a place among modern industrialized nations, the next logical step for the GDR was to show its design expertise in Western countries, facilitated by membership in the International Council of Societies of Industrial Design (ICSID). After earlier positive experiences with the UK, East Germany strove to formalize sporadic and unofficial bilateral cultural and economic relations with Great Britain on the way toward full diplomatic recognition.[31] British companies had regularly participated in the Leipzig Fair in the 1960s and, pursued by GDR diplomats of the MfAA, representatives of British industry, the media, and the two major political parties had visited East Berlin.[32] A parliamentary friendship group with Labour MPs had existed since 1962, yet its members mostly hailed from the left wing of the party.[33] In the international spirit of détente in 1969 the British industry organization CBI and the GDR chamber of foreign commerce signed an initial trade agreement for the years 1970 to 1973. Diplomats worked with the British public relations company Lex Hornsby to promote recognition of the GDR and convey information to support this effort to British newspapers.[34] In addition, a number of cultural exchange events were scheduled, among them UK tours for some of the GDR's finest artistic institutions, such as the Leipzig Gewandhaus Orchestra and the East Berlin's Komische Oper.[35] It became evident that industrial circles were more receptive to establishing contacts with the GDR than their political counterparts.[36]

In an effort to merge political and economic aims, the MfAA commissioned the ZfF in 1970 to put on an industrial design exhibition in London. By displaying products that fulfilled the highest international standards of quality and design with clear usage of GDR insignia, the exhibition planners aimed to impress characteristics of their socialist economy on the British public.[37] What seemed like a straightforward event, however, demanded much diplomatic skill. At first, the general idea of a GDR design exhibition found fertile ground in England. Sir Paul Reilly, the head of the British Council of Industrial Design (CoID) and an active member of ICSID, supported the ZfF and even visited East Berlin in April 1970.[38] The difficulties arose over an exhibition venue. The location had to be humble enough to avoid the impression that the British government entertained quasi-official relations with the socialist GDR, but also a sufficiently representative space not to offend the East German guests. In the end, the Ceylon Tea Center, a Sri Lankan trade forum, served as the exhibition space.

The diplomatic intricacies did not end there. Upon receiving the texts for the placards and the catalog, both loaded with socialist ideologisms, Sir Paul Reilly retracted his agreement to personally open the exhibition. From the outset, he had made it clear that he "was happy to open an exhibition which was entirely on the subject of Design and did not contain any political or ideological allusions, however slight."[39] As head of a government-supported organization, he did not want to be involved with an ideologically inscribed event, he insisted. If the GDR wanted him back on board, Sir Paul Reilly demanded that the ZfF revise the texts.

From this point, opinions within East German official circles sharply diverged. Designers feared that "the revisions would mean abandonment of our socialist point of view."[40] The DAMW, the ZfF's superior governmental institution, pointed to the possibility that others, especially West German officials, could use such altered texts politically against the GDR. The diplomats of the MfAA, on the other hand, preferred changing the texts to losing Sir Paul Reilly's endorsement, which "would hence represent an important precedent for future activities toward the GDR's diplomatic recognition by Great Britain."[41] This stance was in line with GDR foreign policy in the final months of the Ulbricht era, which introduced a cautious opening up to the West from 1970 onward.[42]

Although coordinated with the Soviet Union, Ulbricht's foreign policy maxim of the GDR as the model socialist state, had, with its ambition of an independent *Deutschlandpolitik*, contradicted Soviet western strategy. It was abandoned in recognition of the GDR's geostrategic position and the responsibility this entailed for the country's leadership in East-West rapprochement.[43] In the end, potential diplomatic gains won out over ideological concerns. The ZfF entirely revised the texts and thus gave the presentation of socialist material culture new meaning, one that catered to Western European sensibilities about individuality and that erased any trace of open state socialism from the displays. Original text was phrased as such:

> New standards for the quality of industrial products are derived from the development of the socialist order in the GDR. Manufactures are an essential part of our environment. They influence people's way of living within every area. The quality of material and ideological needs also depend on product design.[44]

The revised, English translation purged the Marxist language from the texts:

> New standards of quality have been set for industrial products. It is recognized that as an essential part of our environment these influence man in all spheres of his life. Ideally, every product should be an expression of certain requirements, both physical and aesthetic.[45]

When the exhibition opened, it underscored the humanistic aspects of GDR design culture. This new stance was further underlined by Martin Kelm's remarks at the show's opening: "It is the goal in our society to positively influence all of the factors affecting human beings and to create an environment in which one can experience the challenging notion of humanism."[46] Yet Kelm used his speech also to reinsert ideological messages with a socialist interpretation of humanism:

> As you know, we abolished the hurdles of private ownership of property as well as means of production in order to undertake planning that serves across societal interests. The people own everything. The people can determine their own fortunes. Hence, we have the potential to design an environment that serves the people's interests. We work on utilizing these opportunities and on putting industrial design to work in creating a complexly designed humanistic environment.[47]

The re-inscription of GDR material culture as an expression of humanistic ideals within socialism was a watershed moment in East Germany's cultural and trade diplomacy: For the first time, political goals became more important than ideological consistency. With this newfound pragmatism with regard to the neo-liberal free trade doctrine, the SED sought to combat the stigma of isolation and provincialism that had attached to the country after the construction of the Wall.[48]

Having appeared in the catalog for the 1967 Warsaw exhibition, the concept of humanism in communism was not entirely new. As a shared concern, it facilitated communication between Eastern Bloc countries at different stages of socialist and industrial development; though in London the ZfF employed it to sway Western audiences. Indeed, in the mid-1960s, "socialist humanism" became a key term in the rapprochement of eastern and western Marxists.[49] This school of Marxist thought opposed the structural mechanisms of state socialism and instead emphasized subjectivity and human agency in socialist theory, and aimed at creating social alliances to win support for reform. Yet using humane socialism to mitigate the ideological opposition between Western democracies and socialist groups, parties, and even states, announced a new stage in diplomatic cultural exchange. It also contributed to a period of Western Eurocommunism in the 1960s and 1970s by enabling the cooperation of bourgeois and leftist parties in Western democratic governments, such as the Labour governments in Britain and the Grand Coalition in West Germany.[50]

At the London exhibition, the GDR thus strategically employed the concept of humane socialism to overcome the ideological barrier. To convey this approach materially, the exhibition consciously minimized the better-developed heavy industrial sector and instead displayed consumer products that related to the everyday.[51] It especially featured objects for leisure activities, such as patio furniture and toys. An East German review mentioned that the toys are "not only very well designed, but also pedagogically valuable and fulfill therapeutic requirements. The colorful, imaginatively arranged, and multiform toys bestow the entire exhibition with a friendly and casual atmosphere."[52] East German products ranging from pictures of heavy work equipment to displays of prized china and glassware created the impression of a progressive material culture. Yet visitors saw more than industrial design. GDR literature and picture albums strategically placed throughout the exhibit for perusal conveyed a better understanding of the socialist country.[53] A color slide presentation about Karl-Marx-Stadt's postwar reconstruction (today Chemnitz) brought all these elements together and transported visitors to an ideal socialist setting where public

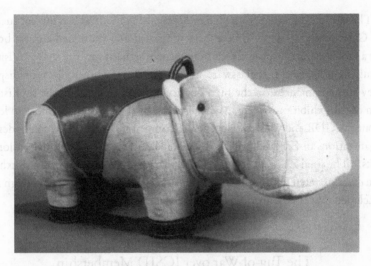

FIGURE 4.1. Children's toy hippo, designed by Renate Müller (1960s)
for VEB Therapeutisches Spielzeug Sonneberg, and exhibited in London
in 1970. Photograph: Klaus Dietrich Zeutschel.

buildings, public art, the health establishment, and urban infrastructure neatly coalesced. Apparently, the message resonated positively with British audiences. On 9 September 1970, even the conservative *Daily Telegraph* titled its story on the GDR design exhibition "Humane East Germans."[54]

In the end, the response to the London exhibition far exceeded the hopes and expectations of diplomats in the GDR. Representatives from several eastern European countries, as well as the cultural attaché of the American embassy in London and a few members of British parliament, among other London notables, attended the opening reception. In his speech, Sir Paul Reilly affirmed the bilateral interest in fostering trade relations between Great Britain and the GDR "whether officially or unofficially."[55] Not to take advantage of this sizable market, he maintained, "would be ludicrous for a trading people like the British." Yet he acknowledged the unusual diplomatic situation, hoping that "no-one here feels any compunction about being present to wish this exhibition well. It is indeed innocent self-interest that brings us all together here, since trade is properly a two-way traffic and cannot be conducted without reasonable personal contacts."[56] Once ideology was set aside, economic interests prevailed. With this event, the GDR moved one step closer to losing pariah status and becoming a desired trade partner.

The exhibition lasted from 7 to 19 September 1970, and was a great success for GDR foreign policy.[57] There were 1067 visitors who signed a guest book, but a CoID report suspected that more people actually saw the show.[58] Visitors nominated the tea china, glassware, and toys as their favorite objects on display. They also commented on the high quality of GDR design and the sophistication of the exhibition system. Many agreed that there was much more to learn about the GDR and wanted to deepen relations with the country. Major design organizations in England proved receptive and invited the GDR delegation to talks.[59] The final ZfF report showed great satisfaction with the way the exhibition demonstrated East German capabilities in the field of industrial design and concluded that this contributed tremendously to GDR diplomacy.[60]

Encounters of Foreign Design: The Tug-of-War over ICSID Membership

The adversarial nature of East and West German cultural diplomacy over industrial design also preoccupied the ICSID. Founded in 1957 out of several industrial design congresses, the ICSID was an organization dedicated to globally advancing and organizing the new professional field of industrial design.[61] Initial members included Denmark, the FRG, France, India, Italy, Japan, Norway, Sweden, the United States, and the United Kingdom. The ICSID quickly became the dominant body defining the profession, finding solutions to contemporary design problems, and setting standards for industrial design education. Its first president, Peter Muller-Munk from the United States, called it "a fine display of transatlantic community and un-selfish professional co-operation."[62] According to his successor Sir Misha Black, officeholders were highly aware that as a nonpolitical professional organization it could play a part in bridging the bipolarity of the Cold War: "Those who will not associate politically are able to meet and talk at the ICSID Assemblies and Conferences."[63] This awareness translated into an inclusive member acquisition policy across the Iron Curtain.

ICSID's eastward expansion emulated a pattern seen in several nongovernmental cultural organizations vying for the United Nations Educational, Scientific, and Cultural Organization (UNESCO) status in the 1960s. Nonaligned Yugoslavia became the first socialist member of the ICSID in 1961, followed by the Soviet Union's All-Union Scientific Research Institute of Industrial Design (VNIITE) as the first Eastern Bloc country in 1965. The novelty of eastward expansion both encouraged Western members to protest on political and technical grounds while the Eastern Bloc members prepared for possible diplomatic fallout and sabotage attempts. A particular concern for ICSID was that Eastern Bloc design councils were often state institutions and not professional associations. Yuri Soloviev, the head of VNIITE, sent the ICSID executive board a long appraisal of the role of industrial design in socialist societies, explaining how the state centrally organized the profession.[64] Despite some initial hesitation on part of the ICSID board, the desire to grow from a transatlantic into a global organization won out over concerns about the nature of the new member societies. To enable national members in addition to professional associations to join the organization, the ICSID constitution was changed, eventually allowing most eastern European industrial design institutions to be admitted.[65] The same applied to the ZfF when it requested membership at the Vienna Congress in 1965.[66] However, the existence of two Germanys complicated this request.

On 9 January 1965, Mia Seeger received a "strictly confidential" letter from her Belgian colleague Josine des Cressonnières. The ICSID secretary general inquired whether Seeger had heard of the ZfF in Berlin, which had approached her about ICSID membership. Des Cressonnières did not know whether the ZfF was located in East or West Berlin and relied on her German friend for information.[67] This rather innocuous letter initiated a two-and-a-half-year-long West German campaign to prevent the GDR from joining the ICSID.

A founding member, the West German RfF had acted as the sole representative of German interests in ICSID since 1957. With ICSID's pending extension into the Eastern Bloc, the worlds of Cold War diplomacy and cultural politics collided.[68] The campaign to isolate the GDR aligned with the Federal Republic's *Deutschlandpolitik* and Cold War foreign policy of nonrecognition regarding the eastern part of Germany. The Hallstein Doctrine prescribed the severing of diplomatic relations with countries that extended diplomatic recognition to the GDR and affirmed the West German claim to sole representation (*Alleinvertretungsanspruch*) for all of Germany in international organizations. The concern was that German-German interaction would become official if the ZfF were to gain ICSID membership. It would take place within an international organization that accepted representatives from diplomatically recognized countries, which would force West Germany to share German representation with East Germans. It was feared that this would open doors to increasing international integration in other contexts and eventually pave the way to recognition of the GDR as a sovereign state.[69] It was thus important, western officials argued, to shut this down. West German professional and academic organizations received recommendations of how to perpetuate the GDR's international nonrecognition at international congresses from the West German Foreign Ministry (AA). For

instance, before any congress or meeting, professional organizations should ensure that the term "GDR" did not find its way into the event program. Both East
and West German participants should be listed simply with "Germany" as their
country of origin.[70] International organizations, the advice circular maintained,
needed to be informed that the separate recognition of the GDR by name or, even
worse, through independent membership would profoundly undermine desired
intra-German cooperation on both the professional and the interpersonal level.

Mia Seeger's successor as general secretary of the RfF, Fritz Gotthelf, intensified the campaign to reject the East Germans after the ICSID executive committee had passed the GDR's application in February 1967 for confirmation by
the General Assembly in Canada.[71] He turned to the Executive Committee,
explaining once more the delicate German political situation and the diplomatic
importance of West Germany's *Alleinvertretungsanspruch*, but to no avail. While
the ICSID executives acknowledged the tenuous relations, they had neither the
interest nor the power to challenge the Cold War status quo of German division.
In July 1967, a few weeks before the Ottawa Congress, Gotthelf received a confidential letter from Des Cressonnières, stating that, after careful consideration,
the board had decided to grant East Germany full membership. Almost humor-
ously, she reported that "the Executive Committee has concluded that it was not
possible to come to a decision, against all existing facts, about the re-unification
of Germany!"[72] Des Cressonnières ended by pointing to a precedent in which
ICSID had already granted provisional membership to a design society from the
People's Republic of China and advised that it ought to extend the same to the
East German ZfF. In face of this, Gotthelf could do little but accept the ICSID's
decision. After more than two years of string-pulling and backdoor diplomacy,
he downplayed the importance of the matter in his response: "One Germany
or two; we aren't politicians." Nevertheless, Gotthelf announced that West
Germany would abstain from the vote on East Germany's membership "in an
elegant manner" by being absent from the Canada congress.[73] This last-minute
effort to save face could not conceal that the Federal Republic and its ICSID
representatives had suffered a significant blow in the struggle for sole German
representation in international bodies.

As the West Germans pushed forward their last intervention against GDR
membership in the summer of 1967, tensions between the ZfF and the ICSID
executive committee rose as well. From the very beginning, the GDR had taken
a "no nonsense" approach to West German attempts to exclude them from this
organization. Having encountered the Federal Republic's *Alleinvertretungsanspruch* in other international bodies, the SED leadership suspected western

conspiracy behind the smallest diplomatic slip-up, and East Berlin became adamant about the correct representation of its country in name, flag, and national anthem.[74] When the program for the ICSID Congress in Ottawa failed to identify the ZfF as an East German institution, Martin Kelm threatened to boycott the congress altogether.[75] Des Cressonnières tried to calm the situation by assuring him that the membership nomination of the ZfF would be listed with the addendum "German Democratic Republic (GDR)."[76]

What might seem like an unnecessary escalation actually represented a fundamental building block of GDR foreign policy to gain formal recognition as a legitimate state from the West. Membership in nongovernmental international organizations moved the country closer to attaining a seat at the United Nations. Moreover, as the tug-of-war over ICSID membership shows, both Germanys knew that each of these incidents raised the stakes in the German-German Cold War over ideology, division, and international recognition. Eventually the ZfF gained membership at the Ottawa Congress, along with the institutes of Poland, Czechoslovakia, and Bulgaria, leveling the diplomatic playing field between eastern and western Europe for the industrial design profession.[77] In fact, a decade later during the Soviet ICSID presidency under Soloviev, it would be the West Germans who complained that their country had been labeled incorrectly as "German Federal Republic" and who would request a correction to the official and UN-recognized "Federal Republic of Germany" in all ICSID documents and papers.[78] This may well have been a squabble over alphabetical order, since the German Democratic Republic would of course appear before the "German Federal Republic" in any listing of members.

That East German cultural diplomacy actually worked was proven by a sudden spike of western interest in GDR design after its acceptance into the ICSID. West German diplomatic circles were not at all pleased with this outcome, but the industrial design community embraced it. *Form*, a leading design publication with significant influence on aesthetic discourse in the Federal Republic, welcomed this as a blessing in disguise as "the membership of the GDR in the ICSID might perhaps offer more opportunities for knowledge exchange."[79] Another article in *Form* recognized the leading East German design publication *Form und Zweck* "as an auxiliary bridge to compensate for the lack of personal exchange of experiences between East and West."[80] While other national design traditions were covered, the journal had largely ignored GDR design for the better part of a decade. This international validation redeemed GDR design in the eyes of West German designers. However, the East German turn toward modern idioms in the mid-1960s no doubt propelled this new interest as well.

Nonetheless, the ICSID mediated exchange did not mean that German-German interaction became less confrontational after 1967. In 1968, for instance, the BMWi supported the then-flailing RfF in building a design center in West Berlin, which remained politically contested territory. The GDR protested the center, which it understood to be a government institution, but of course had no power to block it. When in 1969 the RfF suggested an ICSID expert meeting at the new International Design Centre (IDZ) in West Berlin, Kelm declined the invitation from Des Cressonières.[81] He reasoned that "the fact that recent official efforts on part of the West German Federal Republic to support industrial design are to be implemented of all places in West Berlin, that is outside the borders of the West German state, can only be interpreted as a political act against the GDR."[82] Des Cressonnières, in turn, told the RfF that she had foreseen such complications: "I must admit there is some truth in it.... I told Philip Rosenthal when I saw him: 'Why choose Berlin? It will create difficulties.'"[83] The ICSID executive board quickly found a diplomatic solution and asked Kelm to arrange a visit to the AiF in East Berlin for one of the days of the expert meeting, a request with which he happily complied.

Diplomacy of German Design:
The German-German Basic Treaty

These events demonstrate that industrial designers from both Germanys could not interact easily as long as confrontation dominated Cold War foreign policy. In the absence of official political relations, professional exchanges were seen as part of the struggle for hearts and minds and therefore intrinsically tied to cultural diplomacy.[84] As the general Cold War climate moved from deterrence to dialogue in the late 1960s, the situation slowly changed. Intertwined with détente processes in superpower relations was the ongoing issue of the national status of a divided country and its diplomatic recognition.

In a first step, Chancellor Willy Brandt who had opened up West German diplomacy to negotiations with the Eastern Bloc in his prior position as minister of foreign affairs, intensified these efforts after his election in 1969.[85] Brandt's *Neue Ostpolitik* revised the previous "policy of strength" that the conservative Adenauer and Erhard governments had followed.[86] Adenauer especially had been convinced that West Germany's rearmament, NATO membership, and economic cooperation in western Europe would inevitably lead the Federal Republic from strength to strength and, more importantly, safeguard it from communist political influence and Soviet expansionism or military aggression.

Western integration, however, only deepened German division, and Adenauer knew this.[87] By 1969, the formula "reunification through Western integration," the idea that a politically and economically strong Federal Republic would "attract" East Germany into reunification, had not worked. The Wall stood as a reminder of the limits of Adenauer's strategy.

The construction of the Berlin Wall had taught Brandt, at the time the mayor of West Berlin, important lessons, among them the realization that "the West alone would not solve the problems of German division."[88] Negotiations over minor agreements, such as the 1963 special pass agreement for West Berliners to see East Berlin family for holidays impressed on him and his advisor Egon Bahr the importance of dialogue and exchange with the GDR. Improving relations with the Soviet Union was an important step toward German-German political rapprochement. In the absence of a peace treaty following the Second World War, postwar Germany's former eastern territories had remained a point of contention in Soviet–West German relations. Under the auspices of Brandt's policy of rapprochement, Bonn affirmed the eastern German border, the Oder-Neisse-Line, in 1970 in the Moscow Treaty with the Soviet Union and the Warsaw Treaty with Poland, and renounced any claim to former German territories. The two treaties enabled the Federal Republic to continue to pursue an eastern foreign policy separately from their transatlantic partners, especially the United States. Egon Bahr summarized Bonn's new strategy in the German Question: "Responsibility for Germany had to be borne by Germans themselves."[89]

The ultimate goal of Brandt's *Ostpolitik* was indeed to re-establish some kind of national context for the two German states.[90] It was therefore crucial "to restore at least some aspects of the pre–World War II links between the two halves of Germany."[91] In this way, his policy diverged from superpower détente, because it sought to change the Cold War status quo. To realize the eastern policy regarding East Germany, Brandt needed greater independence from external powers "to create living conditions far better than those enforced by Cold War rivalries."[92] After twenty years, the Federal Republic thus gave up its foreign policy maxim of *Alleinvertretungsanspruch*, abolished the Hallstein Doctrine, and entered into official negotiations with the other part of Germany.[93]

The superpowers on both sides had mixed feelings about this German-German rapprochement. On the one hand, the Germans had to find a way to coexist, but on the other hand, the possibility of German unification under the umbrella of the opposing system, or even a neutral Germany released from any binding partnerships, presented a scenario that neither side wanted. Washington was especially nervous about the degree of independence displayed by West German diplomats and their willingness to cooperate with Soviet diplomats in order to achieve their political goals. Moscow was less nervous about the GDR leadership, especially after the transition from the obstinate Ulbricht to the more pliant Honecker, whom it kept on a short leash throughout the negotiation process.[94] The Soviet Union supported the normalization of German-German relations as far as it fit with the overall détente and economic policy interests of the Bloc leader.[95] While the superpowers saw German division as a means for maintaining peace in Europe, Germans argued with increasing intensity that the division was a major cause of tension.[96]

As the Moscow and Warsaw treaties awaited ratification in the West German parliament, and the Four Power Agreement on Berlin had just been signed, direct talks between East and West Germany commenced.[97] After finalizing the Transit Accord and the Traffic Treaty, which established regulations for the passage of West German citizens and goods through the GDR, negotiations about more substantial issues began in the summer of 1972: the national question, the absence of a peace treaty and the presence of the Four Powers, and the question of citizenship. Both sides signed the Basic Treaty that December after curtailed negotiations left some of the issues unresolved. Over the next two decades, the Federal Republic would spend millions for the Transit Accord annually, which included visa charges and tariffs. Bonn would also pay more than DM 3.5 billion to free roughly 34,000 political prisoners and reunite approximately 250,000 families divided by the Wall.[98]

West German willingness to pay enormous sums for the transit regulations highlights Bonn's efforts to ameliorate interpersonal relations between the East and West German populations. It also demonstrated a new attitude toward the German Question by accepting the realities of the division.[99] At the core of this policy lay the hope that increased interaction between East and West would reignite feelings of national unity, lead to the demise of the GDR, and end German division.[100] However, the SED completely controlled contacts between their population and the West: Visas required a complicated application process, packages and mail from the West were searched, and, as Stasi files later revealed, western visitors were monitored for the majority of their stay in the East. The Brandt government, on the one hand, attempted to reach an agreement that deregulated human interaction and limited institutional or official interference in order to break down the literal and figurative walls that the SED had erected between people who shared cultural and political roots. The Honecker government, on the other hand, continued its approach to the German division via demarcation policies.[101]

The specifics of German-German cultural exchanges agreed upon in the Basic Treaty, namely the Cultural Accord (*Kulturabkommen*), provide an excellent window into the diplomatic efforts to "normalize" East-West relations on both sides. They also reveal West Germany's long-term goal for *Ostpolitik* deregulating cultural exchange by allowing nonstate actors to initiate and conduct cultural events on the other side of the border.[102] Beginning in 1974, the West German Permanent Representative Mission (StäV) in East Berlin, which the Federal Republic had set up instead of an embassy in the aftermath of the Basic Treaty, functioned as a mediator for political issues, economic cooperation, and cultural contacts concerning both parts of Germany. Yet negotiations over the *Kulturabkommen* remained unresolved for twelve years.[103] The initial five rounds of talks between 1973 and 1975 brought no results because the GDR claimed ownership of cultural artifacts that the Federal Republic had included in a new cultural foundation.[104] East Germany also contested the inclusion of West Berlin in the *Kulturabkommen*. Together, these issues brought deliberations to a halt until 1982.[105] As an interim solution, both Germanys agreed on the state-mediated cultural exchange to enable mutual visits of theater companies, choirs, and museum exhibitions.

The disagreements not only stemmed from the hasty and incomplete negotiations over the Basic Treaty but also from the souring German-German relations in the aftermath of the 1975 Helsinki Accords. Suddenly, the GDR reversed its strategy from dialogue to delineation, as "internal problems increased under the influence of détente" and GDR citizens, encouraged by the Helsinki human rights stipulations, began to reject the socialist system openly.[106] Frustrated by the East German change of course, Bonn insisted on continuing the "policy of normalization."[107] Meanwhile, the interim solution of state-regulated cultural exchanges suited the GDR well. With the cultural accords in limbo, the SED maintained control over contacts between East and West and did not shy away from leveraging this power to complicate cultural exchange whenever Cold War tensions flared. The Federal Republic, alternately, participated in the state-mediated cultural exchanges because it saw them as an opportunity to reconnect with the other Germany and to shape East German perceptions of the Federal Republic. Eventually, Honecker dropped East Berlin's unresolved claims to artifacts to the bottom of the negotiation list in order to recommence talks in 1983. After twelve more rounds, negotiations successfully concluded with the signing of the *Kulturabkommen* on 6 May 1986.

West German public discontent with the *Kulturabkommen* certainly grew over the negotiation period. The most prominent critic of the treaty was Nobel

Prize–winning author and artist Günter Grass. In a newspaper interview with the *Rheinischer Merkur*, Grass criticized the diplomatic aspect of the agreement because it was negotiated as if the two Germanys were foreign territory to each other, like a treaty with France or Finland. He warned that the Federal Republic gave up the last piece of commonality between East and West and insisted that "the agreement should have been made on the basis of a shared culture and history."[108] The political and economic division had long been established, but the realm of culture had proven resistant to division, he maintained. The agreement, in Grass's opinion, put survival of a shared German culture into question. Grass had previously approached the federal government with his concerns about the *Kulturabkommen*'s potentially damaging effects. As an alternative, he suggested a German-German national foundation to ensure the continuation of the German *Kulturnation*.[109]

> Such a solution . . . could contribute to the development of a new un-derstanding of 'nation,' which would exclude reunification, but, on the other hand, could assist Germans in two states to find a new, relaxed self-understanding. This would also preclude a renewed political power build-up in the center of Europe. Our neighbors in East and West needn't fear such a development any more.[110]

Apart from his preference for this universalist, postfascist, and pacifist vision for a German culture, Grass was concerned that the *Kulturabkommen* could negatively affect the arts and cultural economies: It would promote only what was officially acceptable art in both German states, thus implicitly censoring artistic expression. Grass exclaimed that "everywhere where art, where literature, where painting is created, it is necessarily subversive, and it will thus be, perhaps even from both sides, be held back."[111] The *Kulturabkommen*, notwithstanding its original intentions of deregulating German-German cultural exchange, could possibly become a tool for state censorship of the arts.

Despite Grass's warnings, the Federal Republic pursued the *Kulturabkommen* to continue the normalization of German-German relations. Rather than heeding Grass's concerns about the treaty's meaning for the German national idea and cultural diversity, politicians in the Federal Republic valued its practical merits: They could hold the GDR leadership accountable to a signed treaty, but not to the lofty idea of a unified *Kulturnation*.

German-German State-Mediated Cultural
Exchange and the *Kulturabkommen*

To a certain extent, Grass was right. The events that came out of the *Kultur-abkommen* indeed centered on promoting cultural products that affirmed official policy and national narratives. Subversive modern art, such as the 1983 postmodern artwork "Consumer's Rest," a re-appropriated and manipulated shopping cart with which West Berlin designer Frank Schreiner playfully critiqued consumer society, did not rank high on the West German priority list for German-German cultural exchange. Too much was at stake as well in the realm of economic culture and industrial design to employ humor, which is evident in the events surrounding the planning and execution of two industrial design exhibitions before and after the signing of the *Kulturabkommen*: the FRG exhibition *Design—Thinking Ahead for Humanity* in East Berlin (1984) and the *Design in the GDR* show in Stuttgart (1988). These exhibitions showcase the political strategies behind intra-German cultural exchanges, while illustrating the significance of the *Kulturabkommen* as a cornerstone for a more self-determined *Deutschlandpolitik*.

The idea for the West German exhibition originated in 1983 against the backdrop of deteriorating East-West relations during the Soviet-American Geneva talks about the American Pershing missiles in the Federal Republic.[112] In this tense atmosphere, Bonn commissioned the RfF to assemble a West German industrial exhibition. The Federal Ministry for Intra-German Relations (BMB)[113] and the BMWi jointly coordinated the planning effort so that the FRG government could pitch the project as part of the interim state-mediated cultural exchange.[114] Emphasizing that it would contribute to peace in Europe, the western side made clear that holding the design exhibition within the same calendar year was of "political significance."[115] Using every available channel, the Federal Republic impressed the event's importance for German-German relations on the SED leadership. Minister for Economic Affairs Otto Graf Lambsdorff even brought the exhibition pitch on a trip to the Leipzig trade fair in the spring of 1984.[116] Nine months after Hans Otto Bräutigam, the head of the Permanent Representative Mission in East Berlin, had first proposed the design exhibition to the GDR deputy foreign minister Kurt Nier, the project came to fruition. The exhibition ran for two weeks in December 1984 as the fourth project the Federal Republic sent as part of the state-mediated cultural exchange since 1975.[117] None of Bonn's initiative had been coordinated with transatlantic partners, signaling to the international community the German determination to

FIGURE 4.2. West Berlin artist Frank Schreiner
designed "Consumer's Rest" as a playful critique
of consumerism in 1983. © DACS 2019.

"insulate inter-German relations from the vicissitudes of relations between the
superpowers."[118]

Initially, the GDR hesitated to support the West German project. Yet after
a few weeks of deliberations, it swallowed the bait that the RfF had put in the
exhibition proposal: a symposium that would convey "specialized technical and
professional details and suggestions."[119] With the exhibition would come an opportunity to inspect West German industrial products and to learn about their
aesthetic, structural, and technological qualities, without the risks and costs associated with industrial espionage. It was a welcome chance for East German

research and development to catch up to world standards, a preoccupation for the GDR.

With the exception of the venue, the preparations for *Design—Thinking Ahead for Humanity* went smoothly, and the exhibition opened on 3 December 1984, in the International Trade Center in the heart of East Berlin. High-ranking East and West German politicians, representatives of GDR cultural organizations, and the industrial designers from the RfF and the AiF attended the opening event.[120] Even Wolfgang Schäuble, the chancellery chief of staff in the first Helmut Kohl government, visited during his first official trip to the GDR. During the opening speech, Martin Kelm highlighted the political significance of German-German rapprochement at this moment: "We regard the fact that this exhibition takes place as a positive sign, particularly at a time when the international situation gives reason for serious concerns. . . . Even the best intentions and the best design achievements would make no sense for humanity if a nuclear inferno cannot be prevented."[121] Hans Otto Bräutigam of the Permanent Mission also commented on the international situation when he greeted the guests:

> The Federal Government is determined to continue the path paved by the Basic Treaty and the Helsinki Accords. We want to extend cooperation and take advantage of every chance to improve relations. We do this conscious of our shared responsibility for peace and stability in Europe and in the interest of the people on both sides. Cultural activities such as this exhibition are the building blocks for good neighborly relations between the two German states.[122]

Such expressions of "mini-détente" in German-German relations solidified the idea of their special role in maintaining East-West dialogue.[123] Sharing concerns about becoming hostages of the superpower arms race with other non-nuclear nations in Europe offered a new vision for pan-German foreign policy: a Germany unified for the universal values of peace and accord.

West Germany's emphasis on interpersonal relations in the German-German rapprochement was expressed by the exhibition's content. From its conception, it was intended to show design's contribution to everyday life by means of selected, progressive solutions.[124] Humans and the social fabric, not the products themselves, stood at the center and provided the premise for "deepening mutual knowledge about cultural and social existence" in the two German states.[125] High-profile guests, diplomatic speeches, and the awareness that this German-German display of harmony stood in stark contrast to the tense Second Cold

FIGURE 4.3. A friendly encounter between RfF president Philip Rosenthal (left)
and AiF director Martin Kelm (second from left) at the second opening of the West
German industrial exhibition *Design—Thinking Ahead for Humanity* in Leipzig, 1985.
Photograph: Waltraud Grubitzsch.

War benefited both sides in the diplomatic arena. The exhibition consciously
continued the Federal Republic's efforts with *Neue Ostpolitik*, to change the
Cold War status quo and the push for direct interaction between the German
populations.

Materially, the West German show was impressive. Nearly two hundred products, systems, and projects from more than a hundred businesses conveyed the
evolution of industrial design in the Federal Republic. A historical section con-
textualized West German design in the Werkbund and the Bauhaus traditions
of modern, functionalist aesthetics.[126] Visitors quickly realized that the exhibition was not a sales show when they saw the lavish products displayed for home
interiors. The luxury furniture company Interlübke sent its high-priced Duo-
Bed, while the furniture cooperative Wohnkultur displayed the top-selling,
yet expensive, WK 470 furniture system, and Vitsoe showed an upholstery
suite.[127] None of the East German visitors could afford such pricey furniture
nor could most West Germans. Rather, the exhibition clearly showcased the
perks of the Western lifestyle with the amenities of high-end designer interiors
and high-technology standards for appliances and tools. In addition to displays

of affluence, the descriptions accompanying the interior designs provoked East German political cadres with a critique of the GDR surveillance society. One read, for example, "In a mass society and an increasingly depersonalized environment, the personal apartment remains one of the few areas where one can realize individual ideas."[128] The home, the text suggested to GDR audiences, offered a space for personal freedom and self-expression, an escape from the state's control over its citizens. Such provocations affected cultural exchanges during the show's two-week run.

The initial impression of a close-knit inter-German relationship created by the exhibition documents' emphasis on "peace in Europe" and "German-German understanding" is quickly nuanced by materials from the East German archives. Unbeknownst to the guests from the Federal Republic, the SED closely monitored and manipulated the exhibition. Event advertisement posters provided by the RfF were only put up in obscure places, if at all.[129] The GDR leadership hoped to keep the number of visitors to a minimum, yet thanks to word of mouth, their numbers rose by the day.[130] In a press release, the Permanent Mission celebrated the fact that 22,000 people had seen the show during its first week. The crowd's youth was noticed; it revealed that the SED populated the West German product show with chosen party-loyal groups, trusted young professionals, and design students.[131] Only about two hundred visitors were "average" GDR citizens on the first day of *Design—Thinking Ahead for Humanity*.[132] In addition to the at best insufficient exhibition promotion, the AiF purposely slowed down the admission into the venue. Each day during opening hours, a queue of 150–200 curious East Germans stood in front of the International Trade Center. Officials from the FRG's Permanent Mission stopped by several times and asked the AiF staff to open more registers to decrease the waiting time. The eastern side withstood the pressure, claimed to have been bullied, and complained that Bonn connected political profitability to attendance.[133] The West Germans decided to ignore this provocation. Overall, 66,000 people visited the exhibition in eighteen days, and the RfF sold every one of the 40,000 available catalogs.

Meanwhile, the AiF feared that the displays of Western affluence might potentially lead to open critique of socialism and its economic shortcomings. Two days before the industrial exhibition opened, it outright confiscated a number of West German design books that the RfF provided in the exhibition.[134] However, after the books were removed, visitors simply turned to the information and technical descriptions provided in the exhibition texts.[135] Moreover, the East German exhibition personnel prevented contact between East German visitors and the RfF staff on hand to answer visitors' questions.[136] As a countermeasure, the AiF outfitted its own staff with a twenty-page disinformation script to enable them to discredit western achievements in conversation with exhibition visitors. Emphasizing the potential negative effects of market capitalism and profitmaking on the social fabric of a country, the text characterized industrial design and its institutions in the Federal Republic as "ineffective."[137]

However, the feared consumer protest failed to materialize. The internal AiF event report described visitors' reactions as "confident and competent-critical with specialized design interest."[138] It is possible that the staff did not record visitors' disgruntlement accurately so as to give the impression that they had the situation under control. Certainly, earlier design shows had attracted critical, if knowledgeable, audiences in the GDR that usually did not hold back with critique. With a public relations fiasco successfully averted, the SED leadership confidently completed the negotiations over the German-German *Kulturabkommen* in 1986 without further complications. Once the West German event had ended, the GDR design institution looked forward to sending an exhibition to the West in accordance with the principle of reciprocity.

Yet it would take more than three years for the GDR industrial design show to finally be sent to West Germany in May 1988. The fact that the AiF, the Foreign Ministry, the DIA, the collectivized industry, and design schools all collaborated on the *Design in the GDR* exhibition illustrates the complex interweaving of industry, industrial design, trade, and cultural foreign policy. However, the extent of the effort did not match the prestige of the resulting industrial exhibition. One of the regional design institutions in the West, the Design Center in Stuttgart, hosted the exhibition in its representative nineteenth-century building, far from Bonn. To ensure the political and economic success of the event, the SED leadership demanded elaborate advertising strategies.[139] But the West German government quickly thwarted these efforts. When the time came to print the catalog, the GDR Permanent Mission in Bonn asked for a short greeting from the chief of staff of the Federal Chancellery to parallel high-ranking GDR politicians' participation in the 1984 exhibition.[140] To their great astonishment, Bonn denied the request, claiming that: "These kinds of forewords were common during the period of rare, individual state-mediated cultural projects in prior years. In the light of the extensive project list agreed upon after the signing of the *Kulturabkommen*, this kind of high-level preface should not generally be planned on; they should be reserved for especially high-ranking projects."[141]

Diplomatic gestures such as an official greeting would only further legitimize the GDR, which Bonn wanted to prevent. With the signing of the cultural agreement in 1986, the Federal Republic had reached its goal of securing German-German exchanges on a nongovernmental level, and this exhibition presented the perfect opportunity to put this achievement into practice. If the East had not noticed the political effects of the *Kulturabkommen* at the time, they surely realized them in 1988.

A loss of diplomatic significance in conjunction with the provincial exhibition location demoted the GDR design show from a national event of political importance to a regional event of purely economic interest. Only one West German regional politician attended the opening event, the RfF did not even pay an official visit. The FRG design journal *Form* covered the exhibition only in an eight-line news item that stated matter-of-factly that 170 products from the GDR were on display in Stuttgart's design center between 26 May and 31 July 1988, providing broader historical as well as recent insights into GDR design development.[142]

Meanwhile, the AiF tried to make the best of the situation. The East German design journal *Form und Zweck* dedicated an entire page to the exhibition. Exaggerating the importance of the Stuttgart Design Center, it described the challenges of putting together the exposition in such a "lavish" environment. "We could not simply present products with 'Design in der DDR' because it was important to depict the way of living and culture, to convey knowledge about the country, its economic potential, and its people," the author explained.[143] In this regard, the GDR project emulated the West German show of 1984—the event aimed at creating a dialogue and deepening mutual understanding, while not shying away from "critical comparison."[144] But the result was quite different. Over the exhibit's long run, it had just 18,000 visitors. According to the *Form und Zweck* article, West German visitors perceived GDR design as high quality in its usefulness and as "aesthetically respectable without attempting to circumvent social responsibility with spectacular pieces."[145] Although not exactly a rave review, the design council staff seemed satisfied with having proven the GDR's prowess as an export nation.

Martin Kelm and Michael Blank, since 1987 the director of the newly established GDR Design Center in East Berlin, visited the RfF that summer. At this occasion, Blank talked about industrial design development in German socialism, mentioning the showcase specifically, with the editor of the RfF journal *Design Report*. In this conversation, he reached far back to Horst Michel's humble beginnings in Weimar during the occupation years to claim a long tradition and continuity in functionalist East German design aesthetics. To the learned observer, the claim just did not match the reality of the hard-fought battles against functionally unnecessary embellishments that socialist realism had bred throughout the 1950s. This was clearly an exercise in emphasizing common ground with the West German host for economic reasons. Blank admitted that some prototypes had been placed in the exhibition to provide stimulation for trade but simultaneously dismissed the notion that the showcase had been conceptualized as a trade fair with a marketing strategy.[146] "We deliberately changed the title [from *Design from the GDR* to *Design in the GDR*] to show how it works here, what we do and how," he assured the *Design Report* editor. When the conversation turned to future exchange projects with the mention of cooperation opportunities in Berlin, Blank quickly reined in the interviewer by invoking Berlin's contested status and reminded him that—from East Germany's perspective—the RfF represented West Germany, but not West Berlin. Cold War politics clearly remained a limiting element in exchanges between the RfF and the AiF until the last days of German division.

Later in 1988, the West German liaison to the GDR Permanent Mission in Bonn summarized the lessons learned from the German-German cultural exchange. Her memo stated that there had been many possibilities for cultural contacts and exchanges with persons and institutions in the GDR, especially since there was no language barrier and plenty of shared traditions. However, "Cooperation in the classical sense was very rare, because the GDR avoids 'the all-German' (*Gesamtdeutsches*)."[147] It was difficult for the GDR to uphold its policy of delineation after the agreed-upon cooperation in the Basic Treaty and the *Kulturabkommen*. From the western perspective relations with the East improved over time, whereas the GDR preferred cultural cooperation with countries of the Eastern Bloc precisely for reasons of demarcation. Nevertheless, the piecemeal effort to improve German-German relations via cultural cooperation paid off for both sides.

While Bonn aborted the Hallstein Doctrine as the international climate shifted from confrontation to détente, it capitalized on this moment to free itself from superpower politics by creating a sustainable German-German dialogue. Of course, the four-power agreements still decided the fate of Germany on a diplomatic level, but the German-German policy of rapprochement clearly improved and facilitated contacts between the East and West on an individual and organizational level. By pushing for nongovernmental relations between East and West Germans, especially in the realm of everyday culture, Bonn achieved its long-term goal of loosening the SED's grip on every aspect of East German social and cultural life. The shared cultural heritage, especially in the case of industrial design, brought each Germany closer to the quotidian reality on the other side of the border. What is more, the FRG thus gave the GDR the chance to "function as an actor on the world stage," despite its lack of autonomy from the Soviet Union.[148] The Bonn–East Berlin negotiations were part and parcel of the GDR's transition from pariah to internationally recognized state. In the process, the GDR successfully broke the West German *Alleinvertretungsanspruch*. Its claim to membership among modern nations, expressed in and communicated through its economic culture, received political legitimization at last.

CHAPTER 5

Conservative Modernity

The Reception of Functionalism in German Living Rooms

ABITATION (*WOHNEN*) IS A PART OF CULTURE," Hans Paul Barhdt expounded in his sociological analysis of the processes at work in the German postwar home. His 1961 book became a seminal sociological text on German urbanization and the tensions between public and private spaces.[1] "A space, an apartment, is comfortable if it provides a cozy-familiar frame to everyday functions, including work—yet not all kinds of work—in a way that these functions not only don't interfere with each other, but rather harmonize with each other. This harmony is a part of culture."[2] With his work Barhdt expanded the West German functionalist debate about domestic culture, aesthetics, and taste. Industrial designers and architects had previously limited functionalism to a specific aesthetic of "good design," which, religiously implemented, expressed support for politically legitimizing national brand narratives. Barhdt reinterpreted functionalism as practicality, the way in which the home and the things in it aligned with the needs of its inhabitants and their everyday routines. His definition included the actual practices involved in the consumption of space, both in terms of the acquisition of objects and their usage. This perspective subordinates material culture to human needs, a position similar to Adorno's call for an extended functionalism.[3]

The sociological approach to material possessions diverges from postwar German design discourse that had put form and political meaning above the necessities of everyday life. As such this point of view offers a different perspective on the complex history of functionalism in Germany and provides an opportunity to look at its implementation in German homes. It adds the social element that was lacking in West German design debates, an aspect that differed between the Federal Republic and the GDR, where it had remained part of the East German industrial design discourse from the states' foundation.

What remained unclear, however, was how, or whether at all, socialist and capitalist modes of habitation differed practically. This chapter seeks to understand how pervasive the German postwar discourse on functionalism was in German everyday life and what elements of the good design education successfully entered consumer practices.

By the 1970s both German states had arrived at functionalist aesthetics as a marker of modern living standards. This raises the question of whether the two German states also shared one vision of modernity. Heretofore, historians of the GDR and other Eastern Bloc countries have put forward the notion of "socialist modernity,"[4] arguing that the Eastern Bloc shared with capitalist modernity progressive forces such as secularization and industrialization, yet that socialism had "a special dynamism" in its scientific approach used to legitimize political action and a "cult of technology and a mania for remaking the world" in its vision for a socialist way of life.[5] This emphasis implies that GDR designers and politicians, producers, and consumers had inherently different ideas about industrial modernity than their western cousins.

While the notion of a socialist path to modernity is certainly useful, it has its limitations when discussing the two postwar German states. In fact, strong similarities existed between the economic cultures in East and West in the later decades of the Cold War, which leads to the conclusion that the earlier diverging concepts of modernity were fueled by the ideological fervor of the GDR's early days under Stalinist influence, traces of which persisted into the 1960s. In the long run, however, the German-German bond that endured despite and because of the eastern demarcation efforts, the reflexes that the ever-present alternative on the other side of the border triggered, led to reflective policymaking and institution building.[6] Approaching this topic from the vantage point of the welfare state, specifically housing policy, offers an exciting opportunity to move beyond discourse on postwar German design that had put form and political meaning above the necessities of everyday life. The existence of a German socialist state helped raise the profile of social policy during the Adenauer years and made progress in housing provision and economic security a foundational issue in debates about human dignity and citizenship in the early Federal Republic. Similarly, West Germany's social market economy and its conservative welfare state, centered on middle-class dreams of homeownership and the male bread-winner model, challenged the GDR leadership to move away from radical socialist ideas and to inch toward a model that Konrad Jarausch has labelled a "welfare dictatorship."[7]

As we have seen, East and West German economic cultures were not dramatically different in terms of expectations for living standards, both expressed in political debate and production culture. However, at the level of execution, the availability and the material quality of furniture and housing remained a challenge for the GDR's economic system throughout the Cold War, as thousands of complaint letters and comments in exhibition guestbooks show. The East German population expected more, especially after the Fifth Party Congress in 1958, when the GDR leadership pitted East German economic performance against the West German benchmark. At the same time, social stratification in West German capitalist society limited the opportunities for participation in progressive lifestyles for those in the low-income brackets.

These limitations, in turn, raise questions about the extent to which the officially promoted political, social, and cultural norms and values embodied in material culture and interior design were able to transcend the divide between public and private in the two German states. This chapter examines these questions through consumer education and consumption practices. The narrativity of material culture can explain consumer choices based on fashions, personal tastes, and projections of self-image. No matter if it is furnished sparsely modern, retro nostalgic, cozy romantic, or expensive luxurious, a home becomes part of a life story. Accordingly, consumers purchase the material representation of values with which they identify.[8] The act of consumption, then, symbolizes the population's acceptance or rejection of foundational values inscribed in the national brand and the economic culture. In this way, consumers became an integral part to the success or failure of official aesthetics in interior design in East and West Germany. But it is important to go beyond consumption statistics to evaluate the relative success of functionalist rhetoric. What did prescriptive visions of domestic modernity mean for the populations' everyday life? How successful were these interjections of public policy into private homes, and how did the individual mitigate them?

Despite the emphasis on modernization and progress on both sides of the border, what emerged in the practices of domestication and privatization, curiously, is a pan-German conservative modernity, a muted rationalism that intertwined progressive cultural policy with conservative social policy. The term conservative modernity warrants further explanation. It links to political conservatism, which revolves around ideas of nationhood that put family at the center of political life. These concerns form the basis for a commitment to safeguarding the limits of acceptable expression of national belonging.[9] Conservatives themselves have explained that their philosophy is not opposed to change, but is a cautious "break" to slow down change, to reform gradually and not to revolutionize.[10] Conservative modernism shares certain concerns and values with political conservatism and has been discussed as a phenomenon that emerged first in the early 20th century as a political reaction to cultural liberalization.[11] The term was also used in architecture discourse in the interwar years and resurfaced during the postwar reconstruction period. Recovering polemics from the 1930s, church architect and moderate modernist Rudolf Schwarz employed the term during the 1953 Bauhaus Debate in West Germany to express "his rejection of any kind of avant-garde."[12] After losing the argument to functionalists Hans Schwippert and Egon Eiermann, he repeatedly took a stance against "monocultures" of glass facades and cubic architecture. A similar conservative resistance to design monocultures was reflected in the consumer behavior of most East and West Germans. Partial integration and "incorrect" appropriation of those modern idioms that the two German states promoted at different points over forty years—be it functionalist modernism, socialist synthetic modernism based on functional product designs, or Adorno's extended functionalism—resulted in a conservative modernism. The intertwining of cultural and economic modernization with, in essence, conservative social policy was another aspect that contributed to an economic culture shared by populations on both sides of the border.

Leading by Example: The Visual Experience of *Wohnkultur*

Implementation of modernization in everyday life happened only gradually for a host of reasons. Social patterns of tradition, the inability of the state—despite growing welfare states—to enable everybody to participate in a modernity that sought a complete break with the past, the authoritative notion that there was only one right way to get to this modernity, and the connection of its fulfillment to competing ideas about national identity or brand narratives all presented hurdles. These parallel challenges came clearly to the fore in state-guided consumer education, political attempts at integrating the population into the nation's cultural-economic aspirations via moderate, rational, and "correct" consumption.[13]

Home ownership quickly became an important issue in bombed-out and refugee-crowded urban areas in the West and was encouraged by local administrations. Under the Adenauer governments, a conservative consensus viewed private property and state welfare as the basis of social security.[14] The exhibition catalog for one of the first postwar interior design exhibitions *How to Dwell?* in Stuttgart in 1949 acknowledged popular ambitions of home ownership: "A house for the family is the dream of many. Rightfully so! A people that cultivates domestic culture does not give up on itself."[15] However, for the time being, the catalog posited that Germans had to content themselves with smaller apartments and simpler, fitting furniture. "The occurring changes require completely different things. . . . The small apartment is not transitional, it is constant."[16] Indeed, the First Housing Law of 1950, describes West German humble beginnings with the so-called small apartment model of 32 to 65 square meters.[17] Between 1950 and 1952, 70 percent of all new-built housing was public housing funded by the state with subsidies or interest-free loans to alleviate the shortage of capital. Private investors received tax cuts and credits in exchange for accepting rent restrictions and an income-defined tenant community. This housing policy aimed at the social integration of a starkly stratified postwar West German society by providing affordable apartments for all, including millions of refugees and expellees.[18] While rental property development had clear priority during the early years with an estimated housing deficit of 4.5 million apartments, private home ownership received equal state support.[19] Meanwhile, the right to housing was not inscribed in the West German constitution, and home ownership remained a distant dream for many.

The GDR faced similarly challenging circumstances. Initial experiments in communal housing and shared spaces faltered in the face of what East German authors also depicted as a "natural" longing for a private apartment and family life without subletters and an army of children.[20] In 1952, the prestige construction project Stalinallee in Berlin promised East Germans family flats with lush amenities, including elevators, modern built-in cupboards, and separate bathrooms. Although about 70 percent of the materials for the first stage of the project had been salvaged from the debris of bombed houses, the lavish architectural style proved too expensive to become the standard blueprint for GDR public housing.

The hardships of the postwar housing situation engendered popular nostalgia for a comfortable past. In an effort to make their new apartments feel like home, many West Germans acquired furnishings that reminded them of better times, much to the disdain of the network of industrial designers, producers, and politicians who had invested in the national aesthetic. Consumer choices, guided by sentimentality rather than the actual limitations of the postwar situation, only confirmed the Werkbund's conviction that public consumption ought to be guided. The liberalization of choice in the climate of incipient economic recovery only exacerbated the problem, which the Federal Republic shared with its European neighbors.[21] The RfF design council promptly nominated itself to supervise this liberalization of choice. During the parliamentary hearings about the council's rationale in 1952, the Werkbund laid out the elitist philosophy for the RfF: "The audience has neither good nor bad taste. Its taste always refers to that of the powerful, who shape the *Zeitgeist*, the meaning of life, and mankind's ambitions and illusions."[22] Such a top-down approach not only ran contrary to West Germany's sociopolitical goals of democratization and liberalization in all areas of cultural, economic, and public life, but it also intentionally capitalized on the principle of pecuniary emulation, canons of taste in modern stratified society, and status consumption.[23]

Similarly, but with a different ideological impetus, Horst Michel and the Weimar Institute organized several kitsch exhibitions to educate the broader public through comparison with well and badly designed products.[24] Michel's understanding of good design was expressed in the same design maxims as the Werkbund: durable and honest materials, the avoidance of modishness, and pretension of value appreciation via "unauthentic" or embellished surfaces. When the regime eventually made a step toward a comprehensive housing policy in the 1960s, people brought their old furniture into new modern housing, which frustrated reformers.

In the 1960s, the Soviet Union had solved a comparable situation with the so-called everyday (*byt*) campaigns. The eradication of petit-bourgeois furniture as "vestiges of the capitalist past hindering the development of late socialism" became one of the central aims of Khrushchev's rationalizing reforms. *Byt* reformers distributed household advice manuals which encouraged behaviors that would conform with socialist ontology through taste education. Stalinist excess could be adequately contained through this disciplining regime of taste. Manuals provided do-it-yourself advice about how to alter the vestiges of petit-bourgeois living to conform to the reformist principles of the leveled domestic landscape. Chopping off the backs of divans and lowering bed frames or disposing completely of such bourgeois furniture were among the recommended measures to guarantee the "horizontality" of the home.[25]

There is no evidence of such campaign measures in the interior design advice literature of the GDR. A possible reason might have been the extreme pressure on the SED to uphold the image of a flourishing economy that could provide for its population, so it instead addressed the problem of outdated interior design choices with the 1964 reform of the furniture industry. But producing modern furniture did not mean that consumers would buy it. Actively shaping consumer taste and influencing decision-making remained the only means to improve future consumption.

It is noteworthy that both Germanys denied that the general public had good taste and therefore elevated design professionals to arbiters of beauty. This elitist worldview and the activities that derived from it expressed what can be called "taste paternalism," a term that encapsulates the missionary zeal with which reformers took up their self-assigned task of enlightening the population about aesthetic principles. "Show and tell" became a popular method to generate public understanding of their respective modern domestic cultures in the two German states. The Werkbund and the ZfF, each in cooperation with regional administration and industry, put together a range of activities that brought their message to the people. They targeted all age groups to ensure the education of present and future consumers to buy the "right" products that supported the construction of socialist and capitalist society. Hands-on taste education, a form of consumer education that relies on clear distinctions between good and bad design, became the logical next step in both Germanys.

In 1954, the Werkbund initiated a program of material culture education in West Berlin's secondary schools that eventually spread to other federal states.[26] To provide teachers with materials for demonstration, the Berliners invented so-called Werkbund boxes (*Werkbundkisten*), which they filled with exemplary objects for the students to see, touch, and utilize. The objects were arranged in the boxes according to their material, function, utility, technology, shape, and color. Each box had a different thematic focus—"the work space," "kitchen appliances," and "the set table." Often, they contained designs of Werkbund members Heinrich Löffelhardt and Wilhelm Wagenfeld, and those of firms close to the association, such as Zwiesel glass, Arzberg china, and Carl Pott cutlery.[27] Some of the boxes, like the ones that focused on table settings, encouraged students to utilize them in simulations of family meals, reproducing conservative social norms of family and domesticity.[28] Growing incomes and more leisure time, the result of the economic miracle, made youth vulnerable to the seduction of the developing consumer society, the Werkbund feared. The objective of this program was to sensitize teenagers to the design of everyday objects and to enhance their critical abilities vis-à-vis the world of consumer products.[29]

After the social critique of functionalism by the 1968 movements, the *Werkbundkisten* initiative began to lose momentum in the early 1970s. One federal state after another ended the program amid the general climate of antiauthoritarianism and youth protest. A final report of the Werkbund in Lower Saxony stated in 1970 that the program had become counterproductive: "The youth's skepticism toward things that they perceive as representations of the establishment lead to a loss of their binding character or even to an urge to fight them."[30]

In the GDR students' education about the material environment had a completely different point of departure. After the secondary school reforms of 1958, the curriculum required polytechnical education and industrial apprentice-ships.[31] The underlying objectives of this program were similar to the *Bitterfelder Weg* in acquainting school students with the means of production in connection with the cultural value of objects.[32] A byproduct of polytechnical training in schools was a preparation for adult life in the GDR economy of scarcity, where do-it-yourself became an important and clandestinely state-supported strategy to fill the gaps of supply shortages.[33] It also aimed at introducing university-bound students to the everyday experiences of workers, familiarizing them with the social foundations of the German socialist state. In the West, professional in-ternships became increasingly common in later decades, but here the goal lay in helping young people choose their future vocations.

To educate the adult population that possessed actual buying power, both Germanys developed an interior design counseling system.[34] In West Germany, the elevation of living standards developed alongside public housing policy. So-called *Wohnberatungen* sprang up around the Federal Republic. The first *Wohnberatung* set to work Mannheim in 1953.[35] The "Second Housing and Family Home Law," which abolished some of the conditions for generous state-supported mortgage systems and tax cuts in 1956, shifted focus from rent-ing to private home ownership.[36] The effect of this housing policy liberalization was further social stratification that disadvantaged lower income groups; in fact, by 1960 working-class families were disproportionally represented in emergency accommodations.[37] The newly introduced term "family home" encapsulates the conservative foundation on which West German society and its growing welfare state would continue to evolve, an anti-collectivism centered on private property. Home ownership never reached the same level as in other European countries: by the 1990s West Germany's 43.1 percent looked unimpressive when compared to 81 percent in Ireland, 78 percent in Spain, and 68 percent in Great Britain. Nevertheless, with 2.3 millions new-built homes and 600,000 rental properties converted to private ownership by 1994, the Federal Republic's policy has been noted as a success because it expanded the circle of home owners to lower in-come groups.[38]

By 1972, sixteen *Wohnberatungsstellen*, a number of them Werkbund-affiliated, received subsidies from the Ministry for Housing and municipalities across the republic.[39] The federal government expected interior design counseling that connected furnishing to the conservative consensus around private homeown-ership and technocratic ideas about social progress. The West German *Wohn-beratungen* tied this message to restrictive taste regimes in domestic culture by impressing the functional aesthetic of "good design" on the population.[40]

Clients received advice from interior decorators who used samples ranging from wallpaper over furniture to tea sets to help them find space-saving solutions for their home. Some of the *Wohnberatungen* even presented life-sized idealized apartment settings. This involvement in all areas of the material environment epitomizes the Werkbund's paternalistic claim that through taste and consumer education they could regulate the way in which the population furnished its homes.[41] In the end, the interior design counseling did not remain untouched by the changes brought about by the protest movements of the late 1960s. It gradually had to move away from "the taste of an elite of sensitive esthetes" but nonetheless remained linked to their political and economic interests.[42]

Wohnberatung was also a byproduct of socialist economic reforms, standardization, and concentration in the GDR. It was a way to achieve greater transparency in the retail sector and thus facilitate better planning. With a change of economic orientation from heavy industry toward consumer good production under Ulbricht's NES, furniture retail morphed from barely meeting the most basic needs of the population to a more service-oriented industry. For example, the *Wohnberatung* in Karl-Marx-Stadt, Ulbricht's model socialist industrial city, joined the regional retail organization in 1964.[43] Just like their western counterparts, interior decorators advised customers with the help of samples, product catalogs, and mini-exhibitions that promoted ideologically correct furniture and advertised new synthetic ersatz materials, such as Melafol. Within the constraints of the planned economy, the mission of the *Wohnberatung* was to create domestic environments that enabled and supported new experiences as well as ignited the population's joie de vivre.[44] Nevertheless, the personal comfort of the home came second to overall economic goals. *Wohnberatung* belonged to an entire institutionalized system that "'trained' consumers to 'want' what the government decided that they 'needed.'"[45]

Despite, or even because of, the failure of design councils and intellectuals to develop a terminology that could give East and West German domestic culture a profound sociocultural meaning, the market for interior design publications boomed by the mid-1960s. This medium communicated trends, new ideas, and tastes through images, allowing citizens to see how one should live in modern postwar Germany. In a survey conducted in 1962 and 1963 in Cologne and its suburbs, sociologist Alphons Silbermann found that among the design interested Cologne inhabitants with basic schooling, 39 percent read articles on furnishings and living spaces. Among those with a secondary education (*Gymnasium*), this number increased to 69 percent.[46] Readers usually referred to special interior design magazines, the daily press, or lifestyle magazines for information on interior design.[47] Consequently, the media catered to a broad audience ranging from experts to the general interest readers. The West German design magazine *Form* moved gradually toward a specialized and professional audience. Along with this specialized audience came increasingly specialized debates, such as the critique of functionalism in the late 1960s. Earlier, such debates had taken place exclusively in the Werkbund newspaper *Werk und Zeit (Work and Time)*, mostly read by its own membership. *Form*, however, was available at newsstands across the country and even in the GDR, where design professionals used it to stay informed about the developments in the West.[48] In contrast, the East German design council's specialized industrial design journal *Form und Zweck* became a forum for institute employees and design professionals to show the connection between politics, ideology, and industrial design but did not provide advice on how Germans should furnish their homes.[49] The debates remained largely scientific and ideological, without any real application to everyday living conditions and practices.

Interior design magazines, alternately, developed a broad popular appeal. Since 1957, the East German magazine *Kultur im Heim* reported on the domestication of socialism and its effect on the New Man. It has been described as part of the effort to implement "a rational 'sensible' modernity in domestic culture."[50] The editors put great emphasis on images for presenting new designs, and the photographs usually showed arranged room settings, though most of them taken from company or fair displays. The logic behind orchestrated displays, rather than depicting single pieces of furniture, was to elicit emotional reactions from readers.[51] Such settings demonstrated a cohesive socialist domestic culture in contexts that the population could easily transfer to their homes.[52]

The practice of arranging settings also profoundly shaped an entire generation of interior designers in the Federal Republic who knew how to find the best light, fashionable color combinations, and cutting-edge designs. One of them, Rolf Heide, oversaw an advice section that responded to reader questions in *Brigitte*, Germany's most successful women's magazine. His designs offered solutions to real world problems, such as how to combine antique with new furniture or cheap furniture with collector's items. This column's success inspired the Hamburg publishing house Gruner and Jahr to publish *Schöner Wohnen (Better Dwelling)* in 1960, the first and most successful magazine to exclusively focus on the domestic environment.[53] Like *Kultur im Heim*, *Schöner Wohnen* used idealized settings to influence German tastes. After its successful first issue in 1960, its readership quickly grew to two million.[54] With pictures of the newest trends in furniture design, color palettes, and room arrangements, *Schöner Wohnen*

FIGURE 5.1. Cover of the East German interior design
journal *Kultur im Heim* 3/1966 showing the furniture
suite "Leipzig 3" produced by VEB Möbelindustrie
Gera. Image courtesy of Stiftung Haus der Geschichte der
Bundesrepublik Deutschland. Photographer unknown.

brought interior design to the masses in an effort to promote aesthetically cohesive living environments. Studio photographs filled the pages of the magazine,
an art form in and of itself, as the founding editor-in-chief Josef Kremerkothen
noted: "Small rooms needn't look cramped, improvisation needn't seem primi-
tive—they had to appear lively . . . , light had to create atmosphere . . . , colors had
to be finely matched with materials."[55] Heide eventually joined *Schöner Wohnen*
where he created idealized room arrangements and continued to exert tremendous influence over shaping the population's interior design taste.

FIGURE 5.2. Cover of the West German interior
design journal *Schöner Wohnen* 4/1968.
Image courtesy of Stiftung Haus der Geschichte
der Bundesrepublik Deutschland.
Photograph: Richard Stradtmann.

By the late 1970s, *Kultur im Heim* had abandoned studio pictures of ideal
room arrangements in favor of actual apartments. This development has been
associated with the loosening of the party's hold on every facet of public and private life.[56] Closer examination of the magazine reveals, however, that this change
in imagery also occurred alongside the stagnation of GDR furniture innovation
during this decade. Showing the same furniture in the domestic context of different subcultures and lifestyles glossed over the unavailability of new designs
and created an illusion of consumer choices. By shifting focus to the makeshift
solutions of their readers' neighbors, editors avoided showy, yet unavailable,
prototypes under Honecker's failing consumer socialism. In this way, *Kultur
im Heim* circumvented the kind of public disgruntlement that earlier interior
design showcases had caused.

Designers, politicians, and retailers hoped that consumers would internalize these images and make consumer choices in support of the aspired national modern brand. By visualizing the spatial context of furniture in arranged displays and on blueprints of family homes at *Wohnberatungen*, the Werkbund and the ZfF brought their vision to the people. This paternalistic attitude toward consumer taste continued interwar-era concerns about German material and economic culture: aesthetic education and the struggle against kitsch in everyday life.

The Multifunctional Living Room

Despite the emphasis on rational technological progress that accompanied economic and social modernization, privacy and emotions had replaced the public "aesthetics of power" of the Nazi period in postwar Germany.[57] Yet the curious combination of the success of modern Bauhaus rationalism with the conservative social climate of the reconstruction decade in the West and the artistic dictat of socialist realism in the East had sidelined emotional needs.[58] Change eventually occurred when the 1970s saw a general shift toward individualization based on postmaterial values in the West and an official acknowledgment of the right to privacy in the East.[59] These developments inserted powerful notions for more freedom of individual expression and emotionality into the discussion. To understand the forces at play requires exploring how Germans navigated the struggle between rigid public taste regimes and desired private coziness, a tension that was nowhere more at play than in the living room.

The extent of urban destruction that wartime bombings had caused made the representational function of the living room in bourgeois homes—a *Gesamtkunstwerk* of strategically placed representative furniture and decorations—seem like a relic of a bygone era. Nevertheless, as a symbolic system of interior design the living room continued to figure largely in debates on lifestyles as codifications of class distinctions, habitus, and socioeconomic aspirations.[60] However, the sociological model of distinctive consumption driven by social aspiration, observable in the late nineteenth and early twentieth centuries, lost its explanatory power as the three-class system was replaced by a growing number of postmodern lifestyle milieus.[61] Moreover, during the housing scarcity of the immediate postwar years, Germans in East and West and from all social backgrounds lived in crowded conditions. As a result, the little space available had to serve multiple functions: as space for receiving guests, eating, sleeping, storing belongings, and working. The postwar German living room therefore became a less formal space. Furniture designers responded, and the two decades immediately following the Second World War saw the most interesting developments in modular system furniture not only in Central Europe but also in the United States and among neutral European powers such as Switzerland and Sweden.[62]

With the economic boom of the 1950s and early 1960s, the West German population experienced a collective increase in living standards, which enabled workers to afford household goods and technical equipment previously only affordable for the educated and upper-middle class.[63] In the GDR, the population worked hard during reconstruction with a view to reaping the promised fruits of their labor in the planned economy, even though this consumer good abundance failed to materialize. Still, they benefitted from the increasing political attention to the pressing needs for more modern housing over the course of the 1960s and 1970s.

One commonality that survived the forty years of partition on either side of the border was the multifunctionality of rooms, originating from necessity during the immediate postwar period and continuing into the years of greater prosperity. This was not an entirely new concept though. Urban working-class housing prior to this period had seldom offered the space for a room that was purely representational. Family life of urban workers had long taken place in the enlarged kitchen. It combined the sociability of a living room or parlor with workroom features, kitchen functions, and sleeping amenities. Typically, furniture was light and easily moveable, as industry workers were "nomads," always on the move to the next place of employment, unlike bourgeois families. Over the course of a century, however, the reality of the working population had changed, especially under the welfare regimes in the GDR, with the inherent right to work and the constitutional right to housing.[64] Social distinctions, naturally more finely nuanced than in the three-class system, were lived out in the private sphere of the home, even under the utopian auspices of a classless socialist society.[65]

Nevertheless, GDR citizens' exploration of the functionality of their living rooms was spatially confined by the highly standardized architecture in the Eastern Bloc. The country used specific crane models and prefabricated construction techniques that both originated in the Soviet Union. The Russian apartment model of the 1950s offered families with two children on average 35–40 square meters with an economical floor plan that predetermined the function of each room.[66] In 1962, the GDR presented its own concept for modern socialist living in the "P2," which became the most common apartment, built until 1990. It consisted of a small, open kitchen that connected to the living room and dining area, thus including the housewife in family activities. This layout departed from traditional worker housing by making the living room the center of family life, reflecting "the idea of the home as primarily a respite of leisure and relaxation."[67] The important point here is not only that with P2 workers' housing had a room for leisure and sociability but that it emphasized family as the central unit in socialism. In this, the architectural design anticipated a profound change in GDR social policy. Three years later in 1965, the SED passed a new Family Law that pronounced the family the "basic cell of society," an effort to combat one of the highest divorce rates worldwide.[68]

By the mid-1960s, planners prioritized the construction of prefabricated buildings with standardized apartments, while inner-city areas with older building structures, for instance in Dresden, Leipzig, and Berlin, fell into disrepair. As such, the historic worker apartments lost appeal due to their outdated sanitary facilities and utilities, such as communal toilets on the landing and coal ovens. When offered an apartment in one of the new, if less aesthetically pleasing, buildings, most families opted for the modern amenities of P2 and, later, the WBS 70 apartments. Housing remained a problematic policy area until Honecker introduced his Unity of Economic and Social Policy program at the Eighth Party Congress in 1971, followed by a promise to solve the housing question in the GDR once and for all. The following year he announced the Housing Construction Program, the largest capital investment program in the country's history: building increased by 78 percent over the course of the decade. By the end of the 1970s, more than one million of these one- to three-bedroom apartments were built, and over all 2.1 million dwellings had been either newly constructed or renovated by 1990.[69]

Such highly standardized architecture reignited concerns about the danger of potential moral degeneration through uniformity in the socialist material environment. Similar to the debates economic planners and industrial designers had in the 1950s and 1960s over the streamlining of furniture production, the concern was that uniformity in construction contributed to a loss in cultural value of GDR living standards. In 1969, attempts to create diversity within the confines of standardized construction techniques through long-term planning, such as the GDR Bauakademie building project "Mutable Living" (*Variables Wohnen*), ended in failure. It became a sobering litmus test for the degree of individuality and flexibility that socialist architecture and the interior design industries could tolerate.[70] The architectural idea was simple: the outer walls would define the apartment while the open interior floor plan could be custom-designed by the tenant. A utilities pipe constituted the only fixture and suggested a logical placement of the bathroom and the kitchen in its vicinity.

FIGURE 5.3. A design collective at the Institute for Industrial Design Halle—Burg
Giebichenstein designed a furniture system that replaced brick-and-mortar walls
in the East German architectural experiment "Variables Wohnen."
SLUB/Deutsche Fotothek, Friedrich Weimer, 1973.

Otherwise, the apartment concept remained open and could be designed according to the number and the needs of the inhabitants. This approach differed
from previous apartment designs, as built-in furniture in the P2 apartments,
such as heating convectors hidden in partitions that did double-duty as desks,
presented limitations and prescribed usage.

In *Variables Wohnen*, storage furniture elements, instead of traditional walls,
divided the space into rooms, offering a high degree of individuality in ascribing
the function of the rooms. The Bauakademie tested this concept in Berlin and
Rostock with twenty-four and eighty apartment units respectively. Furniture
combines were involved in interior design counseling as well as the delivery and
installation of furniture. To gain a better understanding of the array of demands
and needs across the population, the Bauakademie chose tenants from all walks
of life, from cleaning lady to medical doctor and from metalworker to studied

engineer.[71] Its overarching goal was to find patterns for ideal solutions that would serve different age groups, professions, and family structures. However, after five years the organizers realized that, when tenants were given the freedom to fulfill their every housing wish, no apartment would look like the next one. The Bauakademie concluded that "the multitude of functional design solutions stood in stark contrast to the quest for an ideal solution."[72] No such thing as one "socialist way of living" existed; a long-term planning concept, a one-fits-all solution, could not derive from this individual-functional approach to modern housing. The open floor plan posed an insurmountable challenge for East German industry and its five-year planning intervals.[73] What the experiment proved in the end was the point that East German citizens had their own ideas about functionality, which did not necessarily overlap with those of designers, urban planners, and politicians. *Variables Wohnen* was just one of many ideas that the Bauakademie, the ZfF, and furniture companies across the GDR put forward in finding sensible solutions to individualize standardized housing. As the 1970s progressed, the ailing economy allowed for very few of these ideas to be realized.[74]

In the early 1980s, official design discourse in the GDR eventually embraced the idea of the working-class living room, at a time when it had already commonly become the largest room in modern apartments. *Kultur im Heim* posed the ideologically loaded question: "Living or representation room?"[75] The article carefully pointed out that in a nonbourgeois context the living room served multiple functions, such as socializing, eating, playing, and napping, which had once been limited to other rooms. The author saw this socialist development as inherently different from the fragmentation that sociologists had found in Western capitalist societies. There, the article claimed, individualization had led to the compartmentalization of the floor plan, each room serving the desires of one family member. This allegedly eradicated the larger room for communal activities and family time. As a result, conspicuous consumption habits had evolved and nonfunctional furniture, such as the lowered coffee table impractical for family meals, had increasingly entered Western apartments. Accordingly, the article concluded, the "capitalist living room" had exclusively representational properties—nobody lived in it anymore. However, the article completely disregarded the fact that the multifunctional living room was a modern twentieth-century development and that, historically speaking, nobody had "lived" in it much before the war either. Meanwhile, the author saw the socialist living room as a true *living* room (lit.: *Lebensraum*). In this room, communal activities trumped materialism and therefore, almost by definition, the furniture had to be functional. Not in a stylistic sense, but in a pragmatic way: furniture needed to provide storage, work space for adults and children, play areas, and a table for family meals as well as for entertaining guests.[76]

The claim that the eastern living room served no representational function seems to have enjoyed broad acceptance. A multiple response survey conducted in prefab building areas in East German middle-sized and large towns found that none of the study's respondents used the living room for representational purposes. Asked about their regular activities in the living room, 94 percent responded that they used it for reading and writing, 62 percent for crafts and sewing, 53 percent for keeping and nurturing plants and pets, 42 percent for playing instruments and games, and 23 percent for activities connected to collections, such as stamps or glasses.[77] It is noteworthy that entertaining is not listed among the activities, and contemporaries attested that "the GDR is not a leisure-time society and never will be."[78] In recent years, research on state-controlled cultural events and television viewing habits has shown that, on the contrary, East Germans enjoyed both leisure and company in the home, away from forced participation in cultural consumption, campaigns, and mass-organization activities.[79] Evidence of a thriving private party culture supports the conclusion that East Germans hosted guests in their living room as well.[80]

Because of these largely standardized living room functions, a standard in furnishings emerged: a large closet, a couch and easy chairs, and a dinner table plus chairs could be found in the majority of the living rooms.[81] Serially produced storage furniture with functional elements, such as the glass cabinets, mini bars, and desks included in the popular MDW program from Dresden-Hellerau, featured prominently in magazine photographs.[82] By 1981, the study "Wohnen '81" found, 90 percent of living rooms in all prefab buildings contained such a multifunctional *Schrankwand*.[83] This postwar invention epitomized the sociological phenomenon of desired or forced mobility in the age of technology and combined it with the profitability of large-series production in the increasingly mechanized furniture industry.[84] Ninety-six percent of respondents to the "Wohnen '81" study in new workers housing described their dream living room as comfortable and cozy, that is, emotionally fulfilling.[85] Yet when asked to describe the actual living room furniture they owned, respondents listed "practical and purposeful" (39 percent), "factual and neutral" (30 percent), and "timelessly dignified" (12 percent)—a clear break with their declared preferences and emotional needs.[86]

This discrepancy between desire and reality warrants explanation, as it could not solely have been the result of the limited furniture availability. Although

purchases of specific styles could be difficult or take several years due to poor
planning and the organization of consumer good production by district, the
GDR furniture industry produced a range of styles in the 1980s. This ranged
from Biedermeier and Chippendale-inspired furniture at the Zeulenroda
combine, to the postmodern pieces of the Berlin furniture combine. Evolving
pro-family policy in the GDR had made the money available for the consumer
desires that the "Wohnen '81" study implies. Following the 1965 Family Law,
which had aimed at containing the effects of the comparatively liberal divorce
laws, the SED encouraged the founding of new families with so-called marriage
loans (*Ehekredite*). From 1972 onward, interest-free loans of 5,000 Ostmark supported young couples under the age of twenty-seven (increased to 7,000 Ostmark for couples under thirty-one in 1986) in their start to married life. These
loans could be partially "paid back" by having children.[87] Moreover, young married couples and families were statistically over-represented in the new housing
development of Marzahn in East Berlin, for instance, showing that the authorities treated these groups preferentially when allocating the new, modern apartments.[88] With such measures, the state aligned conservative family policy and
progressive housing policy and put young families in a position to participate in
East German consumer culture. Therefore, in combination with a well-devel-
oped do-it-yourself culture, a large part of the population would have had the
means to realize their design preferences to a certain extent.

One possible explanation for the aforementioned discrepancy could be that
the discourse on socialist functionalism had been effective among the GDR population. East German neofunctionalist designers and planners understood functional to mean practical furniture that served the needs of the population. They
considered decorative elements as unnecessary for the function of the piece, as
expensive to produce, and as obstructive to their goal of standardized, more efficient production. They thus dedicated the majority of the furniture production
capacities to serial shelf systems and multifunctional pieces, such as the *MuFuTi*,
a multifunctional table that could be used as a desk or a family dinner table;
it could be extended when hosting guests or lowered to serve the function of
a coffee table. Taken at face value, the broad acceptance of the Schrankwand
in 90 percent of prefabricated building households seems to demonstrate the
pervasiveness of the functionality discourse in the context of standardized
apartments.

A second possible explanation could be that, in the process of self-evalua-
tion, respondents simply reinterpreted their impractical furniture solutions as
practical and, thus, functional. Germans always liked to experience their home

emotionally, not functionally, as renowned architecture critic and journalist Manfred Sack asserts: "Dwelling incites feelings. If an apartment is impractical, one will notice, but get used to it and begin to think that it is practical."[89] Such a cognitive shift can be illustrated with further examination of the Schrankwand and its contents. Its material structure, underpinned by systemic thinking, leads consumers to three main behavioral patterns: orderliness, presentation, and representation.[90] The differentiation between presentation and representation is significant here, as the former is about self-recognition and the latter about impressing visitors. The difference reveals thus how East German consumers thought about personalizing and appropriating the dominant piece of furniture in the living room—or more precisely the ways they had learned how to talk about it.

Displayed objects, collections, or little knick-knacks without immediate everyday function are usually assumed to have a representational purpose as means to impress. In a research study, 100 percent of Schrankwand owners in the GDR reported that they indeed used theirs for storage of porcelain and cut glass. Usually, these collections were put on display in the glass cabinets, like museum objects in vitrines. However, interviewees claimed that such items were put there because the owners liked them, not because they were believed to reflect favorably on the owner's taste or to impress visitors.[91] This response shows a degree of success for the East German official discourse on the working-class living room, in so far as the population accepted that it was by definition not a representational space. Further items, such as photos and personal documents (98 percent), books (91 percent), TV sets and radios (80 percent), hobby materials and collections (65 percent), records and record players (55 percent), and alcoholic beverages (49 percent) also underscore the role of the Schrankwand in leisure time activities and as a personal archive. The storage of tablecloths (72 percent) as well as sheets and towels (43 percent) obviously fall under orderliness.[92] The Schrankwand in its storage capacity thus embodied first and foremost pragmatism, yet it was filled with hobby materials that contributed to personal well-being and expressed the personality of the owner, and finally kept safe personal items such as collections or photographs. This appropriation strategy combined the useful with the emotional.

Taste Appropriation and Obstinacy in the 1980s Living Room

Further insights into the motivations behind furniture consumption are offered by three empirical studies conducted in East and West Germany in the 1980s. All of them share an interest in the object-person relationship but relate their findings to the broader economic culture by investigating the values and norms that informed these relationships. They were conducted in the final decade of Germany's division, thus documenting developments in housing and interior design after thirty years under the socialist and capitalist economic systems and before reunification changed the societal context in the East. Thirty years, or one generation, not only reveals long-term change but also the success of the national brand narrative and the prescriptive design discourse in real German homes.

In the mid-1980s, an East German study supported by the AiF looked behind apartment doors in the GDR. Two cultural studies researchers, Herbert Letsch and Karla Scharf, used autobiographical interviews, photographic documentation, and theoretical analysis of the collected materials to trace the participants' demands on their home environments. The study aimed to contribute to economic planning with a production-oriented aesthetic strategy for domestic everyday design.[93] The project naturally had an ideological angle, operating with a theoretical concept that assumed that aesthetics embody the sensual experience of socialism. It concluded that the way in which the population conceived of domestic aesthetics was always a combination of everyday practical demands and an aesthetic appreciation of cultural and artistic objects. On top of that was the "desire for self-recognition" in the things and spaces in the home.[94]

For the study, Letsch and Scharf interviewed six couples between twenty-five and forty years of age from working-class family backgrounds. Most of them had been trained in industrial jobs, though some of them had gone on to secondary education. Their ages indicate that all of the couples had spent their entire lives in the Soviet occupation zone and the GDR and had been socialized in socialism through membership in political mass organizations and educated in the East German school system. The interview questions included some that addressed furnishing choices and the stories behind individual furniture pieces as well as the respondents' ideas about "the aesthetic" and "the beautiful."[95]

Take, for example, Frank and Marina R., born in 1957 and 1959, respectively. They were employed in working-class professions—he trained as a road construction worker and she worked as a cook. When Letsch and Scharf interviewed them for the first time in 1985, they lived with their two daughters in turn-of-the-century workers' housing near the city center of Dresden. A year later, the family moved to a modern housing development at the outskirts of town, taking the living room furniture with them. The light brown Schrankwand with teak wood finishing, the first major furniture acquisition the couple had made together, they explained, had been chosen not because of any aesthetic objective, but because of the storage space it offered. It was too modern looking for the couple, who preferred ornamentation and dark wood, and underlay purely practical considerations.[96] In the absence of a bedroom closet, Family R. kept bedding, their own clothes, and their children's clothes in it. It also offered a display cabinet for knickknacks and their glass collection, including heavy beer glasses. Mrs. R. explained that these objects add "warmth" to the room. After the move into the modern apartment, they switched the display to their newer collection of cut crystal glasses, because they had changed their taste to more elegant objects.[97] They also moved over their upholstery furniture ensemble, which provided ample seating for guests and neighbors stopping by.

Frank R. was a do-it-yourself home improver, who produced intricate works, such as lanterns and small furniture, for the living room and other rooms. As these items had no commercial value, they were not representational pieces per se, but they illustrate the personality and technical skill of the owner. In the context of an economy where not everything one wanted or needed was available, these were invaluable skills. Materials, equally scarce, could be procured through official and unofficial channels. In 1984 alone, 778,000 Ostmark worth of construction materials, it has been estimated, had been pilfered from industrial workshops and construction sites.[98]

Handmade items were visible in the other respondents' apartments as well. Günter Z. shared Frank R.'s love for wood, and he even lined his entire apartment with wooden panels.[99] This idea came about when he wanted to reintroduce his conservative taste into the prefab apartment. In their previous home in an old building, Günter Z., a car-body constructor turned acrobat, had invested in Chippendale furniture. Although he still liked the furniture, he could not arrange these pieces in a pleasing way in the new space. Even a handmade, complementary room divider could not fit aesthetically, "and so we decided to buy a Schrankwand."[100] His story allows insights into how dominant modern housing architecture was in interior design decisions and goes some way to explaining why the great majority of people living in the new prefab construction apartments eventually turned to functionalist storage furniture to solve their decorating problems. Despite their differences in education, status, taste, and exposure to culture, all of the respondents owned a Schrankwand, and discussed in the interviews the purchasing decision and the functionality of this piece.[101] The conservative wood paneling, on the other hand, illustrates how do-it-yourself not only presented a means to make things that were otherwise unavailable but was also a strategy to undermine the overwhelming modern logic of the prefab architecture. Above Günter Z.'s couch hung samurai swords, a nunchaku, and a samurai symbol, which, he explained, showed his interest in

FIGURE 5.4. The *Schrankwand* with collectables in Frank R.'s living room in a prefab
building in Dresden Gorbitz. Photograph: Christine Starke DGPH, 1989.

Asian culture and admiration for Far Eastern martial arts. He watched samurai
films and read books and also practiced karate himself. The earnestness with
which he described this fascination with Japan stands in complete contrast to
the backdrop of the traditional dark wood paneling and the floral fabric of the
couch. Collecting and displaying objects without use value allowed residents to
recognize themselves in the space and made it feel homey.[102]

The preference for traditional idioms, such as dark woods and handcrafted
furniture, was apparent in most of the apartments in this study. In his leisure
time, lathe operator Achim Sch. customized such objects as picture frames and
semi-antiques, and treated them to look old.[103] He and his wife described these
accessories as "romantic," indicating that some of the do-it-yourself projects catered to the emotional needs of the inhabitants to create coziness and "atmosphere" in their modern housing. Other smaller objects on display, such as a
Chinese tea set, heavy wine glasses, and a silver-plated candelabra, completed
the interior design. About the latter Renate Sch. remarked: "We like old things,
because they have a visual effect and represent a value."[104] Inherited and barely

FIGURE 5.5. Asian influences in Günter Z.'s living room in a prefab building in Dresden Gorbitz. Photograph: Christine Starke DGPH, 1989.

used objects such as the china tea set and the candelabra represented both status and family history, indicating that despite the utopia of a classless society, social differentiation still existed in the GDR.

In contrast, the more educated respondents in the study liked light colors and preferred simpler lines. Engineer Hubertus R. and his wife Martina, who had left her university course after the couple had welcomed their first child, fully committed to functional furniture in their apartment. They spent their interest-free marriage loan on a Schrankwand and later added additional storage pieces in the hallway and the children's room.[105] Their furnishing strategy rendered the home significantly less cluttered than those of the other families. Similarly, the divorced Günter N., who worked in the youth organization Free German Youth as secretary for culture and, after his studies at the SED party school, eventually ran a cultural club for adolescents, came into contact with functionalist aesthetics through his political work. More and more, his job bled into Günter N.'s leisure time activities. He learned to play the guitar, painted, and even turned his living room into a pottery studio, where he created modern-looking vessels and vases.[106] "Flowery pottery," overuse of color, and other decorations bothered him. His austere crafts aesthetic had transferred over to his minimalist furnishing, for example, with a shelving and storage unit that was barely large enough to accommodate the television set. In both cases, jobs and aesthetic education influenced the comfort level of the respondents with functional styles. Hubertus R. and Günter N. worked in fields where cultural and functional aspects of design carried great importance, and this affected their everyday practices. These patterns indicate that the likelihood of accepting functionalism was as much knowledge-driven in eastern socialist society as in western society.

The Schrankwand was ubiquitous in the Federal Republic in the 1980s as well. Despite the populations' differences in education and socioeconomic status, across strata they used the Schrankwand to tie together the different living room designs. In the photographic study *Das deutsche Wohnzimmer* (*The German Living Room*), Herlinde Koelbl documented this room across different socioeconomic groups in urban and rural settings in 1980. Unlike in the GDR, there was no comparable furnishing standard in the Federal Republic, and living rooms varied greatly according to family social and financial situations—with the exception of the Schrankwand.

Working-class families often did not have room to spare for a living room and used the kitchen for eating, working, socializing, and receiving guests. This multifunctionality expressed economic realities. Hannelore P. (30), a housewife with five children and a husband who dealt in scrap metal, lived in an apartment that had no bathroom.[107] The family shared the toilet on the landing with neighbors, and the nearest bathroom was three blocks away. Clearly not everybody could partake in West German modern domestic culture. Social stratification, income, and education determined access to the markers of the promoted conservative middle-class modernity of home ownership, modern household appliances, and correct consumption.

Amid the clashing patterns of wallpapers, floor tiles, couch fabric, and tablecloth, Antoinette S. (47), a housewife with eight children and an unskilled worker husband, attested to the financial strain that urban apartment rents put on the working-class family: "We cannot afford a different apartment. My husband and I sleep in the living room."[108] Indeed, for a working-class household, house ownership in the 1980s entailed large sacrifices, such as foregoing costly hobbies and vacations, and years of saving money. Seated proudly in a comfortably furnished living room, new home owners Alois (55), a crane operator, and his wife Katharina W. (52) declared: "We have arrived." With the table set for a dinner for two, a bottle of wine on display, this living room embodied the reward for all of the hard work of building a safe haven from the daily trials and tribulations where they could recharge: "We have never gone on a vacation trip. First we had to work on the house and now we want to enjoy the fruits of our labor," Alois and Katharina W. explained.[109]

Families living in the countryside, where real estate was less expensive and more abundant, had a different experience altogether. Koelbl photographed a married farming couple, Heinrich (63) and Elfriede B. (71), in two different spaces where they spent their spare time. The first was plainly furnished with a sufficiently comfortable couch behind a small table with two nonmatching easy chairs and a wooden chair assembled around the table. They explain: "We spend our evenings in this room, also because of the television."[110] The other picture was taken in a more representational room with furniture that would be fittingly described as *Gelsenkirchener Barock*, with seating furniture joined by an expensive-looking corner cabinet opposite a large mirror. The mostly dark wood and the busy fabrics on the couch and the easy chairs, ranging from floral print to geometric patterns, were chosen to make an impression. "According to what kind of visitor we receive," they were quoted, "he will be brought into this living room or the other." This comment clearly indicates that the *gute Stube* (parlor) was reserved for important visitors and did not fulfill everyday functions. While this room was a representational space, the other space where family life took place was furnished with functional designs that aligned with their needs for leisure and rest in the evenings. It is difficult to determine whether this separation of representational and functional spaces indicated generational difference, though it seems unlikely. Similarly, the young farming family of Josef (38) and Rosa S. (31) confirmed that "We are in the *gute Stube* just a few times each year."[111] In a context where the home constituted part of professional life and offered spaces for hobbies elsewhere on the premises, the living room could be used exclusively to host guests. Couple S. filled theirs with rustic furniture that expressed their cultural and social identity, but as this room had no function in the rest of their lives, it seemed unnecessary to use it on a daily basis.

On the contrary, educated middle-class families of the 1980s often considered the living room to also be a workspace where reading, thinking, and writing took place. City council woman Inge H. (53) explained: "We are mostly in the kitchen. We use the living room only when we want quiet to read or to work."[112] And cleric Josef W. (51) affirms this sentiment: "I am very seldom at home and thus this room suffices. I use it to work and spend my leisure time."[113] Large bookshelves dominated both Josef W. and Inge H.'s rooms, and the small but functional seating furniture and coffee table were not suitable for hosting a nice afternoon tea or a dinner party. Inge H.'s living room solely contained a desk. These rooms made a purely functional impression by accentuating the need for academic work space. Hosting guests was not a priority, and thus hardly anyone ever saw the only representational element: the books.

This pattern of the multifunctional living room usage among the West German middle class was unlike the way in which Robert N. (40), an administrative clerk, furnished his room. Over the tiled coffee table floated a crystal chandelier, and on the wall hung a print of a painting depicting a young lady in a leisure pose with a book—presumably signifying the importance of education for this family. The silver-plated tea service displayed on an ornamented tea trolley seemed to come from an entirely different time and place when such objects symbolized respectability and high social status. The Schrankwand in dark wood towers over the family in the picture, next to which Robert N. is quoted as self-importantly saying: "Those who come to my home have to follow my volition."[114] The entire room is stuck in the tastes and aspirations of the nineteenth century. Nevertheless, this is an exception and only one of a few pictures showing representational living rooms of the aspirational upper middle-class styles.[115]

Despite what these examples suggest about the multiple functions that the 1980s living room served in the Federal Republic, the foreword by Manfred Sack to Koelbl's photographic study presented a pessimistic viewpoint on the inhabitants' ability to create a functional space to live in, rather than merely to represent its owners.[116] Sack identified the reasons for what he saw as a growing tendency to buy furniture that embodied social aspirations, rather than actual personality and circumstances of the owner, as a disenfranchisement of the population, a lack of education about simple laws of proportion and materiality, and the increasingly predetermined apartment layouts, including bathroom tiling and built-in kitchens. Yet such wide-ranging, unspecific conclusions reveal more about Sack than about the people depicted in the study. His claims ignored the photographic evidence in favor of architectural trends and a personal bias toward functionalist styles, and thus missed an opportunity to actively engage with the inhabitants' appropriation of spaces and their everyday relationship with objects.

Offering a more deeply engaged approach, Gert Selle and Jutta Boehe's ethnological study of West German living cultures in the early to mid-1980s rebuts Sack's pessimistic claims.[117] Their method resembles that of Letsch and Scharf's parallel study in Leipzig. Three couples, all of them homeowners, were chosen from three different middle-class backgrounds: Mr. (41) and Mrs. S. (42) held white-collar jobs as a technician and a secretary at a TV station and came from a working-class background; Mr. and Mrs. Z. (both 43) came from the well-educated middle class, having earned degrees as an engineer and a teacher, with a petit-bourgeois background; Mr. (45) and Mrs. H. (40) had an upper middle-class background, working as a social worker and a dentist. Their names were anonymized and the location of the study remained undisclosed. Photographic documentation in combination with couple interviews as well as individual interviews detail the history and context of the families' acquisition choices. The analysis evaluated furnishing habits vis-à-vis the participants' personal past to explain the relationships the respondents had to the objects in their homes. The study's subjects had been infants at the end of the Second World War and grew up in the western zones of occupation and later the Federal Republic, with one exception. They thus were completely socialized in the West; only Mrs. S. spent her childhood in the eastern zone of occupation and the GDR before her family moved to the West.

Only one of the three houses fit the state-promoted modernity of the Federal Republic. Couple H.'s house, a bungalow made of white brick, steel, glass, and a little bit of wood, was the only one that the researchers call "functionalist-modern."[118] The bungalow had a special place in Bonn's official architecture. In 1963, Sep Ruf built a flat-roofed bungalow as residence and reception building for the West German chancellor, expressing the values of political horizontality and transparency with large windows and unassuming architecture.[119] Couple H.'s heightened awareness of modernist idioms could be due to the fact that they both had been married before to spouses who worked in artistic professions, a painter and an architect respectively. With its low ceilings and skylight bands in place of windows, the architecture dominated the atmosphere of the dim-lit house. The mix of furniture styles, ranging from functionalist electronic gadgets over mainstream modern furniture to Ikea pieces and do-it-yourself shelving on trestles, interrupts the austere look of the bungalow's severe construction materials. Meanwhile, large oriental rugs introduced a noticeably competing aesthetic into this house, adding warmth to the cold, drab concrete floors.

The other couples described their houses and their furniture as functional as well, although the architectural shells of their homes cannot be described as functionalist-modern. While the furniture did not closely resemble Bauhaus designs, they were simple with clear lines and practical shapes. One or two pieces were embellished, but the majority of the furniture served clearly the functions of storing, eating, working, hosting, and playing. Based on their preconceptions

FIGURE 5.6. Living room interior of Couple H.'s house. Gert Selle and Jutta Boehe,
Leben mit den schönen Dingen. ©1985, Rowohlt Verlag GmbH, Hamburg.

about the age and profession of the couple, Selle and Boehe remark that they
would have expected less educated Mr. and Mrs. S. to represent themselves
differently, perhaps with *Stilmöbel* or modish furniture, and that they were
surprised by the "sober" impression of the house during their first visit.[120] The
couple explained that after the expense of the house they were unable to invest
in expensive furniture as well. They therefore made do with hand-me-downs
and acquired functional pieces bit by bit. Expensive fantasies, such as a modern
Interlübke bedroom furniture ensemble, had remained financially out of reach.
A skilled handyman, Mr. S. built a similar looking set with his wife's help.[121] Do-
it-yourself thus flourished on both sides of the border and became an important
strategy for consumers navigating the power relations between official taste paternalism and production.[122] It has been estimated that do-it-yourself activities,
such as fancywork and redecorations, cost the economy around 4 percent of
West Germany's annual GDP in the 1970s and 1980s.[123] One could go as far as
claiming that this practice undermined the modernization effort. Yet, considering its broad application, it also implies that it was part of the economic culture
in East and West, which idealized a conservative appreciation of the crafts.

Two of the couples recognized that certain corners of their houses exclusively served emotional purposes, such as the decorative and historical objects assembled on an old wooden trunk and the kitschy stoneware plates ornamented with birds hanging next to the fireplace and above a rock collection in couple Z.'s living room.[124] A porcelain piggybank sat as a lucky charm in couple S.'s living room. And they kept some needlework pillowcases, which had been gifted to them. Mrs. S. commented that she always kept handicrafts out of respect for the work that went into making them, even if they did not suit her taste.[125] Just like the respondents in Letsch and Scharf's East German study,[126] these West German couples explain their strong relationship to knickknacks and handmade objects through symbolic, emotional value. They remarked that these objects had been given or made by relatives and that these objects symbolized happy memories. The porcelain piggy bank in couple S.'s living room was a wedding present, and couple Z. had accumulated the rock collection during their travels.[127]

In both houses, these knickknacks co-existed, or rather clashed, with the iconic, modern Braun Hi-Fi stereo. Braun became a household name for user-friendly electronic gadgets that conformed to the aesthetic austerity of neofunctionalism. Braun designer Dieter Rams's own design principles aligned with the functionalist mantras of honesty, innovation, durability, and unobtrusiveness.[128] In the Z. and S. households, the functionalist stereo sat right next to memorabilia and other objects that had only decorative functions. In this way, the couples developed strategies to co-opt prescriptive taste regimes, and in some places in the house, they outright rejected the functionalist vision that the Federal Republic had modeled since the 1950s. They counterbalanced the accepted maxim of practicality with emotionally laden objects to add warmth and coziness to their house interiors.

At the same time, such things also presented the character of their owners to guests. These were not aspirational pieces meant to represent their status or even pretend to a higher status. The objects in the house of couple Z. demonstrated five different interior design styles, Selle and Boehe reported: (1) timid versions of Stilmöbel, (2) functional-classical modernism (such as the Braun stereo and the TV), (3) Scandinavian influences (Ikea), (4) historical pieces with decorative character, and (5) inherited designs from the 1950s and 1960s.[129] Whereas this style mix confused the research team, to the couple it did not present a contradiction. Couple Z. had personal relationships to all of these objects that rendered them practical from their viewpoint. The researchers supposed that "In this tendency [toward heavy mixing of styles] strong contradictions emerge; however, these are presumably largely resolved through invisible interpretational

FIGURE 5.7. Living room interior of Couple Z.'s house. Gert Selle and Jutta Boehe, *Leben mit den schönen Dingen.* ©1985, Rowohlt Verlag GmbH, Hamburg.

and practical factors in the respondents' consciousness."[130] It is therefore important to understand that individuals with high awareness of questions of taste consciously justify furnishing solutions that do not fit any design prescription to overcome the embarrassment of their lacking rationality. In this justification process, functionality and practicality derive from the usage of objects in combination with the accommodation of emotional needs to create homeliness.[131] Individuals satisfy these needs by surrounding themselves with objects that contain memories, carry familiarity, or are the products of their hobbies, resulting in an eclectic style mix.

It is interesting to note that neither the photographic study by Koelbl nor the ethnological study by Selle and Boehe included the numerous high-rises and so-called *mehrparteien* apartment blocks in the city centers of the Federal Republic. In fact, the prefab tower-and-slab developments, once considered at the forefront of modern postwar architecture, had already fallen from grace by the 1970s.[132] Rather, the studies explore—with the few exceptions in Koelbl's book—the state-funded ideal of middle-class home ownership, emphasizing West German social conservatism enshrined in a housing policy that celebrated family and respectability. The East German studies, meanwhile, seem to trace young families' processes of becoming "bourgeois" in the GDR, which the state supported through a systematic combination of conservative family laws and progressive housing policy. The result was, in both cases, a conservative modernism in German homes by the 1980s.

The photographic sources and field notes from the sociological studies in East and West show that even after forty years, despite the best efforts of taste reformers, functionalism as an aesthetic remained elitist. In both Germanys, the better educated showed a higher likelihood of adopting modern-functionalist idioms and did this in a more cohesive fashion.[133] They tended to surround themselves less with bric-a-brac. One difference that did emerge between East and West was the fact that West Germans looked at their kitschy belongings and emotional affection for things with a good amount of irony and self-mockery.[134] This indicates that lacking refinement in taste, as it was understood according to the prescriptive aesthetics of the RfF, was something of which West German consumers were conscious. In the GDR, however, kitsch objects were treated with the same respect as the most practical of objects. This might stem from the general experience of material scarcity and the effort that had gone into acquiring or making these objects in the first place.

Most important, the studies show that, over many decades of modernist design discourse, the populations of both East and West Germany appropriated functionalism as individual practicality. The interviews indicate that functionality, interpreted as pragmatic and useful, was held in high esteem across the two Germanys. Yet the distancing irony with which West Germans talked about their bric-a-brac showed that the discourse of taste education was more pervasive in the West than in the East. This finding is not surprising considering that the SED rehabilitated functionalism only in the 1960s. Some solutions that found approval from designers, politicians, and economic planners, such as the Schrankwand, were convincing to the population because of the storage they provided or the multifunctionality they offered. The pattern that emerges in postwar Germany shows that the population had a good grasp of what functionalist furniture does and is.

The overall impression that the interiors of houses and apartments offered, however, was far removed from the aesthetics of modernist designers and design councils who adopted functionalism as a political style, symbolizing modernity. Consumption choices proved that the population did not wholeheartedly buy into the political constructions that both the FRG and the GDR had tried to create around functionalism as a source of national belonging. In the early postwar decades, consumer counseling and taste education continued the prewar discourse on what it meant to live like a German.[135] Once functionalism revealed itself as a dogma in the late 1960s, the national emphasis on correct consumption stopped, yet the striving for modernity continued in both parts of Germany. The population did develop a sensitivity to practical design that served the needs of their family life. However, they accepted the functionality discourse on their own terms and created areas that fulfilled their emotional needs.

The analysis suggests that functionalist discourse diffused German society, yet not with the consistency that the disciples of modernism would have liked. It was a conservative modernity that showed widespread awareness of the right materials, the wrong embellishments, and the need for the emotional comfort of traditions and social relations. The population accepted the practicality of functionalism's clear lines and rectangular shapes for small apartments. However, it did not accept the emotional emptiness of the functionalist extreme. These conclusions align with sociologists' findings about the diversification of lifestyles gaining momentum in the 1960s. Individualization of space through the personal appropriation of general guidelines for functional living, in the end, made the populations of the GDR and the Federal Republic cautious participants in an economic culture in which, for quite different motives in East and West, class lines became increasingly blurred and the material codification of status diversified.

Conclusion

The Ties That Never Broke

B Y THE LATE 1980S, the dynamics of German-German economic competition in the realm of living standards had created an unsustainable situation for the GDR. The high costs of the promised socialist consumer society under Honecker's Unity of Economic and Social Policy program had incurred mounting debts, a strategy that relied on short-term borrowing from the West to patch holes in domestic consumer good production. This entanglement with the Federal Republic opened up the possibility of rethinking the German-German relationship. In early winter of 1989, East German demonstrators changed their chant from "We are the people" to "We are *one* people." What turned a gentle revolution, or an insistence on long-overdue reforms within socialism, to a clear avowal for German unity that December? The question is particularly important because it became quite quickly evident that such a course of action would mean the disappearance of the GDR as a state and, with it, the end of the socialist experiment on German soil.

Much of the historical discussion addressing this question has centered on the economic performance of the GDR and the consumer history of its population's privations. What has been less analyzed is the courage East Germans displayed in turning the very understandable request for reform of an oppressive state system, one that spied on its own citizens, decisively hindered their mobility, infringed on their civil rights, and was unable to deliver on its consumer promises, into a complete rejection of that state and the social security it provided. East Germans voluntarily left behind the safety net of the GDR, where the "welfare dictatorship" protected them against poverty, offered high social wages, and heavily subsidized consumer goods that qualified as a "need."[1] This study suggests that, long before 1989, the two Germanys came to operate under one economic culture marked by interdependencies and shared expectations, which made the transition from reform to unity plausible and feasible in German minds. Moreover, the dynamics that four decades of intra-German trade had created also put West German politicians in a position to shape East Germany's future. For all intents and purposes, the Federal Republic had co-financed the economic reforms in the East, supporting Honecker's Unity of Economic and Social Policy via generous Swing credits in the intra-German trade. When the new GDR head of government Hans Modrow asked West German chancellor Helmut Kohl for a DM 15 billion solidarity payment to avoid state bankruptcy during the tumultuous days in late 1989, Kohl contemplated helping at first, yet withdrew this commitment in January 1990.[2] With this the Federal Republic finally pulled the plug on an economic *Deutschlandpolitik* that had propped up the East German regime. It also foreclosed any chance for survival of a reformed GDR, as financial solidarity was now closely linked to political unity.

Across four decades of *Deutschlandpolitik* the Federal Republic consistently supported intra-German trade, not least by providing credit to the GDR. Yet the more important point is that it upheld the line that economic exchanges did not imply de facto political recognition. The government minimized regulation of the economic contacts with the GDR but rather let the private sector deal directly with the economic structures in the East. In this way, the political question remained separate from private economic interests in the West, and this depoliticization decoupled intra-German trade from party politics to some extent. Of course, one must not forget the many heated debates among and between CDU and SPD over *Ostpolitik* in its different iterations ranging from Adenauer's policy of strength to Brandt's policy of compromise.[3] The economic principles on which German-German trade relations were built, namely the 1951 Berlin Agreement and the 1958 Protocol on Intra-German Trade, spanned, however, both major parties' periods in government. Hence, there was a basic political consensus on this kind of cooperation across the forty years of German division, broadly supported by the West German population, who continued to feel a bond with their socialist neighbors to a certain degree.

Western modes of rapprochement eventually engaged people in the GDR on all levels, ranging from politicians to company managers to workers who did contractual work for the West. Meanwhile, the GDR utilized West German interest in a sustainable relationship via intra-German trade to increase exports and to yield more foreign currency. In order to establish itself and survive in an international market, the East German production aesthetic converged with western ones. With the continuous interconnection of the two national economies, and the relatively high level of living standards in the GDR that western credits enabled, East and West Germans, knowingly or not, worked on designing one nation. These ties facilitated making the step from reforming communism to joining the capitalist system.

With the conceptual framework of the economic culture approach it is possible to explore the intricate nature of the German Cold War in the realm of the economy, looking at possibilities, rather than solely at outcomes, and the opportunities and limitations that designers faced in the implementation of aesthetic discourse in the production and consumption processes. In the early reconstruction years, elites focused on pronounced national aesthetics for political rather than social purposes. Alongside the cultural identification with the West, such aesthetics expressed Adenauer's policy of strength on the German Question, based on the logic that *Westbindung*, rearmament, and NATO membership would eventually bring about German unification. In reaction to Bonn's position, the GDR followed a policy of demarcation from the West by showing allegiance to the Eastern Bloc, both ideologically and culturally. However, when one examines design discourse beyond initial bloc alliances, it becomes evident that the ideologically loaded Cold War climate limited the elite's ability to inscribe material culture with a spirit of social reform. These developments contributed to an emerging economic culture that was profoundly outward looking, while deeply imbedding production ethics that would come to be known as the "made in Germany" brand: durability, functionality, material thrift, and modern aesthetics.

Looking at values and norms inscribed in product culture, the economic culture approach levels the playing field for the GDR, which from the outset was disadvantaged in its economic competition with the Federal Republic. The transfer of goods across the border shaped eastern and western understandings of what it meant to be a modern industrial nation. The economy served as a field for competition until these adversaries developed a shared language of progress and security, enabling trade contacts and mutual projects that reproduced interconnections on the institutional and the personal level. The two German states, located geographically at the heart of the confrontation between Eastern and Western ideologies, created a political space that magnified the precariousness of the Cold War in Europe. At the same time, this space also amplified the moments of rapprochement in later decades that unfolded on a global scale in the East-West conflict: economic cooperation, political détente, and peaceful coexistence. Bringing these areas of cooperation into focus enables an appreciation of the continuous ties between the FRG and GDR that opened up a sustainable dialogue and maintained a certain degree of mutual understanding throughout the Cold War.

Significantly, what this process produced were not two different kinds of modernity, a socialist and a capitalist one, but one German conservative modernity based on a shared value system in the production and consumption processes, a pan-German economic culture that emerged due to the diplomatic necessities and economic practicalities of the German Cold War. It developed between the extremes of fast-paced American production cycles, creating demand by bringing the next big thing to the market, and the static structures of the Soviet-style centrally planned economy that supplanted market mechanisms with state interests. Industrial design, which had for so long served as a field for Cold War competition, became an arena in which to mediate inter-German relations. The pan-German economic culture developed a vocabulary of transparency, humanity, and morality that shaped German efforts for peace in Europe in the 1980s. When the superpowers ended global détente and entered the Second Cold War by stationing new nuclear missiles in Europe, the two German states took the opportunity to define their own positions.

This outcome was not clear from the beginning. From the 1950s to the building of the Berlin Wall in 1961 was a time of pronounced demarcation and adversarial relations from both sides. Yet this period of delineation proved to be only a prelude to the détente of the 1970s. Many of the early policies that facilitated East-West contacts, such as the Berlin Agreement and the EEC Protocol on Intra-German Trade, in fact papered over major cracks. Contemporaries feared that European integration and German unity were necessarily opposed to each other, and it was therefore imperative to develop a European economic foreign policy that achieved maximum flexibility in the German Question. Therefore a "natural" alignment of West German national interests and European integration during the Cold War, which current debates often assume, cannot be claimed. Similarly, Germany's change from reflexive multilateralism, expressed in Germany as a reliable partner of the Western alliance with a normative commitment to European integration, to a more instrumentalized multilateralism in the service of post-reunification national interest has been deemed a new phenomenon.[4] The opposite was in fact the case; postwar Germany has always followed a national interest–guided policy in Europe. This conclusion is supported by the way in which the Federal Republic handled the question of intra-German trade within the EEC.

It was this early foundation on which a thriving economic and even cultural exchange across the inner-German border were built. The decisive later decades, in which GDR decline became palpable on an everyday level, show how delineation and demarcation policies were overcome on political, economic, and personal levels. Additionally, the examination of the 1970s and 1980s introduces the relational aspect of trade with the West into East German efforts to build a sustainable vision of GDR modernity, which indicates where propaganda ended and economic reality set in. Pragmatism not only trumped ideological dogma, but also revealed the GDR's underlying economic-cultural values and aspirations for a place among modern industrial nations, a goal the Federal Republic shared. By creating direct contact between the populations of East and West Germany with a gradual decrease in state involvement, which came to a head with the opening of the Berlin Wall on 9 November 1989, the German Question moved beyond the reach of the GDR government and eventually co-opted even the staunchest critics among the Allies into a plan for a unified German future.

Despite their systemic differences, the FRG and GDR co-created an economic culture in which designer, producers, retailers, and consumers increasingly agreed on the same values and norms that governed economic interaction and inspired shared ideas of modern living standards. It was conservative not just in form, but also in content. Two Germanys developed large welfare states to democratize industrialization under the auspices of both capitalism and socialism. The fact that the Federal Republic had such a security net in place, to some extent thanks to the pressures exerted by the socialist alternative across the border, enabled a rather smooth reunification, where East Germans were successfully integrated in the pension insurance scheme and unemployment benefits, even at high costs and with enormous effort on the part of the German tax payers. Of course, there is much evidence that suggests that the realities of the market quickly disillusioned enthusiastic East Germans; it took time to adjust to the level of personal initiative needed to succeed in the labor market or to navigate the commodified insurance sector. Industrial output in the *neue Bundesländer* contracted by 60 percent in the first two years following unification.[5] Many hard lessons were learned. A term was dubbed for the long-term unemployed and those in the low-income groups in Eastern Germany: *Einheitsverlierer*, literally losers of unification.[6] This experience of displacement has given rise to *Ostalgie*, nostalgia for the East German past, a much-debated phenomenon, especially in the realm of consumer goods.[7]

Indeed, the country's collapse immediately endangered its material culture. Not only did GDR industrial production slow down, but, once the border was open, the novelty of the western product culture also attracted GDR citizens who could cross the border unhindered. East German interior design was quickly replaced with western furniture and domestic appliances. Wolfgang Becker's film *Good Bye Lenin* approaches the topic from a tragic-comical perspective.[8] To shelter his fragile mother from the fatal shock after a long coma, a young man re-creates a socialist lifestyle to keep her from learning that her beloved GDR was about to disappear. The ruse quickly turns into a struggle because East German food products already begin to disappear from store shelves. Several scenes show sidewalks filled with discarded furniture that neighbors who moved to the West left behind or those who stayed traded for western items. Ikea posters advertise affordable storage furniture, some of which ironically was produced in the GDR.[9]

Entertaining as this film is, it blends reality with fiction not just through its use of archival footage. A sense of looming loss set in as soon as the first free East German elections in March 1990 paved the road to reunification. AiF employees and affiliates of the institute's design product collection *Sammlung industrielle Gestaltung* went on a last shopping spree across East Berlin in the spring of 1990.[10] The approaching monetary union of 1 July jeopardized the future of thousands of East German companies. Outdated machinery and low technical standards clearly disadvantaged them on the capitalist market. With the arrival of the D-Mark their products became more expensive, and when European socialism collapsed the following year, the COMECON market broke away as well. Privatization of national industries kept many workers in limbo until mostly western investors bought a company, only to sell it for parts or restructure it for greater profitability after years of Treuhand trusteeship.[11]

The western Werkbund noted as well that reunification had strained East German product culture and made an effort to engage with it. The design show *From Bauhaus to Bitterfeld: 41 Years of GDR Design* of December 1990 and the accompanying exhibition catalog aimed to address "the difficulties of transitioning from one social order to another" and to document "the work done to avoid loss of identity."[12] Nonetheless, in the catalog West German design historian Gert Selle observed that "the people have not only had their national state supplanted by a foreign state but also seem to have lost the world of their experienced material and immaterial cultures. Objects that once filled the stage of daily ritual as familiar props and that, in their meager charm, could remind one of the dead or dying culture, now age at a highly accelerated rate."[13] Among the catalog's contributors were a number of East German industrial designers, art historians, architects, and former AiF employees who joined in this requiem for GDR product culture. To explain the fast depreciation, they quickly pointed to the country's inability to reform economically, the scarcity of resources, and empty ideological discourse about certain design styles and products. These voices solidified the picture of a bygone era already in the process of being historicized. The usage of black-and-white photography in the catalog further underpinned this obsolescence.

But it was not only the populations' excitement for western consumer goods, a lack of sentimentality among East German professionals, or a lack of awareness on the part of western investors that sidelined GDR material culture and industrial design after 1990. Political circumstances necessitated an immediate confrontation of dictatorial power structures in the former GDR. Infiltration of institutions and organizations by informants especially came to the forefront of discussion when the Stasi files were declassified in 1992. Two organizations that had represented industrial design interests, the Association of Artists in the Applied Arts (Verband Bildender Künstler, VBK) and the AiF, were questioned about the nature of their support for the SED regime. Former VBK president Clauss Dietel defended the association but claimed to speak for many GDR industrial designers when he criticized the AiF's style diktat and ideologization of aesthetics.[14] These comments were made in an interview with RfF magazine *Design Report* in response to the question "What remains of GDR design?" It thus seems that what remained was a politically implicated profession and its products, which had given shape to the goals of German socialism, but had no place in the newly reunified Germany because of the complexity of this past association.

Thirty years after the fall of the Wall, a united Germany has developed not only domestic stability but also leadership in Europe and international diplomacy. As one of the worldwide leading export nations, Germany receives international acknowledgment for its economic policies and contributions to European integration and peace. Here the experience of the economic foreign policy strategy vis-à-vis the GDR seems to inform Germany's current position as a "reluctant hegemon" in Europe and its continued skepticism toward military leadership.[15] The checkbook diplomacy of the Cold War era has set the tone for a foreign policy that uses economic cooperation as a means for conflict resolution and a path toward increasing political opponents' receptiveness for German interests.

Trade policy, it has been argued here, provided similar incentives for modernization in East and West and forged conditions conducive to deepened cultural relations, which in turn rekindled notions of a pan-German identity. Design, taste, and consumption were at the center of this postwar identity discourse in both parts of Germany. These realms help to explain why German unity came about without further great social upheavals or political disruptions in the fall of 1990. Shared visions of economic prowess, cultural belonging, and Germany taking its place among modern industrialized nations in a sense paved the way for reunification. Given the challenging process of two different political and economic systems growing together, it is remarkable that such past negotiations in the field of economic culture have not played a greater role in the current debate over united Germany's identity, especially because its economic strength continues to decisively shape German political culture and foreign policy. *Designing One Nation* thus proposes that we need to stop thinking about the two Germanys in isolation from each other in order to see how much they still had in common in 1989, after forty years of separation, and how this shared past affects Germany today.

NOTES

Introduction

1 For example, see "Was bleibt vom DDR-Design? Elke Trappschuh trifft Clauss Dietel," *Design Report* 22 (1992): 24; and Gert Selle, "The Lost Innocence of Poverty: On the Disappearance of a Culture Difference," *Design Issues* 8, no. 2 (1992): 64. Selle originally wrote the text in 1990 for the exhibition catalog *Vom Bauhaus bis Bitterfeld: 41 Jahre DDR-Design* (Giessen: Anabas, 1991).

2 Francis Fukuyama discusses the collapsing socialism of the 1980s as the last, dying alternative to Western liberalism. See Fukuyama, "The End of History?" *National Interest* (Summer 1989): 3–18.

3 In my usage of nouns describing the eastern and the western part of Germany, I have tried to refrain from employing ideologically loaded language. I use the terms "Federal Republic of Germany," "Federal Republic," "German Democratic Republic," and "GDR" as they would be employed in German—without any ideological connotation. But the different linguistic traditions in the English language make it necessary also to point out that the abbreviation "FRG" as well as "West Germany" and "East Germany" are value-free denominations for the two German states. The latter especially allows for an easy geographical identification. I have tried to avoid the shorthand East and West as to not confuse my readers when I am addressing the larger East-West conflict between the superpowers. However, if I have used East and West in relation to the two German states, then I have made the specific meaning evident through context. Similarly, I have capitalized "Eastern" and "Western" to mark phenomena and processes that were politicized in the global Cold War.

4 The first stanza of the *Lied der Deutschen* (Song of the Germans) began with the words "*Deutschland, Deutschland über alles, über alles in der Welt*" (Germany, Germany above everything, above everything in the world). In the wake of the Second World War, these lines had received a strong negative meaning as they were now connected to expansionist nationalism.

5 See, for example, Mark E. Spicka, *Selling the Economic Miracle: Economic Reconstruction and Politics in West Germany, 1949–1957* (New York: Berghahn, 2007); James C. Van Hook, *Rebuilding Germany: The Creation of the Social Market Economy* (Cambridge: Cambridge University Press, 2004); André Steiner, *Von Plan zu Plan: Eine Wirtschaftsgeschichte der DDR* (Munich: Deutsche Verlagsanstalt, 2004); Christoph

Buchheim, *Die Wiedereingliederung Westdeutschlands in die Weltwirtschaft, 1945–1958* (Munich: Oldenbourg, 1990).

6 Paul Egon Rohrlich, "Economic Culture and Foreign Policy: The Cognitive Analysis of Economic Policy Making," *International Organization* 41, no. 1 (1987): 66.

7 See Jeffrey Kopstein, *The Politics of Economic Decline in East Germany, 1945–1989* (Chapel Hill: University of North Carolina Press, 1997); Jaap Sleifer, *Planning Ahead and Falling Behind: The East German Economy in Comparison with West Germany, 1936–2002*, Jahrbuch für Wirtschaftsgeschichte Beiheft 8 (Berlin: Akademie, 2006).

8 Scholarly explanations for the GDR's stability range from the intimidation of the population via constant surveillance (*Überwachungsstaat*), the population's political mobilization in SED mass organizations, and the relatively expansive welfare state (*Fürsorgestaat*) inducing a social consensus, to a "niche society" (*Nischengesellschaft*) allowing the population to escape the SED's grip, if just for short periods of time. West German diplomat and head of the FRG Permanent Mission in East Berlin Günter Gaus coined the phrase "niche society" to describe a population that followed policies just to meet expectations about what good socialist citizens should behave like but did not care about socialism in the privacy of their homes. Gaus, *Wo Deutschland liegt: Eine Ortsbestimmung* (Hamburg: Hoffmann und Campe, 1983). In England, a group of scholars has focused on the seemingly contradictory ways in which the stability of the GDR worked in the social realm. Mary Fulbrook, *Anatomy of a Dictatorship: Inside the GDR, 1949–1989* (Oxford: Oxford University Press, 1995); Jeannette Z. Madarász, *Conflict and Compromise in East Germany, 1971–1989: A Precarious Stability* (Houndmills: Macmillan, 2003); Catherine Epstein, *The Last Revolutionaries: German Communists and Their Century* (Cambridge, MA: Harvard University Press, 2003). A similar approach has been taken by Andrew I. Port, *Conflict and Stability in the German Democratic Republic* (New York: Cambridge University Press, 2007).

9 For example, see Volker Berghahn, *The Americanisation of West German Industry, 1945–1973* (Cambridge: Cambridge University Press, 1986).

10 East and West German consumption has been studied extensively. For example, see Ina Merkel, *Utopie und Bedürfnis: Die Geschichte der Konsumkultur in der DDR* (Cologne: Böhlau, 1999); Judd Stitziel, *Fashioning Socialism: Clothing, Politics, and Consumer Culture in East Germany* (Oxford: Berg, 2005); David E. Crew, ed., *Consuming Germany in the Cold War* (Oxford: Berg, 2003); Jennifer A. Loehlin, *From Rugs to Riches: Housework, Consumption and Modernity in Germany* (Oxford: Berg, 1999); NGBK, ed., *Wunderwirtschaft: DDR-Konsumgeschichte in den 6oer Jahren* (Cologne: Böhlau, 1996). A general shift in postwar European economic behavior occurred in the postwar period when consumption started to take precedence over social security, trading rights for goods. See Victoria De Grazia, *Irresistible Empire: America's Advance through 20th-Century Europe* (Cambridge, MA: Belknap Press of Harvard University Press, 2005), 341.

11 Paul Betts, *The Authority of Everyday Objects: A Cultural History of West German Industrial Design* (Berkeley: University of California Press, 2004) and Eli Rubin,

Synthetic Socialism: Plastics and Dictatorship in the German Democratic Republic (Chapel Hill: University of North Carolina Press, 2008) offer the most widely read interpretations of industrial design in postwar Germany. German literature on the topic is represented by Christopher Oestereich, *"Gute Form" im Wiederaufbau: Zur Geschichte der Produktgestaltung in Westdeutschland nach 1945* (Berlin: Lukas, 2000); Gert Selle, "Das Produktdesign der 50er Jahre: Rückgriff in die Entwurfsgeschichte, vollendete Modernisierung des Alltagsinventars oder Vorbote der Postmoderne?" in *Modernisierung im Wiederaufbau: Die westdeutsche Gesellschaft der 50er Jahre*, ed. Axel Schildt and Arnold Sywottek, 612–624 (Bonn: Dietz, 1993); Gert Selle, *Geschichte des Design in Deutschland*, 2nd ed. (Frankfurt: Campus, [1994] 2007). Ronald Stade explores the politics behind GDR aesthetics in "Designs of Identity: The Politics of Aesthetics in the GDR," *Ethnos* 58, no. 3/4 (1993): 241–258. For a discussion of the predominately separate nature of East and West German historiography, see H-German Forum on "Integrating Post-1945 German History," January and February 2011, http://h-net.msu. edu/cgi-bin/logbrowse.pl?trx=lm&list=H-German. However, a number of edited volumes and monographs have looked at the two Germanys in conjunction. For example, see Henry Ashby Turner Jr., *The Two Germanies Since 1945* (New Haven, CT: Yale University Press, 1987); Christoph Kleßmann, ed., *The Divided Past: Rewriting Post-War German History* (Oxford: Berg, 2001); Uta Balbier, *Kalter Krieg auf der Aschenbahn: Deutsch-deutscher Sport, 1950–72, eine politische Geschichte* (Paderborn: Schöningh, 2007); Udo Wengst and Hermann Wentker, eds., *Das doppelte Deutschland: 40 Jahre Systemkonkurrenz* (Berlin: Ch. Links, 2008); Erica Carter, Jan Palmowski, and Katrin Schreiter, eds., *German Division as Shared Experience: Interdisciplinary Perspective on the Postwar Everyday* (Berghahn: New York, 2019).

12 For example, see Hans-Ulrich Wehler, *Deutsche Gesellschaftsgeschichte IV* (Munich: C. H. Beck, 2008), xv–xvi; Heinrich August Winkler, *Der lange Weg nach Westen II: Deutsche Geschichte, 1933–1990* (Munich: C. H. Beck, 2000); Edgar Wolfrum, *Die geglückte Demokratie: Geschichte der Bundesrepublik Deutschland von ihren Anfängen bis zur Gegenwart* (Stuttgart: Klett-Cotta, 2006).

13 For example, see Katherine Pence and Paul Betts, *Socialist Modern: East German Everyday Culture and Politics* (Ann Arbor: University of Michigan Press, 2008); Rubin, *Synthetic Socialism*.

14 Konrad Jarausch, "Divided, Yet Reunited—The Challenge of Integrating German Post-War Histories," contribution to *H-German Forum*, 1 February 2011, http://h-net. msu.edu/cgi-bin/logbrowse.pl?trx=vx&list=h-german&month=1102&week=a&msg=lNK7XIEc2qqANKFyP6tmew&user=&pw=, accessed 13 October 2015.

15 Renewed interest in the German Cold War has brought forth studies that approach it from both cultural and political perspectives. Diplomatic and international historians have looked at the German Question mostly within the context of East and West German superpower alignment. See, for example, M. E. Sarotte, *Dealing with the Devil: East Germany, Détente, and Ostpolitik, 1969–1973* (Chapel Hill: University of North Carolina Press, 2001); William Glenn Gray, *Germany's Cold War: The Global*

Campaign to Isolate East Germany, 1949–1969 (Chapel Hill: University of North Carolina Press, 2003). American and Soviet attempts at containing each part of Germany within their sphere of influence has led cultural historians of the Cold War to look at German political, cultural, and economic development through the lenses of Americanization and Sovietization. For example, see Norman Naimark, *The Russians in Germany: A History of the Soviet Zone of Occupation, 1945–1949* (Cambridge, MA: Harvard University Press, 1995); Konrad Jarausch and Hannes Siegrist, eds., *Amerikanisierung und Sowjetisierung in Deutschland, 1945–1970* (Frankfurt am Main: Campus, 1997); Uta Poiger, *Jazz, Rock, and Rebels: Cold War Politics and American Culture in a Divided Germany* (Berkeley: University of California Press, 2000); Petra Goedde, *GIs and Germans: Culture, Gender, and Foreign Relations, 1945–1949* (New Haven, CT: Yale University Press, 2003). On the topic of domestic culture and interior design, Greg Castillo's seminal study compares how the two superpowers operationalized modern design principles diplomatically. Castillo, *Cold War on the Home Front: The Soft Power of Midcentury Design* (Minneapolis: University of Minnesota Press, 2010).

16 Scholarship has explored a variety of factors that played a role in the sudden collapse of the GDR: the changing international system of the Cold War, the lacking political-military support by the Soviet Union, the immanent state bankruptcy after four decades of centrally planned economy, and the resulting failure to fulfill the population's consumer demands. What is striking is the isolated examination of the GDR—the Federal Republic plays only a role insofar as it is the objectionable opposite and representative of the ideology to be defeated. See Merkel, *Utopie und Bedürfnis*; Raymond Stokes, *Constructing Socialism: Technology and Change in East Germany, 1945–1990* (Baltimore, MD: Johns Hopkins University Press, 2000); Jonathan R. Zatlin, *The Currency of Socialism: Money and Political Culture in East Germany* (Cambridge: Cambridge University Press, 2007).

17 Some of the most influential voices in the convergence theory literature include Walt Whitman Rostow, *The Stages of Economic Growth: A Non-Communist Manifesto* (Cambridge: Cambridge University Press, 1960); Raymond Aron, *Dix-Huit Leçons sur la Société Industrielle* (Paris: Gallimard, 1963); Jan Tinbergen, "Kommt es zu einer Annäherung zwischen den kommunistischen und den freiheitlichen Wirtschaftsordnungen?" *Hamburger Jahrbuch für Wirtschafts und Gesellschaftspolitik* 8 (1963): 11–20. Rostow represents the more extreme point of view of unilateral convergence, predicting that the socialist economies will eventually adapt their economic structures to the global capitalist system, while capitalist economies will remain mainly unchanged.

18 See Jutta Kneissel, "The Convergence Theory: The Debate in the Federal Republic of Germany," *New German Critique* 2, special issue on the German Democratic Republic, trans. Andreas Huyssen and Johanna Moore (Spring 1974): 16–27. Kneissel provides a broad overview of the 1960s convergence theory debates and also offers a treatment of its reception in the GDR.

19 In recent years, GDR design has been rediscovered by design historians. Examples of this burgeoning literature include Katharina Pfützner, *Designing for Socialist Need:*

Industrial Design Practice in the German Democratic Republic (Oxon: Routledge, 2018); and Christian Wölfel, Sylvia Wölfel, and Jens Krzywinski, eds., *Gutes Design: Martin Kelm und die Designförderung in der DDR* (Dresden: Thelem, 2014).

20 See, for example, Johannes Paulmann, ed., *Auswärtige Repräsentationen: Deutsche Kulturdiplomatie nach 1945* (Cologne: Böhlau, 2005); Frank Trommler, *Kulturmacht ohne Kompass: Deutsche auswärtige Kulturbeziehungen im 20. Jahrhundert* (Cologne: Böhlau, 2014); Greg Castillo, "Domesticating the Cold War: Household Consumption as Propaganda in Marshall Plan Germany," *Journal of Contemporary History* 40, no. 2 (April 2005): 261–288.

21 By the 1980s, Germans entertained a multitude of perspectives on the German Question. The traditionalist view saw the question in freeing the GDR from the shackles of communism with the ultimate goal of forming a nation-state. Policies that represented this view usually came from the conservative political spectrum. The Europeanist view centered on Germany's role in Europe, trying to move Germany from the periphery of the Western Alliance to the center in an increasingly significant political entity. This conception has less to do with the notion of German unity than with the re-establishment of its economic and political significance. This view was held by liberal parties. The universalist view followed a contrary idea that saw Germans overcome their political division and their past by promoting universal values such as peace, social justice, and environmental preservation. The Green Party as well as segments of the cultural elite supported this approach. At one time or the other, the underlying premises of these conceptions informed in different ways East and West German decision-making in Western relations, East-West relations, and especially in the internal German relationship. Anne-Marie Burley, "The Once and Future German Question," *Foreign Affairs* 68, no. 5 (1989): 66.

Chapter 1

1 Bundesarchiv (hereafter BArch), B102/207796, Walter Gropius to Karl Schiller, 18 December 1967.

2 It should be noted that the postwar economic situation developed differently in East and West. Some of the reasons were the differing extent of reparations taken by the Allies and the Soviet Union, the varying results of socialism and capitalism, and the positive effects of the Marshall Plan in the Federal Republic. See Greg Castillo, "Exhibiting the Good Life: Marshall Plan Modernism in Divided Berlin," in *Cold War Modern: Art and Design in a Divided World, 1945–1975,* ed. David Crowly and Jane Pavett, 66–71 (London: Victoria and Albert Museum, 2008); Zatlin, *The Currency of Socialism*; Naimark, *The Russians in Germany.*

3 Design Council, "Our history," http://www.designcouncil.org.uk/en/Design-Council/1/Our-history/ accessed on 10 July 2008. On the constitution and immediate postwar activities of the Council of Industrial Design, see Patrick J. Maguire

and Jonathan M. Woodham, eds., *Design and Cultural Politics in Post-War Britain: The Britain Can Make It Exhibition of 1946* (London: Leicester University Press, 1997).

4 The first national design council, the Swedish Society for Industrial Design, was founded in 1845 to safeguard the quality of Swedish handmade crafts and "to counter the perceived threat from industrial mass production and from the poor quality products made by craftsmen who were not trained by the guilds." In the early twentieth century, the society accepted the predominance of industrial goods and thereafter sought to guide industrial production aesthetics. Svensk Form, "How It All Started," http://www.svenskform.se/english/ accessed on 10 July 2008.

5 See, for example, April A. Eisman, "East German Art and the Permeability of the Berlin Wall," *German Studies Review* 38, no. 3 (2015): 597–616; Poiger, *Jazz, Rock and Rebels*.

6 This stereotype has contributed to the near omission of GDR design in German postwar design history, for example, see Marion Godau and Bernd Polster, *Design Lexikon Deutschland* (Cologne: DuMont, 2000). See also Pfützner, *Designing for Socialist Need*, 3.

7 Betts, *Authority of Everyday Objects*, 11.

8 For a detailed account of the Werkbund from its founding to the Third Reich, see Joan Campbell, *The German Werkbund: The Politics of Reform in the Applied Arts* (Princeton, NJ: Princeton University Press, 1978). See also Oestereich, *"Gute Form" im Wiederaufbau*, 53–55.

9 The complex history and legacy of the Bauhaus cannot be treated here, but myriad works on the avant-garde of Weimar's Bauhaus have been published in the past four decades. See Anja Baumhoff and Magdalena Droste, eds., *Mythos Bauhaus: Zwischen Selbsterfindung und Enthistorisierung* (Berlin: Reimer, 2009); Wulf Herzogenrath, "Zur Rezeption des Bauhauses," in *Beiträge zur Rezeption der Kunst des 19. und 20. Jahrhunderts*. Studien zur Kunst des neunzehnten Jahrhunderts 29, ed. Wulf Schadendorf, 129–141 (Munich: Prestel, 1975). Christina Biundo, Kerstin Eckstein, Petra Eisele, Carolyn Graf, Gabriele Diana Grawe, and Claudia Heitmann, *Bauhaus-Ideen, 1919–1994: Bibliographie und Beiträge zur Rezeption des Bauhausgedankens* (Berlin: Reimer, 1994) provide a comprehensive overview of literature and sources on the Bauhaus up to its date of publication.

10 Mark Jarzombek, "The *Kunstgewerbe*, the *Werkbund*, and the Aesthetics of Culture in the Wilhelmine Period," *Journal of the Society of Architectural Historians* 53, no. 1 (1994): 8.

11 Jeremy Aynsley, *Designing Modern Germany* (London: Reaktion Books, 2009), 50.

12 The founding of the Austrian Werkbund in 1912 and the Swiss Werkbund in 1913 show how influential the Werkbund movement was across the German-speaking lands.

13 *Neues Bauen* in Frankfurt and the 1927 Weissenhofsiedlung in Stuttgart remain the most consistent testimony to the period. See Betts, *Authority of Everyday Objects*, 30.

14 Ibid., 23–72.

15 Campbell, *The Werkbund*, 224–226.

16 Campbell finds that the Werkbund leaders Ernst Jäckh and Hans Peolzig tried to work the Nazi machinery and appease the party structures in order to maintain control over the coordination process (*Gleichschaltungsprozess*). Nevertheless, by the autumn of 1933 the Werkbund had come completely under the domination of the Nazi state.

17 Nazism's co-option of modernism has been discussed by numerous authors, for example, see Andrew Hewitt, *Fascist Modernism: Aesthetics, Politics, and the Avant-Garde* (Stanford, CA: Stanford University Press, 1993). For an overview of the debate, see Winfried Nerdinger, "Modernisierung: Bauhaus Nationalsozialismus," in *Bauhaus-Moderne im Nationalsozialismus*, ed. Andrew Hewitt (Munich: Prestel, 1993), 9–23.

18 Frederic J. Schwartz, "'Funktionalismus heute': Adorno, Bloch und das Erbe des Modernismus der BRD," in *Mythos Bauhaus: Zwischen Selbsterfindung und Enthistorisierung*, ed. Anja Baumhoff and Magdalena Droste (Berlin: Reimer, 2009), 320–321.

19 Ibid.

20 Herbert Steinwarz, *Wesen, Aufgaben, Ziele des Amtes Schönheit der Arbeit* (Berlin, 1937), 5–6.

21 Oestereich, *"Gute Form" im Wiederaufbau*, 23.

22 Ibid., 267.

23 Aynsley, *Designing Modern Germany*, 151.

24 Castillo, *Cold War on the Home Front*, 7–8.

25 The concept of "kitsch" originated in the nineteenth century in reaction to Romanticism in literature and painting. With the rise of aesthetic education in the early twentieth century, criticism gave kitsch a pejorative meaning of cheapness—an illusion that betrays the audience. In the interwar years, kitsch became associated with cultural crisis and social decay. Walter Benjamin was one of the first thinkers to explore production of kitsch in the mechanical age. He posits that by substituting a plurality of copies for a unique existence, the object loses its authenticity, which he understands to be the artistic essence of things. These copies can be put "into situations which would be out of reach for the original itself." Walter Benjamin, *Illuminations*, ed. Hannah Arendt, trans. Harry Zohn (New York: Schocken Books, 2007), 220–221. After 1945, the negative conception of kitsch continued to influence aesthetic discourse and education. Katrin Pallowski, "Zur Kontinuität der 'klassischen Moderne' in den 50er Jahren," in *Design in Deutschland, 1933–45*, ed. Sabine Weißler (Gießen: Anabas, 1990), 133–134. For an overview of the kitsch debate over the course of two centuries, see Ute Dettmar and Thomas Küpper, *Kitsch: Texte und Theorien* (Stuttgart: Philipp Reclam jun., 2007).

26 For a detailed description of the exhibition and the reactions to it, see Castillo, *Cold War on the Home Front*, 7–8.

27 Oestereich, *"Gute Form" im Wiederaufbau*, 283.

28 Ibid., 284.

29 With the help of the Soviet occupiers, the German Communist Party forced a merger with the Social Democratic Party in the eastern zone of occupation in April 1946.

30 For a detailed account of Soviet cultural occupation policy between 1945 and 1949, see Naimark, *Russians in Germany*.

31 Bruno Paul's furniture designs figure among the most prominent works of German art nouveau at the turn of the century. Shortly thereafter, Paul became one of the driving members behind the Deutscher Werkbund.

32 Petra Eisele, "Ist Geschmack Glücksache? Horst Michel und das Weimarer Institut für Innengestaltung," in *Horst Michel—DDR-Design: Tagungsband zum Kolloquium*, ed. Petra Eisele and Siegfried Gronert (Weimar: Universitätsverlag, 2004), 27.

33 Sammlung Industrielle Gestaltung, Stiftung Haus der Geschichte der Bundesrepublik Deutschland (hereafter SiG), box "AIF Diverses ungeordnet," handwritten notes, "Horst Michel," 20 November 1984. The foundation *Haus der Geschichte der Bundesrepublik Deutschland* has taken over the former library, photography archive, and product collection of the East German design council *Amt für industrielle Forgestaltung* (AiF). This industrial design collection contains uncataloged primary sources in a number of boxes and binders. Some of the materials contain research for AiF publications, others document the rich exhibition activity of the AiF and its predecessor organizations. I used the labeling on the boxes and binders to make the sources traceable, and included additional information where possible.

34 Law quoted in Eisele, "Ist Geschmack Glücksache?," 27.

35 See Heinz Hirdina, *Gestalten für die Serie* (Dresden: Verlag der Kunst, 1988), 216; Ronald Stade, "Designs of Identity," 245.

36 "Horst Michel," 20 November 1984.

37 "Richtlinien für die Kulturabteilungen der SED," 15 June 1946, in *Politik und Kultur in der Sowjetischen Besatzungszone Deutschlands (SBZ), 1945–1949*, ed. Gerd Dietrich (Berlin: Peter Lang, 1993), 254–255; and "Entschließung zur Kulturpolitik, angenommen vom Ersten Kulturtag der SED in Berlin," 7 May 1948," in ibid., 310–314.

38 "Schreiben der Abteilung Parteischulung, Kultur und Erziehung beim Zentralsekretariat an die Landes-und Kreisvorstände der SED," May 1948, in ibid., 315–320.

39 For discussions of 1949 and the resulting German-German competition for national legitimacy and international recognition, see Wilfried Loth, *Stalin's Unwanted Child: The Soviet Union, the German Question, and the Founding of the GDR*, trans. Robert F. Hogg (Houndmills, Basingstoke, Hampshire: Macmillan Press, 1998); Naimark, *Russians in Germany*; Ronald J. Granieri, *The Ambivalent Alliance: Konrad Adenauer, the CDU/CSU, and the West, 1949–1966* (New York: Berghahn Books, 2003); Gray, *Germany's Cold War*; Jarausch and Siegrist, ed., *Amerikanisierung und Sowjetisierung in Deutschland*.

40 Antonio Gramsci, "Questions of Culture," in *Selections from Cultural Writings*, ed. by David Forgacs and Geoffrey Nowell-Smith, trans. by William Boelhower (Cambridge, MA: Harvard University Press, 1985), 41. [Originally published in *Avanti!*, Piedmont edition, 14 June 1920.]

41 Boris Groys, *Gesamtkunstwerk Stalin: Die gespaltene Kultur in der Sowjetunion* (Munich: Carl Hanser, 1988), 27.

42 Christina Kiaer called it the "social use value for art," which operated through

the creation of democratic objects for the everyday. Kiaer, *Imagine No Possessions: The Socialist Objects of Russian Constructivism* (Cambridge, MA: MIT Press, 2005), 4.

43 The emotionality of cultural Stalinism is especially evident in literature, as Katerina Clark has skillfully illustrated in her work on the ritualistic socialist realist novel. Clark, *The Soviet Novel: History and Ritual* (Bloomington: Indiana University Press, [1981] 2000). For more information about the role of human emotions in socialist thought turn to Derek Müller, "Das Menschenbild im Stalinismus," in *Der Topos des Neuen Menschen in der russischen und sowjetrussischen Geistesgeschichte*, 220–246 (Bern: Peter Lang, 1998).

44 Müller called the style of socialist realist culture "pathetic, heroic, and neo-classical." Müller, "Das Menschenbild im Stalinismus," 234.

45 See Naimark, *Russians in Germany*.

46 For a discussion of the social impetus in East German design, see Pfützner, *Designing for Socialist Need*.

47 Wagenfeld quoted in Oestereich, *"Gute Form" im Wiederaufbau*, 285. One of the few industrial designers who had continuously worked during the Weimar Republic, the Third Reich as well as postwar Germany, Wagenfeld left an impressive body of work ranging from lamp designs to glassware. Throughout these decades he stayed true to his leftist politics, which he openly displayed in his extensive written work about the relationship between design and society. Betts, *Authority of Everyday Objects*, 79.

48 A. Dirk Moses, *German Intellectuals and the Nazi Past* (Cambridge: Cambridge University Press, 2007), 42.

49 See Mark E. Spicka, *Selling the Economic Miracle: Economic Reconstruction and Politics in West Germany, 1949–1957* (New York: Berghahn, 2007), 3–5; Wolfrum, *Die geglückte Demokratie*, 75–77; Konrad Jarausch, *Die Umkehr: Deutsche Wandlungen 1945–1995* (Bonn: Bundeszentrale für politische Bildung, 2004), 117; Heinrich August Winkler, *Der lange Weg nach Westen: Deutsche Geschichte 1933–1990*, vol. 2 (Bonn: Bundeszentrale für politische Bildung, 2005), 160–161; Axel Schildt, *Ankunft im Westen: Ein Essay zur Erfolgsgeschichte der Bundesrepublik* (Frankfurt am Main: Fischer 1999), 49–86, for a selection of the literature on the 1948 currency reform and its effects on the West German economy.

50 BArch, B102/1964 Heft 1, text draft, Ludwig Erhard, "The Purpose of the German Industrial Exhibition in New York," 25 January 1949.

51 Ibid.

52 A detailed discussion of postwar German cultural diplomacy with a shift in emphasis from cultural imperialism to cultural exchange is provided by Paulmann, *Auswärtige Repräsentationen*, and Trommler, *Kulturmacht ohne Kompass*.

53 Konrad Jarausch introduced the concept of recivilization, a depiction of four decades of German division as a constant struggle to instill the publics and political cultures in both German states with lasting postfascist ethical standards. While he does not treat artistic expression and material culture, these fields are indispensable for an

analysis that seeks to connect the public to the private. See Jarausch, *After Hitler: Recivilizing Germans, 1945–1995* (Oxford: Oxford University Press, 2006).

54 See Castillo for a verbatim excerpt from German émigré and Museum of Modern Art (MoMA) assistant curator Herwin Schaefer's critique. Castillo, *Cold War on the Home Front*, 34–35.

55 Betts, *Authority of Everyday Objects*, 179–180. Betts provides an in-depth account of the international critique of the German display at the New York "Decorate Your House" show.

56 In reaction to the late nineteenth-century British disdain for German wares—the label "Made in Germany" was first introduced with Britain's 1887 Merchandise Marks Act to warn English consumers of German low-quality products—the prevention of kitsch became a guiding idea in the aesthetic reform movements of the early twentieth century. See Maiken Umbach, "Made in Germany," in *Deutsche Erinnerungsorte II*, ed. Etienne Francois and Hagen Schulze (Munich: C. H. Beck, 2001), 407.

57 Oestereich, *"Gute Form" im Wiederaufbau*, 285.

58 For the details of the parliamentary proceedings, see ibid., 286–289.

59 BArch, B102/34493, Heinrich König, presentation "Rat für Formgebung," 25 October 1950.

60 BArch, B102/34493, Max Wiederanders, report before the Bundestag Committee on Cultural Policy, 25 October 1950.

61 Oestereich, *"Gute Form" im Wiederaufbau*, 288.

62 *Wir bauen ein besseres Leben: Eine Ausstellung über die Produktivität der Atlantischen Gemeinschaft auf dem Gebiet des Wohnbedarfs* (Stuttgart: Gerd Hatje, 1952), 3.

63 Greg Castillo, "Marshall Plan Modernism in Divided Germany," in *Cold War Modern*, ed. David Crowley and Jane Pavitt (London: Victoria and Albert Museum, 2008), 66–67.

64 The West German daily newspaper *Der Tag*, 22 September 1952, quoted in Castillo, "Marshall Plan Modernism in Divided Germany," 68.

65 BArch, B102/34493, Walter Kersting to Ludwig Erhard, 30 September 1951.

66 Aynsley, *Designing Modern Germany*, 179–180.

67 Max Bill quoted in Betts, *Authority of Everyday Objects*, 142.

68 For an extensive treatment of the programmatic and ideological linkages between Bauhaus and HfG Ulm, see Claudia Heitmann, "Die Bauhaus-Rezeption in der Bundesrepublik Deutschland von 1949–1968—Etappen und Institutionen" (PhD diss. Hochschule der Künste Berlin, 2001), 98–223; Thilo Hilpert, "The Postwar Dispute in West Germany: The Renewal of Rationalism," in *Bauhaus Conflicts, 1919–2009*, ed. Stiftung Bauhaus Dessau, 128–148 (Ostfildern: Hatje Cantz, 2009); Betts, *Authority of Everyday Objects*, 149.

69 Aynsley, *Designing Modern Germany*, 181.

70 Martin Bober, "Von der Idee zum Mythos: Die Rezeption des Bauhaus in beiden Teilen Deutschlands in Zeiten des Neuanfangs (1945 und 1989)" (PhD diss., Universität Kassel, n.d.), 134.

71 Clark, *Soviet Novel: History and Ritual*, 34 and 150.

72 Sächsisches Staatsarchiv Dresden (hereafter SächsStA-D), 11764/3131, Kant to Wurzler and Weber, "Vorbereitung KAS und BKV," here: Note from Weber, 10 November 1954.

73 An official photographer captured the open house exhibition on film, see BArch, 14 565/5N, E IV b1, 3 May 1952.

74 See Bober, "Von der Idee zum Mythos," 143; Rubin, *Synthetic Socialism*, 45; and Selle, *Geschichte des Design*. However, Betts and Castillo have noted the discursive quality of the debate. See Castillo, *Cold War on the Home Front*, esp. 51; Paul Betts, "Building Socialism at Home: The Case of East German Interiors," in *Socialist Modern: East German Everyday Culture and Politics*, ed. Katherine Pence and Paul Betts (Ann Arbor: University of Michigan Press, 2008), 102.

75 Martin Kelm, in discussion with the author, 4 May 2009.

76 Aynsley, *Designing Modern Germany*, 177.

77 Ernst May went to the Soviet Union to support the construction of Soviet socialism between 1930 and 1933. His team included the Austrian architect Margarete Schütte-Lihotzky, who invented the famous functional Frankfurt kitchen, the precursor to the modern kitchens that are designed rationally around the individual work steps of cooking, cleaning, and washing. Most of the Brigade members left the Soviet Union disheartened by the restrictions that the bleak economic and political reality set to their idealistic vision of a holistic approach to housing.

78 SiG, 14/A/3, folder "Materialien zur Designgeschichte der DDR," Selman Selmanagic, interview by Siegfried Zoel, transcript, 19 September 1985.

79 Selmanagic interview. For his biography, see Sonja Wüsten, "Selman Selmanagić Biographisches," in *Selman Selmanagić: Festgabe zum 80. Geburtstag am 25. April 1985*, ed. Sonja Wüsten, Dietmar Kuntzsch, and Hans Menday (Berlin, 1984), 6–41.

80 Selmanagic, interview.

81 The Bundesarchiv Berlin (BArch) holds most of the AiF documents (DF 7) that cover political and economic work. The source base on the first years of design institutionalization is surprisingly slim, which might have resulted from its humble beginnings at Weißensee before it integrated into the state apparatus via the Ministry of Culture.

82 Eli Rubin, "The Form of Socialism without Ornament: Consumption, Ideology, and the Fall and Rise of Modernist Design in the German Democratic Republic," *Journal of Design History* 19, no. 2 (2006): 160.

83 BArch, B102/34493, Bundestag minutes, 129th session, 4 April 1951.

84 BArch, B102/3449, information leaflet, "Rat für Formgebung: Stiftung zur Förderung der Formgestaltung," n.d., 2.

85 Michael Erlhoff (executive manager of the Rat für Formgebung, 1984–90), in discussion with the author, 6 July 2009.

86 BArch, B102/34492, information leaflet, "Rat für Formgebung: Stiftung zur Förderung der Formgestaltung," n.d.

87 Betts, *Authority of Everyday Objects*, 184.

88 Stadtarchiv Stuttgart (hereafter StAS), Estate Mia Seeger, 2068/A 81, Heinrich König to Arno Henning (MdB), 30 June 1951.

89 StAS, Estate Mia Seeger, 2068/A 81, Schwippert to Hinsch, 15 June 1952.

90 König to Henning, 30 June 1951.

91 The Werkbund had issued a memorandum "Zur Einrichtung eines Rat für Formgebung," in which it proposed the founding of a second body to the actual design council. This task force of representatives from all tiers of the economic system was to help implement the Rat für Formgebung's decisions. Among the memorandum's signatories were Heinrich König, Karl Ott, Egon Eiermann, and Mia Seeger. StAS, Estate Mia Seeger, 2068/A 81, memorandum, August 1951.

92 One of the first projects that Mia Seeger completed with the support of the design council structures was the four-volume opus *Deutsche Warenkunde* (published between 1955 and 1961), which she co-edited with Stephan Hirzel. This project continued and updated the 1915 *Deutsches Warenbuch* of the Werkbund, one of the first collections of German manufactured wares that embodied the simplified, functionalist aesthetic of *Gute Form*. The *Weissenhofsiedlung*, a modernist architecture and interior design exhibition at the outskirts of Stuttgart in 1927, was her first project of international significance. At Weissenhof she worked with architects of international acclaim, such as Mies van der Rohe, Le Corbusier, El Lissitzky, and Ernst May. In 1930, Seeger organized the German exhibitions at the Société Artistes Décorateurs in the Paris Grand Palais in collaboration with the director of the Bauhaus Walter Gropius and helped design the German presentation at the Milan Triennials of 1930 and 1936. Karin Kirsch, "Mia Seeger 1903–1991," in *Baden-Württembergische Portraits: Frauengestalten aus fünf Jahrhunderten*, ed. Elisabeth Nölle-Neumann (Stuttgart: Deutsche Verlags-Anstalt, 2000), 247–254.

93 "Der Rat für Formgebung: Stiftung zur Förderung der Formgestaltung."

94 BArch, B102/34492, statutes, "Stiftung zur Förderung der Formgestaltung," April 1953.

95 Werkbundarchiv, Berlin (hereafter WBA-MdD), Hartmann Estate, Binder 13, ADK 7–1384/52, memo, Bundesverband der Deutschen Industrie, Arbeitskreis für industrielle Formgestaltung, "Bericht über die Arbeitstagung am 28./29.10.52 in Darmstadt," 8 December 1952. Jonathan Wiesen, *West German Industry and the Challenge of the Nazi Past, 1945–1955* (Chapel Hill: University of North Carolina Press, 2001), 159–163.

96 The government budget allocated annual funds of DM 70,000 under title 604 to support "rationalization, standardization, and design." This amount was raised to DM 120,000 in 1957–58 by the addition of title 601 for the "promotion of crafts." BArch, B120/34492, itemized budget, "Aufwendungen des Bundes zur Förderung des 'Rat für Formgebung.'"

97 At that time, the exchange rate between the West and East German marks was 1:1.

98 BArch, DF 7/3, Zentralinstitut für Formgestaltung, "Budget 1964," 25 November 1963.

99 BArch, B102/227796, memorandum "Formgestaltung als wirtschafts-und kultur-politischer Faktor," 8 June 1967.

100 Steiner, *Von Plan zu Plan*, 73.

101 On the link between the work quotas and supply shortages in consumer goods, see Katherine Pence, "'You as a Woman Will Understand': Consumption, Gender and the Relationship between State and Citizenry in the GDR Crisis of 17 June 1953," *German History* 19, no. 2 (2001): 218–252.

102 For a discussion of the refocused New Course after 17 June 1953, see Mark Landsman, *Dictatorship and Demand: The Politics of Consumerism in East Germany* (Cambridge, MA: Harvard University Press, 2005), 115–148.

103 Ibid., 118–119.

104 See Armin Grünbacher, "Sustaining the Island: Western Aid to 1950s West Berlin," *Cold War History* 3, no. 3 (2003): 1–23.

105 BArch, DF 7/3167, "Die Arbeit der Redaktion 'Bildende Kunst' am Jahrgang 1963," n.d.

106 BArch, DF 7/3057, statutes, Rat für Industrieform, 1 July 1962.

107 For Martin Kelm's career path, see Rubin, "The Form of Socialism," 160.

108 BArch, DF 7/2207, Entwurf der Sekretariats-Vorlage "Über die Änderung der Unterstellung des Rates für Industrieform und des Zentralinstitutes für Formgestaltung sowie über weitere Maßnahmen zur Verbesserung der Industrieformgestaltung," 26 September 1964.

109 See Rubin, "Form of Socialism," 161–162.

110 Ibid.

111 Selmanagic interview.

112 The significance of party credentials for upward mobility within the state apparatus of the GDR has been discussed by Epstein, *Last Revolutionaries*.

113 Rubin, "Form of Socialism," 161.

114 BArch, DF 7/2207, Culture Department of the ZK, draft "Über die Änderung der Unterstellung des Rates für Industrieform und des Zentralinstitutes für Formgestaltung sowie über weitere Maßnahmen zur Verbesserung der Industrieformgestaltung," 26 September 1964.

115 Ibid.

116 For example, Rubin proposes that the worker protests of 17 June 1953 already marked the shift from cultural Stalinism to functionalism. See Rubin, "The Form of Socialism," 158.

117 On the history of Berlin prefab housing, see Florian Urban, *Tower and Slab: Histories of Global Mass Housing* (London: Routledge, 2012), 59–78.

118 See Loth, *Stalin's Unwanted Child*; Hope M. Harrison, *Driving the Soviets Up the Wall: Soviet-East German Relations, 1953–1961* (Princeton, NJ: Princeton University Press, 2003).

119 Martin Kelm, in discussion with the author, 4 May 2009.

120 For a detailed description of the German pavilion at Brussels, see Aynsley,

Designing Modern Germany, 156–161. As discussed earlier in this chapter, the Hitler regime did employ modernism for its own goals. During the Cold War, however, the complexity of Nazi culture was deflated into essentially "blood and soil" pastoralism and antimodernism. Betts, *Authority of Everyday Objects*, 187.

121 WBA-MdD, Hartmann Estate, folder 13, correspondence between Eiermann, Seeger, Schneider, and G. v. Hartmann, May–August 1954.

122 "So urteilte die Welt," *Werk und Zeit* 6, no. 7 (1958): 7.

123 See Johannes Paulmann, "Representation without Emulation: German Cultural Diplomacy in Search of Integration and Self-Assurance during the Adenauer Era," *German Politics and Society* 25, no. 2 (2007): 180–181.

124 In successive years, the values of humility and transparency also found its way into state architecture. In 1963, Ludwig Erhard, new chancellor of the Federal Republic, chose Sep Ruf, co-designer of the Brussel pavilion, as the architect for the *Kanzlerbungalow*, the official residence of the chancellor in Bonn. Carola Ebert, "Into the Great Wide Open: The Modernist Bungalow in 1960s West Germany/Avaryyseihalus. Modernistlik bangalo 1960. aastate Lääne-Saksamaal," in *Constructed Happiness: Domestic Environment in the Cold War Era/Võistlevad õnned: Elukeskkond külma sõja perioodili*, ed. Mart Kalm and Ingrid Ruudi, proceedings of a conference held at the Institute of Art History, Estonian Academy of Arts in Tallinn, 20–22 May 2004 (Tallinn: Trükk, 2005), 148.

125 Oestereich, *"Gute Form" im Wiederaufbau*, 298–299.

126 BArch, B102/151283, Schneider to Schmücker, 28 June 1965.

127 Manfred Sack, "Unter drückendem Hut der Industrie: Wie der Rat für Formgebung sein Unabhängigkeit verlor," *Zeit* 51, 20 December 1968.

128 The East German leadership contested the establishment of the IDZ in West Berlin, as it saw the center as a governmental institution. Britsch to Schiller, von Dohnanyi, Rat für Formgebung; Re: Denkschrift des RfF vom 8. Juni 1967, Besprechung bei Staatssekretär von Dohnanyi, 22 August 1968, BArch B102/151284.

129 The disagreement between the Werkbund and the BDI is well documented in *Werk und Zeit* 17, no. 11 (1968); and *Werk und Zeit* 18, no. 6/7 (1969). See also Max Peter Maass, "Was kann den Rat für Formgebung noch retten?," *Darmstädter Tagblatt*, 29 May 1969.

130 Betts, *Authority of Everyday Objects*, 252.

131 WBA-MdD, folder "Rat für Formgebung I," Deutscher Werkbund statement, 27 June 1969.

132 WBA-MdD, folder "Rat für Formgebung/AOU I," Jochen Rahe (chair of the board Deutscher Werkbund Hessen e.V.) to Dieter Rams (RfF president), 5 May 1989.

133 WBA-MdD, ADO 7–1615/55, Mia Seeger, catalog *Deutsche Wohnung: Ausstellung Hälsingborg H55*, 1955.

134 Thilo Hilpert, "The Postwar Dispute in West Germany: The Renewal of Rationalism," in *Bauhaus Conflicts, 1919–2009*, ed. Stiftung Bauhaus Dessau (Ostfildern: Hatje Cantz, 2009), 129.

135 Ibid., 132–135.

136 On the connections of this debate to the closing of the Bauhaus, see Betts, *Authority of Everyday Objects*, 85.

137 Josef Kremerskothen, "Wohnen wie noch nie," in *Rolf Heide—Designer, Architekt, Querdenker*, ed. Dirk Meyhöfer (Ludwigsburg: Avedition, 2000), 13.

138 Josef Kremerskothen, "Wegstücke," in *Peter Maly*, Designermonographien 5, ed. Alex Buck and Matthias Vogt (Frankfurt am Main: Form, 1998), 18.

139 Peter Maly, in discussion with the author, 6 May 2009. Rolf Heide, in discussion with the author, 5 May 2009.

140 Dieter Rams and Hans Gugelot's work for the radio company Braun was the most successful merging of Ulm's functionalist dogmatism with industrial design. This collaboration broke with radio design conventions and was highly influential in shaping West German progressive aesthetics in consumer goods.

141 Heitmann, "Bauhaus-Rezeption in der Bundesrepublik Deutschland," 134.

142 "Auf dem Kuhberg," *Der Spiegel*, 20 March 1963, 71–75.

143 See Betts, *Authority of Everyday Objects*, 174–176.

144 For a discussion of the effects of nuclear deterrence policy in Cold War society, see Jeremi Suri, *Power and Protest: Global Revolution and the Rise of Détente* (Cambridge, MA: Harvard University Press, 2003), 7–43.

145 Theodor W. Adorno, "Funktionalismus heute," in *Gesammelte Schriften* 10.1, ed. Rolf Tiedemann, 375–395 (Frankfurt am Main: Suhrkamp, 1977).

146 Ibid., 380.

147 Robert Twombly, ed., *Louis Sullivan: The Public Papers* (Chicago: University of Chicago Press, 1988), xii.

148 Abraham A. Moles, "Die Krise des Funktionalismus," *Form* 41 (1968): 36; Werner Nehls, "Die heiligen Kühe des Funktionalismus müssen geopfert werden," *Form* 43 (1968): 4; Hartmut Seeger, "Funktionalismus im Rückspiegel des Design," ibid., 10–11; Gerda Müller-Krauspe, "Opas Funktionalismus ist tot—Der Standort des Industrial Design—gestern, heute und morgen," *Form* 46 (1969): 29–32. See also Betts's discussion of Adorno and the demise of functionalism. Betts, *Authority of Everyday Objects*, 254–257.

149 See Adorno, "Funktionalismus heute," 381; Hartmut Seeger, "Syntaktik und Semantik," *Form* 46 (1969): 34–36.

150 "Fortschrittliche Möbelkultur—behagliches Wohnen und gute Arbeit," *Berliner Zeitung*, special edition for the 1950 Leipzig Fair, 27 August–1 September 1950.

151 Horst Michel, "Verbindung von Zweck und Anmut: Sinn und Unsinn unseres Gebrauchsgeräts," in *Nationalzeitung* (Berlin Ost), 15 October 1950.

152 Michel cit. after J. W. "Möbel als Ausdruck unseres Kulturwillens," in *Nationalzeitung* (Berlin Ost), 6 June 1952, n.p.

153 Eisele, "Ist Geschmack Glücksache?," 46.

154 By holding official industrial design competitions across industrial sectors, economic planners attempted to include the working people in the process of finding a socialist culture that corresponded to the needs and tastes of the population. In this

way, they believed, waste and kitsch would be avoided. See SächsStA-D, 11764/2222, Ministry for Light Industries, "Aufruf zum Wettbewerb zur Erlangung von Entwürfen auf der Grundlage des Ministerratsbeschlusses vom 12.1.1954"; BArch, B102/284972–2, "DDR Presse-Informationen," 17 January 1984.

155 Michel, *Der Industrieformgestalter auf dem Bitterfelder Weg*, Institut für Innengestaltung an der Hochschule für Architektur und Bauwesen Weimar (Weimar: Buch- und Kunstdruckerei Johannes Keipert, n.d.), 7.

156 M.P., "Wohnraumkultur trotz Standardisierung?," *Kultur im Heim* 1 (1960): 3.

157 "Ist Standard gleich uniform?," *Kultur im Heim* 1 (1960): 4.

158 Giulio Carlo Argan as quoted by Ekkehard Bartsch, "Standardisierung—Vielfalt—Formgestaltung," *Form und Zweck* 2 (1965): 9. Quoted from Giulio Carlo Argan, *Gropius und das Bauhaus* (1962), 31.

159 Bartsch, "Standardisierung—Vielfalt—Formgestaltung," 12.

160 Interview with Horst Heyder, "Erfahrungen," *Form und Zweck* 5 (1979): 22.

161 SiG, "Ausstellungen AIF, diverse Fotos," exhibition concept "Vom Bauhaus bis Bitterfeld," Frankfurt am Main, December 1990, n.d.

162 For instance, an official interior design advice publication of the early 1960s contained illustrations for both traditional and modern worker housing that showed functionalist furniture. A. G. Schuchardt, *Wie wohnen?*, 3rd ed. (Berlin: Institut für angewandte Kunst, 1962).

163 Horst Michel, "Forderungen an den Gestalter von Industrieprodukten fur den Wohnbereich," in *Informationen Rat fur Industrieform* 2, ed. Zentralinstitut für Formgestaltung (Berlin, 1964), 13.

164 SiG, "Ausstellungen AIF, diverse Fotos," "Abschlussbericht zur Austellung 'Modernes Wohnen' in Hoyerswerda, Tiergartenmuseum," 8 November 1965.

165 SiG, "Ausstellungen AIF, diverse Fotos," folder "1965 Ausstellung 'Modernes Wohnen' Hoyerswerda," Zentralinstitut für Formgestaltung, 1965. These visitor comments echoed the sentiment expressed at an exhibition that the ZfF organized in Neubrandenburg earlier that year. SiG, "Ausstellungen AIF, diverse Fotos," folder "Ausstellung 'Form' Neubrandenburg," Zentralinstitut für Formgestaltung, 1965.

166 Ibid.

167 BArch, DE1/26539, Großmann, "Bericht über die Beratung am 24.2.1959," 14 March 1959.

168 SiG, "Ausstellungen AIF, diverse Fotos," "Konzeption der Ausstellung 'Gestaltete Umwelt für den Menschen' zum 20. Jahrestag der Gründung der DDR 1969," 1 February 1968.

169 See Wolfgang Thöner, "State Doctrine or Criticism of the Regime: On the Reception of the Bauhaus in East Germany, 1963–1990," in *Bauhaus Conflicts*, ed. Stiftung Bauhaus Dessau (Ostfildern: Hatje Cantz, 2009), 226–242.

170 Paul Betts, *Within Walls: Private Life in the German Democratic Republic* (Oxford: Oxford University Press, 2010), 130.

171 Karin Hirdina quoted in Georg Bertsch, Ernst Hedler, and Matthias Dietz,

SED—Schönes Einheits Design (Cologne: Taschen Verlag, 1994), 28. This quotation originated in the 1975 article "Der Funktionalismus und eine Kritiker" in the East German design journal *Form und Zweck*.

172 It would take another ten years until the Bauhaus reopened as an educational institution that celebrated the leftist avant-gardism of former director Hannes Meyer. See Thöner, "State Doctrine or Criticism of the Regime," 237–240.

173 Betts, "Building Socialism at Home."

Chapter 2

1 Nation branding has been used for analysis of other national furniture industries, see Per Hansen, "Co-branding Product and Nation: Danish Modern Furniture and Denmark in the United States, 1940–1970," in *Trademarks, Brands, and Competitiveness*, ed. Teresa de Silva Lopes and Paul Duguid (New York: Routledge, 2010), 77–101; Per Hansen, *Danish Modern Furniture, 1930–2016: Rise, Decline and Re-emergence of a Cultural Category*, trans. Mark Mussari (Odense: University Press of Southern Denmark, 2018), esp. 4–5, 18–24.

2 Rafael Castro and Patricio Sáiz, "Cross-cultural Factors in International Branding," *Business History* 62, no. 1 (2020), special issue The Brand and Its History, Part II: Branding, Culture, and National Identity: 4–5.

3 Grant McCracken, "Culture and Consumption: A Theoretical Account of the Structure and Movement of the Cultural Meaning of Consumer Goods," *Journal of Consumer Research* 13, no. 1 (1986): 76.

4 Rohrlich, "Economic Culture and Foreign Policy," 69.

5 See Susan E. Reid, "Who Will Best Whom? Soviet Popular Reception of the American National Exhibition in Moscow, 1959," *Kritika: Explorations in Russian and Eurasian History* 9, no. 4 (2008): 855–904.

6 Michael E. Porter, "The Competitive Advantage of Nations," *Harvard Business Review* (March–April 1990): 73–93.

7 Drawing on Roland Barthes's concept of the "fashion system," Per Hansen points to the importance of coherent narratives in the successful transformation of a product into a national brand. Per Hansen, "Networks, Narratives, and Markets: The Rise and Decline of Danish Modern Furniture, 1930–1970," *Business History Review* 80, no. 3 (2006): 449–483.

8 For example, historians have contrasted the locally anchored concept of homeland (*Heimat*) with the nineteenth-century struggle for a German national identity. Celia Applegate, *A Nation of Provincials: The German Idea of Heimat* (Berkeley: University of California Press, 1990); Alon Confino, *The Nation as a Local Metaphor: Württemberg, Imperial Germany, and National Memory, 1871–1918* (Chapel Hill: University of North Carolina Press, 1997); Peter Heil, *"Gemeinden sind wichtiger als Staaten": Idee und Wirklichkeit des kommunalen Neuanfangs in Rheinland-Pfalz, 1945–1957.*

Veröffentlichung der Kommission des Landtages für die Geschichte des Landes Rheinland-Pfalz 21 (Mainz: v. Hase & Koehler, for the Kommission des Landtages, 1997); Katharina Wiegand, ed., *Heimat: Konstanten und Wandel im 19./20. Jahrhundert: Vorstellungen und Wirklichkeiten* (Munich: Deutscher Alpenverein, 1997); Benjamin Ziemann, *Front und Heimat: Ländliche Kriegserfahrungen im südlichen Bayern, 1914–1923*. Veröffentlichungen des Instituts zur Erforschung der europäischen Arbeiterbewegung, Schriftenreihe A: Darstellungen, no. 8 (Essen: Klartext. 1997); James Retallack, "'Why Can't a Saxon Be More Like a Prussian?' Regional Identities and the Birth of Modern Political Culture in Germany, 1866–67," *Canadian Journal of History* 32 (1997): 26–55. On the meaning of *Heimat* in German socialism, see Jan Palmowski, *Inventing a Socialist Nation: Heimat and the Politics of Everyday Life in the GDR, 1945–1990* (Cambridge: Cambridge University Press, 2009).

9 Karlheinz Hottes, "Regional Variations of the Economic Development in the Federal Republic of Germany," in *American German International Seminar. Geography and Regional Policy: Resource Management by Complex Political Systems*, ed. John S. Adams, Werner Fricke, and Wolfgang Herden (Heidelberg: Geographische Institut Universität Heidelberg, 1983), 41–42.

10 Lorenz Eitner, "Industrial Design in Postwar Germany," *Design Quarterly* 40 (1957): 13.

11 For literature on the Federal Republic's state-building and the social market economy, see Mark E. Spicka, *Selling the Economic Miracle: Economic Reconstruction and Politics in West Germany, 1949–1957* (New York: Berghahn, 2007), 3–5; Wolfrum, *Die geglückte Demokratie*, 75–77; Jarausch, *Die Umkehr*, 117; Winkler, *Der lange Weg nach Westen*, 160–161; Axel Schildt, *Ankunft im Westen: Ein Essay zur Erfolgsgeschichte der Bundesrepublik* (Frankfurt am Main: Fischer 1999), 49–86; and Erica Carter, *How German Is She? Postwar West German Reconstruction and the Consuming Woman* (Ann Arbor: University of Michigan Press, 1997), 5.

12 See Lutz Niethammer's analysis of interviews with workers in the Ruhr region. Lutz Niethammer, "Normalization in the West: Traces of Memory Leading Back into the 1950s," in *The Miracle Years: A Cultural History of West Germany, 1949–1968*, ed. Hanna Schissler (Princeton, NJ: Princeton University Press, 2001), 239.

13 As Mark E. Spicka's examination of Christian Democrats' election campaigns in the 1950s reveals, the Adenauer government understood popular sentiment and used it to form consensus by forging national identities deliberately around economic policies and the social market economy. Spicka, *Selling the Economic Miracle*, 3.

14 Werner Abelshauser, "Ansätze 'Korporativer Marktwirtschaft' in der Koreakrise der frühen fünziger Jahre: Ein Briefwechsel zwischen dem Hohen Kommissar John McCloy und Bundeskanzler Konrad Adenauer," *Vierteljahreshefte für Zeitgeschichte* 30, no. 4 (1982): 715–756.

15 Wolfrum, *Die geglückte Demokratie*, 79.

16 Corporatism (business, labor, government interaction) describes the instrumentalization of large organizations toward administrative activity that has traditionally fallen

to the state. For a detailed discussion of lobbyism, associations, and corporatism in Germany and an overview of scholarly works, see Peter Lösche, *Verbände und Lobbyismus in Deutschland* (Stuttgart: Kohlhammer, 2007); Eberhard Schütt-Wetschky, *Interessenverbände und Staat* (Darmstadt: Primus, 1997); Gerhard Lehmbruch, "Wandlungen der Interessenpolitik im liberalen Korporatismus," in *Verbände und Staat*, ed. Ulrich von Alemann and Rolf G. Heinze (Opladen: Westdeutscher, 1979), 51.

17 Bibliothek Bundesverband der Deutschen Industrie (hereafter BDI), statutes, "Kulturkreis im Bundesverband der Deutschen Industrie e.V.," 1952, Preamble.

18 *Gustav Stein: Sammler—Förderer—Freund*, ed. Wilhelm-Lehmbruck-Museum Duisburg (Duisburg: Stadt Duisburg, 1983), 13.

19 See Bührer, "Der Kulturkreis im Bundesverband der Deutschen Industrie und die 'kulturelle Modernisierung' der Bundesrepublik in den 50er Jahren"; BDI, Gustav Stein, "Das sechste Arbeitsjahr," in *Jahrestagung Lübeck 57*, ed. Kulturkreis im Bundesverband der Deutschen Industrie e.V., n.d., 24.

20 Gustav Stein, *Unternehmer als Förderer der Kunst* (Frankfurt am Main: August Lutzeyer, 1952), 2.

21 Werner Bührer, "Der Kulturkreis im Bundesverband der Deutschen Industrie und die 'kulturelle Modernisierung' der Bundesrepublik in den 50er Jahren," in *Modernisierung im Wiederaufbau: Die westdeutsche Gesellschaft der 50er Jahre*, ed. Axel Schildt and Arnold Sywottek (Bonn: Dietz, 1993), 584; S. Jonathan Wiesen, *West German Industry and the Challenge of the Nazi Past, 1945–1955* (Chapel Hill: University of North Carolina Press, 2001), 165–170.

22 Annual reports by the Rat für Formgebung provide a detailed description of the design council's activities and consulting contracts. For example, Bibliothek Rat für Formgebung (hereafter BRfF), Mia Seeger, "Rat für Formgebung—Darmstadt—Bericht für das Jahr 1956/1957," Darmstadt 8 April 1957.

23 Oestereich, *"Gute Form" im Wiederaufbau*, 230–231.

24 WBA-MdD, Hartmann Estate, ADK 7–1384/52, BDI Arbeitskreis für industrielle Formgestaltung, 8 December 1952.

25 BArch, B102/34492, Carl Hundhausen to Ludwig Erhard, 3 September 1958.

26 Ibid.

27 Stein, *Unternehmer als Förderer der Kunst*, 15–16.

28 BArch, B102/21240, Arbeitskreis für industrielle Formgebung im BDI, Rundschreiben Nr. 29, 8 November 1960.

29 There was obviously no singular "business interest" and "business community." They are used here as shorthand to identify mainstream attitudes and general tendencies among entrepreneurs, not to ignore diverse entrepreneurial opinions and management styles in industrial organizations.

30 Geyer in interview with Johann Klöcker, "Industrial Design: Neue Aufgaben des Unternehmers," *Süddeutsche Zeitung*, 14 April 1965, 35–36.

31 Ibid.

32 See also Betts, *Authority of Everyday Objects*, 251–252.

33 BArch, B102/21240, Arbeitskreis für industrielle Formgebung im BDI, "Anlage zu Rundschreiben Nr. 30," 20 February 1961.

34 BArch, B102/206848, BMWi Report, "Lage der Holz, Zellstoff, Papier und Druckindustrie in Baden-Württemberg," 10 November 1980; Gesellschaft für Konsumforschung (hereafter GfK), S 1979 262-2, *Der Markt für Wohnmöbel in der Bundesrepublik Deutschland: Ergebnisse einer repräsentativen Verbraucherbefragung*, volume 2, ed. Institut der Deutschen Möbelwirtschaft e.V., (Nuremberg: Matthias Ritthammer, 1979), table 15.1/A, 15.1/B, and 15.1/C.

35 University of Brighton Design Archives (hereafter UoBDA), 10-10-2, Herbert Ohl to Helene de Callatay, October 1978.

36 Privately owned industry was successively expropriated and brought under state ownership (nationalization/socialization), a process completed in 1972. Craft businesses were mostly converted to group ownership (collectivization) and often remained in private hands. Nevertheless, collectivization meant that formerly independent crafts businesses were forced to work together as production co-operatives. As furniture industry and crafts interweaved in the furniture production process, this study needs to consider both processes alongside each other. For a more detailed discussion of business ownership in the GDR, see Rainer Geißler, *Die Sozialstruktur Deutschlands: Zur gesellschaftlichen Entwicklung mit einer Bilanz zur Vereinigung*, 5th ed. (Wiesbaden: Verlag für Sozialwissenschaften, 2008), 145–146.

37 The shortcomings of centralized planning have been discussed widely by GDR economic historians. See, for example, Sleifer, *Planning Ahead and Falling Behind*; Hartmut Berghoff and Uta Balbier, eds., *The East German Economy, 1945–2010: Falling Behind or Catching Up?* (Cambridge: Cambridge University Press, 2014). Small pockets of private ownership persisted in the GDR economy. For instance, segments of the crafts remained in private hands. See Geißler, *Die Sozialstruktur Deutschlands*, 146.

38 The GDR design institution changed names and institutional affiliation several times: Institute for Applied Art under the Ministry of Culture (*Institut für angewandte Kunst, Kulturministerium*, 1952–62), Central Institute for Design under the Ministry of Culture (*Zentralinstitut für Formgestaltung, Kulturministerium*, 1963–65), Central Institute for Design under the German Office for Standardization and Product Testing (*Zentralinstitut für Gestaltung, Deutsches Amt für Messwesen and Warenprüfung*, 1965–72), and Office for industrial Design (*Amt für industrielle Formgestaltung*, 1972–90).

39 Reimer Dohrn, "A View from Port to City: Inland Waterway Sailors and City-Port Transformation in Hamburg," in *Port Cities as Areas of Transition: Ethnographic Perspectives*, ed. Waltraud Kokot, Mijal Gandelsman-Trier, Kathrin Wildner, Astrid Wonneberger (Bielefeld: Transcript, 2008),102–103.

40 Hottes, "Regional Variations of the Economic Development in the Federal Republic of Germany," 41.

41 See A. J. Nicholls, *Freedom with Responsibility: The Social Market Economy in Germany, 1918–1963* (Oxford: Oxford University Press, 1994); Gerold Ambrosius, *Die Durchsetzung der sozialen Marktwirtschaft in Westdeutschland, 1945–1949* (Stuttgart:

Deutsche Verlagsanstalt, 1977); James C. Van Hook, *Rebuilding Germany: The Creation of the Social Market Economy* (Cambridge: Cambridge University Press, 2004), Christoph Buchheim, *Die Wiedereingliederung Westdeutschlands in die Weltwirtschaft, 1945–1958* (Munich: Oldenbourg, 1990).

42 It should be noted, however, that the destruction of industrial infrastructure in the western part of Germany was greater, which also explains why less reparations in form of production machinery or entire industrial complexes were extracted from the American, British, and French zones of occupation. For a detailed treatment of postwar reparations, see Oskar Schwarzer, *Sozialistische Zentralplanwirtschaft in der SBZ/DDR: Ergebnisse eines ordnungspolitischen Experiments, 1945–1989*, Vierteljahrschrift für Sozial-und Wirtschaftsgeschichte 143 (Stuttgart: Franz Steiner, 1999), 21–30.

43 Norman Naimark estimates that the occupiers took about a third of all industrial structures in the Soviet zone of occupation. Naimark, *Russians in Germany*, 169.

44 Thomas Nabert, *Möbel für Alle: Die Geschichte der sächsischen Möbelindustrie* (Leipzig: Pro Leipzig, 2014), 192.

45 André Steiner, "From the Soviet Occupation Zone to the 'New Eastern States': A Survey," in *The East German Economy, 1945–2010: Falling Behind or Catching Up?*, ed. Hartmut Berghoff and Uta Andrea Balbier (Cambridge: Cambridge University Press, 2014), 24.

46 The planning happened in stages that combined multilevel proposal structures from the individual company to the Planning Commission. The Planning Commission then aligned these aggregated proposals with political aims and macroeconomic targets, and passed it on to the state and party leadership for approval and ratification into law. For a detailed discussion of the GDR economic planning process, see Ralf Ahrens, *Gegenseitige Wirtschaftshilfe? Die DDR im RGW: Strukturen und handelspolitische Strategien, 1963–1976* (Cologne: Böhlau, 2000), 30–31. Much earlier discussions of systemic problems of centrally planned economies of the Soviet kind include the Socialist Calculation Debate of the 1920s, when Ludwig van Mises put forward the point that, without market mechanisms, price and cost developments are arbitrary, which undermines realistic company-level calculations and planning. Van Mises, "Die Wirtschaftsrechung im sozialistischen Gemeinwesen," *Archiv für Sozialwissenschaft und Sozialpolitik* 47 (1920).

47 For example, see Oskar Schwarzer, *Sozialistische Zentralplanwirtschaft in der SBZ/DDR: Ergebnisse eines ordnungspolitischen Experiments, 1945–1989*, Vierteljahrschrift für Sozial-und Wirtschaftsgeschichte 143 (Stuttgart: Franz Steiner, 1999). Jaap Sleifer blames the slow improvement of labor productivity. See Sleifer, *Planning Ahead and Falling Behind*, 157–161. Social historian Andrew I. Port takes this argument further and maintains that dysfunctional labor relations not only explain the inefficiency of the economy, but also the relative stability of the GDR. Without worker solidarity, he argues, there was little potential for organized challenges to the SED leadership. See Port, "East German Workers and the 'Dark Side' of *Eigensinn*: Divisive Shop-Floor Practices and the Failed Revolution of June 17, 1953," in *The East German Economy*, ed. Berghoff and Balbier, 111–130.

48 André Steiner's findings suggest that the Plan set "soft" goals as economic policy-makers in the GDR were never fully knowledgeable about the real potential of material and human resources, which, he argues, could have yielded much higher returns. Steiner, *Von Plan zu Plan*, 7 and 13. See also Steiner, "From the Soviet Occupation Zone to the 'New Eastern States': A Survey," 22.

49 For a discussion of structural factors hampering innovation in the GDR economy, see Hans-Jürgen Wagener, "Zur Innovationsschwäche der DDR-Wirtschaft," in *Innovationsverhalten und Enscheidungsstrukture: Vergleichende Studien zur wirschaftlichen Entwicklung im geteilten Deutschland*, ed. Johannes Bähr and Dietmar Petzina (Berlin: Dunker und Humblot, 1996), 21–48.

50 See Katrin Schreiter and Davide Ravasi, "Institutional Pressures and Organizational Identity: The Case of Deutsche Werkstätten Hellerau in the GDR and Beyond, 1945–1996," *Business History Review* 92, no. 3 (2018): 453–481.

51 For a detailed history of the Deutsche Werkstätten Hellerau of the Wilhelminian period and Weimar, see Owen Harrod, "The Deutsche Werkstätten and the Dissemination of Mainstream Modernity," *Studies in Decorative Arts* 10, no. 2 (2003): 21–41, and *Mythos Hellerau: Ein Unternehmen meldet sich zurück*. Catalog for the Exhibition in the Deutsche Architektur Museum (Darmstadt: Druckhaus, n.d.), 13.

52 For a detailed treatment of Paul's pioneering aesthetic in standardized furniture, see Sonja Günther, *Bruno Paul, 1874–1968* (Berlin: Gebrüder Mann, 1992). DWH has been deemed more influential than the Bauhaus in anchoring modernism in German everyday life. See W. Owen Harrod, "The Deutsche Werkstätten and the Dissemination of Mainstream Modernity," *Studies in the Decorative Arts* 10, no. 2 (2003): 39–40.

53 BArch, DC20/3945, Ulbricht to Amt für Literatur und Verlagswesen, 30 November 1953.

54 Hans W. Aust, "Hausfrauen wollen keine Diplomatenschreibtische," *Berliner Rundschau*, 22 November 1953.

55 SächsStA-D, 11764/3131, Kant, Aktennotiz über die Besprechung am 6.3.1954 in Leipzig, betreffs der Entwicklungsstellen für die Entwicklung für Möbeln, 8 March 1954.

56 SächsStA-D, 11764/3131, Bericht über die Ausstellung von Möbel-Entwürfen unserer Techniker, 20 April 1954.

57 SächsStA-D, 11764/3131, Kant to Wurzler and Weber, 11 October 1954.

58 While many studies of popular conduct under the GDR dictatorship, such as the concept of a niche society, find acts of nonconformity mostly in the private sphere of the home, disobedience also happened in plain sight—even in one of the most significant political arenas of state socialism: the centrally planned economy.

59 By 1980, Hellerau consisted of forty-six companies in one combine structure. In comparison, the second largest furniture combine Zeulenroda had only twenty-eight production sites. Andreas Lauber, *Wohnkultur in der DDR—Dokumentation ihrer materiellen Sachkultur: Eine Untersuchung zu Gestaltung, Produktion und Bedingungen des Erwerbs von Wohnungseinrichtungen in der DDR* (Eisenhüttenstadt: Dokumentationszentrum Alltagskultur der DDR, 2003), 89–92.

60 See *Protokoll der Verhandlungen des V. Parteitages der Sozialistischen Einheitspartei Deutschlands. 10. bis 16. Juli 1958,* 2 vol. (Berlin: Dietz, 1959).

61 BArch, DE1/26547, Planning Commission, "Offener Brief an alle Möbelwerker der Deutschen Demokratischen Republik," c. 1959.

62 The influence of Western consumer culture on the East German population has been well documented in the works of Merkel, *Utopie und Bedürfnis;* Stitziel, *Fashioning Socialism;* Crew, ed., *Consuming Germany in the Cold War.*

63 BArch, DE1/26547, Aktionsprogramm der VVB Zeulenroda, 15 June 1958, Strukturpapier zur Stellung und Rolle der VVB, n.d.

64 Ian Jeffries and Manfred Melzer, "The New Economic System of Planning and Management 1963–70 and Recentralization in the 1970s," in *The East German Economy,* ed. Ian Jeffries and Manfred Melzer (London: Croom Helm, 1987), 28. In the case of the furniture industry, the steering activities of the *Bauakademie* in the field of design had started earlier, as discussed above.

65 BArch, DE1/26547, draft, "Beschluss der zentralen Möbelwerker-Konferenz vom 14. and 15. Mai 1959," n.d. Lauber, *Wohnkultur in der DDR,* 30.

66 BArch, DE1/26547, "Betriebsliste VVB (B) Möbel Zeulenroda/Thüringen, Stand vom 1.7.1958," n.d.

67 BArch, DE1/26547, Planning Commission, "Offener Brief an alle Möbelwerker der Deutschen Demokratischen Republik," c. 1959.

68 BArch, DE1/ VS II 12173, concept, "Zur Entwicklung der Möbelindustrie der Deutschen Demokratischen Republik Berlin," September 1964.

69 Ibid., 15.

70 Ibid., 26.

71 Ibid., 27. See also Lauber, *Wohnkultur in der DDR,* 30.

72 This trajectory ironically represents rather traditional patterns of labor division in the German industrial sector. Similar networks formed organically in Western capitalism.

73 "Zur Entwicklung der Möbelindustrie," 17.

74 For an in-depth discussion of Ulbricht's motivations and goals for NES, see Kopstein, *Politics of Economic Decline in East Germany,* 41–72.

75 Jeffries and Melzer, "New Economic System of Planning and Management," 27.

76 "Zur Entwicklung der Möbelindustrie," 7.

77 Ibid., 8 and 20. Eli Rubin describes this alternative, synthetic East German modernity as a strategy by which the GDR sought to construct socialist economic superiority. See Rubin, *Synthetic Socialism.*

78 Horst Redeker, *Chemie gibt Schönheit.* Institut für angewandte Kunst 4, ed. Hanna Schönherr (Berlin: VEB Mitteldeutsche Kunstanstalt Heidenau, 1959).

79 See, for example, BArch, DF7/2207, "Statement regarding the implementation of additional permanent positions for the Central Institute for Design," not signed, n.d.; BArch, DF7/197, "AiF conception division research and development," 22 July 1974.

80 BArch, DF7/00198, AiF Memo, n.d.

81 Ibid., AiF Memo, 26 April 1978.

82 Ibid.

83 The 1961 program of the Communist Party of the Soviet Union equated scientific and technological progress with social progress, thus introducing the idea that machines not only contributed to the efficiency of everyday chores, but that "the regular use of new technology would also modernize its users, inculcating the scientific consciousness requisite for the transition to communism." Susan E. Reid, "The Khrushchev Kitchen: Domesticating the Scientific-Technological Revolution," *Journal of Contemporary History* 40, no. 2 (2005): 313.

84 BArch, DE1/48691, Gruppe Holz und Kulturwaren—Fachgebiet Möbel, "Arbeitsprogramm-Entwurf der Arbeitsgruppe 'Standardisierung,'" 28 June 1960; and BArch, DE1/48691, DAMW-Gütebericht 1. Jhg. '63, 24 July 1963.

85 SiG, folder "Ausstellung Funktion—Form—Qualität Warschau 1967—Texte," Rudolf Horn, "Zur Gestaltung und Konstruktion eines Industriemöbelprogramms für den VEB Deutsche Werkstätten Hellerau," c. fall 1967.

86 For more details about the design history of MDW, see Andreas Ludwig, "'Hunderte von Varianten': Das Möbelprogramm Deutsche Werkstätten (MDW) in der DDR," *Zeithistorische Forschungen/Studies in Contemporary History*, no. 3 (2006): 449–459.

87 Rudolf Horn (designer and lecturer for design at the school for applied arts Burg Halle-Giebichenstein), conversation with the author, 9 February 2009.

88 Walter Ulbricht quoted by Rudolf Horn, "Zur Gestaltung und Konstruktion eines Industriemöbelprogramms."

89 Werner Glöckner, "Komplette Innenräume," *Form und Zweck* 5 (1980): 12.

90 BArch, DG4/1130, "Entwurf zum Referat der Parteiaktivtagung des Industriezweigs Möbel in Zeulenroda," 16–20.

91 Raymond Stokes has described technological advances as the key to West Germany's reappearance as a serious competitor on the world market in the chemical industry. Stokes, *Opting for Oil: The Political Economy of Technological Change in the West German Chemical Industry, 1945–1961* (Cambridge: Cambridge University Press, 1994). Michael E. Porter's general study of the Federal Republic's competitive advantage points to its high level of education, resulting technological expertise, and inventiveness as the feature of West German economic success. Porter, *The Competitive Advantage of Nations* (New York: Free Press, 1990), 369–370.

92 Gary Herrigel, *Industrial Constructions: The Sources of German Industrial Power* (Cambridge: Cambridge University Press, 1996). For a detailed discussion of Germany's industrial development in the twentieth century, see Harm G. Schröter, "The German Question, the Unification of Europe, and the European Market Strategies of Germany's Chemical and Electrical Industries, 1900–1992," *Business History Review* 67, no. 3 (1993): 369–405.

93 While the term cannot be directly translated, Hartmut Berghoff defines the *Mittelstand* as "the 'golden middle,' something that strikes a balance between grinding poverty and immoral riches." Membership of the *Mittelstand* remains an attractive

social concept, because it projects the notion of solid, but legitimate wealth. Berghoff, "The End of Family Business? The Mittelstand and German Capitalism in Transition, 1949–2000," *Business History Review* 80, no. 2 (2006): 264.

94 In her study on corporate governance in West German family businesses, Christina Lubinski provides an overview of the rudimentary state of the literature. Lubinski, *Familienunternehmen in Westdeutschland: Corporate Governance und Gesellschafterkultur seit den 1960er Jahren* (Munich: C. H. Beck, 2010), 10–18. See also Toni Pierenkemper, "Sechs Thesen zum gegenwärtigen Stand der deutschen Unternehmensgeschichtsschreibung: Eine Entgegnung auf Manfred Pohl," *Zeitschrift für Unternehmensgeschichte/ Journal of Business History* 45, no. 2 (2000): 158–166.

95 Herrigel, *Industrial Constructions*; Berghoff, "The End of Family Business?," 268.

96 Baden-Württemberg's furniture industry was slightly larger with 330 furniture companies employing 33,000 and earning DM 3.7 billion in 1979. BArch, B102/285299, BMWi, "betr. Lage der Holz, Zellstoff, Papier und Druckindustrie in Baden-Württemberg," 10 November 1980.

97 Ibid. This number is not adjusted for inflation over time.

98 For instance, between 1977 and 1981 the number of wood furniture producers in Bavaria decreased from 267 to 264 with a corresponding reduction in work force from 24,000 to 23,000. Meanwhile, earnings increased over the same period from about DM 2 billion to 2.25 billion, with revenues from exports going up as well from DM 120 million to 180 million. Seventy-seven upholstery companies counting 11,500 employees completed the furniture industry landscape in Bavaria, earning an additional DM 1.5 billion, of which DM 136 million were export revenues. See BArch, B102/285299, Bayer. Staatsministerium für Wirtschaft und Verkehr, "Lagebericht über die Holz,-Zellstoff-, Papier-und Druckindustrie in Bayern," n.d.; Bayer. Staatsministerium für Wirtschaft und Verkehr, "Lagebericht über die Holz,-Zellstoff-, Papier-und Druckindustrie in Bayern," 14 May 1982.

99 Detlef Mika (executive manager for marketing and production at Interlübke), in discussion with the author, 4 June 2009.

100 Oestereich, *"Gute Form" im Wiederaufbau*, 230–231.

101 For an in-depth discussion of the restructuring of West German industry after 1945 and its integration into the world market, see Volker Berghahn, *The Americanisation of West German Industry, 1945–1973* (Cambridge: Cambridge University Press, 1986). Edgar Wolfrum notes, though, that this slow process was diversified and that especially the *Mittelstand* businesses held on to German traditions. Wolfrum, *Die geglückte Demokratie*, 82.

102 Scholarly debate has been careful to differentiate between cultural and economic Americanization. Anselm Doering-Manteuffel defines the concept of Americanization as "the dominance of US American cultural patterns in a different national and cultural context." Doering-Manteuffel, *Wie westlich sind die Deutschen? Amerikanisierung und Westernisierung im 20. Jahrhundert* (Göttingen: Vandenhoeck & Ruprecht, 1999), 15. See also Jarausch and Siegrist, ed. *Amerikanisierung und Sowjetisierung in Deutschland*.

For discussions of economic Americanization, see Paul Erker, "'Amerikanisierung' der westdeutschen Wirtschaft? Stand und Perspektiven der Forschung," in *Amerikanisierung und Sowjetisierung in Deutschland*, ed. Jarausch and Siegrist, 137–145; Susanne Hilger, *"Amerikanisierung" deutscher Unternehmen: Wettbewerbsstrategien und Unternehmenspolitik bei Henkel, Siemens und Daimler-Benz, 1945/49–1975* (Stuttgart: Steiner, 2004); Harm G. Schröter, *Americanization of the European Economy: Comparative Survey of American Economic Influence in Europe since the 1880s* (Dordrecht: Springer, 2005).

103 Johann Klöcker, "Die Industrie übernimmt die Verantwortung selbst: Zur Gründung des Gestaltkreis im Bundesverband der Deutschen Industrie," *Süddeutsche Zeitung*, 14 April 1965; see also Stein, *Unternehmer als Förderer der Kunst*, 15. Different German attitudes toward longevity in production and consumption are discussed in Aynsely, *Designing Modern Germany*, 192.

104 Klöcker, "Die Industrie übernimmt die Verantwortung selbst," 35.

105 "Zur Entwicklung der Möbelindustrie," 6. See also Eli Rubin's discussion of the chemical industry in Rubin, *Synthetic Socialism*, 225.

106 BArch, DL102/VA1751, Angelika Werner, "Die Entwicklung des Bedarfs nach Möbeln und Polsterwaren im Zeitraum bis 1990," 20 November 1985.

107 Johannes Bähr, "Firmenabwanderung aus der SBZ/DDR und aus Berlin-Ost (1945–1953)," in *Wirtschaft im Umbruch: Strukturveränderungen und Wirtschaftspolitik im 19. und 20. Jahrhundert*, ed. Wolfram Fischer, Uwe Müller, and Fran Zasvhaler (St. Katharinen: Scripta-Mercaturae, 1997), 229–249.

108 Wolfrum, *Die geglückte Demokratie*, 146 and 196.

109 Most of the works on East German economic development look at nationalized large-scale industries, such as machine tools, optics, chemicals, and electronics. See Vincent Edwards and Peter Lawrence, *Management Change in East Germany: Unification and Transformation* (London: Routledge, 1994); Johannes Bähr and Dietmar Petzina, eds., *Innovationsverhalten und Entscheidungsstrukturen: Vergleichende Studien zur wirtschaftlichen Entwicklung im geteilten Deutschland, 1945–1990* (Berlin: Duncker & Humblot, 1996); Kopstein, *Politics of Economic Decline in East Germany*; Stokes, *Constructing Socialism*; Dolores Augustine, *Red Prometheus: Engineering and Dictatorship in East Germany, 1945–1990* (Cambridge, MA: MIT Press 2007); Steiner, *Von Plan zu Plan*.

110 BArch, DE1/48691, "DAMW-Gütebericht 1. Jhg. '63," 24 July 1963, 50.

111 Axel Bruchhäuser Private Collection, IM "Ulrich," Hinweise und Einschätzung zur Entwicklung der Fa. Bruchhäuser KG Güstrow, zu Problemen des Ex-und Importes und zum Verhalten von Herrn Bruchhäuser, 22 October 1969.

112 Axel Bruchhäuser Private Collection, BStU File "Axel Bruchhäuser," "Betriebsparteiorganisation und Betriebsführung Fa. P. Bruchhäuser & Sohn KG," 23 July 1969.

113 Ibid.

114 Axel Bruchhäuser Private Collection, BStU File "Axel Bruchhäuser."

115 Ibid., Sender and Erpel, Informationen über den Kandidaten, n.d.

116 The Stasi purchased a West German car, an Opel Commodore, for him to travel around the Federal Republic with more ease. Axel Bruchhäuser in conversation with the author, 5 June 2009.

117 Axel Bruchhäuser Private Collection, BStU File "Axel Bruchhäuser," Sender and Erpel, "Instructions for Axel Bruchhäuser's recruitment," c. January 1970, 15–16.

118 The psychology of ownership in family businesses and its relation to concepts of family identity has been documented in Lubinski, *Familienunternehmen in West-deutschland*, 116.

119 Axel Bruchhäuser Private Collection, BStU File "Axel Bruchhäuser," Axel Bruch-häuser to Ludwig Hoffmann, 15 July 1974. The Tecta company still thrives under Axel Bruchhäuser's leadership. .

120 See, for example, Axel Bruchhäuser Private Collection, BStU File "Axel Bruch-häuser," General Director "Holz und Papier," directive, 9 March 1970.

121 Axel Bruchhäuser Private Collection, BStU File "Axel Bruchhäuser," Axel Bruch-häuser to Ludwig Hoffmann, 15 July 1974.

122 See Dolores L. Augustine, "Innovation and Ideology: Werner Hartmann and the Failure of the East German Electronics Industry," in *The East German Economy*, ed. Berghoff and Balbier, 108–110.

123 This is not to say that innovation only came from family businesses. Dolores L. Augustine has shown that research and development experts in state-owned industries such as microelectronics similarly encountered the distrust of the SED and endured persecution that hindered innovation. Augustine, "Innovation and Ideology: Werner Hartmann and the Failure of the East German Electronics Industry."

124 Paul Betts notes that the styles referenced in the making of national aesthetics in GDR furniture design were ironically international by definition, for example, Chippendale. However, these former bourgeois styles "could be safely rediscovered under the umbrella of a broadly defined 'socialist style.'" Betts, "Building Socialism at Home: The Case of East German Interiors," in *Socialist Modern: East German Everyday Culture and Politics*, ed. Katherine Pence and Paul Betts (Ann Arbor: University of Michigan Press, 2003), 106.

125 SiG, Industriewaren von Heute. Wir bitten um Ihre Beurteilung, Institut für angewandte Kunst, Berlin, 1952.

126 SiG, I. Hämmerling, guestbook "Industriewaren—zweckmäßig und schön," June 1956.

127 For more information on the GDR's strategies for domestic stability, see Madarász, *Conflict and Compromise*.

128 SiG, signature illegible, guestbook "Industriewaren."

129 Ibid. Ernst Riech.

130 Ibid. Dieter Chartie.

131 SiG, Manfred Müller, guestbook "Modernes Wohnen," 1965.

132 Ibid.

133 BArch, DL102/72, Herbert Fischer and Georg Wittek, "Ergebnisse der Untersu-chungen des Teilabschnittes Warenbewegung Möbel," 28 February 1959, 21.

134 Mark Landsman offers an insightful discussion of what the GDR understood socialist demand to be, exploring the meanings of the German terms for demand (*Nachfrage*) and need (*Bedürfnis*). He finally places it "between *Nachfrage* and *Bedürfnis*, as a metaphor for the regime's ambivalent, ongoing struggle with a consumer demand it needed to keep within limits but also desired to satisfy." Landsman, *Dictatorship and Demand*, 156–157.

135 Scholarship has put special emphasis on this Party Congress as a course correction, reorienting the industrial production of the GDR toward consumer goods. See Rubin, *Synthetic Socialism*, 33.

136 BArch, DL102/VA268, "Die Anwendung der Motivforschung in der sozialistischen Konsumgüterforschung," n.d.

137 For a detailed discussion of GDR consumer behavior and the Plan, see Merkel, *Utopie und Bedürfnis*, 119–160. See also Steiner, *Von Plan zu Plan*.

138 Landsman, *Dictatorship and Demand*, 149–172.

139 Paul Betts offers an analysis of East German domestic modernization, see Betts, "Building Socialism at Home," 108–119.

140 BArch, DL102/554, Werner Bischoff and Waltraud Nieke, "Grundlagen für die Gestaltung des Möbelsortiments im Perspektiv- und Prognosezeitraum (Ergebnisse einer Bevölkerungsbefragung) Teil 2: Meinungen der Bevölkerung zur Einrichtung der Wohnzimmer mit Möbeln 1971," 23 July 1971.

141 BArch, DC20/20265, Work Group for Organization and Inspection at the Ministers' Council, "Bericht über Möglichkeiten und zu lösende Probleme der Reparatur, Modernisierung und Mehrfachverwendung gebrauchter Möbel sowie zur Gewinnung von Sekundärrohstoffen aus den nicht mehr gebrauchsfähigen Erzeugnissen," 1983.

142 "Biedermeier im Neubau?" in *Kultur im Heim* 3 (1981): 30–33; "Möbel aus zweiter Hand," in *Kultur im Heim* 5 (1985): 35–37.

143 BArch, DL102/VA1751, Angelika Werner, "Die Entwicklung des Bedarfs nach Möbeln und Polsterwaren im Zeitraum bis 1990," 20 November 1985.

144 Ibid.

145 For a sample study with calculations analyzing consumer needs, see BArch, DL102/208, Harald Zappe and J. Braungart, "Der Einfluss einer Neubauwohnung auf die Anschaffung von Wohnraummöbeln und Beleuchtungskörpern," Institut für Marktforschung, 1967.

146 Joachim Staadt, *Eingaben: Die institutionalisierte Meckerkultur in der DDR* (Berlin: Freie Universität Berlin, 1996); Ina Merkel, ed., *"Wir sind doch nicht die Mecker-Ecke der Nation": Briefe an das DDR*-Fernsehen (Cologne: Böhlau, 1998); Eli Rubin, "The Order of Substitutes: Plastic Consumer Goods in the Volkswirtschaft and Everyday Domestic Life in the GDR," in *Consuming Germany in the Cold War*, ed. David F. Crew (Oxford: Berg, 2003), 104.

147 Merkel, "Wir sind doch nicht die Mecker-Ecke," 24–27.

148 Jonathan Zatlin provides a detailed analysis of the development that turned the

initial intention behind citizens' petitions as an instrument of political control into a rhetorical battle over unfulfilled material promises by the late 1980s. In 1989 alone more than 100,000 petitions contributed to the legitimacy crisis of the GDR leadership. Zatlin, *Currency of Socialism*, 286–320.

149 Some surviving *Eingaben* addressed to the furniture industry, retailers, and design magazines can be found in BArch, DG5/6054–6059.

150 BArch, DG5/6057, "Abteilung Verwaltungsorganisation, Analyse über die Arbeit mit Eingaben im Ministerium für Bezirksgeleitete Industrie und Lebensmittelindustrie im 1. Halbjahr 1987," n.d.

151 BArch, DG5/6055, Family R. Licht to VEB Möbelkombinat Hellerau, 24 June 1987.

152 BArch, Zsg 132, Institut für Demoskopie Allensbach, "Wohnstil (1): Einrichtung, Möbel, Lampen," 1954.

153 Alphons Silbermann, *Vom Wohnen der Deutschen: Eine soziologische Studie über das Wohnerlebnis* (Cologne: Westdeutscher Verlag, 1963), 68.

154 BRfF, Annual report, "Rat für Formgebung—Tätigkeitsbericht '70," Darmstadt, n.d.

155 "Der Markt für Wohnmöbel in der Bundesrepublik Deutschland," table 28.2/A.

156 Interview with designer Rolf Heide, "Wunschtraum: Einfache Möbel für einfache Leute," in *Grundbedürfnisse im Wohnbereich*, ed. Rat für Formgebung (Darmstadt: Rat für Formgebung, 1973), 31.

157 For a detailed history of the *Gesellschaft für Konsumforschung*, see Wilfried Feldenkirchen and Daniela Fuchs, *Die Stimme des Verbrauchers zum Klingen bringen* (Munich: Piper, 2009).

158 GfK, S 1972 001, "Der Möbeleinzelhandel in den Stadt- und Landkreisen der BRD," March 1972.

159 Ibid.; S 1978 083, "Der Möbeleinzelhandel in den Stadt- und Landkreisen der BRD," September 1978.

160 Interview with Eckart Rittmeyer, "Beim Versandhaus: Abneigung gegen avantgardistische Designer," in *Grundbedürfnisse im Wohnbereich*, ed. Rat für Formgebung (Darmstadt: Rat für Formgebung, 1973), 26.

161 Interview with Gerhard Krahn, "Der Möbelhändler: Kein Stilapostel," in *Grundbedürfnisse im Wohnbereich*, ed. Rat für Formgebung, 27.

162 Ibid., 28. Europa-Möbel, a national furniture retailer chain, was known to 65 percent of the population in the Federal Republic. *Der Markt für Wohnmöbel in der Bundesrepublik Deutschland*, table 11.

163 Joachim Pietsch, "Gelsenkirchener Barock und Drittes Reich," in *Gelsenkirchener Barock*, ed. Stadt Gelsenkirchen Städtisches Museum (Heidelberg: Edition Braus, 1991), 74.

Chapter 3

1 BArch, DF7/3084, Friedrich Koslowsky, "Wohnen heißt Leben—Das Haus des Lebens," Frankfurt am Main, 10 September 1963.

2 Peter E. Fäßler, *Durch den "Eisernen Vorhang": Die deutsch-deutschen Wirtschaftsbeziehungen, 1949–1969* (Cologne: Böhlau, 2006), 3.

3 For detailed treatments of Deutschlandpolitik in a global context, see Gray, *Germany's Cold War*; Werner Kilian, *Die Hallstein-Doktrin: Der Diplomatische Krieg zwischen der BRD und der DDR, 1955–1973. Aus den Akten der beiden deutschen Außenministerien* (Berlin: Duncker & Humblot, 2001); Joachim Scholtyseck, "Im Schatten der Hallstein-Doktrin: Die globale Konkurrenz zwischen Bundesrepublik und DDR," in *Die Herausforderung des Globalen in der Ära Adenauer*, ed. Eckart Conze (Bonn: Bouvier, 2010), 79–97.

4 Sidney Pollard, "Probleme für europäische Integration im 19. und 20. Jahrhundert," in *Wirtschaftliche und politische Integration in Europa im 19. und 20. Jahrhundert*, Geschichte und Gesellschaft 10, ed. Helmut Berding (Göttingen: Vandenhoek and Ruprecht, 1985), 9–33.

5 This perspective is inspired by European integration scholarship. See, for example, Tanja A. Börzel and Diana Panke, "Europäisierung—ein politikwissenschaftliches Laboratorium," in *Les identités européennes au XXe siècle: Diversités, convergences et solidarités*, ed. Robert Frank and Gérard Bossuat (Paris: Sorbonne Press, 2004), 53–71. Historians have joined this debate on Europeanization, yet they are usually less interested in the institutionalized Europe and more attracted to long-term social and cultural processes. For a critique of the institutional approach to Europeanization from a historical point of view, see Ulrike von Hirschhausen and Kiran Klaus Patel, "Europäisierung," Version: 1.0, in *Docupedia-Zeitgeschichte*, 29 November 2012, https://docupedia.de/zg/Europ.C3.A4isierung?oldid=76143. See also Hartmut Kaelble and Martin Kirsch, eds., *Selbstverständnis und Gesellschaft der Europäer: Aspekte der sozialen und kulturellen Europäisierung im späten 19. und 20. Jahrhundert* (Frankfurt am Main: Peter Lang, 2008); Martin Conway and Kiran Klaus Patel, eds., *Europeanization in the Twentieth Century: Historical Approaches* (New York: Palgrave Macmillan, 2010); Silvio Vietta and Michael Gehler, eds., *Europa—Europäisierung—Europäistik: Neue wissenschaftliche Ansätze, Methoden und Inhalte* (Wien: Böhlau, 2010).

6 For examples of this debate, see Ann Laura Stoler and Frederick Cooper, eds., *Tensions of Empire: Colonial Cultures in a Bourgeois World* (Berkeley: University of California Press, 1997) and Sebastian Conrad and Jürgen Osterhammel, eds., *Das Kaiserreich transnational: Deutschland in der Welt, 1971–1914* (Göttingen: Vandenhoek and Ruprecht, 2004).

7 See Paolo Graziano and Maarten Peter Vink, eds., *Europeanization: New Research Agendas* (New York: Palgrave Macmillan, 2007); Gunnar Folke Schuppert, ed., *The Europeanization of Governance* (Baden-Baden: Nomos, 2006); Robert Harmsen and Thomas Wilson, "Introduction: Approaches to Europeanization," *Yearbook of European Studies* 14 (2004): 13–26.

8 This approach is inspired by concepts of cultural nationalism, a school of thought represented by Benedict Anderson, *Imagined Communities: Reflections on the Origin and Spread of Nationalism*, 2nd ed. (New York: Verso, 1991).

9 European identity should not be understood as a variation of its national predecessor. Unlike national identity that represses regional or international identity, European identity recognizes a multitude of coexisting identities. See Luisa Passerini and Hartmut Kaelble, "European Identity, the European Public Sphere, and the Future of Europe," in *Nationale Identität und transnationale Einflüsse, Amerikanisierung, Europäisierung und Globalisierung in Frankreich nach dem Zweiten Weltkrieg*, ed. Reiner Marcowitz (Munich: Oldernbourg, 2007), 97–98.

10 Leora Auslander has dubbed this process the "communicative capacity of objects." Auslander, *Taste and Power: Furnishing Modern France* (Berkeley: University of California Press, 1996).

11 Marcus Schüller, *Wiederaufbau und Aufstieg der Kölner Messe, 1946–1956* (Stuttgart: Franz Steiner Verlag, 1999), 33.

12 BArch, B102/20344, memo, Baum, "Besprechung betreffend Interzonenhandel mit Möbeln auf der Internationalen Kölner Möbelmesse," 24 February 1960.

13 For a discussion of East German price policy, see Sleifer, *Planning Ahead*, 31–36.

14 The history of the Leipzig fair began in 1165, when Otto the Rich, Margrave of Meissen, gave the town its charter and started to hold market events twice yearly. In 1497, Emperor Maximillian I granted Leipzig the privilege of holding fairs. Since then the fair grew into the modern trading place of international significance that it is today. "Historie," http://www.leipziger-messe.com/, accessed 17 March 2012.

15 Leipziger Messe, ed., *"Dienst am Ganzen"* (Leipzig: Messeamt, 1947). See also Achim Beier, "Die Stellung der Leipziger Messe in der DDR bis zum Mauerbau (1949 bis 1961)," in *Leipzigs Messen 1497–1997, Teilband 2: 1914–1997*, ed. Hartmut Zwahr, Thomas Topfstedt, and Günter Bentele (Cologne: Böhlau Verlag, 1999), 655.

16 Leipziger Messe, *"Dienst am Ganzen."*

17 The meaning of the border in the immediate postwar years has been examined in Edith Sheffer, *Burned Bridges: How East and West Germans Made the Iron Curtain* (Oxford: Oxford University Press, 2011).

18 Dr. Vollrath von Maltzahn, interview by Mitteldeutscher Rundfunk, fall 1947.

19 Schüller, *Wiederaufbau und Aufstieg der Kölner Messe*, 65–76.

20 H. J. Taepper, "Messepolitik von Köln aus gesehen," *Handelsblatt* 83, 20 July 1951.

21 Ibid., 224–225.

22 Politisches Archiv des Auswärtigen Amtes (hereafter PA AA), B38-IIA1 38, Inter Nationes, "Der interzonale Handel zwischen der Bundesrepublik und der sowjetisch besetzten Zone Deutschlands," June 1962.

23 BArch, B102/1931, Dr. Kaumann to Dr. Vollrath von Maltzahn, "Leipziger Frühjahrsmesse 1949," 29 January 1949.

24 Helene Seppain, *Contrasting US and German Attitudes to Soviet Trade, 1917–91: Politics by Economic Means* (London: St. Martins, 1992), 127.

25 See Ahrens, *Gegenseitige Wirtschaftshilfe?*, 99–103.

26 During the reforms between 1963 and 1970 and again from 1978 onward, the GDR experimented with more direct involvement of large combines in foreign trade, yet in practice the monopoly remained with the Central Planning Commission and the Council of Ministers. See BArch, B288/146, Gesamtdeutsches Institut Bundesanstalt für Gesamtdeutsche Aufgaben, Hansjörg Buck, "Erhöhung der Außenhandelseffizienz der DDR durch Unternehmenskooperation zwischen Ost und West und Umbau der Außenhandelsorganization? Zur Krise der Außenwirtschaft der DDR, ihren Ursachen und den Möglichkeiten zu ihrer Überwindung," 13 June 1979, 68–76.

27 See Ulrich Dietsch, *Außenwirtschaftliche Aktivitäten der DDR: Maßnahmen gegenüber westlichen Industriestaaten* (Hamburg: Weltarchiv, 1976), and Benno-Eide Siebs, *Die Außenpolitik der DDR, 1976–1989: Strategien und Grenzen* (Paderborn: Schöningh, 1999).

28 Achim Beier claims that the reintroduction of semiannual fairs in Leipzig signified the East's future submission to Western capitalist markets. However, especially in light of the roadblocks set for West German businesses that wanted to exhibit in Leipzig, and in the context of the late 1940s and early 1950s when the GDR focused on economic integration in the COMECON, his claims are premature. It seems more likely that Leipzig developed the semiannual schedule to reclaim its prewar status as the most important German universal trade fair and to counter fair competition from West Germany. Beier, "Die Stellung der Leipziger Messe in der DDR," 656–657.

29 BArch, B102/245211, Report, "Abwicklung und Entwicklung des innerdeutschen Handels (idH)," n.d.

30 See Fäßler, *Durch den "Eisernen Vorhang,"* 3.

31 Seppain, *Contrasting US and German Attitudes*, 128.

32 In reality, the Ostmark was never equivalent to the D-Mark, but this garnered public support for the East German currency. To the population it signaled that prices in the GDR remained more stable and were lower than in the West. "Thus, the SED's assertion of equivalence helped bolster its political legitimacy and create the illusion that the purchasing power of the East German mark was equivalent to the D-Mark's." Zatlin, *Currency of Socialism*, 116.

33 Ibid., 58.

34 Inter Nationes, "Der interzonale Handel."

35 Baum, "Besprechung betreffend Interzonenhandel mit Möbeln," 4.

36 BArch, B102/20433, Lieberich to BMWi Fachreferat Holz und Papier, "Beschwerden über die Möbeleinfuhr im Interzonenhandel," 11 April 1960.

37 Ibid.; BArch, B102/20433, G. Bauer (BMWi) to Referat IV B 4 (BMWi), "Interzonenhandel, hier: (a) Bezug von Möbeln, (b) Zulassung westdeutscher Möbelhersteller zur Leipziger Messe," 31 May 1960.

38 Baum, "Besprechung betreffend Interzonenhandel mit Möbeln, 2.

39 Ibid., 3.

40 Ibid.

41 Ibid., 1.

42 Ibid.

43 Ibid., 3.

44 BArch, DF5/5585, DAMW, "Ordnung für die Auszeichnung von Exponaten mit Goldmedaillen und Diplomen auf den Leipziger Messen," 29 July 1964.

45 For example, see BArch, DF5/5526, evaluation form, "VEB Sitzmöbel Waldheim: Sofa Excelsior, Sessel Excelsior," 5 September 1965.

46 For materials on awarded gold medals in 1964 and thereafter, see BArch, DF5/5585.

47 BArch, DF5/5041, fair report DAMW, 4 September 1970.

48 Ibid.

49 Carsten Schreiber, "Die Inszenierung des Erfolgs: Zur Funktion der Leipziger Messe in den 1970er Jahren," in *Leipzigs Messen 1497–1997, Teilband 2: 1914–1997*, ed. Hartmut Zwahr, Thomas Topfstedt, and Günter Bentele (Cologne: Böhlau Verlag, 1999), 676.

50 Inter Nationes, "Der interzonale Handel."

51 Ibid.

52 PA AA, MfAA C528/72, report, "Der Wirtschaftskrieg der BRD in den Handelsbeziehungen mit der DDR," n.d. (c. 1970). The Federal Republic helped procuring consumer goods for the GDR from other Western countries; this part of intra-zonal trade depended on the foreign currency liquidity of the GDR. See Inter Nationes, "Der interzonale Handel."

53 Ibid.

54 PA AA, B 38-IIAI 38, Embassy Washington to AA, 9 August 1963.

55 Heretofore unseen documents from the Federal Ministry of Economics and the West German Permanent Representative Mission (*Ständige Vertretung*) in East Berlin allow for new insights into the diplomacy of intra-German trade and its development.

56 For a detailed description of the SPD's strategy behind *Neue Ostpolitik*, see Egon Bahr and Michel Vale, "Bearing Responsibility for Germany: Twenty Years of the Wall—Ten Years of the Four-Power Agreement," *International Journal of Politics* 13, no. 1/2, Germany Debates Defense (1983): 69–82.

57 Zatlin, *Currency of Socialism*, 6.

58 BArch, B102/106247, Memo, Leipziger Herbstmesse 1971, 16 September 1971.

59 The GDR presented the Soviet Union as the largest foreign participant, yet the Soviet Union's exhibition area was only half the size of that of the Federal Republic. BArch, B102/106247 Bd. 1, DPA news, "Bundesrepublik größter Aussteller in Leipzig nach der DDR," 2 February 1972. See also BArch, B102/106247, Sonnenburg, note, 16 September 1971, 2.

60 Ibid., 4.

61 BArch, B 102/106247, fair report, Sonnenburg, "Messebericht Leipziger Herbstmesse 1971," October 1971.

62 BArch, B102/396753, TSI, "Lieferungen in die DDR," 18 August 1971.

63 BArch, B102/396753, Dr. Sieben (TSI), "Prognose Nr. 2-1972," 15 April 1972; TSI, "Neue Einblicke in die Struktur des innerdeutschen Handels," 13 December 1971, 11. One accounting unit was worth DM 1.

64 Ibid., 2–3 and 7.

65 Ibid., 6.

66 Ibid., 1–2.

67 Ibid.

68 Dr. Sieben (TSI), "Prognose Nr. 2-1972."

69 For an in-depth analysis of the dilemmas that the GDR faced under Honecker's economic policy, see "The New Economic System of Planning and Management 1963–70 and Recentralization in the 1970s," in *The East German Economy*, ed. Ian Jeffries and Manfred Melzer (London: Croom Helm, 1987), 26–40.

70 Dr. Sieben (TSI), "Prognose Nr. 2-1972."

71 Ibid.

72 Zatlin, *Currency of Socialism*, 126. See also Jeffries and Melzer, "New Economic System of Planning and Management," 37.

73 For details on the dynamics between supply and demand, see Merkel, *Utopie und Bedürfnis*; Kaminsky, *Wohlstand, Schönheit, Glück*; Stitziel, *Fashioning Socialism*; Pence and Betts, *Socialist Modern*.

74 It is important to note that economic historians have doubted the veracity of the GDR accounting. According to Jonathan Zatlin, the GDR's long-serving minister of economics Günter Mittag forged trade statistics and intentionally inflated the national debt to impress on the SED leadership the notion that his subsequent planning strategies were successful at decreasing it. Zatlin, *Currency of Socialism*, 124.

75 BArch, B102/284973, Wilitzki to BMWi, "Besuchsbeschränkungen auf den Leipziger Messen," 27 June 1974.

76 Ibid.

77 Dr. Sieben (TSI), "Prognose Nr. 2-1972."

78 BArch, B102/180511, BMWi, "Entwicklung des innerdeutschen Handels im Jahre 1972."

79 BArch, B102/396753, memo, Referat W/IV 1, "Aussichten des innerdeutschen Handels; hier: Besprechung in der Kaufhof AG in Köln," 14 December 1971.

80 SiG, "Materialien zur Designgeschichte der DDR," Horst Michel, interview by Prof. Laux and Siegfried Zoels, transcript, 18 September 1975 in Weimar.

81 SächsStA-D, 11764/2390, "Fachbericht zur Dienstreise vom 02.12. bis 05.12.1985 zur Firma RKL-I, Firma Lübke und Messeleitung Köln," 7 December 1985.

82 BArch, B102/206958, Weinbeer to Friderichs, 17 October 1974.

83 BArch, B102/206958, Schwab (BMWi) to Referat IV C 4 (BMWi), "Umsatzsteuerbegünstigung für Polstermöbel," October 1974. The special regulation for turnover tax was used from 1968 onward as a mechanism to balance intra-German trade. The percentage changed according to complex macroeconomic considerations that

factored in the domestic dynamics of GDR price policy and FRG currency revaluation. See BArch, B288/147, Wagner, "Die umsatzsteuerliche Behandlung des innerdeutschen Handels," Seminar des Handelsvereins, 12 November 1981.

84 GDR minister for foreign trade Horst Sölle remarked in his opening speech at the 1971 Leipzig Fall Fair that the 1969 revaluation of western currency negatively affected East German exports. BArch, B102/106247, Sonnenburg, "Messebericht Leipziger Herbstmesse 1971," October 1971. See BArch, B102/206958, Loos, "Finanzierungshilfen für die Polstermöbelindustrie, bezug: Schreiben des Fachverbandes der Bayerischen Polstermöbelindustrie e.V. vom 17. Oktober 1974."

85 BArch, B102/206958, Friderichs to Weinbeer, 26 November 1974.

86 BArch, B102/396753, Note, Schaefer, "Ergebnisse des IdH im 1. Halbjahr 1981," 24 August 1981; Note, Schaefer, "Ergebnisse des IdH im 1. Halbjahr 1982," 23 August 1982.

87 Schaefer, Ergebnisse des IdH im 1. Halbjahr 1981, 24 August 1981.

88 BArch, B102/236619, transcript, conference "Internationale Politik 1981," 7 October 1981.

89 Ibid.

90 BArch, B102/236619, Dr. Volze (BMB), "Zur DDR-Plandirektive 1981/85," 16 June 1981.

91 Harm G. Schröter, "The German Questions, the Unification of Europe, and the European Market Strategies of Germany's Chemical and Electrical Industries, 1900–1992," *Business History Review* 67, no. 3 (1993): 373.

92 West German furniture trade grew from DM 25.5 million in 1953 to DM 115.4 million in 1959, after it stagnated between 1957 and 1958. *Statistisches Jahrbuch für die Bundesrepublik Deutschland 1953* (Wiesbaden: Metzler Poeschl, 1954), 305; *Statistisches Jahrbuch für die Bundesrepublik Deutschland 1957* (Wiesbaden: Metzler Poeschl, 1958), 299; *Statistisches Jahrbuch für die Bundesrepublik Deutschland 1960* (Wiesbaden: Metzler Poeschl, 1961), 305.

93 BArch, B102/1523-1, Report, "Lagebericht Aussenhandel für 4. Quartal 1954, Exportausschuss Holzverarbeitung," 22 January 1955.

94 Ibid.

95 For a discussion of the goals of French diplomacy, see A. W. Lovett, "The United States and the Schuman Plan: A Study in French Diplomacy, 1950–1952," *Historical Journal* 39, no. 2 (1996): 425–455; and William I. Hitchcock, *France Restored: Cold War Diplomacy and the Quest for Leadership in Europe, 1944–1954* (Chapel Hill: University of North Carolina Press, 1998).

96 High Authority of the European Coal and Steel Community, "Treaty Establishing the European Coal and Steel Community," 1951.

97 Hottes, "Regional Variations," 42.

98 Ibid., 41.

99 Protocol about Intra-German Trade and Connected Issues, Paragraph 1, 25 March 1957.

100 Ibid., Paragraph 2.

101 Ibid., Paragraph 3. See also BArch, B102/180511, Kommission der Europäischen Gemeinschaften, "Handelsbeziehungen mit der Deutschen Demokratischen Republik" (Mitteilung von der Kommission an den Rat), 18 April 1973.

102 BArch, B102/245206, Commentary on Protocol about Intra-German Trade and Connected Issues. Emphasis in the original. This special relationship is further explained in BArch, B102/245206, Dr. Schlebitz an AA, "Sonderbeschluss des Ministerrats zur gemeinsamen Handelspolitik betreffend Staatshandelsländer; Behandlung der SBZ in diesem Beschluss," 21 August 1961.

103 See also PA AA, B 38-IIA1 141, AA, Harmonisierung der Zollwertvorschriften in der EWG, 1 Dezember 1965.

104 Dr. Schlebitz to AA.

105 BArch, B102/180605, Ostausschuss der deutschen Wirtschaft, Entschließung betr. längerfristige Kreditgewährung an die Staatshandelsländer des Ostens, 1 December 1964.

106 BArch, B102/180605, attachment, Ost-Ausschuss der deutschen Wirtschaft, Memorandum betr. Frage der Kreditgewährung bei Investitionsgüter-Lieferungen an Ostblockstaaten, 1 December 1964.

107 Inter Nationes, "Der interzonale Handel."

108 BArch, B102/180605, Dr. Heise, betr.: Grosse Anfrage der Abgeordneten Freiherr von Kühlmann-Stumm und Gen. betr. EWG Politik, 10 June 1966.

109 BArch, B102/180605, Sach (BMWi), Fernschreiben 188, Tagung des EWG-Ministerrats am 13./14.6.66, 15 June 1966. The archival documentation of German involvement in the question of western state-backed credits ends here, and it is therefore plausible to assume that these matters continued to be discussed in one of the two other organizations.

110 BArch, DF5/5041, Mitteilung des Ministerrats der DDR, "Zu den Außenwirtschaftsbeziehungen der DDR mit der BRD," 3 June 1970.

111 Ibid.

112 For a detailed account of the COMECON trading mechanisms, see Ahrens, *Gegenseitige Wirtschaftshilfe?*, 27–87.

113 Inter Nationes, "Der interzonale Handel."

114 Ahrens, *Gegenseitige Wirtschaftshilfe?*, 36–39.

115 Suvi Kansikas, "Acknowledging Economic Realities: The CMEA policy change vis-à-vis the European Community, 1970–3," *European Review of History/Revue européenne d'histoire* 21, no. 2 (2014): 324. On the principle of solidarity in the COMECON and its significance as a cornerstone of the Eastern Bloc solidarity, see Simon Godard, "Construire le bloc de l'Est par l'économie? La delicate émergence d'une solidarité internationale socialiste au sein du Conseil d'aide économique mutuelle," *Vingtième Siècle. Revue d'histoire*, no. 109 (2011): 45–58.

116 Angela Romano, "Untying Cold War Knots: The EEC and Eastern Europe in the Long 1970s," *Cold War History* 14, no. 2 (2014): 153–173.

117 BArch, B102/301093, Brüssel Eurogerma to BMWi u.a., betr Bundesaussenminister beim EP am 16.9.1970, 18 September 1970.

118 See BArch, B102/180511, Kommission der Europäischen Gemeinschaften, "Handelsbeziehungen mit der Deutschen Demokratischen Republik" (Mitteilung von der Kommission an den Rat), 18 April 1973.

119 BArch, B102/180511, memo, Einleitende Aufzeichnung für die Sitzung der Staatssekretäre für Europafragen am 21. Februar 1973, 16 February 1973.

120 Ibid.

121 On the negative dependencies that developed from western credits, see Ralf Ahrens, "Außenwirtschaftspolitik zwischen Ostintegration and Westverschuldung," in *Die Zentrale Wirtschaftsverwaltung in der SBZ/DDR: Akteure, Strukturen, Verwaltungspraxis*, Wirtschaftspolitik in Deutschland 1917-1990 vol. 3, ed. Dierk Hoffmann (Berlin: De Gruyter Oldenbourg, 2016), 510–590.

122 BArch, B102/180512, Dr. Schreiber (BMWi), Vermerk betr. Sitzung der Gruppe Handelsfragen des Rates am 19. November 1974 in Brüssel, 21 November 1974; ibid., Fernschreiben aus Brüssel an AA, betr. EWG-DDR, 20 November 1974.

123 Ibid., Dr. v. Arnim (BMWi), Vermerk betr.: Verhältnis EWG-DDR Hier: Niederländische Beschwerde über Abschirmung des Marktes der Bundesrepublik gegenüber in die Niederlande aus der DDR eingeführte Waren, 2 December 1974.

124 Ibid., "Meeting mit Benelux-Delegation, Erläuterungen unserer Delegation," February 1975.

125 The EEC countries signed trade agreements with the GDR in the aftermath of the Basic Treaty. Commission des Communautes Europeennes, *Accord de Cooperation bilateraux entre des Etats Membres et la RDA* signed by France on 19 July 1973, England on 18 December 1973, Italy on 18 April 1973, Belgium/Luxemburg on 31 August 1974, Netherlands on 12 June 1974, Denmark on 21 February 1974.

126 BArch, B102/180512, Dr. Groß, Vermerk betr. Freiverkehrsfähigkeit von im innerdeutschen Handel bezogenen Waren, 11 April 1975.

127 Dr. v. Arnim (BMWi), Niederländische Beschwerde.

128 "Meeting mit Benelux-Delegation, Erläuterungen unserer Delegation." This was twice the amount of GDR goods that had entered the Benelux via the FRG in the previous year.

129 BArch, B288/75, public hearing, Sachverständige zur Deutschlandpolitik, 11 October 1977.

130 Ibid.

131 Lauber, *Wohnkultur in der DDR*, 41.

132 BArch, B102/285299. "Niederschrift über die Arbeitstagung Holz, Zellstoff, Papier und Druck am 13. November 1980 in Bonn," 15 January 1981.

133 See, for example, BArch, DF5/5082, Dr. Lindenhayn (DAMW) to Köppen (chair of the economic council Neubrandenburg), 4 June 1971.

134 Ibid.

135 BArch, DF5/5041, DAMW fair report, Leipziger Herbstmesse 1970, 4 September 1970.

136 Ibid.

137 SächsStA-D, 11764/1897, travel reports.

138 BArch, B102/206958, Weinbeer to Friedrichs, Betr.: Beschäftigungslage in der Polstermöbelindustrie—Wettbewerbsverzerrung durch DDR-Billigimporte, 9 August 1976.

139 BArch, DF7/534, 535, 536, 537, 538 product index, "Produktkartei Wohnraummöbel"; BArch DF7/509, 510, 511, 512, 514, 515, 516, 517, 518, "Produktkartei Sitzmöbel."

140 Karin Hirdina quoted in Georg Bertsch, Ernst Hedler, and Matthias Dietz, *SED—Schönes Einheits Design* (Cologne: Taschen Verlag, 1994), 28. This quote was originally published in the East German design journal *Form und Zweck* in 1975.

141 SächsStA-D, 11764/1897, Guntscheff (export department of VVB Möbel Dresden), Teilreisebericht über die Teilnahme am 10. Internationalen Möbelsalon Paris vom 11.–15.1.1979, 23 January 1979; Großpietzsch (head of R&D Hellerau), Teil-Reisebericht vom Besuch der Deutschen Möbelmesse Köln 1979, n.d., 9.

142 The *Dokumentationszentrum Alltagskultur der DDR* in Eisenhüttenstadt keeps a number of modern storage furniture from the 1970s and 1980s. Close up these *Schrankwände* look cheap due to the decorative foil technique and their poor construction despite the neofunctionalist design.

143 Lauber, *Wohnkultur in der DDR*, 42.

144 BArch, B102/285299, Niederschrift über die Arbeitstagung Holz, Zellstoff, Papier und Druck am 13. November 1980 in Bonn, 15 January 1981.

145 Aynsley, *Designing Modern Germany*, 204.

146 For a detailed discussion of Italian influences in German furniture design of the 1980s, see Selle, *Geschichte des Design in Deutschland*, 267–272; and Aynsley, *Designing Modern Germany*, 202–207.

147 Herbert Pohl (architect and designer) in discussion with the author in Berlin on 13 January 2009. Design historian Gert Selle claims that the playful, Italian-influenced furniture style did not exist in the GDR. However, Pohl worked with an entire team of designers and architects who created similarly experimental furniture that did not comply with former style ideals, such as production-minded functionalist furniture or decorative furniture with mass appeal. Selle, *Geschichte des Designs in Deutschland*, 270.

148 The reluctance to use the term "postmodern" in German illustrates this interpretation of postmodernism as a return to the past. The title of Jean-François Lyotard's epoch defining work *The Postmodern Condition: A Report on Knowledge* (1979) was translated into "The Presence of the Past" in both Italian and German. Design historian Jeremy Aynsely has shown how these translation questions started a debate about "the 'return' to history" in architecture and design with significant implications for European countries. Aynsley, *Designing Modern Germany*, 202.

149 Ibid., 205–206.

150 BArch, DF 7/1072, Gerhard Wetzig, Dienstreisebericht Möbelmesse Köln 19.1.–22.1.1982, 1 February 1982.

151 BArch, B457/8, Danish Design Council to Bieberstein (BMWi), The European Design Prize, 23 February 1987; Statutes for the European/EEC Design Prize, 21 February 1987.

152 BArch, B457/150, project proposal, "La Casa Europea—European Design Day on European TV, Anhang zum summary of the meeting of the expert-group 'La CASA Europea'" day in Luxembourg am 18.12.1989, n.d.

153 Ibid.

154 BArch, B288/256, Ambassador Juan J. Rubio de Urquia, "Culture in the GDR: Possibilities of EC Cultural Activities in the GDR," 2 March 1989, 8.

155 BArch, B457/129, Dieter Rams to MAHO AG, 7 September 1989.

156 For a detailed account of the events of 1989 and 1990, in particular the French conditions for German reunification, see Mary E. Sarotte, *1989: The Struggle to Create Post–Cold War Europe* (Princeton, NJ: Princeton University Press, 2009).

Chapter 4

1 See, for example, PA AA, B112/6 Embassy Rio de Janeiro to AA, "Umgravierung des Tafelsilbers," 4 July 1952; AA to Rio de Janeiro, 21 July 1952; AA B112/8, Herrmann to AA, "Aufzeichnung," 12 May 1952.

2 PA AA, B112/3, Von Hentig to AA, "Ausstattung der Botschaft Djakarta," 26 August 1953; Von Hentig to AA, "Dekorationsstoffe für Repräsentationsräume," 23 October 1953.

3 Von Hentig to AA, 26 August 1953.

4 PA AA, B112/6, Hausenstein to Schliep, 10 October 1952.

5 An overview of BDI foreign trade diplomacy is provided in Werner Bührer, "Die Wirtschaftsdiplomatie des BDI von 1949 bis Mitte der 1970er Jahre," in *Auswärtige Repräsentationen*, ed. Johannes Paulmann, 121–137.

6 In 1949, only eleven countries had recognized the GDR, and all of them were communist. See Gray, *Germany's Cold War*, 3.

7 For example, architectural historian Greg Castillo has analyzed the "soft power of mid-century design" to evaluate American influence in Germany during what he calls a "culture battle" (*Kulturkampf*) between Americanization and Sovietization in the 1950s. Castillo, *Cold War at the Home Front*, xv. The diplomatic use of American-style consumerism in the Cold War setting has also been explored by De Grazia, *Irresistible Empire*; Sheryl Kroen, "Negotiating the American Way: The Consumer and the Social Contract in Post-war Europe," in *Consuming Cultures, Global Perspectives: Historical Trajectories, Transnational Exchanges*, ed. John Brewer and Frank Trentmann (Oxford: Berg, 2006), 251–278; Susan Reid, "Who Will Beat Whom: Soviet Popular Reception of the American National Exhibition in Moscow, 1959," *Kritika* 9 (2008): 855–905.

8 Martin Greiffenhagen, "The Dilemma of Conservatism in Germany," *Journal of Contemporary History* 14 (1979): 613.

9 For an example in the context of decolonization in developing countries, see Katherine Pence, "Showcasing Cold War Germany in Cairo: 1954 and 1957 Industrial Exhibitions and the Competition for Arab Partners," *Journal of Contemporary History* 47, no. 1 (2012): 69–95.

10 StAS, Mia Seeger Estate, A 139, private and professional correspondence from Szydlowska to Seeger, 1965–1967.

11 Seeger quoted in Karin Kirsch, "Mia Seeger, 1903–1991," in *Baden-Württembergische Portraits: Frauengestalten aus fünf Jahrhunderten*, ed. Elisabeth Nölle-Neumann (Stuttgart: Deutsche Verlags-Anstalt, 2000), 252.

12 StAS, Mia Seeger Estate, A 139, Szydlowska to Seeger, 15 December 1965.

13 For the aims and development of *Ostpolitik* toward Poland, see Krzysztof Ruchniewicz, "Ostpolitik and Poland," in *Ostpolitik, 1969–1974: European and Global Responses*, ed. Carole Fink and Bernd Schaefer (Cambridge: Cambridge University Press, 2009), 39–57.

14 Peter Frank, "Westdeutsches Design in Polen," in *Werk und Zeit*, July 1967.

15 Peter Frank, "Deutsches Design in Polen," in *Form* 38 (1967).

16 Peter Frank (Mia Seeger's assistant and former head of the Essen and Stuttgart design councils) in discussion with the author, April 2009.

17 Frank, "Westdeutsches Design in Polen."

18 Ibid.

19 Kirsch, "Mia Seeger, 1903–1991," 252

20 Poland and the FRG established diplomatic relations and officially recognized each other when the Bundestag ratified the Warsaw Treaty in 1972.

21 SiG, folder "Ausstellung 'Funktion—Form—Qualität' Warschau 1967 Berichte/Verträge," Besprechung am 14. September 1967, Zentralinstitut für Gestaltung, Abt. IV, Sektor Ausstellungen, betr. "Ausstellung 'Funktion—Form—Qualität' Warschau," 18 September 1967.

22 SiG, folder "Ausstellung 'Funktion—Form—Qualität' Warschau 1967/Texte," opening speech, Martin Kelm, 13 September 1967.

23 Responses from the German, Finnish, and English design councils, see SiG, folder "Ausstellung 'Funktion—Form—Qualität' Warschau 1967 Berichte/Verträge."

24 G. Knobloch, "Form—Funktion—Qualität: Das Zentralinstitut für Gestaltung stellte in Warschau aus," *Silikattechnik* 19, no. 4 (1968): 122.

25 For more examples of GDR diplomatic representation strategies and narratives, see Peter E. Fäßler, "'Antifaschistisch,' 'friedliebend,' und 'fortschrittlich': Botschaften und Formen Aussenwirtschaftlicher Repräsentationen der DDR während der 1950er und 1960er Jahre," in Paulmann, *Auswärtige Repräsentationen*, 139–161.

26 SiG, folder "Ausstellung 'Funktion—Form—Qualität' Warschau 1967 Berichte/Verträge u.ä.," T. Reindl, "Report on the exhibition Formgestaltung der DDR (FFQ)," undated translation (c. spring 1968).

27 Ibid., "Funktion—Form—Qualität," 1967.

28 SiG, folder "Funktion—Form—Qualität UdSSR 1969," catalog text, "Funktion—Form—Qualität 1969 in the Soviet Union," 3 March 1969.

29 SiG, folder "Ausstellung 'Funktion—Form—Qualität' Warschau 1967 Berichte/Verträge u.ä.," German translations of "Wystawa Wzornictwa z NRD," *Zycie Warszawa*, 12 December 1967 and "Wystawa wzornictwa przemyslowege NRD," *Trybuna Ludu*, 12 December 1967.

30 Economic historian János Kornai coined the term "economics of shortage" to point out that the scarcity was not the fault of economic planners or ill-advised price policies, but rather had systemic causes. Kornai, *Economics of Shortage* (Amsterdam: North-Holland, 1980).

31 In 1959, for instance, the GDR had sponsored an exhibition called "Life in the GDR" in London, accompanied by a DEFA cinema program and talks in Coventry and London. The British reaction was, if not enthusiastic, at least not belligerent. PA AA, MfAA B3.337, press report, "Einschätzungen der englischen Pressestimmen anlässlich der Ausstellung 'Das Leben in der DDR' in London 28.9.-11.10.1959," 16 October 1959.

32 PA AA, MfAA A15830 (1963) and MfAA C147 (1967).

33 PA AA, MfAA C160/73, report, "Stand der Beziehungen DDR-Grossbritannien," n.d. (c. 1970).

34 Fäßler describes the East German diplomatic efforts in Western countries before official international recognition as a "policy of small steps" that built awareness for the de facto sovereignty of the GDR among political actors and would pave the way for judicially codified recognition at a later point in time. Fäßler, "'Antifaschistisch,' 'friedliebend' und 'fortschrittlich,'" 154.

35 PA AA, MfAA C160/73, report, "Stand der kulturellen und wissenschaftlichen Beziehungen DDR-Grossbritannien," 27 August 1970.

36 PA AA, MfAA C 160/73, "Jahresanalyse 1969," n.d. (c. 1970).

37 SiG, folder "Ausstellung London 1970—Schriftwechsel," German British Association, protocol, "Über die Beratung zur DDR-Design-Ausstellung am 4.2.1970," 5 February 1970.

38 SiG, folder "Ausstellung London 1970—Schriftwechsel," Sir Paul Reilly to Kelm, 20 May 1970.

39 Ibid.; SiG, folder "Ausstellung London 1970—Schriftwechsel," Lex Hornsby to Knobloch, 3 July 1970.

40 SiG, "Information über die Vorbereitung der Ausstellung 'GDR Design '70' in London," internal memo, Reißmann to Zipfel, 8 July 1970.

41 Ibid.

42 Benno-Eide Siebs, *Die Außenpolitik der DDR, 1976–1989: Strategien und Grenzen* (Paderborn: Schöningh, 1999), 118.

43 Ibid., 37.

44 SiG, folder "Ausstellung London 1970—Texte," draft, "Ausstellungstexte: Englische Endfassung," n.d.

45 Ibid., ZfF, "Entwürfe für Ausstellungstexte: Englische Endfassung," n.d.

46 Ibid., Kelm, opening speech for "DDR-Design 70" in London, 7 September 1970.

47 Ibid.

48 See Fäßler, "'Antifaschistisch,' 'friedliebend' und 'fortschrittlich,'" 149.

49 In the mid-1960s, leftist writers from East and West came together by invitation of Erich Fromm to contribute to the publication of *An International Symposium of Socialist Humanism* (1965) to stimulate global East-West dialogue.

50 See Jean-François Revel, "The Myths of Eurocommunism," *Foreign Affairs* 56, no. 2 (1978).

51 Ekkehard Bartsch, "DDR-Design am Londoner Piccadilly Square," *Sonntag* 43 (1970): 15.

52 Knobloch, "DDR-Design in Großbritannien," *Silikattechnik* 21, no. 9 (1970): 318.

53 SiG, folder "Ausstellung London 1970—Texte," memo, "Ergebnisse der Ausstellung 'DDR-Design '70' in London in der Zeit vom 7. bis 19.9.1970 und Schlußfolgerungen für künftige Ausstellungsvorhaben," n.d.

54 "Humane East Germans," *Daily Telegraph*, 9 September 1970.

55 SiG, folder "Ausstellung London 1970—Texte," Sir Paul Reilly, opening speech at the "GDR Design '70" exhibition in the Ceylon Tea Center, 7 September 1970.

56 Ibid.

57 Ibid., Lex Hornsby & Partner Ltd, press release, "GDR Design '70."

58 Ibid., CoID report on the exhibition, translated from the English original, n.d.

59 "'DDR-Design '70' in London," in *Form* 2 (1970): 62.

60 SiG, folder "Ausstellung London 1970—Texte," memo, "Ergebnisse der Ausstellung 'DDR-Design '70' in London in der Zeit vom 7. bis 19.9.1970 und Schlußfolgerungen für künftige Ausstellungsvorhaben," n.d.

61 UoBDA, 03-1-2, ICSID Constitution, adopted 17 September 1959, 2.

62 UoBDA, Peter Muller-Munk quoted in Misha Black, "The History of ICSID" (1975), 2.

63 Ibid., 3.

64 UoBDA, 10-27-1, Yuri Soloviev, "Le Design et la Politique d'Etat dans les Pays Socialistes (sur l'Exemple de l'Union Sovietique et de la Republique Democratique Allemande)," n.d.

65 UoBDA, 10-27-1, Des Cressonnières to Soloviev, 9 July 1965.

66 UoBDA, 10-10-1, Des Cressonnières (secretary general) to Kelm, 17 January 1965.

67 UoBDA, 10-11-1, Des Cressonnières to Seeger, 9 January 1965.

68 The ambiguous concept of cultural politics has been defined by Peter Jackson as "the view that 'cultural' questions of aesthetics, taste and style cannot be divorced from 'political' questions about power, inequality and oppression. Conversely, the concept refers to the way that contemporary politics have been 'aestheticized,'" Jackson, "Towards a Cultural Politics of Consumption," in *Mapping the Futures: Local Cultures, Global Change*, ed. John Bird et al. (Oxford: Routledge, 1993), 208.

69 PA AA, B38-IIA1 31, Von Schenk to Referat IB1, "Das deutsche Alleinvertretungs-recht in den internationalen Organizationen," 29 June 1965.

70 PA AA, B38-IIA1 31, "Empfehlungen für Kongressteilnehmer aus der BRD zur Wahrung gesamtdeutscher Interessen," n.d. (c. 1965).

71 UoBDA, 10-10-1, Des Cressonnières to Kelm, 13 February 1967.

72 UoBDA, 10-11-1, Des Cressonnières to Gotthelf, 31 July 1967.

73 Ibid., Gotthelf to Des Cressonnières, 2 August 1967.

74 See also Fäßler, "'Antifaschistisch,' 'friedliebend' und 'fortschrittlich,'" 139–161.

75 UoBDA, 10-10-1, Kelm to Des Cressonnières, 15 June 1967.

76 Ibid., Des Cressonnières to Kelm, 16 July 1967.

77 UoBDA, 03-1-1, ICSID minutes, "Second General Assembly in Venice, Italy, 14 to 16 of September 1961." There was no debate over East German membership in the minutes—it seems that the GDR membership was guaranteed by the Chinese precedent and the membership of the FRG, see UoBDA, 03-03-1, ICSID minutes, "Fifth General Assembly in Ottawa, 11 and 12 September 1967."

78 UoBDA, 08-06-6, Herbert Ohl to Helene de Callantay, 21 December 1977.

79 "DDR im ICSID," in *Form*, 40/1967, 64.

80 "Aus der DDR: *Form und Zweck* 1/67," in *Form* 40 (1967): 75.

81 UoBDA, 10-10-1, Kelm to Des Cressonnières, 18 April 1969.

82 Ibid.

83 UoBDA, 10-11-1, Des Cressonnières to Gutman, 25 April 1969.

84 For details on the limited extent of German-German political relations, see Stefan Creuzberger, *Kampf um die Einheit: Das gesamtdeutsche Ministerium und die politische Kultur des Kalten Krieges, 1949–1969.* Schriften des Bundesarchivs 69 (Düsseldorf: Droste, 2008).

85 Hans Otto Bräutigam, *Ständige Vertretung: Meine Jahre in Ost-Berlin* (Hamburg: Hoffmann und Campe, 2009), 29–30.

86 The continuity of the policy of strength under Erhard is discussed in Christoph Kleßmann, "Adenauers Deutschland-und Ostpolitik, 1955–1963," in *Adenauer und die Deutsche Frage*, ed. Josef Foschepoth (Göttingen: Vandenhoeck & Ruprecht, 1988), 64.

87 For a detailed discussion of Adenauer's reunification politics, see Josef Foschepoth, "Westintegration statt Wiedervereinigung: Adenauers Deutschlandpolitik, 1949–1955," in ibid., 29–60. The continuity of the policy of strength under Erhard is also discussed by Christoph Kleßmann, "Adenauers Deutschland-und Ostpolitik, 1955–1963," ibid., 64.

88 Sarotte, *Dealing with the Devil*, 11.

89 Egon Bahr and Michel Vale, "Bearing Responsibility for Germany: Twenty Years of the Wall—Ten Years of the Four-Power Agreement," *International Journal of Politics* 13, no. 1/2, German Debates Defense (1983): 74.

90 For an in-depth discussion of the Federal Republic's Eastern policy, see Timothy Garton Ash, *In Europe's Name: Germany and the Divided Continent* (New York: Random House, 1993).

91 Sarotte, *Dealing with the Devil*, 175.

92 Suri, *Power and Protest*, 220.

93 Bräutigam, *Ständige Vertretung*, 30.

94 Sarotte offers a detailed discussion of the negotiations and diplomatic contacts between the two German states and the American and Soviet superpowers, see *Dealing with the Devil*, 129 and 167.

95 See Siebs, *Die Außenpolitik der DDR*.

96 Gert Krell, "West German Ostpolitik and the German Question," *Journal of Peace Research* 28, no. 3 (1991): 315. See also Ulrich Albrecht, "Security and the German Question," *World Policy Journal* 1, no. 3 (1984): 575–602. Germans were joined by other Europeans, like the Swedish disarmament expert Alva Myrdal, who realized the "touchiness" of the German situation during the reinvigorated Cold War of the early 1980s. Herbert Ammon and Peter Brandt, "The Relevance of the German Question for Peace in Europe," *International Journal of Politics* 13, no. 1/2, Germany Debates Defense (1983): 96.

97 Egon Bahr maintained in 1983 that the Four-Power Agreement on Berlin would have not materialized without the active contribution of the two German states. He concluded that the four powers "could no longer undertake any measures in the center of Europe that touched Germany without the two German states also participating." Bahr and Vale, "Bearing Responsibility for Germany," 78.

98 Sarotte, *Dealing with the Devil*, 149.

99 Krell, "West German Ostpolitik and the German Question," 318.

100 Suri, *Power and Protest*, 218.

101 Siebs, *Die Außenpolitik der DDR*, 122.

102 The East German–Austrian cultural accords served as an inspiration for this part of the German-German agreement.

103 Treaty on Cultural Cooperation Between the Governments of the Federal Republic of Germany and the German Democratic Republic, 6 May 1986.

104 BArch, B288/481, internal memo, Mahnke, Kulturabkommen, 28 April 1986.

105 It was impossible for the FRG to meet this request, as the claim to West Berlin had constituted an integral part of its diplomacy vis-à-vis the Eastern Bloc. Excluding West Berlin, arguably a culturally striving city by the mid-1970s, from the agreement would have meant a great loss of diplomatic and cultural prowess for the FRG.

106 BArch, B288/75, Bräutigam, note for Gaus, "Gespräch mit dem Chefredakteur der außenpolitischen Zeitschrift 'Horizont' am 20. Oktober 1976," 25 October 1976.

107 BArch, B288/75, Foreign Ministry to StäV, NfD, 21 January 1977. Despite the technical agreements reached between the FRG and the GDR, East German diplomats complicated the interaction with West Germany's Permanent Mission to such a degree that Chancellor Helmut Schmidt protested this behavior in a public speech. He called it "a sign of lacking confidence of the GDR leadership's in its own political position."

108 Günter Grass, "Wir geben das letzte aus der Hand, was grenzübergreifend ist.

Günter Grass im Interview über das Kulturabkommen mit der DDR," interview with Stephan Lohr, *Rheinischer Merkur*, 1 April 1986.

109 BArch, B288/493, Dr. von Richthofen to MD Meichsner (BMB), 21 October 1985.

110 Ibid., Günter Grass to President Richard von Weizsäcker, 6 September 1985.

111 Grass, interview with Stephan Lohr.

112 See BArch, B288/481, Bräutigam, betr. Gespräch mit SED-Parteibüromitglied Kurt Hager am 28.9.1983, 29 September 1983; BArch, B288/481, Bräutigam (StäV) to BMB and BK, betr. Projekt einer Design-Ausstellung aus der Bundesrepublik Deutschland in der DDR, 1 March 1984.

113 The Ministry for Pan-German Affairs (*Bundesministerium für Gesamtdeutsche Fragen*, BMG) was renamed Federal Ministry for Intra-German Relations (*Bundesministerium für innerdeutsche Beziehungen*, BMB) in 1969. For a history of the ministry up to this point, see Creuzberger, *Kampf für die Einheit.*

114 BArch, B288/481, Dr. Klaus-Eberhard Murawski (BMB) to BK, "Offiziel vermittelte Projekte in der kulturellen Zusammenarbeit mit der DDR; hier: Vorschlag zur Design-Ausstellung," 30 January 1984.

115 Ibid., Bräutigam (StäV) to BMB and BK, 1 March 1984.

116 Ibid., note, Girardet (StäV), 24 February 1984.

117 BArch, B288/482, bulletin, "Bundesministerium für innerdeutsche Beziehungen," Nr. 60/84, 22 November 1984.

118 Elizabeth Harvey, "The Two Germanies: Recent Publications on the Federal Republic, the German Democratic Republic and the German Question," *Historical Journal* 33, no. 4 (1990): 968.

119 BArch, B288/481, exhibition proposal, attached to Bräutigam (StäV) to BMB and BK, "Projekt einer Design-Ausstellung aus der Bundesrepublik Deutschland in der DDR," 1 March 1984.

120 BArch, B288/482, list, "Teilnehmer an der Eröffnung der Ausstellung."

121 Ibid., Kelm, opening speech, 3 December 1984.

122 Ibid., Bräutigam, opening speech, 3 December 1984.

123 Renata Fritsch-Bournazel, *Confronting the German Question: German on the East-West Divide* (New York: Berg, 1988). This mini-détente started a wave of research on the German Question that reached publication just before the GDR collapsed in 1989. For example, see Edwina Moreton, ed., *Germany Between East and West* (Cambridge: Cambridge University Press, 1987).

124 BArch, B288/481, concept, "Design-Ausstellung des Rat für Formgebung in der Deutschen Demokratischen Republik 1984, Manuskript: Dipl. Ing. Herbert Ohl, Dipl.—Des. Eckhard Neumann," December 1983.

125 BArch, B288/482, Bundesministerium für innerdeutsche Beziehungen, Nr. 60/84, 22 November 1984.

126 Ibid., press release, "Vorausdenken für den Menschen. Design-Ausstellung des Rates für Formgebung in Berlin (Ost)," n.d.

127 Concept, "Design-Ausstellung des Rat für Formgebung in der Deutschen Demokratischen Republik 1984."

128 SiG, folder "BRD Ausstellung," RfF, "Ausstellungstext Tafel 012," n.d.

129 Michael Blank, "Tagesinformationen zur BRD-Ausstellung," 2 December 1984.

130 Rotraud und Herbert Pohl (textile and furniture designers) in conversation with the author, 13 January 2009.

131 BArch, B288/482, press release, "Erfolgreich: Design-Ausstellung in Berlin (Ost), n.d.

132 SiG, folder "Ausstellungen BRD," Michael Blank, "Tagesinformationen zur BRD-Ausstellung," 4 December 1984.

133 Ibid., Blank, "Tagesinformationen zur BRD-Ausstellung," 11 December 1984.

134 Ibid., Blank, "Tagesinformationen zur BRD-Ausstellung," 1 December 1984.

135 Ibid., Blank, "Tagesinformationen zur BRD-Ausstellung," 4 December 1984.

136 Ibid., Blank, "Tagesinformationen zur BRD-Ausstellung," 6 December 1984.

137 SiG, folder "BRD-Ausstellung 3.—20.12.1984," AiF, "Argumentationsmaterial für die Betreuer der Ausstellung 'Design—Vorausdenken für den Menschen. Eine Ausstellung aus der Bundesrepublik Deutschland' zur Situation des Design in der BRD," 15 November 1984.

138 SiG, folder "Ausstellungen BRD," AiF, "Bericht über die Durchführung der Ausstellung 'Design—Vorausdenken für den Menschen. Eine Ausstellung aus der Bundesrepublik Deutschland' im Internationalen Handelszentrum, in Berlin, Hauptstadt der DDR," 20 December 1984, 5.

139 BArch, B288/497, "Organisationsprojekt und 1. Ideenskizze: Zur Ausstellung des Amtes für industrielle Formgestaltung der DDR in der BRD 1988, Berlin 1. Juli 1987."

140 Ibid., Dr. Thunig-Nittner, Sekretär Brandstädter von der StäV/DDR und Frau Dr. Thunig-Nittner vom BK, 1. December 1987.

141 Ibid., Dr. Thunig-Nittner, betr. Geleitwort für Katalog, 23 December 1987.

142 "Design der DDR erstmals in der Bundesrepublik," *Form* 2 (1988): 64.

143 Michael Blank, "Design in der DDR: Ausstellung in Stuttgart, BRD," *Form und Zweck* 6 (1988): 48.

144 SiG, folder "BRD 1988," concept, Organisationsprojekt und 1. Ideenskizze zur Ausstellung des Amtes für industrielle Formgestaltung der DDR in der BRD 1988.

145 Blank, "Design in der DDR," 48.

146 Michael Blank, "Wir müssen aufhören, in Tassen und Tellern zu denken," *Design Report* 6 (1988): 27.

147 BArch, B288/256, Thunig-Nittner to Gerz, "EC-Meeting 10. 11.1988, hier: Bereich Kultur," 9 November 1988.

148 Sarotte, *Dealing with the Devil*, 3.

Chapter 5

1 Ulfert Herlyn in Hans-Paul Barhdt, *Die moderne Großstadt: Soziologische Überlegungen zum Städtebau*, ed. Ulfert Herlyn (Wiesbaden: Springer Fachmedien, 1998), 7.

2 Hans-Paul Barhdt quoted in Herlinde Koelbl and Manfred Sack, *Das deutsche Wohnzimmer*, with a foreword by Andreas Mitscherlich (Munich: List, 1980), 16. The photo pages of the book are not paginated.

3 Adorno, "Funktionalismus heute," 377.

4 See, for example, Pence and Betts, *Socialist Modern*; Kimberly Zarecor, *Manufacturing a Socialist Modernity: Housing in Czechoslovakia, 1945–1960* (Pittsburgh: University of Pittsburgh Press, 2011); Marie-Janine Calic, Dietmar Neutatz, and Julia Obertreis, eds., *The Crisis of Socialist Modernity: The Soviet Union and Yugoslavia in the 1970s* (Göttingen: Vandenhoeck and Ruprecht, 2011). The socialist modernity concept aligns with the sociological "varieties of modernity" paradigm that emerged in the 2000s inspired by the political economy literature on "varieties of capitalism." It critiques modernization theory of the 1950s and 1960s, which saw modernization as a homogenizing process that would ultimately lead to convergence of societies undergoing it. The "varieties of modernity" perspective meanwhile emphasizes cultural and institutional diversity, concluding that there are several paths to modernity, also within Europe, the region which modernization theorists have used as the yardstick for comparison. See Volker H. Schmidt, "Multiple Modernities or Varieties of Modernity?," *Current Sociology* 54, no. 1 (2006): 77–97.

5 Calic, Neutatz, and Obertreis, *The Crisis of Socialist Modernity*, 12.

6 Peter Beilharz, *Socialism and Modernity* (Minneapolis: University of Minnesota Press, 2009), 140; see also Benjamin Robinson, *The Skin of the System: On Germany's Socialist Modernity* (Stanford, CA: Stanford University Press, 2009).

7 Konrad Jarausch, "Care and Coercion: The GDR Welfare Dictatorship," in *Dictatorship as Experience: Towards a Socio-Cultural History of the GDR*, ed. Konrad Jarausch and Eve Duffy (New York: Berghahn, 1999), 47–70.

8 Hansen, "Networks, Narratives, and Markets," 452.

9 Alison Light has used the term "conservative modernity" in her work *Forever England: Femininity, Literature and Conservatism between the Wars* (Routledge: London, 1991). The concept has been applied to other countries in a special journal issue edited by David Glover and Cora Kaplan. "Introduction," *New Formations* 28, Conservative Modernity (1996). Light, *Forever England*, 17–18.

10 Lord Hugh Cecil, *Conservatism* (London: Williams & Norgate, 1912), 14.

11 See, for example, Nicholas Attfield, *Conservative Modern: Conservative Revolution in German Music, 1918–1933* (Oxford: Oxford University Press, 2017); Michael Minden, *Modern German Literature* (Cambridge: Polity, 2011), 114–148; Jeffrey Herf identified a related, yet more intense cultural politics in what he has called "reactionary modernism." Through this concept he sought to explain and reconcile the rejection of Enlightenment reason, from which modernization has grown, with the simultaneous

embrace of technology by the political Right during the Weimar years and under National Socialism. Jeffrey Herf, *Reactionary Modernism: Technology, Culture, and Politics in Weimar and the Third Reich* (Cambridge: Cambridge University Press, 1984), 16.

12 Hilpert, "The Postwar Dispute in Germany," 132.

13 For detailed studies on the corrective systems of consumer education, see Crew, *Consuming Germany*; Merkel, *Utopie und Bedürfnis*; Carter, *How German Is She?*

14 See Eric Weitz, "The Ever-Present Other: Communism in the Making of West Germany," in *The Miracle Years: A Cultural History of West Germany, 1949–1968*, ed. Hannah Schissler (Princeton, NJ: Princeton University Press, 2001), 219–232.

15 Josef Alfons Thuma, "Einiges zur Frage 'wie wohnen?'" in Gedanken und Bilder zur Ausstellung "wie wohnen": Bautechnik, Möbel, Hausrat," Stuttgart-Karlsruhe, 1949–1950 (Stuttgart: Verlag Gerd Hatje, 1950).

16 Schnellbach, "Möbel," in Gedanken und Bilder zur Ausstellung "wie wohnen."

17 See Oestereich, "Gute Form" im Wiederaufbau, 320.

18 See Tilman Harlander, "Wohnungspolitik," in *Handwörterbuch der Stadt- und Raumentwicklung*, ed. Akademie für Raumforschung und Landesplanung (Hanover: Akademie für Raumforschung und Landesplanung, 2018), 2957–9.

19 Clemens Zimmermann, "Wohnungspolitik—Eigenheim für alle?" in *Villa und Eigenheim: Suburbaner Städtebau in Deutschland*, ed. Tilman Harlander (Stuttgart: Deutsche Verlags-Anstalt, 2001), 67.

20 See SiG, Herbert Letsch and Karla Scharf, "Ästhetische Sinnlichkeit und Subjektentfaltung: Dargestellt an der ästhetischen Problematik sozialistischen Wohnens," Berlin 1988/89, unpublished, 8. Karla Scharf published parts of this study as "Wohnwelt als Teil der Alltagswelt und der ästhetischen Kultur," in *Lebens-Formen: Alltagsobjekte als Darstellung von Lebensstilveränderungen am Beispiel der Wohnung und Bekleidung der "Neuen Mittelschichten,"* ed. Susanne S. Reich (Berlin: Akademie der Künste, 1991), 103–120.

21 In her study of the British furniture market, Judy Attfield explores this question in the context of the sea change from legal design regulations and rationing in the immediate postwar period to the increasing popularity of all types of furniture in later postwar decades. Judy Attfield, "'Give 'em something dark and heavy': The Role of Design in the Material Culture of Popular British Furniture, 1939–1965," *Journal of Design History* 9 (1996): 185–201.

22 BArch, B102/34493, Wiederanders, report, 25 October 1950.

23 See Thorstein Veblen, *The Theory of the Leisure Class: An Economic Study of Institutions* (Oxford: Oxford University Press, [1899] 2007).

24 SiG, box "Diverses AIF ungeordnet," handwritten notes, "Horst Michel," 20 November 1984.

25 Victor Buchli, "Khrushchev, Modernism, and the Fight against 'Petit-bourgeois' Consciousness in the Soviet Home," *Journal of Design History* 10, no. 2, Design, Stalin and the Thaw (1997): 161–170. Aesthetics as a fundamental building block for debates

about de-Stalinization are also discussed by Susan Reid, "De-Stalinization and Taste," *Journal of Design History* 10, no. 2, Design, Stalin and the Thaw (1997): 177–201.

26 See Stefan Jungklaus, "Werkbundkisten—Erziehung zum vernünftigen Konsumenten," in *Kampf der Dinge: Der Deutsche Werkbund zwischen Anspruch und Alltag*, ed. Werkbundarchiv (Leipzig: Werkbundarchiv Museum der Dinge, 2008), 126–133; Betts, *Authority of Everyday Objects*, 103–104.

27 Ibid., 129.

28 The conservative nature of social policy in the Federal Republic of the 1950s has been acknowledged by scholarship. See, for example, Robert G. Moeller, ed., *West Germany under Construction: Politics, Society, and Culture in the Adenauer Era* (Ann Arbor: University of Michigan Press, 1997).

29 Jungklaus, "Werkbundkisten—Erziehung zum vernünftigen Konsumenten," 126.

30 WBA, WBK-I, ADO 9-316/70, final report, "Werkbundkisten," ed. Deutscher Werkbund Niedersachsen-Bremen, 1970.

31 Rotraud Pohl (former designer at the Berlin Furniture Combine) in discussion with the author, 13 January 2009.

32 Horst E. Wittig, *Pläne und Praktiken der polytechnischen Erziehung in Mitteldeutschland* (Bad Harzburg: Verlag für Wissenschaft, Wirtschaft und Technik, 1962). For a discussion of the connections between ideology and education, see Mary Fulbrook, *Anatomy of a Dictatorship: Inside the GDR, 1949–1989* (Oxford: Oxford University Press, 1995), 80–81.

33 Jonathan Voges, *"Selbst ist der Mann": Do-It-Yourself und Heimwerken in der Bundesrepublik Deutschland* (Göttingen: Wallstein Verlag 2017), 215.

34 Betts, *Authority of Everyday Objects*, 97–101.

35 Heinrich König, "Erste Wohnberatungsstelle in Mannheim," *Werk und Zeit* 17 (1953).

36 Axel Schild and Arnold Sywottek, eds., *Massenwohnung und Eigenheim: Wohnungsbau und Wohnen in der Großstadt seit dem Ersten Weltkrieg* (Frankfurt am Main: Campus, 1988), esp. Günther Schulz, "Eigenheimpolitik und Eigenheimförderung im ersten Jahrzehnt nach dem Zweiten Welkrieg," in ibid., 409–439; Günther Schulz, *Wiederaufbau in Deutschland: Die Wohnungsbaupolitik in den Westzonen und der Bundesrepublik von 1945 bis 1957* (Düsseldorf: Droste, 1994).

37 See Adelheid von Saldern, *Häuserleben: Die Geschichte des Arbeiterwohnens vom Kaiserreich bis heute* (Bonn: Dietz, 1995), 268–270.

38 Zimmermann, "Wohnungspolitik—Eigenheim für alle?" 64–65.

39 Hedwig Meermann, "Wohnberatung als politische Aufgabe," *Werk und Zeit* 3 (1972).

40 For a history of the Werkbund's involvement in creating German *Wohnkultur*, see Nicola von Albrecht, "'Klärung des Wohnwillens' oder die Wohnberatung," in *Kampf der Dinge: Der Deutsche Werkbund zwischen Anspruch und Alltag*, ed. Werkbundarchiv, 114–121 (Leipzig: Werkbundarchiv Museum der Dinge, 2008).

41 Von Albrecht, "'Klärung des Wohnwillens' oder die Wohnberatung," 120.

42 Michael Andritzky, "Die Zukunft der Wohnberatung," *Werk und Zeit*, 5/1971; Michael Andritzky, "Neue Ziele und Methoden für Wohnberatungen," *Werk und Zeit* 1/1972.

43 Manfred Goerke, "Wohnberatung des Bezirkes Karl-Marx-Stadt," *Kultur im Heim* 4 (1964): 12–14.

44 Bernd Wurlitzer, "Vorbildlicher Kundendienst," *Kultur im Heim* 2 (1972): 4.

45 Rubin, *Synthetic Socialism*, 103.

46 Silbermann, *Vom Wohnen der Deutschen*, 213.

47 Ibid., 212.

48 Until the building of the Berlin Wall in August 1961, West German magazines and scholarly periodicals were easily accessible. East German design schools continued to hold subscriptions for their libraries throughout the years of partition.

49 See, for example, Dr. Walter Besenbruch, "Die Künstler und die Partei," *Form und Zweck* (1957/58): i–viii; Hans W. Aust, "Bessere Industrieform—eine wichtige Aufgabe beim Aufbau des Sozialismus," *Form und Zweck* (1958/59): 25–35.

50 Andreas Ludwig, "Vorwort," in *Fortschritt, Norm und Eigensinn: Erkundungen im Alltag der DDR*, ed. Dokumentationszentrum Alltagskultur der DDR e.V. (Berlin: Christoph Links, 1999), 12–13.

51 Michel, "Industrieformgestalter auf dem Bitterfelder Weg," 5.

52 For a discussion of privacy in the GDR, see Betts, *Within Walls*, 119–147.

53 Kremerskothen, "Wohnen wie noch nie," in *Rolf Heide—Designer, Architekt, Querdenker*, ed. Dirk Meyhöfer (Ludwigsburg: Avedition, 2000), 16.

54 With a distribution of more than 3 million readers in 2011, it has grown into one of the biggest European lifestyle magazines, http://www.gujmedia.de/print/portfolio/schoener-wohnen/profil/, accessed on 18 February 2012.

55 Kremerskothen, "Wegstücke," 25.

56 Betts, *Within Walls*, 141.

57 The aesthetics of power in Nazi Germany and the Soviet Union under Stalin have been excellently explained in the exhibition catalog Irina Antonowa and Jörn Merkert, eds., *Berlin—Moskau, 1900–1950*, 2nd ed. (Munich: Prestel, 1995).

58 For a discussion of Bauhaus rationalism, see Hilpert, "The Postwar Dispute in West Germany," 138–146.

59 Christopher Neumaier and Andreas Ludwig, "The Individualization of Everyday Life: Consumption, Domestic Culture, and Family Structures," in *A History Shared and Divided: East and West Germany since the 1970s*, ed. Frank Bösch (New York: Berghahn, 2018), 293–347.

60 For example, see Adelheid von Saldern, "Bürgerliche Repräsentationskultur: Konstanz und Wandel der Wohnformen im Deutschen Reich und in der Bundesrepublik (1900–1980)," *Historische Zeitschrift* 284 (2007): 348–359, or Silbermann, *Vom Wohnen der Deutschen*. Pierre Bordieu observed that "It is in the relationship between the two capacities which define the habitus, the capacity to produce classifiable practices and works, and the capacity to differentiate and appreciate these practices and products

(taste), that the represented social world, i.e., the space of life-styles, is constituted." Bordieu, *Distinction: A Social Critique of the Judgment of Taste* (Oxon: Routledge, [1984] 2010). See the first chapter of Wolfgang Ruppert, ed., *Fahrrad, Auto, Fernsehschrank: Zur Kulturgeschichte der Alltagsdinge* (Frankfurt am Main: Fischer, 1993), 14–36, for a discussion of the theoretical literature that brought forward material culture studies as a social history approach to explore society in the age of mass production.

61 See Hansen, *Danish Modern Furniture*, 28.

62 Hans Wichmann, "System-Möbel: Ein Novum unseres Jahrhunderts," in *Möbeldesign: Made in Germany*, ed. Zentrum Baden-Württemberg (Stuttgart: Landesgewerbeamt Baden-Württemberg, 1985), 152.

63 German sociologist Ulrich Beck coined the term *Fahrstuhleffekt* ("elevator effect") to describe the collective improvement in living standards in his work *Risikogesellschaft: Auf dem Weg in eine andere Moderne* (Frankfurt am Main: Suhrkamp, 1986). This concept observes that increased wealth across all social strata dissolves class distinctions, because lower classes gain access to goods and services that were once reserved for the privileged. It started a snowball effect that eradicated the markers of class-specific habitus and led, according to Beck, to the individualization tendencies that the field of sociology has attested for the later postwar decades.

64 The right to housing is guaranteed in Article 37 of the 1968 Constitution of the German Democratic Republic.

65 See Betts, *Within Walls*, 141–147.

66 BArch, DH2/23618, Entwicklung einer vielgeschossigen Typenserie 1954, 21.

67 Betts, *Within Walls*, 132.

68 Donna Harsch, "Between State Policy and Private Sphere: Women in the GDR in the 1960s and 1970s," *Clio* 41, "Real socialism" and the Challenge of Gender (2015): 96.

69 Emily Pugh, *Architecture, Politics and Identity in Divided Berlin* (Pittsburgh: University of Pittsburgh, 2014), 289.

70 BArch, DH2/23621, Herwig Loeper, "Experimente Variables Wohnen in Berlin und Rostock."

71 BArch, DF 7/544, questionnaires "Variables Wohnen," May 1975. The composition of the test housing block expressed what Ina Merkel has described as a process of "de-differentiation" by letting people from different backgrounds live in the same environment. Merkel, *Utopie und Bedürfnis*, 348–455. For more information about the processes and mechanisms behind GDR urban planning, see Christian Rau, *Stadtverwaltung im Staatssozialismus: Kommunalpolitik und Wohnungswesen in der DDR am Beispiel Leipzigs, 1957–1989*, Beiträge zur Stadtgeschichte und Urbanisierungsforschung 20 (Stuttgart: Franz Steiner Verlag, 2017); and Annemarie Sammartino, "The New Socialist Man in the *Plattenbau*: The East German Housing Program and the Development of the Socialist Way of Life," *Journal of Urban History* 44, no. 1 (2018): 78–94.

72 BArch, DH2/23621, final report "Experiment Variables Wohnen in Berlin und Rostock," 53.

73 Ibid., 24.

74 "Variables Wohnen: Pläne für die nahe Zukunft," *Kultur im Heim* 5 (1979): 28–31.

75 "Das Wohnzimmer: Lebens-oder Repräsentationsraum?," *Kultur im Heim* 5 (1986): 2.

76 Ibid., 3.

77 Pohl Private Collection, Rotraud Pohl, "Soziologische Untersuchung zum Wohnen," 5. Multiple choice questionnaires.

78 Helmut Hanke and Michel Vale, "Leisure Time in the GDR: Trends and Prospects," *International Journal of Sociology* 18, no. 4 (1988/1989): 167.

79 See, for example, Axel Schmidt, "Zwei Staaten eine Fernsehgeneration: Überlegungen zur Bedeutung der elektronischen Massenmedien in der Geschichte der Kommunikation zwischen der Bundesrepublik und der DDR," in *Doppelte Zeitgeschichte: Deutsch-deutsche Beziehungen, 1945–1990*, ed. Arnd Bauernkämper, Martin Sabrow, and Bernd Stöver (Bonn: Dietz, 1998), 58–71, and Esther von Richthofen, *Bringing Culture to the Masses: Control, Compromise and Participation in the GDR* (New York: Berghahn, 2009).

80 Interviews in Letsch and Scharf, "Ästhetische Sinnlichkeit und Subjektentfaltung," 28 and 44.

81 Pohl, "Soziologische Untersuchung zum Wohnen," 4.

82 "Wir wohnen im Neubau," *Kultur im Heim* 4 (1980): 3–15.

83 Pohl Private Collection, "Kurzfassung zum Forschungsbericht 'Wohnen '81,'" 5. The study "Wohnen '81" interviewed and observed 777 people in development areas in Potsdam and Leipzig. The results returned 95 percent statistical significance.

84 See Wichmann, "System-Möbel: Ein Novum unseres Jahrhunderts."

85 As the questionnaire allowed for multiple responses, the rest of the answers to the question about what style of living room furniture would cater to their personal taste included 66 percent for "modern and fashionable," 65 percent "solid and timeless," and 64 percent preferred "pragmatic and functional." Only 38 percent liked a "representative" living room, 37 percent pictured "modern pieces mixed with antique ones," 25 percent would have liked to furnish their living rooms entirely with antique pieces, 22 percent described their taste as "out of the ordinary," and 12 percent as "daring and bold." Pohl, "Soziologische Untersuchung zum Wohnen," 10. See also Rotraud Pohl, "Wohnzimmer-Wünsche im Test: Ergebnisse einer wohnsoziologischen Untersuchung," *Kultur im Heim* 1 (1984): 16–19.

86 "Kurzfassung zum Forschungsbericht 'Wohnen '81,'" 7.

87 The 1986 marriage loan reform set the loan reduction at Ostmark 1,000 for the first child, Ostmark 1,500 for the second, and Ostmark 2,500 for the third. Roland Merten, "Junge Verlierer in den neuen Bundesländern: Die vergessenen Verlierer im Prozeß der deutschen Vereinigung," *Sozialer Fortschritt* 42, no. 12 (December 1993): 298. See also Heike Trappe, *Emanzipation oder Zwang? Frauen in der DDR zwischen Beruf, Familie und Sozialpolitik* (Berlin: Akademie, 1995); Michael Schwartz, "Emanzipation zur sozialen Nützlichkeit: Bedingungen und Grenzen von Frauenpolitik in der DDR," in *Sozialstaatlichkeit in der DDR: Sozialpolitische Entwicklungen im Spannungsfeld von*

Diktatur und Gesellschaft, 1945/49–1989, ed. Dierk Hoffmann and Michael Schwartz, Schriftenreihe der Vierteljahrshefte für Zeitgeschichte, special issue (Munich: Oldenbourg, 2005): 47–88.

88 See Eli Rubin, *Amnesiopolis: Modernity, Space, and Memory in East Germany* (New York: Oxford University Press, 2016), 87–88.

89 Sack, "Das deutsche Wohnzimmer," 12.

90 See also Anke te Heesen and Anette Michels, "Der Schrank als wissenschaftlicher Apparat," in *auf/zu: Der Schrank in den Wissenschaften,* ed. Anke te Heesen and Anette Michels (Berlin: Akademie, 2007), 10.

91 Letsch and Scharf, "Ästhetische Sinnlichkeit und Subjektentfaltung."

92 "Kurzfassung zum Forschungsbericht 'Wohnen '81,'" 6.

93 Letsch and Scharf, "Ästhetische Sinnlichkeit und Subjektentfaltung."

94 Ibid., 3. See also Dominique Krössin, "Kultur ins Heim: Geschmackserziehung versus Eigensinn," in *Fortschritt, Norm und Eigensinn. Erkundungen im Alltag der DDR,* ed. Dokumentationszentrum Alltagskultur der DDR e.V. (Berlin: Christoph Links, 1999), 151–163.

95 Ibid., 17.

96 Ibid., 25.

97 Ibid., 33.

98 Voges, "Selbst ist der Mann," 210.

99 Letsch and Scharf, "Ästhetische Sinnlichkeit und Subjektentfaltung," 34 and 79.

100 Ibid., 79.

101 Ibid., 25, 46, 56, 85, and 99.

102 Marcus Felson, "The Differentiation of Material Life Styles, 1925–1966," *Social Indicators Research* 3 (1976): 414; Grant McCracken, "Homeyness: A Cultural Account of One Constellation of Consumer Goods and Meanings," in *Culture and Consumption II: Markets, Meaning, and Brand Management,* ed. Grant McCracken (Bloomington: Indiana University Press, 2005), 26.

103 "Letsch Ästhetische Sinnlichkeit und Subjektentfaltung," 46.

104 Ibid.

105 Ibid., 56.

106 Ibid., 97.

107 Koelbl and Sack, *Das deutsche Wohnzimmer,* n.p.

108 Ibid.

109 Ibid.

110 Ibid.

111 Ibid.

112 Ibid.

113 Ibid.

114 Ibid.

115 Von Saldern describes how "the vertical borders between lifestyles and mentalities of the upper and lower classes persisted even in the last third of the twentieth century"

yet finds that these were less polarized than in the first half of the century. "Bürgerliche Repräsentationskultur," 382.

116 Herlinde Koelbl, and Manfred Sack, eds., *Das deutsche Wohnzimmer* (München: List, 1980), 7–19.

117 Gert Selle and Jutta Boehe, *Leben mit den schönen Dingen: Anpassung und Eigensinn im Alltag des Wohnens* (Reinbek: Rowohlt, 1986).

118 Selle and Boehe, *Leben mit den schönen Dingen*, 175.

119 Ebert, "Into the Great Wide Open: The Modernist Bungalow in 1960s West-Germany," 144–155.

120 Selle and Boehe, *Leben mit den schönen Dingen*, 60.

121 Ibid., 75.

122 While in the GDR the motivation for DIY projects often resulted from scarcity, scholars of the Federal Republic find that the West German DIY culture developed as a bourgeois pasttime around the increasing availability of leisure time for the middle classes; home ownership, which provided the space for DIY activities; and mostly conservative ideas of masculinity. Voges, *"Selbst ist der Mann,"* 32–61 and 221–264. West German DIY has also been linked to social protest movements and the squatter scene, see Reinhild Kreis "Heimwerken als Protest: Instandbesetzer und Wohnungsbaupolitik in West Berlin während der 1980er Jahre," *Zeithistorische Forschungen/Studies in Contemporary History* 14 (2017): 41–67.

123 See Andreas Buehn, Alexander Karmann, and Friedrich Schneider, "Shadow Economies and Do-It-Yourself Activities: The German Case," *Journal of Institutional and Theoretical Economics* 165, no. 4 (2009): 701–722.

124 Selle and Boehe, *Leben mit den schönen Dingen*, 123.

125 Ibid., 62.

126 See Letsch and Scharf, "Ästhetische Sinnlichkeit und Subjektentfaltung," 73.

127 Selle and Boehe, *Leben mit den schönen Dingen*, 83–84, 135, and 146–147.

128 Aynsley, *Designing Modern Germany*, 182.

129 Selle and Boehe, *Leben mit den schönen Dingen*, 134.

130 Ibid., 135.

131 Grant McCracken posits that "arrangements are homey when they combine diverse styles of furnishings in a single room. They are also homey when they establish patterns of asymmetrical balance and when they pair and center heterogeneous objects. Homeyness can also be achieved by the judicious combinations of particular colors, fabrics, and pieces of furniture." McCracken, "Homeyness," 26.

132 Urban, *Tower and Slab*, 64.

133 For similar findings in different cultural contexts, see Felson, "The Differentiation of Material Life Styles" (Detroit); McCracken, "Homeyness" (southern Ontario); Attfield, "Give 'em something dark and heavy" (Great Britain); Hansen, *Danish Modern Furniture* (Denmark).

134 Voges finds this distancing irony also to be a part of West German media discourse on do-it-yourself projects. *"Selbst ist der Mann,"* 263.

135 For a provocative discussion of the prewar discourse on interior design aesthetics and German identity, see Jarzombek, "The *Kunstgewerbe*, the *Werkbund*, and the Aesthetics of Culture in the Wilhelmine Period," 7–19.

Conclusion

1 Zatlin, *Currency of Socialism*, 53–54.

2 Konrad Jarausch, *The Rush to Unity* (New York: Oxford University Press, 1994), 108–109. The timeline Mary Sarotte meticulously puts together in her seminal work on the unification process makes clear that West German chancellor Kohl threw caution to the wind once he heard the chants for unity during his visit to Leipzig on 18 December 1989. Mary E. Sarotte, *1989: The Struggle to Create Post–Cold War Europe* (Princeton, NJ: Princeton University Press, 2009), 85–86.

3 See Krell, "West German Ostpolitik and the German Question"; Granieri, *The Ambivalent Alliance*, 10.

4 For example, see Kai Oppermann, "National Role Conceptions, Domestic Constraints and the New 'Normalcy' in German Foreign Policy: The Eurozone Crisis, Libya and Beyond," *German Politics* 21, no. 4 (2012): 502–519.

5 Hans Werner Sinn, "Germany's Economic Unification: An Assessment after Ten Years," National Bureau of Economic Research, Working Paper 7586 (Cambridge, MA, 2000), 9.

6 See, for example, Helmut Wiesenthal, "Die Transformation der DDR: Ein analytischer Rückblick auf Verfahren und Resultate," Gutachten für die Forschungsgruppe Europa, Centrum für angewandte Politikforschung (München, 1998).

7 Paul Betts, "Twilight of the Idols: East German Memory and Material Culture," *Journal of Modern History* 72, no. 3 (2000): 731–765.

8 *Good Bye Lenin!* Wolfgang Becker, director, 2003.

9 SächsStA-D, 11764/2390, Telex VE MK Dresden-Hellerau to VEB DW Hellerau, betr. Reklamationseinsatz gen. Krebs bei Fa. IKEA, 28 May 1986. Western businesses and their GDR suppliers have come under scrutiny by historians over allegations that they used forced and unpaid labor of political and criminal prisoners. For example, see Nicholas Kulish and Julia Werdiger, "Ikea Admits Forced Labor Was Used in 1980s," *New York Times*, 16 November 2012.

10 Johanna Sänger, "Zwischen allen Stühlen: Die Sammlung Industrielle Gestaltung als Archiv zur materiellen Kultur der DDR," *Zeithistorische Forschungen/Studies in Contemporary History*, no. 12 (2015): 138. Although only about 10,000 of the *Sammlung*'s 160,000 objects had been acquired before reunification, it has arguably become the most multifaceted and comprehensive collection of GDR design.

11 See Schreiter and Ravasi, "Institutional Pressures and Organizational Identity."

12 Hermann Glaser and Regine Halter, "Vorwort," *Vom Bauhaus bis Bitterfeld. 41 Jahre DDR-Design* (Gießen: Anabas, 1991), 9.

13 Gert Selle, "Die verlorene Unschuld der Armut—Über das Verschwinden einer Kulturdifferenz," in ibid., 54.

14 "Was bleibt vom DDR-Design?" 19–22.

15 See the *Economist*, Special Report Germany, "Europe's Reluctant Hegemon," June 2013. For the scholarly debate, see, for example, Ulrike Guérot and Mark Leonard, "The New German Question: How Europe Can Get the Germany It Needs," *Policy Brief*, European Council on Foreign Relations (April 2011): 1–13; and W. E. Paterson, "Does Germany Still Have a European Vocation?" *German Politics* 19, no. 1 (2010): 41–52.

BIBLIOGRAPHY

Archival Sources

Bibliothek Bundesverband der Deutschen Industrie, Berlin (BDI)
Bibliothek Rat für Formgebung, Frankfurt (BRfF)
Bundesarchiv Berlin (BArch)
    DC 20 Ministerrat
    DE 1 Staatliche Plankommission
    DG 4 Ministerium für Leichtindustrie
    DG 5 Ministerium für Bezirksgeleitete und Lebensmittelindustrie
    DF 5 Amt für Standardisierung
    DF 7 Amt für industrielle Formgestaltung
    DH 2 Baukademie der DDR
    DL 2 Ministerium für Außenhandel
    DL 102 Institut für Marktforschung
Bundesarchiv Koblenz (BArch)
    B 102 Bundesministerium für Wirtschaft
    B 288 Ständige Vertretung
    B 457 Rat für Formgebung
    Zsg 132 Institut für Demoskopie Allensbach
Design Archives, University of Brighton, UK (UoBDA)
    International Council of Societies of Industrial Designers
Dokumentationszentrum Alltagskultur der DDR, Eisenhüttenstadt
Gesellschaft für Konsumforschung, Nürnberg (GfK)
Politisches Archiv des Auswärtigen Amtes, Berlin (PA AA)
Sächsisches Staatsarchiv Dresden (SächsStA-D)
    Bestand Deutsche Werkstätten Hellerau
Sammlung Industrielle Gestaltung, Stiftung Haus der Geschichte der Bundesrepublik
    Deutschland (SiG)
Stadtarchiv Stuttgart (StAS)
    2068 Estate Mia Seeger
Werkbundarchiv - Museum der Dinge, Berlin (WBA-MdD)
    Estate Gustav Brakas von Hartmann
    Bestand Rat für Formgebung

Private Collections

Axel Bruchhäuser
Herbert and Rotraud Pohl

Interviews

Michael Blank
Uta Brandes
Axel Bruchhäuser
Michael Erlhoff
Peter Frank
Rolf Heide
Karin Hirdina
Günther Höhne
Rudolf Horn
Bernd Göbel
Martin Kelm
Karin Kirsch
Lore Kramer
Peter Maly
Detlef Mika
Herbert Pohl
Rotraud Pohl
Renate Sigwart

On-Site Visits

Deutsche Werkstätten Hellerau, Dresden
Interlübke, Rheda-Wiedenbrück
Hülsta, Stadtlohn
Möbel Wallach, Celle
Tecta, Lauenförde
Walter Knoll, Stuttgart

Published Primary Sources

Berliner Rundschau
Berliner Zeitung
Brigitte
Daily Telegraph

Darmstädter Tagblatt
Design Report
Form
Form und Zweck
Handelsblatt
Kultur im Heim
Nationalzeitung
Rheinischer Merkur
Schöner Wohnen
Silikattechnik
Sonntag
Spiegel
Süddeutsche Zeitung
Werk und Zeit

Gedanken und Bilder zur Ausstellung "wie wohnen": Bautechnik, Möbel, Hausrat. Stuttgart-Karlsruhe, 1949–1950. Stuttgart: Verlag Gerd Hatje, 1950.

Gustav Stein: Sammler—Förderer—Freund. Edited by Wilhelm-Lehmbruck-Museum Duisburg. Duisburg: Stadt Duisburg, 1983.

Dietrich, Gerd, ed. *Politik und Kultur in der Sowjetischen Besatzungszone Deutschlands (SBZ), 1945–1949.* Berlin: Peter Lang, 1993.

Koelbl, Herlinde, and Manfred Sack, eds. *Das deutsche Wohnzimmer.* München: List, 1980.

Leipziger Messe, ed. "Dienst am Ganzen." Leipzig: Messeamt, 1947.

Letsch, Herbert, and Karla Scharf. "Ästhetische Sinnlichkeit und Subjektentfaltung. Dargestellt an der ästhetischen Problematik sozialistischen Wohnens." Berlin 1988/89, unpublished, Sammlung industrielle Gestaltung, Haus der Geschichte Berlin.

Michel, Horst. *Der Industrieformgestalter auf dem Bitterfelder Weg.* Institut für Innengestaltung an der Hochschule für Architektur und Bauwesen Weimar. Weimar: Buch-und Kunstdruckerei Johannes Keipert, n.d.

Protokoll der Verhandlungen des V. Parteitages der Sozialistischen Einheitspartei Deutschlands. 10. bis 16. Juli 1958, 2 vol. Berlin: Dietz, 1959.

Rat für Formgebung. *Gründbedürfnisse des Wohnens.* Darmstadt: Rat für Formgebung, 1973.

Redeker, Horst. *Chemie gibt Schönheit.* Institut für angewandte Kunst 4. Edited by Hanna Schönherr. Berlin: VEB Mitteldeutsche Kunstanstalt Heidenau, 1959.

Schuchardt, A. G. *Wie wohnen?* 3rd ed. Berlin: Institut für angewandte Kunst, 1962.

Selle, Gert, and Jutta Boehe. *Leben mit den schönen Dingen: Anpassung und Eigensinn im Alltag des Wohnens.* Reinbek: Rowohlt, 1986.

Statistisches Jahrbuch für die Bundesrepublik Deutschland 1953. Wiesbaden: Metzler Poeschl, 1954.

Statistisches Jahrbuch für die Bundesrepublik Deutschland 1957. Wiesbaden: Metzler Poeschl, 1958.

Statistisches Jahrbuch für die Bundesrepublik Deutschland 1960. Wiesbaden: Metzler Poeschl, 1961.

Stein, Gustav. "Das sechste Arbeitsjahr." In *Jahrestagung Lübeck 57*, edited by Kulturkreis im Bundesverband der Deutschen Industrie e.V. N.d.

Stein, Gustav. *Unternehmer als Förderer der Kunst.* Frankfurt am Main: August Lutzeyer, 1952.

Vom Bauhaus bis Bitterfeld. 41 Jahre DDR-Design. Gießen: Anabas, 1991.

Wir bauen ein besseres Leben: Eine Ausstellung über die Produktivität der Atlantischen Gemeinschaft auf dem Gebiet des Wohnbedarfs. Stuttgart: Gerd Hatje, 1952.

Secondary Sources

Abelshauser, Werner. "Ansätze 'Korporativer Marktwirtschaft' in der Koreakrise der frühen fünziger Jahre: Ein Briefwechsel zwischen dem Hohen Kommissar John McCloy und Bundeskanzler Konrad Adenauer." *Vierteljahreshefte für Zeitgeschichte* 30, no. 4 (1982): 715–756.

Adam, Peter. *Art of the Third Reich.* New York: H. N. Abrams, 1992.

Adorno, Theodor W. "Funktionalismus heute." In *Gesammelte Schriften* 10.1, edited by Rolf Tiedemann. Frankfurt am Main: Suhrkamp, 1977.

Ahrens, Ralf. "Außenwirtschaftspolitik zwischen Ostintegration und Westverschuldung." In *Die Zentrale Wirtschaftsverwaltung in der SBZ/DDR: Akteure, Strukturen, Verwaltungspraxis*, Wirtschaftspolitik in Deutschland 1917-1990 vol. 3, edited by Dierk Hoffmann, 510-590. Berlin: De Gruyter Oldenbourg, 2016.

Ahrens, Ralf. *Gegenseitige Wirtschaftshilfe? Die DDR im RGW: Strukturen und handelspolitische Strategien, 1963–1976.* Cologne: Böhlau, 2000.

Albrecht, Nicola von. "'Klärung des Wohnwillens' oder die Wohnberatung." In *Kampf der Dinge: Der Deutsche Werkbund zwischen Anspruch und Alltag*, edited by Werkbundarchiv, 114–121. Leipzig: Werkbundarchiv Museum der Dinge, 2008.

Albrecht, Ulrich. "Security and the German Question." *World Policy Journal* 1, no. 3 (1984): 575–602.

Allen, Christopher S. "Corporatism and Regional Economic Policies in the Federal Republic of Germany: The 'Meso' Politics of Industrial Adjustment." *Publius* 19, no. 4, Federalism and Intergovernmental Relations in West Germany: A Fortieth Year Appraisal (1989): 147–164.

Ambrosius, Gerold. *Die Durchsetzung der sozialen Marktwirtschaft in Westdeutschland, 1945–1949.* Stuttgart: Deutsche Verlagsanstalt, 1977.

Ammon, Herbert, and Peter Brandt. "The Relevance of the German Question for Peace in Europe." *International Journal of Politics* 13, no. 1/2, Germany Debates Defense (1983): 83–96.

Anderson, Benedict. *Imagined Communities: Reflections on the Origin and Spread of Nationalism*. 2nd ed. New York: Verso, 1991.

Antonowa, Irina, and Jörn Merkert, eds. *Berlin–Moskau, 1900–1959*. 2nd ed. Munich: Prestel, 1995.

Applegate, Celia. *A Nation of Provincials: The German Idea of Heimat*. Berkeley: University of California Press, 1990.

Aron, Raymond. *Dix-Huit Leçons sur la Société Industrielle*. Paris: Gallimard, 1963.

Ash, Timothy Garton. *In Europe's Name: Germany and the Divided Continent*. New York: Random House, 1993.

Attfield, Judy. "'Give 'em something dark and heavy': The Role of Design in the Material Culture of Popular British Furniture, 1939–1965." *Journal of Design History* 9 (1996): 185–201.

Attfield, Nicholas. *Conservative Modern: Conservative Revolution in German Music, 1918–1933*. Oxford: Oxford University Press, 2017.

Augustine, Dolores. *Red Prometheus: Engineering and Dictatorship in East Germany, 1945–1990*. Cambridge, MA: MIT Press, 2007.

Augustine, Dolores. "Innovation and Ideology: Werner Hartmann and the Failure of the East German Electronics Industry." In *The East German Economy, 1949–2010*, edited by Hartmut Berghoff and Uta Balbier, 95–110. Cambridge: Cambridge University Press, 2014.

Auslander, Leora. *Taste and Power: Furnishing Modern France*. Berkeley: University of California Press, 1996.

Aynsley, Jeremy. *Designing Modern Germany*. London: Reaktion Books, 2009.

Bähr, Johannes, and Dietmar Petzina, eds. *Innovationsverhalten und Entscheidungsstrukturen: Vergleichende Studien zur wirtschaftlichen Entwicklung im geteilten Deutschland, 1945–1990*. Berlin: Duncker & Humblot, 1996.

Bähr, Johannes. "Firmenabwanderung aus der SBZ/DDR und aus Berlin-Ost (1945–1953)." In *Wirtschaft im Umbruch: Strukturveränderungen und Wirtschaftspolitik im 19. und 20. Jahrhundert*, edited by Wolfram Fischer, Uwe Müller, and Fran Zasvhaler, 229–249. St. Katharinen: Scripta-Mercaturae, 1997.

Bahr, Egon, and Michel Vale. "Bearing Responsibility for Germany: Twenty Years of the Wall—Ten Years of the Four-Power Agreement." *International Journal of Politics* 13, no. 1/2, Germany Debates Defense (1983): 69–82.

Barhdt, Hans-Paul. *Die moderne Großstadt: Soziologische Überlegungen zum Städtebau*. Edited by Ulfert Herlyn. Wiesbaden: Springer Fachmedien, 1998.

Balbier, Uta. *Kalter Krieg auf der Aschenbahn: Deutsch-deutscher Sport, 1950–72, eine politische Geschichte*. Paderborn: Schöningh, 2007.

Barron, Stephanie, ed. *Degenerate Art: The Fate of the Avant-Garde in Nazi-Germany*. Los Angeles: Los Angeles County Museum, 1991.

Baumhoff, Anja, and Magdalena Droste, eds. *Mythos Bauhaus: Zwischen Selbsterfindung und Enthistorisierung*. Berlin: Reimer, 2009.

Bauernkämper, Arnd, Martin Sabrow, and Bernd Stöver, eds. *Doppelte Zeitgeschichte: Deutsch-deutsche Beziehungen, 1945–1990*. Bonn: Dietz, 1998.

Beck, Ulrich. *Risikogesellschaft: Auf dem Weg in eine andere Moderne*. Frankfurt am Main: Suhrkamp, 1986.

Beier, Achim. "Die Stellung der Leipziger Messe in der DDR bis zum Mauerbau (1949 bis 1961)." In *Leipzigs Messen, 1497–1997, Teilband 2: 1914–1997*, edited by Hartmut Zwahr, Thomas Topfstedt, and Günter Bentele, 655–665. Cologne: Böhlau Verlag, 1999.

Beilharz, Peter. *Socialism and Modernity*. Minneapolis: University of Minnesota Press, 2009.

Benjamin, Walter. *Illuminations*. Edited by Hannah Arendt, translated by Harry Zohn. New York: Schocken Books, 2007.

Berghahn, Volker. *The Americanisation of West German Industry, 1945–1973*. Cambridge: Cambridge University Press, 1986.

Berghoff, Hartmut. "The End of Family Business? The Mittelstand and German Capitalism in Transition, 1949–2000." *Business History Review* 80, no. 2 (2006): 263–295.

Berghoff, Hartmut, and Uta Balbier, eds. *The East German Economy, 1949–2010*. Cambridge: Cambridge University Press, 2014.

Bertsch, Georg, Ernst Hedler, and Matthias Dietz. *SED—Schönes Einheits Design*. Cologne: Taschen Verlag, 1994.

Betts, Paul. *Within Walls: Private Life in the German Democratic Republic*. Oxford: Oxford University Press, 2010.

Betts, Paul. *The Authority of Everyday Objects: A Cultural History of West German Industrial Design*. Berkeley: University of California Press, 2004.

Betts, Paul. "Building Socialism at Home: The Case of East German Interiors." In *Socialist Modern: East German Everyday Culture and Politics*, edited by Katherine Pence and Paul Betts, 96–132. Ann Arbor: University of Michigan Press, 2003.

Betts, Paul. "Twilight of the Idols: East German Memory and Material Culture." *Journal of Modern History* 72, no. 3 (2000): 731–765.

Biundo, Christina, Kerstin Eckstein, Petra Eisele, Carolyn Graf, Gabriele Diana Grawe, and Claudia Heitmann. *Bauhaus-Ideen, 1919–1994: Bibliographie und Beiträge zur Rezeption des Bauhausgedankens*. Berlin: Reimer, 1994.

Bober, Martin. "Von der Idee zum Mythos: Die Rezeption des Bauhaus in beiden Teilen Deutschlands in Zeiten des Neuanfangs (1945 und 1989)." PhD diss., Universität Kassel, n.d.

Börzel Tanja A., and Diana Panke. "Europäisierung—ein politikwissenschaftliches Laboratorium." In *Les identités européennes au XXe siècle: Diversités, convergences et solidarités*, edited by Robert Frank and Gérard Bossuat, 53–71. Paris: Sorbonne Press, 2004.

Bordieu, Pierre. *Distinction: A Social Critique of the Judgment of Taste*. Oxon: Routledge, [1984] 2010.

Bräutigam, Hans Otto. *Ständige Vertretung: Meine Jahre in Ost-Berlin.* Hamburg: Hoffmann und Campe, 2009.

Buchheim, Christoph. *Die Wiedereingliederung Westdeutschlands in die Weltwirtschaft, 1945–1958.* Munich: Oldenbourg, 1990.

Buchli, Victor. "Khrushchev, Modernism, and the Fight against 'Petit-bourgeois' Consciousness in the Soviet Home." *Journal of Design History* 10, no. 2, Design, Stalin and the Thaw (1997): 161–170.

Buehn, Andreas, Alexander Karmann, and Friedrich Schneider. "Shadow Economies and Do-It-Yourself Activities: The German Case." *Journal of Institutional and Theoretical Economics* 165, no. 4 (2009): 701–722.

Bührer, Werner. "Die Wirtschaftsdiplomatie des BDI von 1949 bis Mitte der 1970er Jahre." In *Auswärtige Repräsentationen: Deutsche Kulturdiplomatie nach 1945*, edited by Johannes Paulmann, 121–137. Cologne: Böhlau, 2005.

Bührer, Werner. "Der Kulturkreis im Bundesverband der Deutschen Industrie und die 'kulturelle Modernisierung' der Bundesrepublik in den 50er Jahren." In *Modernisierung im Wiederaufbau: Die westdeutsche Gesellschaft der 50er Jahre*, edited by Axel Schildt and Arnold Sywottek, 583–595. Bonn: Dietz, 1993.

Burley, Anne-Marie. "The Once and Future German Question." *Foreign Affairs* 68, no. 5 (1989): 65–83.

Busch, Andreas. "Globalisation and National Varieties of Capitalism: The Contested Viability of the 'German Model.'" *German Politics* 14, no. 2 (2005): 125–139.

Butter, Andreas. *Neues Leben, Neues Bauen: Die Moderne in der Architektur der SBZ/DDR, 1945–1951.* Berlin: Hans Schiller, 2006.

Calic, Marie-Janine, Dietmar Neutatz, and Julia Obertreis, eds. *The Crisis of Socialist Modernity: The Soviet Union and Yugoslavia in the 1970s.* Göttingen: Vandenhoeck and Ruprecht, 2011.

Campbell, Joan. *The German Werkbund: The Politics of Reform in the Applied Arts.* Princeton, NJ: Princeton University Press, 1978.

Carter, Erica. *How German Is She? Postwar West German Reconstruction and the Consuming Woman.* Ann Arbor: University of Michigan Press, 1997.

Carter, Erica, Jan Palmowski, and Katrin Schreiter, eds. *German Division as Shared Experience: Interdisciplinary Perspective on the Postwar Everyday.* Berghahn: New York, 2019.

Castillo, Greg. *Cold War on the Home Front: The Soft Power of Midcentury Design.* Minneapolis: University of Minnesota Press, 2010.

Castillo, Greg. "Domesticating the Cold War: Household Consumption as Propaganda in Marshall Plan Germany." *Journal of Contemporary History* 40, no. 2 (April 2005): 261–288.

Castillo, Greg. "Exhibiting the Good Life: Marshall Plan Modernism in Divided Berlin." In *Cold War Modern: Art and Design in a Divided World, 1945–1975*, edited by David Crowley and Jane Pavett, 66–71. London: Victoria & Albert Museum, 2008.

Castro, Rafael, and Patricio Sáiz, "Cross-cultural Factors in International Branding,"

Business History 62, special issue The Brand and Its History, Part II: Branding, Culture, and National Identity, no. 1 (2020): 1–25.

Cecil, Lord Hugh. *Conservatism.* London: Williams & Norgate, 1912.

Clark, Katerina. *The Soviet Novel: History and Ritual.* Bloomington: Indiana University Press, 2000.

Confino, Alon. *The Nation as a Local Metaphor: Württemberg, Imperial Germany, and National Memory, 1871–1918.* Chapel Hill: University of North Carolina Press, 1997.

Conrad, Sebastian, and Jürgen Osterhammel, eds. *Das Kaiserreich transnational: Deutschland in der Welt, 1971–1914.* Göttingen: Vandenhoek and Ruprecht, 2004.

Conway, Martin, and Kiran Klaus Patel, eds. *Europeanization in the Twentieth Century: Historical Approaches.* New York: Palgrave Macmillan, 2010.

Creuzberger, Stefan. *Kampf um die Einheit: Das gesamtdeutsche Ministerium und die politische Kultur des Kalten Krieges, 1949–1969.* Schriften des Bundesarchivs 69. Düsseldorf: Droste, 2008.

Crew, David E., ed. *Consuming Germany in the Cold War.* Oxford: Berg, 2003.

Danyel, Jürgen, ed. *Die geteilte Vergangenheit. Zum Umgang mit Nationalsozialismus und Widerstand in beiden deutschen Staaten.* Berlin: Akademie, 1995.

De Grazia, Victoria. *Irresistible Empire: America's Advance through 20th-Century Europe.* Cambridge, MA: Belknap Press of Harvard University Press, 2005.

Dettmar, Ute, and Thomas Küpper. *Kitsch: Texte und Theorien.* Stuttgart: Philipp Reclam jun., 2007.

Deutsche Werkstätten Hellerau. *Mythos Hellerau: Ein Unternehmen meldet sich zurück.* Catalog for the Exhibition in the Deutsche Architektur Museum. Darmstadt: Druckhaus, n.d.

Dietsch, Ulrich. *Außenwirtschaftliche Aktivitäten der DDR: Maßnahmen gegenüber westlichen Industriestaaten.* Hamburg: Weltarchiv, 1976.

Dohrn, Reimer. "A View from Port to City: Inland Waterway Sailors and City-Port Transformation in Hamburg." In *Port Cities as Areas of Transition: Ethnographic Perspectives*, edited by Waltraud Kokot, Mijal Gandelsman-Trier, Kathrin Wildner, Astrid Wonneberger, 99–110. Bielefeld: Transcript, 2008.

Doering-Manteuffel, Anselm. *Wie westlich sind die Deutschen? Amerikanisierung und Westernisierung im 20. Jahrhundert.* Göttingen: Vandenhoeck and Ruprecht, 1999.

Ebert, Carola. "Into the Great Wide Open: The Modernist Bungalow in 1960s West Germany/Avaryyseihalus. Modernistlik bangalo 1960. aastate Lääne-Saksamaal." In *Constructed Happiness: Domestic Environment in the Cold War Era/Võistlevad õnned: Elukeskkond külma sõja perioodili*, edited by Mart Kalm and Ingrid Ruudi, 144–155. Proceedings of a conference held at the Institute of Art History, Estonian Academy of Arts in Tallinn, 20–22 May 2004. Tallinn: Trükk, 2005.

Edwards, Vincent, and Peter Lawrence. *Management Change in East Germany: Unification and Transformation.* London: Routledge, 1994.

Eisele, Petra. "Ist Geschmack Glücksache? Horst Michel und das Weimarer Institut für Innengestaltung." In *Horst Michel—DDR-Design*. Tagungsband zum Kolloquium, edited by Petra Eisele and Siegfried Gronert, 22–73. Weimar: Universitätsverlag, 2004.

Eisman, April A. "East German Art and the Permeability of the Berlin Wall." *German Studies Review* 38, no. 3 (2015): 597–616.

Eitner, Lorenz. "Industrial Design in Postwar Germany." *Design Quarterly* 40 (1957): 1–27.

Epstein, Catherine. *The Last Revolutionaries: German Communists and Their Century*. Cambridge, MA: Harvard University Press, 2003.

Erker, Paul. "'Amerikanisierung' der westdeutschen Wirtschaft? Stand und Perspektiven der Forschung." In *Amerikanisierung und Sowjetisierung in Deutschland, 1945–1970*, edited by Konrad Jarausch and Hannes Siegrist, 137–145. Frankfurt am Main: Campus, 1997.

Fäßler, Peter E. *Durch den 'Eisernen Vorhang': Die deutsch-deutschen Wirtschaftsbeziehungen, 1949–1969*. Cologne: Böhlau, 2006.

Felson, Marcus. "The Differentiation of Material Life Styles, 1925–1966," *Social Indicators Research* 3 (1976): 397–421.

Foschepoth, Josef. "Westintegration statt Wiedervereinigung: Adenauers Deutschlandpolitik, 1949–1955." In *Adenauer und die Deutsche Frage*, edited by Yvonne Kipp, 29–60. Göttingen: Vandenhoeck & Ruprecht, 1988.

Frevert, Ute. "Europeanizing Germany's Twentieth Century." *History and Memory* 17, no. 1–2 (Spring–Winter 2005): 87–116.

Fritsch-Bournazel, Renata. *Confronting the German Question: German on the East-West Divide*. New York: Berg, 1988.

Fukuyama, Francis. "The End of History?" *The National Interest* (Summer 1989): 3–18.

Fulbrook, Mary. *Anatomy of a Dictatorship: Inside the GDR, 1949–1989*. Oxford: Oxford University Press, 1995.

Gaus, Günter. *Wo Deutschland liegt: Eine Ortsbestimmung*. Hamburg: Hoffmann und Campe, 1983.

Geißler, Rainer. *Die Sozialstruktur Deutschlands: Zur gesellschaftlichen Entwicklung mit einer Bilanz zur Vereinigung*. 5th ed. Wiesbaden: Verlag für Sozialwissenschaften, 2008.

Glover, David, and Cora Kaplan, eds. *New Formations* 28. Special issue "Conservative Modernity." 1996.

Goedde, Petra. *GIs and Germans: Culture, Gender, and Foreign Relations, 1945–1949*. New Haven, CT: Yale University Press, 2003.

Godard, Simon. "Construire le bloc de l'Est par l'économie? La delicate émergence d'une solidarité internationale socialiste au sein du Conseil d'aide économique mutuelle." *Vingtième Siècle. Revue d'histoire*, no. 109 (2011): 45–58.

Godau, Marion, and Bernd Polster. *Design Lexikon Deutschland*. Cologne: DuMont, 2000.

Golsan, Richard, ed. *Fascism, Aesthetics, and Culture*. Hanover, NH: University Press of New England, 1992.

Gramsci, Antonio. "Questions of Culture." In *Selections from Cultural Writings*, edited by David Forgacs and Geoffrey Nowell-Smith. Translated by William Boelhower. Cambridge, MA: Harvard University Press, 1985.

Granieri, Ronald J. *The Ambivalent Alliance: Konrad Adenauer, the CDU/CSU, and the West, 1949–1966*. New York: Berghahn Books, 2003.

Gray, William Glenn. *Germany's Cold War: The Global Campaign to Isolate East Germany, 1949–1969*. Chapel Hill: University of North Carolina Press, 2003.

Graziano, Paolo, and Maarten Peter Vink, eds. *Europeanization: New Research Agendas*. New York: Palgrave Macmillan, 2007.

Greiffenhagen, Martin. "The Dilemma of Conservatism in Germany." *Journal of Contemporary History* 14 (1979): 611–625.

Groys, Boris. *Gesamtkunstwerk Stalin: Die gespaltene Kultur in der Sowjetunion*. Munich: Carl Hanser, 1988.

Grünbacher, Armin. "Sustaining the Island: Western Aid to 1950s West Berlin." *Cold War History* 3, no. 3 (2003): 1–23.

Guérot, Ulrike, and Mark Leonard. "The New German Question: How Europe Can Get the Germany It Needs." *Policy Brief*, European Council on Foreign Relations (April 2011): 1–13.

Gunlicks, Arthur B. "The German Federal System Today: National, State, and Local Relations in an Era of Cooperative Federalism." In *Subnational Politics in the 1980s: Organization, Reorganization and Economic Development*, edited by Louis A. Picard and Raphael Zariski, 89–102. New York: Praeger, 1987.

Günther, Sonja. *Bruno Paul, 1874–1968*. Berlin: Gebrüder Man, 1992.

Harlander, Tilman. "Wohnungspolitik." In *Handwörterbuch der Stadt- und Raumentwicklung*, edited by Akademie für Raumforschung und Landesplanung, 2953–2968. Hanover: Akademie für Raumforschung und Landesplanung, 2018.

Hanke, Helmut, and Michel Vale. "Leisure Time in the GDR: Trends and Prospects." *International Journal of Sociology* 18, no. 4 (1988/1989): 167–181.

Hansen, Per. "Co-branding Product and Nation: Danish Modern Furniture and Denmark in the United States, 1940–1970." In *Trademarks, Brands, and Competitiveness*, edited by Teresa de Silva Lopes and Paul Duguid, 77–101. New York: Routledge, 2010.

Hansen, Per. *Danish Modern Furniture, 1930–2016: Rise, Decline and Re-emergence of a Cultural Category*. Translated by Mark Mussari. Odense: University Press of Southern Denmark, 2018.

Hansen, Per. "Networks, Narratives, and Markets: The Rise and Decline of Danish Modern Furniture, 1930–1970." *Business History Review* 80, no. 3 (2006): 449–483.

Harmsen, Robert, and Thomas Wilson. "Introduction: Approaches to Europeanization." *Yearbook of European Studies* 14 (2004): 13–26.

Harrison, Hope M. *Driving the Soviets Up the Wall: Soviet-East German Relations, 1953–1961*. Princeton, NJ: Princeton University Press, 2003.

Harrod, Owen. "The Deutsche Werkstätten and the Dissemination of Mainstream Modernity." *Studies in Decorative Arts* 10, no. 2 (2003): 21–41.

Harsch, Donna. "Between State Policy and Private Sphere: Women in the GDR in the 1960s and 1970s." *Clio* 41, "Real Socialism" and the Challenge of Gender (2015): 85–105.

Harvey, Elizabeth. "The Two Germanies: Recent Publications on the Federal Republic, the German Democratic Republic and the German Question." *Historical Journal* 33, no. 4 (1990): 953–970.

Heil, Peter. *"Gemeinden sind wichtiger als Staaten": Idee und Wirklichkeit des kommunalen Neuanfangs in Rheinland-Pfalz, 1945–1957*. Veröffentlichung der Kommission des Landtages für die Geschichte des Landes Rheinland-Pfalz 21. Mainz: v. Hase & Koehler, für die Kommission des Landtages, 1997.

Heitmann, Claudia. "Die Bauhaus-Rezeption in der Bundesrepublik Deutschland von 1949–1968—Etappen und Institutionen." PhD diss., Hochschule der Künste Berlin, 2001.

Herf, Jeffrey. *Reactionary Modernism: Technology, Culture, and Politics in Weimar and the Third Reich*. Cambridge: Cambridge University Press, 1984.

Herrigel, Gary. *Industrial Constructions: The Sources of German Industrial Power*. Cambridge: Cambridge University Press, 1996.

Herzogenrath, Wulf. "Zur Rezeption des Bauhauses." In *Beiträge zur Rezeption der Kunst des 19. und 20. Jahrhunderts*. Studien zur Kunst des neunzehnten Jahrhunderts 29, edited by Wulf Schadendorf, 129–141. Munich: Prestel, 1975.

Hewitt, Andrew. *Fascist Modernism: Aesthetics, Politics, and the Avant-Garde*. Stanford, CA: Stanford University Press, 1993.

Hilger, Susanne. *"Amerikanisierung" deutscher Unternehmen: Wettbewerbsstrategien und Unternehmenspolitik bei Henkel, Siemens und Daimler-Benz, 1945/49–1975*. Stuttgart: Steiner, 2004.

Hilpert, Thilo. "The Postwar Dispute in West Germany: The Renewal of Rationalism." In *Bauhaus Conflicts, 1919–2009*, edited by Stiftung Bauhaus Dessau, 128–148. Ostfildern: Hatje Cantz, 2009.

Hirdina, Heinz. *Gestalten für die Serie*. Dresden: Verlag der Kunst, 1988.

Hirdina, Heinz. *Neues Bauen, Neues Gestalten: Das neue Frankfurt/Die neue Stadt: Eine Zeitschrift zwischen 1926 und 1933*. Edited by Amt für Industrielle Formgestaltung. Berlin: Elefanten, 1984.

Hirschhausen, Ulrike von, and Kiran Klaus Patel. "Europäisierung," Version: 1.0, in Docupedia-Zeitgeschichte, 29 November 2012, https://docupedia.de/zg/Europ. C3.A4isierung?oldid=76143.

Hitchcock, William I. *France Restored: Cold War Diplomacy and the Quest for Leadership in Europe, 1944–1954*. Chapel Hill: University of North Carolina Press, 1998.

Hoffmann, Charles W. "Opposition und Innere Emigration: Zwei Aspekte des 'Anderen

Deutschlands.'" In *Exil und Innere Emigration II: Internationale Tagung in St. Louis*, edited by Peter Uwe Hohendahl and Egon Schwarz, 119–140. Frankfurt am Main: Athenäum, 1973.

Hottes, Karlheinz. "Regional Variations of the Economic Development in the Federal Republic of Germany." In *American German International Seminar: Geography and Regional Policy: Resource Management by Complex Political Systems*, edited by John S. Adams, Werner Fricke, and Wolfgang Herden, 38–52. Heidelberg: Geographische Institut Universität Heidelberg, 1983.

Jackson, Peter. "Towards a Cultural Politics of Consumption." In *Mapping the Futures: Local Cultures, Global Change*, edited by John Bird et al., 207–228. Oxford: Routledge, 1993.

Jarausch, Konrad. "Divided, Yet Reunited: The Challenge of Integrating German Post-War Histories." Contribution to *H-German Forum*, 1 February 2011, http://h-net.msu.edu/cgi-bin/logbrowse.pl?trx=vx&list=h-german&month=1102 &week=a&msg=lNK7XIEc2qqANKFyP6tmew&user=&pw=; accessed 13 October 2015.

Jarausch, Konrad. *After Hitler: Recivilizing Germans, 1949–1995*. Oxford: Oxford University Press, 2006.

Jarausch, Konrad. *Die Umkehr: Deutsche Wandlungen, 1945–1995*. Bonn: Bundeszentrale für politische Bildung, 2004.

Jarausch, Konrad. "Care and Coercion: The GDR Welfare Dictatorship." In *Dictatorship as Experience: Towards a Socio-Cultural History of the GDR*, edited by Konrad Jarausch and Eve Duffy, 47–70. New York: Berghahn, 1999.

Jarausch, Konrad. *The Rush to Unity*. New York: Oxford University Press, 1994.

Jarausch, Konrad, and Hannes Siegrist, eds. *Amerikanisierung und Sowjetisierung in Deutschland, 1945–1970*. Frankfurt am Main: Campus, 1997.

Jarzombek, Mark. "The *Kunstgewerbe*, the *Werkbund*, and the Aesthetics of Culture in the Wilhelmine Period." *Journal of the Society of Architectural Historians* 53, no. 1 (1994): 7–19.

Jeffries, Ian, and Manfred Melzer. "The New Economic System of Planning and Management 1963–70 and Recentralization in the 1970s." In *The East German Economy*, edited by Ian Jeffries and Manfred Melzer, 26–40. London: Croom Helm, 1987.

Jungklaus, Stefan. "Werkbundkisten—Erziehung zum vernünftigen Konsumenten." In *Kampf der Dinge: Der Deutsche Werkbund zwischen Anspruch und Alltag*, edited by Werkbundarchiv, 126–133. Leipzig: Werkbundarchiv Museum der Dinge, 2008.

Kaelble, Hartmut, and Martin Kirsch, eds. *Selbstverständnis und Gesellschaft der Europäer: Aspekte der sozialen und kulturellen Europäisierung im späten 19. und 20. Jahrhundert*. Frankfurt am Main: Peter Lang, 2008.

Kaminsky, Annette. *Wohlstand, Schönheit, Glück: Kleine Konsumgeschichte der DDR*. Munich: Beck, 2001.

Kiaer, Christina. *Imagine No Possessions: The Socialist Objects of Russian Constructivism*. Cambridge, MA: MIT Press, 2005.

Kilian, Werner. *Die Hallstein-Doktrin: Der Diplomatische Krieg zwischen der BRD und der DDR 1955–1973. Aus den Akten der beiden deutschen Außenministerien*. Berlin: Duncker & Humblot, 2001.

Kirsch, Karin. "Mia Seeger, 1903–1991." In *Baden-Württembergische Portraits: Frauengestalten aus fünf Jahrhunderten*, edited by Elisabeth Nölle-Neumann, 247–254. Stuttgart: Deutsche Verlags-Anstalt, 2000.

Kleßmann, Christoph, ed. *The Divided Past: Rewriting Post-War German History*. Oxford: Berg, 2001.

Kleßmann, Christoph. "Adenauers Deutschland-und Ostpolitik, 1955–1963." In *Adenauer und die Deutsche Frage*, edited by Josef Foschepoth, 61–79. Göttingen: Vandenhoeck & Ruprecht, 1988.

Kneissel, Jutta. "The Convergence Theory: The Debate in the Federal Republic of Germany." *New German Critique* 2, special issue on the German Democratic Republic, translated by Andreas Huyssen and Johanna Moore (Spring 1974): 16–27.

Kopstein, Jeffrey. *The Politics of Economic Decline in East Germany, 1945–1989*. Chapel Hill: University of North Carolina Press, 1997.

Kornai, János. *Economics of Shortage*. Amsterdam: North-Holland, 1980.

Kraehe, Enno E. "Practical Politics in the German Confederation: Bismarck and the Commercial Code." *Journal of Modern History* 25, no. 1 (1953): 13–24.

Kreis, Reinhild. "Heimwerken als Protest: Instandbesetzer und Wohnungsbaupolitik in West Berlin während der 1980er Jahre." *Zeithistorische Forschungen/Studies in Contemporary History 14* (2017): 41–67.

Krell, Gert. "West German Ostpolitik and the German Question." *Journal of Peace Research* 28, no. 3 (1991): 311–323.

Kremerskothen, Josef. "Wegstücke." In *Peter Maly, Designermonographien* 5, edited by Alex Buck and Matthias Vogt, 16–31. Frankfurt am Main: Form, 1998.

Kremerskothen, Josef. "Wohnen wie noch nie." In *Rolf Heide—Designer, Architekt, Querdenker*, edited by Dirk Meyhöfer, 13–17. Ludwigsburg: Avedition, 2000.

Kroen, Sheryl. "Negotiating the American Way: The Consumer and the Social Contract in Post-war Europe." In *Consuming Cultures, Global Perspectives: Historical Trajectories, Transnational Exchanges*, edited by John Brewer and Frank Trentmann, 251–278. Oxford: Berg, 2006.

Krössin, Dominique. "Kultur ins Heim: Geschmackserziehung versus Eigensinn." In *Fortschritt, Norm und Eigensinn: Erkundungen im Alltag der DDR*, edited by Dokumentationszentrum Alltagskultur der DDR e.V., 151–163. Berlin: Christoph Links, 1999.

Landsman, Mark. *Dictatorship and Demand: The Politics of Consumerism in East Germany*. Cambridge, MA: Harvard University Press, 2005.

Lauber, Andreas. *Wohnkultur in der DDR—Dokumentation ihrer materiellen Sachkultur: Eine Untersuchung zu Gestaltung, Produktion und Bedingungen des Erwerbs von Wohnungseinrichtungen in der DDR*. Eisenhüttenstadt: Dokumentationszentrum Alltagskultur der DDR, 2003.

Lehmbruch, Gerhard. "Wandlungen der Interessenpolitik im liberalen Korporatismus." In *Verbände und Staat*, edited by Ulrich von Alemann and Rolf G. Heinze, 50–70. Opladen: Westdeutscher, 1979.

Light, Alison. *Forever England: Femininity, Literature and Conservatism Between the Wars*. Routledge: London, 1991.

Lindenberger, Thomas. "Ist die DDR ausgeforscht? Phasen, Trends und ein optimistischer Ausblick." *Aus Politik und Zeitgeschichte* 24–26 (2014), http://www.bpb .de/apuz/185600/ist-die-ddr-ausgeforscht-phasen-trends-und-ein-optimistischer -ausblick.

Loehlin, Jennifer A. *From Rugs to Riches: Housework, Consumption and Modernity in Germany*. Oxford: Berg, 1999.

Lösche, Peter. *Verbände und Lobbyismus in Deutschland*. Stuttgart: Kohlhammer, 2007.

Loth, Wilfried. *Stalin's Unwanted Child: The Soviet Union, the German Question, and the Founding of the GDR*. Translated by Robert F. Hogg. Houndmills, Basingstoke, Hampshire: Macmillan, 1998.

Lovett, A. W. "The United States and the Schuman Plan: A Study in French Diplomacy, 1950–1952." *Historical Journal* 39, no. 2 (1996): 425–455.

Lubinski, Christina. *Familienunternehmen in Westdeutschland: Corporate Governance und Gesellschafterkultur seit den 1960er Jahren*. Munich: C. H. Beck, 2010.

Ludwig, Andreas. "'Hunderte von Varianten': Das Möbelprogramm Deutsche Werkstätten (MDW) in der DDR." *Zeithistorische Forschungen/Studies in Contemporary History*, no. 3 (2006): 449–459.

Ludwig, Andreas. "Vorwort." In *Fortschritt, Norm und Eigensinn. Erkundungen im Alltag der DDR*, edited by Dokumentationszentrum Alltagskultur der DDR e.V., 7–15. Berlin: Christoph Links, 1999.

Madarász, Jeannette Z. *Conflict and Compromise in East Germany, 1971–1989: A Precarious Stability*. New York: Palgrave Macmillan, 2003.

Maguire, Patrick J., and Jonathan M. Woodham, eds. *Design and Cultural Politics in Post-war Britain: The Britain Can Make It Exhibition of 1946*. London: Leicester University Press, 1997.

Markusen, Ann, Gregory H. Wassall, Doug De Natale, and Randy Cohen. "Defining the Creative Economy: Industry and Occupational Approaches." *Economic Development Quarterly* 22 (2008): 24–45.

McCracken, Grant. "Homeyness: A Cultural Account of One Constellation of Consumer Goods and Meanings." In *Culture and Consumption II: Markets, Meaning, and Brand Management*, edited by Grant McCracken, 22–47. Bloomington: Indiana University Press, 2005.

McCracken, Grant. "Culture and Consumption: A Theoretical Account of the Structure and Movement of the Cultural Meaning of Consumer Goods." *Journal of Consumer Research* 13, no. 1 (1986): 71–84.

Meikle, Jeffrey L. "Material Virtues: On the Ideal and the Real in Design History." *Journal of Design History* 11, no. 3 (1998): 191–199.

Merkel, Ina. *Utopie und Bedürfnis: Die Geschichte der Konsumkultur in der DDR*. Cologne: Böhlau, 1999.

Merkel, Ina, ed. *"Wir sind doch nicht die Mecker-Ecke der Nation": Briefe an das DDR-Fernsehen*. Cologne: Böhlau, 1998.

Merten, Roland. "Junge Verlierer in den neuen Bundesländern: Die vergessenen Verlierer im Prozeß der deutschen Vereinigung." *Sozialer Fortschritt* 42, no. 12 (December 1993): 295–302.

Michaud, Eric. *The Cult of Art in Nazi Germany*. Translated by Janet Lloyd. 1996. Reprint, Stanford, CA: Stanford University Press, 2004.

Miller, Daniel. *Material Culture and Mass Consumption*. London: Basil-Blackwell, 1987.

Minden, Michael. *Modern German Literature*. Cambridge: Polity, 2011.

Mises, Ludwig van. "Die Wirtschaftsrechung im sozialistischen Gemeinwesen." *Archiv für Sozialwissenschaft und Sozialpolitik* 47 (1920): 86–121.

Moeller, Robert G., ed. *West Germany under Construction: Politics, Society, and Culture in the Adenauer Era*. Ann Arbor: University of Michigan Press, 1997.

Moreton, Edwina, ed. *Germany Between East and West*. Cambridge: Cambridge University Press, 1987.

Moses, A. Dirk. *German Intellectuals and the Nazi Past*. Cambridge: Cambridge University Press, 2007.

Müller, Derek. *Der Topos des Neuen Menschen in der russischen und sowjetrussischen Geistesgeschichte*. Bern: Peter Lang, 1998.

Nabert, Thomas. *Möbel für Alle: Die Geschichte der sächsischen Möbelindustrie*. Leipzig: Pro Leipzig, 2014.

Naimark, Norman. *The Russians in Germany: A History of the Soviet Zone of Occupation, 1945–1949*. Cambridge, MA: Harvard University Press, 1995.

Nerdinger, Winfried. "Modernisierung: Bauhaus Nationalsozialismus." In *Bauhaus-Moderne im Nationalsozialismus*, edited by Winfried Nerginger, 9–23. Munich: Prestel, 1993.

Neumaier, Christopher, and Andreas Ludwig. "The Individualization of Everyday Life: Consumption, Domestic Culture, and Family Structures." In *A History Shared and Divided: East and West Germany Since the 1970s*, edited by Frank Bösch, 293–347. New York: Berghahn, 2018.

NGBK, ed. *Wunderwirtschaft: DDR-Konsumgeschichte in den 6oer Jahren*. Cologne, Böhlau, 1996.

Nicholls, A. J. *Freedom with Responsibility: The Social Market Economy in Germany, 1918–1963*. Oxford: Oxford University Press, 1994.

Niethammer, Lutz. "Normalization in the West: Traces of Memory Leading Back into the 1950s." In *The Miracle Years: A Cultural History of West Germany, 1949–1968*, edited by Hanna Schissler, 237–265. Princeton, NJ: Princeton University Press, 2001.

Oestereich, Christopher. *"Gute Form" im Wiederaufbau: Zur Geschichte der Produktgestaltung in Westdeutschland nach 1945*. Berlin: Lukas, 2000.

Oppermann, Kai. "National Role Conceptions, Domestic Constraints and the New

'Normalcy' in German Foreign Policy: The Eurozone Crisis, Libya and Beyond."
   German Politics 21, no. 4 (2012): 502–519.

Pallowski, Katrin. "Zur Kontinuität der 'klassischen Moderne' in den 50er Jahren."
   In *Design in Deutschland, 1933–45*, edited by Sabine Weißler, 132–141. Gießen:
   Anabas, 1990.

Palmowski, Jan. *Inventing a Socialist Nation: Heimat and the Politics of Everyday Life in
   the GDR, 1945–1990*. Cambridge: Cambridge University Press, 2009.

Passerini, Luisa, and Hartmut Kaelble. "European Identity, the European Public Sphere,
   and the Future of Europe." In *Nationale Identität und transnationale Einflüsse, Amerikanisierung, Europäisierung und Globalisierung in Frankreich nach dem Zweiten
   Weltkrieg*, edited by Reiner Marcowitz, 90–99. Munich: Oldenbourg, 2007.

Paterson, W. E. "Does Germany Still Have a European Vocation?" *German Politics* 19,
   no. 1 (2010): 41–52.

Paulmann, Johannes, ed. *Auswärtige Repräsentationen: Deutsche Kulturdiplomatie nach
   1945*. Cologne: Böhlau, 2005.

Paulmann, Johannes. "Representation without Emulation: German Cultural Diplomacy in Search of Integration and Self-Assurance during the Adenauer Era." *German
   Politics and Society* 25, no. 2 (2007): 168–200.

Pazaurek, Gustav Edmund. *Guter und schlechter Geschmack im Kunstgewerbe*. Stuttgart:
   Deutsche Verlags Anstalt, 1912.

Pence, Katherine. "Showcasing Cold War Germany in Cairo: 1954 and 1957 Industrial
   Exhibitions and the Competition for Arab Partners." *Journal of Contemporary History* 47, no. 1 (2012): 69–95.

Pence, Katherine. "'You as a Woman Will Understand': Consumption, Gender and the
   Relationship Between State and Citizenry in the GDR Crisis of 17 June 1953." *German History* 19, no. 2 (2001): 218–252.

Pence, Katherine, and Paul Betts, eds. *Socialist Modern: East German Everyday Culture
   and Politics*. Ann Arbor: University of Michigan Press, 2008.

Pfützner, Katharina. *Designing for Socialist Need: Industrial Design Practice in the German Democratic Republic*. Oxon: Routledge, 2018.

Pierenkemper, Toni. "Sechs Thesen zum gegenwärtigen Stand der deutschen Unternehmensgeschichtsschreibung: Eine Entgegnung auf Manfred Pohl." *Zeitschrift für Un-
   ternehmensgeschichte/Journal of Business History* 45, no. 2 (2000): 158–166.

Pietsch, Joachim. "Gelsenkirchener Barock und Drittes Reich." In *Gelsenkirchener Barock*, edited by Stadt Gelsenkirchen Städtisches Museum, 71–81. Heidelberg: Edition
   Braus, 1991.

Poiger, Uta. *Jazz, Rock, and Rebels: Cold War Politics and American Culture in a Divided Germany*. Berkeley: University of California Press, 2000.

Pollard, Sidney. "Probleme für europäische Integration im 19. und 20. Jahrhundert."
   In *Wirtschaftliche und politische Integration in Europa im 19. und 20. Jahrhundert*.
   Geschichte und Gesellschaft 10, edited by Helmut Berding, 9–33. Göttingen: Van-
   denhoek and Ruprecht, 1985.

Port, Andrew I. *Conflict and Stability in the German Democratic Republic*. New York: Cambridge University Press, 2007.

Port, Andrew I. "East German Workers and the "Dark Side" of Eigensinn: Divisive Shop-Floor Practices and the Failed Revolution of June 17, 1953." In *The East German Economy, 1945–2010: Falling Behind or Catching Up?*, edited by Hartmut Berghoff and Uta Balbier, 111–130. Cambridge: Cambridge University Press, 2014.

Porter, Michael E. *The Competitive Advantage of Nations*. New York: Free Press, 1990.

Porter, Michael E. "The Competitive Advantage of Nations." *Harvard Business Review* (March–April 1990): 73–93.

Pugh, Emily. *Architecture, Politics and Identity in Divided Berlin*. Pittsburgh: University of Pittsburgh, 2014.

Rabinbach, Anson G. "The Aesthetics of Production in the Third Reich." *Journal of Contemporary History* 11, no. 4, Theories of Fascism (1976): 43–74.

Rau, Christian. *Stadtverwaltung im Staatssozialismus. Kommunalpolitik und Wohnungswesen in der DDR am Beispiel Leipzigs, 1957–1989*, Beiträge zur Stadtgeschichte und Urbanisierungsforschung 20. Stuttgart: Franz Steiner Verlag, 2017.

Reich, Susanne S., ed. *Lebens-Formen: Alltagsobjekte als Darstellung von Lebensstilveränderungen am Beispiel der Wohnung und Bekleidung der "Neuen Mittelschichten."* Berlin: Akademie der Künste, 1991.

Reid, Susan E. "De-Stalinization and Taste." *Journal of Design History* 10, no. 2, Design, Stalin and the Thaw (1997): 177–201.

Reid, Susan E. "The Khrushchev Kitchen: Domesticating the Scientific-Technological Revolution." *Journal of Contemporary History* 40, no. 2 (2005): 289–316.

Reid, Susan E. "Who Will Best Whom? Soviet Popular Reception of the American National Exhibition in Moscow, 1959." *Kritika: Explorations in Russian and Eurasian History* 9, no. 4 (2008): 855–904.

Revel, Jean-François. "The Myths of Eurocommunism." *Foreign Affairs* 56, no. 2 (1978): 295–305.

Retallack, James. "'Why Can't a Saxon Be More Like a Prussian?' Regional Identities and the Birth of Modern Political Culture in Germany, 1866–67." *Canadian Journal of History* 32 (1997): 26–55.

Richthofen, Esther von. *Bringing Culture to the Masses: Control, Compromise and Participation in the GDR*. New York: Berghahn, 2009.

Robinson, Benjamin. *The Skin of the System: On Germany's Socialist Modernity*. Stanford, CA: Stanford University Press, 2009.

Rohrlich, Paul Egon. "Economic Culture and Foreign Policy: The Cognitive Analysis of Economic Policy Making." *International Organization* 41, no. 1 (1987): 61–92.

Romano, Angela. "Untying Cold War Knots: The EEC and Eastern Europe in the Long 1970s." *Cold War History* 14, no. 2 (2014): 153–173.

Rostow, Walt Whitman. *The Stages of Economic Growth: A Non-Communist Manifesto*. Cambridge: Cambridge University Press, 1960.

Rubin, Eli. "The Form of Socialism without Ornament: Consumption, Ideology, and the Fall and Rise of Modernist Design in the German Democratic Republic." *Journal of Design History* 19, no. 2 (2006): 155–168.

Rubin, Eli. "The Order of Substitutes: Plastic Consumer Goods in the Volkswirtschaft and Everyday Domestic Life in the GDR." In *Consuming Germany in the Cold War*, edited by David F. Crew, 87–119. Oxford: Berg, 2003.

Rubin, Eli. *Amnesiopolis: Modernity, Space, and Memory in East Germany*. New York: Oxford University Press, 2016.

Rubin, Eli. *Synthetic Socialism: Plastics and Dictatorship in the German Democratic Republic*. Chapel Hill: University of North Carolina Press, 2008.

Ruchniewicz, Krzysztof. "Ostpolitik and Poland." In *Ostpolitik, 1969–1974: European and Global Responses*, edited by Carole Fink and Bernd Schaefer, 39–57. Cambridge: Cambridge University Press, 2009.

Ruppert, Wolfgang, ed. *Fahrrad, Auto, Fernsehschrank: Zur Kulturgeschichte der Alltagsdinge*. Frankfurt am Main: Fischer, 1993.

Saldern, Adelheid von. "Bürgerliche Repräsentationskultur: Konstanz und Wandel der Wohnformen im Deutschen Reich und in der Bundesrepublik (1900–1980)." *Historische Zeitschrift* 284 (2007): 348–359

Saldern, Adelheid von. *Häuserleben: Die Geschichte des Arbeiterwohnens vom Kaiserreich bis heute*. Bonn: Dietz, 1995.

Sammartino, Annemarie. "The New Socialist Man in the *Plattenbau*: The East German Housing Program and the Development of the Socialist Way of Life." *Journal of Urban History* 44, no. 1 (2018): 78–94.

Sarotte, Mary E. *Dealing with the Devil: East Germany, Détente, and Ostpolitik, 1969–1973*. Chapel Hill: University of North Carolina Press, 2001.

Sarotte, Mary E. *1989: The Struggle to Create Post–Cold War Europe*. Princeton, NJ: Princeton University Press, 2009.

Schildt, Axel. *Ankunft im Westen: Ein Essay zur Erfolgsgeschichte der Bundesrepublik*. Frankfurt am Main: Fischer 1999.

Schildt, Axel, and Arnold Sywottek, eds. *Massenwohnung und Eigenheim: Wohnungsbau und Wohnen in der Großstadt seit dem Ersten Weltkrieg*. Frankfurt am Main: Campus, 1988.

Schlereth, Thomas J. "Material Culture Studies and Social History Research." *Journal of Social History* 16, no. 4 (Summer 1983): 111–143.

Schlereth, Thomas J. "Material Culture Research and Historical Explanation." *Public Historian* 7, no. 4 (Autumn 1985): 21–36.

Schmidt, Axel. "Zwei Staaten eine Fernsehgeneration: Überlegungen zur Bedeutung der elektronischen Massenmedien in der Geschichte der Kommunikation zwischen der Bundesrepublik und der DDR." In *Doppelte Zeitgeschichte: Deutsch-deutsche Beziehungen, 1945–1990*, edited by Arnd Bauernkämper, Martin Sabrow, and Bernd Stöver, 58–71. Bonn: Dietz, 1998.

Scholtyseck, Joachim. "Im Schatten der Hallstein-Doktrin: Die globale Konkurrenz zwischen Bundesrepublik und DDR." In *Die Herausforderung des Globalen in der Ära Adenauer*, edited by Eckart Conze, 79–97. Bonn: Bouvier, 2010.

Schreiber, Carsten. "Die Inszenierung des Erfolgs: Zur Funktion der Leipziger Messe in den 1970er Jahren." In *Leipzigs Messen 1497–1997, Teilband 2: 1914–1997*, edited by Hartmut Zwahr, Thomas Topfstedt, and Günter Bentele, 667–677. Cologne: Böhlau Verlag, 1999.

Schreiter, Katrin, and Davide Ravasi. "Institutional Pressures and Organizational Identity: The Case of Deutsche Werkstätten Hellerau in the GDR and Beyond, 1945–1996." *Business History Review* 92, no. 3 (2018): 453–481.

Schröter, Harm G. *Americanization of the European Economy: Comparative Survey of American Economic Influence in Europe since the 1880s*. Dordrecht: Springer, 2005.

Schröter, Harm G. "The German Questions, the Unification of Europe, and the European Market Strategies of Germany's Chemical and Electrical Industries, 1900–1992." *Business History Review* 67, no. 3 (1993): 369–405.

Schüller, Marcus. *Wiederaufbau und Aufstieg der Kölner Messe, 1946–1956*. Stuttgart: Franz Steiner Verlag, 1999.

Schütt-Wetschky, Eberhard. *Interessenverbände und Staat*. Darmstadt: Primus, 1997.

Schulz, Günther. "Eigenheimpolitik und Eigenheimförderung im ersten Jahrzehnt nach dem Zweiten Welkrieg." In *Massenwohnung und Eigenheim: Wohnungsbau und Wohnen in der Großstadt seit dem Ersten Weltkrieg*, edited by Axel Schild and Arnold Sywottek, 409–439. Frankfurt am Main: Campus, 1988.

Schulz, Günther. *Wiederaufbau in Deutschland: Die Wohnungsbaupolitik in den Westzonen und der Bundesrepublik von 1945 bis 1957*. Düsseldorf: Droste, 1994.

Schuppert, Gunnar Folke, ed. *The Europeanization of Governance*. Baden-Baden: Nomos, 2006.

Schwarzer, Oskar. *Sozialistische Zentralplanwirtschaft in der SBZ/DDR: Ergebnisse eines ordnungspolitischen Experiments, 1945–1989*. Vierteljahrschrift für Sozial-und Wirtschaftsgeschichte 143. Stuttgart: Franz Steiner, 1999.

Schwartz, Frederic J. "'Funktionalismus heute': Adorno, Bloch und das Erbe des Modernismus der BRD." In *Mythos Bauhaus: Zwischen Selbsterfindung und Enthistorisierung*, edited by Anja Baumhoff and Magdalena Droste, 325–335. Berlin: Reimer, 2009.

Schwartz, Michael. "Emanzipation zur sozialen Nützlichkeit: Bedingungen und Grenzen von Frauenpolitik in der DDR." In *Sozialstaatlichkeit in der DDR: Sozialpolitische Entwicklungen im Spannungsfeld von Diktatur und Gesellschaft, 1945/49–1989*, edited by Dierk Hoffmann and Michael Schwartz, Schriftenreihe der Vierteljahrshefte für Zeitgeschichte, Sondernummer, 47–88. Munich: Oldenbourg, 2005.

Sänger, Johanna. "Zwischen allen Stühlen: Die Sammlung Industrielle Gestaltung als Archiv zur materiellen Kultur der DDR." *Zeithistorische Forschungen/Studies in Contemporary History*, no. 12 (2015): 124–139.

Selle, Gert. *Geschichte des Design in Deutschland*. Ext. ed. Frankfurt am Main: Campus, [1994] 2007.

Selle, Gert. "Das Produktdesign der 50er Jahre: Rückgriff in die Entwurfsgeschichte, vollendete Modernisierung des Alltagsinventars oder Vorbote der Postmoderne?" In *Modernisierung im Wiederaufbau: Die westdeutsche Gesellschaft der 50er Jahre*, edited by Axel Schildt and Arnold Sywottek, 612–624. Bonn: Dietz, 1993.

Selle, Gert. "The Lost Innocence of Poverty: On the Disappearance of a Culture Difference." *Design Issues* 8, no. 2 (1992): 61–73.

Seppain, Helene. *Contrasting US and German Attitudes to Soviet Trade, 1917–91: Politics by Economic Means*. London: St. Martins, 1992.

Sheffer, Edith. *Burned Bridge: How East and West Germans Made the Iron Curtain*. Oxford: Oxford University Press, 2011.

Siebs, Benno-Eide. *Die Außenpolitik der DDR, 1976–1989: Strategien und Grenzen*. Paderborn: Schöningh, 1999.

Silbermann, Alphons. *Vom Wohnen der Deutschen: Eine soziologische Studie über das Wohnerlebnis*. Cologne: Westdeutscher Verlag, 1963.

Sinn, Hans Werner. "Germany's Economic Unification: An Assessment after Ten Years." National Bureau of Economic Research, Working Paper 7586. Cambridge, MA, 2000.

Sleifer, Jaap. *Planning Ahead and Falling Behind: The East German Economy in Comparison with West Germany, 1936–2002*. Jahrbuch für Wirtschaftsgeschichte 8. Berlin: Akademie, 2006.

Schmidt, Volker H. "Multiple Modernities or Varieties of Modernity?" *Current Sociology* 54, no. 1 (2006): 77–97.

Spicka, Mark E. *Selling the Economic Miracle: Economic Reconstruction and Politics in West Germany, 1949–1957*. New York: Berghahn, 2007.

Staadt, Joachim. *Eingaben: Die institutionalisierte Meckerkultur in der DDR*. Berlin: Freie Universität Berlin, 1996.

Stade, Ronald. "Designs of Identity: Politics of Aesthetics in the GDR." *Ethnos* 58, no. 3/4 (1993): 241–258.

Steinberg, Rolf, ed. *Nazi-Kitsch*. Darmstadt: Melzer, 1975.

Steiner, André. "From the Soviet Occupation Zone to the 'New Eastern States': A Survey." In *The East German Economy, 1945–2010: Falling Behind or Catching Up?*, edited by Hartmut Berghoff and Uta Balbier, 17–52. Cambridge: Cambridge University Press, 2014.

Steiner, André. *Von Plan zu Plan: Eine Wirtschaftsgeschichte der DDR*. Munich: Deutsche Verlags-Anstalt, 2004.

Steinwarz, Herbert. *Wesen, Aufgaben, Ziele des Amtes Schönheit der Arbeit*. Berlin, 1937.

Stites, Richard. *Revolutionary Dreams: Utopian Vision and Experimental Life in the Russian Revolution*. Oxford: Oxford University Press, 1989.

Stitziel, Judd. *Fashioning Socialism: Clothing, Politics, and Consumer Culture in East Germany*. Oxford: Berg, 2005.

Stoler, Ann Laura, and Frederick Cooper, eds. *Tensions of Empire: Colonial Cultures in a Bourgeois World*. Berkeley: University of California Press, 1997.

Stokes, Raymond. *Opting for Oil: The Political Economy of Technological Change in the West German Chemical Industry, 1945–1961*. Cambridge: Cambridge University Press, 1994.

Stokes, Raymond. *Constructing Socialism: Technology and Change in East Germany, 1945–1990*. Baltimore, MD: Johns Hopkins University Press, 2000.

Suri, Jeremi. *Power and Protest: Global Revolution and the Rise of Détente*. Cambridge, MA: Harvard University Press, 2003.

Taylor, Brandon, and Winfried van der Will, eds. *The Nazification of Art: Art, Design, Music, Architecture, and Film in the Third Reich*. Winchester, England: Winchester Press, 1990.

Te Heesen, Anke, and Anette Michels, "Der Schrank als wissenschaftlicher Apparat." In *auf/zu: Der Schrank in den Wissenschaften*, edited by Anke te Heesen and Anette Michels, 10. Berlin: Akademie, 2007.

Thöner, Wolfgang. "State Doctrine or Criticism of the Regime: On the Reception of the Bauhaus in East Germany, 1963–1990." In *Bauhaus Conflicts*, edited by Stiftung Bauhaus Dessau, 226–242. Ostfildern: Hatje Cantz, 2009.

Tinbergen, Jan. "Kommt es zu einer Annäherung zwischen den kommunistischen und den freiheitlichen Wirtschaftsordnungen?" *Hamburger Jahrbuch für Wirtschafts-und Gesellschaftspolitik* 8 (1963): 11–20.

Trappe, Heike. *Emanzipation oder Zwang?: Frauen in der DDR zwischen Beruf, Familie und Sozialpolitik*. Berlin: Akademie, 1995.

Trommler, Frank. *Kulturmacht ohne Kompass: Deutsche auswärtige Kulturbeziehungen im 20. Jahrhundert*. Cologne: Böhlau, 2014.

Turner, Henry Ashby, Jr. *The Two Germanies Since 1945*. New Haven, CT: Yale University Press, 1987.

Twombly, Robert, ed. *Louis Sullivan: The Public Papers*. Chicago: University of Chicago Press, 1988.

Umbach, Maiken. "Made in Germany." In *Deutsche Erinnerungsorte II*, edited by Etienne Francois and Hagen Schulze, 405–418. Munich: C. H. Beck, 2001.

Urban, Florian. *Tower and Slab: Histories of Global Mass Housing*. London: Routledge, 2012.

Van Hook, James C. *Rebuilding Germany: The Creation of the Social Market Economy*. Cambridge: Cambridge University Press, 2004.

Van Laak, Dirk. "Zwischen 'organisch' und 'organisatorisch': 'Planung' als politische Leitkategorie zwischen Weimar und Bonn." In *Griff nach dem Westen: Die "Westforschung" der völkisch-nationalen Wissenschaften zum nordwesteuropäischen Raum, 1919–1960*, vol. 1, edited by Burkhard Dietz, Helmut Gabel, and Ulrich Tiedau, 67–90. Münster: Waxmann, 2003.

Voges, Jonathan. *"Selbst ist der Mann": Do-It-Yourself und Heimwerken in der Bundesrepublik Deutschland*. Göttingen: Wallstein Verlag, 2017.

Veblen, Thorstein. *The Theory of the Leisure Class: An Economic Study of Institutions*. Oxford: Oxford University Press, [1899] 2007.

Vietta, Silvio, and Michael Gehler, eds. *Europa—Europäisierung—Europäistik. Neue wissenschaftliche Ansätze, Methoden und Inhalte.* Wien: Böhlau, 2010.

Wagener, Hans-Jürgen. "Zur Innovationsschwäche der DDR-Wirtschaft." In *Innovationsverhalten und Enscheidungsstrukturen: Vergleichende Studien zur wirschaftlichen Entwicklung im geteilten Deutschland*, edited by Johannes Bähr and Dietmar Petzina, 21–48. Berlin: Dunker und Humblot, 1996.

"Was bleibt vom DDR-Design? Elke Trappschuh trifft Clauss Dietel." *Design Report* 22 (1992): 18–29.

Wehler, Hans-Ulrich. *Deutsche Gesellschaftsgeschichte IV.* Munich: C. H. Beck, 2008.

Weitz, Eric. "The Ever-Present Other: Communism in the Making of West Germany." In *The Miracle Years: A Cultural History of West Germany, 1949–1968*, edited by Hannah Schissler, 219–232. Princeton, NJ: Princeton University Press, 2001.

Weißler, Sabine, ed. *Design in Deutschland, 1933–45.* Gießen: Anabas, 1990.

Wengst, Udo, and Hermann Wentker, eds. *Das doppelte Deutschland: 40 Jahre Systemkonkurrenz.* Berlin: Ch. Links, 2008.

Werkbundarchiv, ed. *Kampf der Dinge: Der Deutsche Werkbund zwischen Anspruch und Alltag.* Leipzig: Werkbundarchiv Museum der Dinge, 2008.

Wichmann, Hans. "System-Möbel: Ein Novum unseres Jahrhunderts." In *Möbeldesign: Made in Germany*, edited by Zentrum Baden-Württemberg, 146–163. Stuttgart: Landesgewerbeamt Baden-Württemberg, 1985.

Wiegand, Katharina, ed. *Heimat: Konstanten und Wandel im 19./20. Jahrhundert: Vorstellungen und Wirklichkeiten.* Munich: Deutscher Alpenverein, 1997.

Wiesen, Jonathan. *West German Industry and the Challenge of the Nazi Past, 1945–1955.* Chapel Hill: University of North Carolina Press, 2001.

Wiesenthal, Helmut. "Die Transformation der DDR: Ein analytischer Rückblick auf Verfahren und Resultate." Gutachten für die Forschungsgruppe Europa, Centrum für angewandte Politikforschung. München, 1998.

Winkler, Heinrich August. *Der lange Weg nach Westen II: Deutsche Geschichte, 1933–1990.* Bonn: Bundeszentrale für politische Bildung, 2005.

Wittig, Horst E. *Pläne und Praktiken der polytechnischen Erziehung in Mitteldeutschland.* Bad Harzburg: Verlag fiir Wissenschaft, Wirtschaft und Technik, 1962.

Wolfrum, Edgar. *Die geglückte Demokratie: Geschichte der Bundesrepublik von ihren Anfängen bis zur Gegenwart.* Stuttgart: Klett-Cotta, 2006.

Wüsten, Sonja. "Selman Selmanagić Biographisches." In *Selman Selmanagić: Festgabe zum 80. Geburtstag am 25. April 1985*, edited by Sonja Wüsten, Dietmar Kuntzsch, and Hans Menday, 6–41. Berlin, 1984.

Zarecor, Kimberly. *Manufacturing a Socialist Modernity: Housing in Czechoslovakia, 1945–1960.* Pittsburgh: University of Pittsburgh Press, 2011.

Zatlin, Jonathan R. *The Currency of Socialism: Money and Political Culture in East Germany.* Cambridge: Cambridge University Press, 2007.

Ziemann, Benjamin. *Front und Heimat: Ländliche Kriegserfahrungen im südlichen*

Bayern, 1914–1923. Veröffentlichungen des Instituts zur Erforschung der europäischen Arbeiterbewegung, Schriftenreihe A: Darstellungen 8. Essen: Klartext, 1997.

Zimmermann, Clemens. "Wohnungspolitik—Eigenheim für alle?" In *Villa und Eigenheim: Suburbaner Städtebau in Deutschland*, edited Tilman Harlander, 64-75. Stuttgart: Deutsche Verlags-Anstalt, 2001.

INDEX